Iron Ore Transport
on the Great Lakes

Iron Ore Transport on the Great Lakes

The Development of a Delivery System to Feed American Industry

W. BRUCE BOWLUS

McFarland & Company, Inc., Publishers
Jefferson, North Carolina, and London

Unless otherwise indicated, images are from the Charles E.
Frohman Collection located at the Rutherford B. Hayes
Presidential Center in Fremont, Ohio.

LIBRARY OF CONGRESS CATALOGUING-IN-PUBLICATION DATA

Bowlus, W. Bruce, 1946–
    Iron ore transport on the Great Lakes : the development of a
delivery system to feed American industry / W. Bruce Bowlus.
      p.   cm.
    Includes bibliographical references and index.

    ISBN 978-0-7864-3326-1
    softcover : 50# alkaline paper ∞

    1. Shipping — Great Lakes (North America) — History.
2. Iron ores — Transportation.   3. Industries — United States.
I. Title.
HE631.G74B69   2010
    386'.5440977 — dc22   2010011981

British Library cataloguing data are available

On the cover: Great Lakes schooners in the harbor at Frankfort,
Michigan, 1890 (Charles E. Frohman Collection, Rutherford B.
Hayes Presidential Center in Fremont, Ohio); background
©2010 Shutterstock.

Manufactured in the United States of America

McFarland & Company, Inc., Publishers
  Box 611, Jefferson, North Carolina 28640
  www.mcfarlandpub.com

To my mother,
Virginia Teachout Bowlus

Table of Contents

Acknowledgments

Researching, organizing, and writing this manuscript has left me owing a profound debt of gratitude to a considerable number of people. I wish to thank the following, freely admitting that I undoubtedly overlooked individuals whom I should have included. To them I offer my sincerest apologies.

I have nothing but the greatest respect for the staffs of the Western Reserve Historical Society located in Cleveland and the National Archives and Records Administration, Great Lakes Region, in Chicago. The personnel of both archives were infinitely patient and demonstrated professionalism of the highest caliber. I gained much from my visits to both locations.

I was fortunate to have been able to complete a considerable amount of my research at two excellent archives within 30 miles of one another. One, the Rutherford B. Hayes Presidential Center, contains numerous contemporary periodicals, government documents, manuscript collections, and secondary sources that were of tremendous value to me. The Hayes Center also is the repository for the Frank E. Hamilton Collection, part of the Charles E. Frohman Collection, which includes extensive files of pictorial and manuscript records dealing with Great Lakes maritime history. I consistently enjoyed the unwavering support of three different directors of the Center — Leslie Fishel, Jr., Roger Bridges, and Thomas Culbertson. In addition, the library staff, under the direction of Becky Hill, provided me with unequaled assistance in my research efforts. Nan Card, John Ransom, Merv Hall, Marie Paulson, and Gil Gonzalez eagerly responded to my many and varied requests for material over the years. I truly appreciate all their efforts.

The second archive, the Historical Collections of the Great Lakes in the Center for Archival Collections, is located at Bowling Green State University. Its extensive collection of photographs, manuscripts, government records, ships' logs, company records, and maps proved invaluable. The directors of the Great Lakes Collection, both the late Stuart R. Givens and his successor Robert Graham, always exhibited an enthusiastic willingness to lend assistance. Bob Graham's knowledge of the archives helped me uncover some remarkable material.

I was fortunate to have the assistance of the knowledgeable members of the Association of Great Lakes Maritime History in helping me to understand the evolution of maritime history on the Great Lakes. Many eagerly supplied me with explanations of nautical terminology and ship development peculiar to the Lakes. C. Patrick Labadie especially has been a patient and invaluable resource for understanding ship evolution on the Lakes. He likewise provided me with useful editorial comments and suggestions for this manuscript. I also learned much from my diving partners: the late Joyce Hayward, Kathryn Hayes, and Jay Martin. Their enthusiasm for the shipping history of the Lakes and their expertise in wreck diving immeasurably helped my understanding of ship construction and design.

I owe much to the late Richard J. Wright and the late Frank E. Hamilton, although I never met them. Both were scholars of Great Lakes shipping, and each amassed an extensive collection of remarkable insights, manuscripts, and photographs. Fortunately, these collections were preserved and formed the foundation of much of my research. Their eagerness to search out and compile all sorts of information on Great Lakes maritime history saved me an enormous amount of time and helped direct my inquiries.

I am likewise indebted to the late Dr. David C. Roller, Dr. David Curtis Skaggs, and Dr. William R. Rock for their support. Dr. Edmund J. Danziger, Jr., needs to be singled out for special commendation. As my major professor and as a friend, he, without fail, has provided much needed guidance and encouragement over the years.

Early in my career, I was fortunate to enjoy a brief correspondence with the late Stephen E. Ambrose. His kindnesses and unqualified support of my work proved to be a strong motivation for me. I am sorry that I only now have the opportunity to thank him.

The administration of Tiffin University, particularly Vice President for Academic Affairs Charles Christensen, and Dean of the School of Arts and Sciences Miriam Fankhauser, has consistently encouraged my efforts, for which I am most appreciative. The university's library staff, Fran Fleet, Susan Halen, and Karen Miller, have repeatedly assisted me and I am truly grateful for their help. I am also indebted to Dr. Sherry Truffin for her suggestions and insights.

Dr. and Mrs. Robert Blankenburg, Robert and Annette Rideout, and Dr. and Mrs. Walter Verdon were kind enough to provide me with lodging on research trips. I sincerely appreciate their hospitality and friendship.

Finally, I wish to thank my wife, Lucianne, for her gentle prodding, remarkable patience, and unwavering support over the years it took to bring this project together.

Preface

I was raised about 15 miles from the southwestern shore of Lake Erie. Many of my childhood memories revolve around trips to the nearby beaches on Catawba Island, which is really a peninsula extending into Lake Erie just northeast of Port Clinton, Ohio. I remember the sand dunes we ran through to the beach reminded me of pictures I had seen of the shores of Cape Cod. Other times our family rented a cottage overlooking the Lake Erie near Port Clinton for a week. No matter where we went, most of my time was spent in the water. Although I had taken swimming lessons, this was where I really learned how to swim, mostly on my own.

In the midst of my aquatic activities, I sometimes stopped to gaze out at the various pleasure craft cruising between coastal harbors and the islands scattered within Erie's western basin. Without fail, one or more large Lake freighters downbound to points east or upbound to the Upper Lakes soon caught my eye. They passed slowly, almost imperceptibly, along the shipping lanes three to five miles out. Although the power boats and sailboats of various sizes and colors vied for my attention, I repeatedly found myself drawn back to the lumbering freighters as they methodically worked their way past me and disappeared into the distance. Eventually, I was even able to recognize familiar ones that I had seen over the years by their distinctive shapes or company logos. Unlike my friends and others around me at the time, who were either in or on the water to enjoy themselves, the men aboard those ships were working. What, I wondered, would it be like to be aboard such a vessel looking back at the shoreline? And what were these boats carrying? Where had they come from? Where were they bound? As I got older, trips to the lake became less frequent, and my curiosity about these ships was stored away along with other fond memories of those days.

My interest in water sports, however, continued through high school and college, leading me, it seemed inevitably, into scuba diving as an adult. Scuba training and early practice dives were restricted to swimming pools and some of the numerous flooded quarries that dotted northwestern Ohio. But my desire to do something more exciting with my scuba training and practice helped to generate a curiosity about some of the mysteries that I had heard could be found beneath the waters of the nearby Great Lakes. I remembered when the *Edmund Fitzgerald* sank in Lake Superior in November of 1975 because one of the crewmen had been from my hometown. And through my growing contacts in the diving community I learned about many other wrecks, some dating back into the 19th century, resting at the bottom of the Great Lakes waiting to be explored. The transition, however, between controlled dives in the enclosed and frequently supervised environment I was used to and open-water dives, where one enters choppy, dark waters off the stern of a rocking, unsteady dive boat, proved to be dramatic. Yet, I found it exhilarating, especially after I dove on my first shipwreck, the wooden freighter *Prince*, which had sunk in shallow water off the shore of Kelly's Island in Lake Erie in 1911.

Depending on where one dives in the Lakes, the water can be numbingly cold, surprisingly strong currents often disrupt dive plans, underwater visibility is unpredictable, and the diving season is normally only six months long. But I quickly learned that the Lakes contained something not found in many others places, and especially not in saltwater — an abundance of reasonably well-preserved shipwrecks. Unlike the oceans, where warm saltwater and sea life can make quick work of wooden shipwrecks and coral tends to encrust and obscure metal wrecks, the cold, fresh water of the Lakes actually works to preserve sunken vessels, especially wooden ones. These fascinating vessels are time capsules of Great Lakes history, offering a first-hand account of ship evolution in the region. These now became the focus of my dives. Courses in underwater archaeology followed, as did diving trips to search for selected underwater wrecks among the hundreds resting at the bottom of the Lakes. Not surprisingly, the prospect of investigating shipwrecks reignited my childhood curiosity about Lake freighters.

In the course of diving trips to Lake Superior, I took the opportunity to visit the locks at Sault Ste. Marie, Michigan, through which every boat leaving or entering Lake Superior must pass. Standing on the visitors' platform next to the MacArthur Lock, one of four on the American side, I was awed by the immense freighters — some quite possibly ones I had seen years before while at the beach — passing through. What, I wondered, prompted such a massive construction project as these locks in a relatively remote part of the country? Who had built them, and who had paid for them? Why were they necessary? While traveling west from there, I noticed that my map was dotted with references to mines and mining. There were towns named Atlantic Mine, National Mine, Copper Harbor, Iron River, and Iron Mountain. Negaunee, I discovered, was home to the Michigan Iron Industry Museum. I had been vaguely aware that this area had a history of iron and copper mining, but knew little more than that. Arriving in Marquette, I couldn't miss a large, rather unusual dock protruding out into Lake Superior. I learned that this was a pocket ore dock, the first one built in the Upper Lakes. It still loads iron ore from local mines into ships, some of them reaching 1,000 feet in length. I speculated that the ships I had seen both above and below the waters of the Great Lakes, the locks at Sault Ste. Marie, the mining activity on Michigan's Upper Peninsula, and the loading docks at Marquette were somehow connected. But how? And why was this activity separated from the more familiar centers of commerce and industry in Pittsburgh, Chicago, or Detroit? How long had it been going on? What had motivated the builders, investors, workers, and engineers who brought all this to life?

The foregoing questions and experiences came with me to graduate school and directed a good deal of my studies there. I was fortunate to be employed as an editor at the Rutherford B. Hayes Presidential Center at the time. This afforded me free access to the many contemporary periodicals, atlases, manuscripts, and government documents in the Center's extensive collection. It also provided me with ability to investigate Great Lakes shipping through the eyes of a retired Great Lakes ship captain, Frank E. Hamilton, who had accumulated thousands of photographs, numerous ships' logs, annual registration records, and countless other valuable documents relating to the Lakes over the course of his life. This material had come to the Hayes Center as part of the larger Charles E. Frohman Collection. My graduate work was undertaken at Bowling Green State University, which gave me the opportunity to delve into the even more comprehensive Historical Collections of the Great Lakes, an important part of the university's Center for Archival Collections (CAC). Here more photographs, manuscripts, charts, and maps, as well as detailed ship blueprints, much of it painstakingly compiled over a lifetime by the late Great Lakes ship historian Richard Wright, complemented the material available at the Hayes Center. Together, these two collections formed the basis for much of my research then, and continue to do so today.

I augmented the information I found at the Hayes Center and the CAC with trips to libraries and archives around the Great Lakes. These included, but were not limited to, The Clements Library at the University of Michigan, the Burton Historical Collection at the Detroit Public Library, the

National Archives Regional Records Service Center in Chicago, and the Western Reserve Historical Society in Cleveland. In addition, I visited libraries and historical societies in the Duluth-Superior area, Sault Ste. Marie, Toledo, Cleveland, LaCrosse (Wisconsin), and Oberlin (Ohio). I also had the good fortune to be part of a network of Great Lakes scholars and divers who freely shared their knowledge and experiences with me. I likewise gained valuable insight through numerous trips and dives around the Lakes.

The goal throughout my research has been to better understand how the various components involved in the mining and transportation of iron ore from the Lake Superior region interacted. The process that emerged, I discovered, was not simply a matter of independently enlarging ships or deepening channels or designing unloading equipment that operated more efficiently. Rather, these and other elements functioned synergistically, with alterations or improvements in one prompting changes in one or more of the others. But I also learned that the system's evolution was comprised of more than mechanical improvements. Values and long-held political and legal positions needed to be changed before a successful system could appear. Along the way I uncovered compelling stories of some truly remarkable individuals, most of whom have been forgotten, whose contributions were crucial in building this system. In the end, these disparate elements coalesced, making it possible to transport iron ore economically on the Great Lakes. The system that emerged played an indispensable role in the rise of American industrialization late in the 19th century and, by extension, the country's emergence as a world power in the 20th.

Introduction

In an age of electronics and plastics, where jet airliners take travelers to Europe in a matter of hours, technology provides instant communication among people around the world, and consumers have come to expect product change as the normal state of affairs, it has become convenient to ignore the fact that the foundations of the prosperity necessary to create all this rests, if somewhat uncomfortably, on the shoulders of late 19th century industrialization. We are uncomfortable with the period because manufacturing in the United States, while still important, has lost its vitality and influence as the country's economy has become increasingly focused on the service sector and technology. Although once the basis for an improved standard of living for many, manufacturing likewise has been chastised for introducing labor-saving technology and, more recently, moving their operations to other countries. Although done to improve efficiency and make them more competitive, both have displaced workers and, consequently, have generated considerable controversy. But even more troubling have been the revelations of environmental damage arising from decades of indifference and shortsightedness that accompanied the appearance and rapid expansion of countless competing firms dating back to the heady early stages of industrialization.

Yet, one would be hard pressed to discount the contributions made by industrialization to the rapidly expanding wealth of the nation in the late 19th century. Manufacturing for much of the century had been designed for regional consumption; limitations in transportation, both in receiving raw materials and moving finished products to market, prevented most firms from entertaining greater aspirations. This changed after the Civil War. Railroads not only expanded at a prodigious rate, but their operations also became highly organized and coordinated. Receiving and sending items around the country efficiently became possible, opening up opportunities for firms with a national focus. Banks and investors, both foreign and domestic, concluded that such an environment was rich with possibilities and quickly concluded arrangements with railroads and manufacturers. All this coincided with the largest influx of immigrants in United States history, which provided workers for factories springing up in cities in the East and Midwest. This work force was complemented by the arrival of young men and women from the nation's rural areas, where improvements in agricultural methods and technology had rendered their large numbers redundant. Together these elements generated an unprecedented expansion of the nation's economy.

The proliferation of railroads and industries, as well as growth of urban areas where expansion was increasingly growing vertically, all shared a common need for iron and steel. If steam could be considered the 19th century equivalent of jet power, then steel was the "plastic" of the latter part of the century. It was the foundation of industrialization. As a result, the demand for iron ore was unrelenting and efforts to keep the mills supplied with it were at times frenzied. "Iron production in the United States seems to have gone mad and is clearly rushing to a calamitous result," exclaimed the *Chicago Tribune* in 1880. Under these circumstances, the nation was fortunate to have numerous reserves of iron ore, most of which were scattered throughout the states east of the Mississippi River. But they varied in purity, a crucial issue with the introduction of mass-produced Bessemer steel in the 1880s. The two purest fields were centered around Missouri's Iron Mountain and along the southern shores of Lake Superior. While the iron beds of the former were quickly exhausted, deposits of Lake Superior ore seemed endless. And the quality of the iron remained consistently high. But retrieving the ore was not to be easy.[1]

The dilemma facing those seeking to exploit Lake Superior iron ore was overcoming the distance and isolation of the region. To begin, how could the ore reach the shoreline from the inland mines through the unforgiving terrain of Michigan's Upper Peninsula? While transportation by water was generally viewed as the best way to move the ore, Great Lakes ships were poorly designed for handling ore, especially in the volume anticipated. And even if redesigned, the boats would encounter reefs, shoals, tortuous channels, and rapids that threatened to impede their passage to the mills on the southern Lakes. Would state and/or federal government assistance be available to help overcome such obstacles? Once the boats arrived, they would find that the methods for unloading the ore were primitive at best. Could private investors be found who were willing to provide the necessary funding for upgraded equipment? And could all of these activities be somehow organized into a coordinated system that acted in concert rather than at odds? My challenge was to understand how these issues were resolved.

As I began my research, it became clear to me that a considerable number of books, articles, pamphlets, and photographs dealing with Great Lakes maritime history were available. I soon discovered, however, that many of the books and articles dealt with the losses of ships and sailors that had occurred on the Lakes over the years. Designed for a popular audience, they made exciting reading. But they generally lacked professional rigor and tended to concentrate on catastrophes rather than the normal, if less titillating, operations of Lake ships. I also found a considerable collection of travel books, camping guides, and "coffee table" tomes that sought to market the region to potential visitors. While frequently providing interesting anecdotal information, these types of books did little to answer my broader questions.

Fortunately, I also uncovered other writers who demonstrated a very high level of professionalism. Richard J. Wright's *Freshwater Whales: A History of the American Shipbuilding Company and Its Predecessors,* for example, was an exhaustive investigation of one of the largest and most influential shipbuilders in the United States, which happened to be located on the Lakes. Walter Havighurst skillfully presented the iron mining operations of the Pickands Mather Company in *Vein of Iron.* In doing so, he was one of the few who demonstrated an appreciation for the interaction of various phases of mining operations, the inevitable result of the company's early vertical integration. John Dickenson's 1981 *To Build a Canal: Sault Ste. Marie, 1853–1854 and After,* provided an outstanding study of the construction of the first locks at Sault Ste. Marie. Writers, like Peter White and Alexander McDougall, left contemporary records of their roles in events on the Lakes in the 19th century. Although sometimes uneven, and with frustrating gaps in information, they did provide invaluable insights into critical phases of the Great Lakes history. Undoubtedly, the most exhaustive study of the Great Lakes ever undertaken, *History of the Great Lakes,* edited by J. B. Mansfield, was published in 1899. While it covered, among a myriad of other topics, all facets of Great Lakes transportation, it did so without fully demonstrating how these aspects interacted.

For the most part, then, Great Lakes scholars tended to focus on areas of specialization. Countless researchers, engineers, and enthusiasts, for example, painstakingly traced, and continue to follow, the evolution of Great Lakes ships and shipping. I came to know and admire some of these remarkably dedicated, knowledgeable people during my years of wreck diving in the

Lakes. Others, I discovered, were fascinated by loading or unloading operations at iron ore docks or grain elevators, the challenges facing dock workers, or the development of maritime trade unions. Researchers likewise have delved into the history of the locks at the Sault, the operations of the U. S. Army Corps of Engineers on the Lakes, or the expansion of facilities at various harbors around the Lakes. At one time, there was even a particularly knowledgeable, and vocal, group working to "Save the Huletts," iron ore unloading machines, from the City of Cleveland, which sought to tear down these antiquated "eyesores." Yet, despite the first-rate studies relating to the history of commerce on the Lakes, there had not been very much research to find out how all the pieces fit together. Was there a common theme that could be found running through any this? Or was the maritime history of the Lakes simply comprised of dozens of independent themes that only intersected accidentally?[2]

I eventually concluded that the demand for iron ore prompted many of the changes to Lake vessels, waterways, and dockside equipment, with much of the transformation occurring in the last two decades of the 19th century. Before the Civil War, for example, commercial shipping activities on the Lakes were divided between steamboats, transporting passengers and some package freight, and independent sailing vessels of various sizes and descriptions either hauling assorted cargoes or fishing. By the late 1890s, despite serious interruptions caused by the depressions of 1873 and 1893, revolutionary changes in ship propulsion, construction, and design resulted in the creation of a standardized Lake bulk freighter that dwarfed any vessel that had existed before the war. While passenger ships remained popular into the 1950s, they remained a specialized and small segment of Lake shipping. But it was becoming clear by the 1870s that sailing ships were in decline.

I also discovered that many of the changes involved in the mining and transportation of Lake Superior iron ore coincided with the rise of American industrialization during the period. But more than that, this transformation was instrumental in fostering the industrialization itself. In fact, I argue, without the remarkable discoveries, innovations, and improvements occurring on the Lakes at that time, it is questionable whether the United States would have been able to achieve a position of economic leadership in the 20th century.

If scholars of Great Lakes history by and large focused on single themes, I discovered that historians outside of the region have underestimated, or ignored altogether, the importance of the region's maritime history. Historian Alan Nevins wrote two massive biographies of John D. Rockefeller, who played an important role in helping to open what became the largest iron range in history. Nevins saw "great men" as the key to understanding industrialization in the late 19th century. To be sure, Rockefeller, Andrew Carnegie, and others formed a pantheon that dominated industry of the period. But both these businessmen, and the corporations beginning to direct commerce late in the century, enjoyed unparalleled success in large part because governmental regulation was in its infancy, giving them unparalleled flexibility in their business dealings. In a nation with a burgeoning, if erratic, economy, the success of powerful industrialists was also the result of good fortune every bit as much as individual initiative or business acumen. Often, as demonstrated in the following chapters, it was the drive and imagination of numerous, if lesser known, entrepreneurs that provided the impetus for change and progress. The foundation of American commercial success during the late 19th and much of the 20th centuries, in the end, rested on the availability of rich iron ore and the ability to efficiently process it into steel. Events that took place on the Lakes in the 19th century played a pivotal role in allowing this to happen.[3]

Other histories of the period, most notably W. W. Rostow's 1971 *The Stages of Economic Growth: A Non-Communist Manifesto*, have viewed the development of the railroad as the key element spurring industrialization. John Garraty concluded, "The expansion and integration of the railroad network between 1877 and 1890 was probably the most significant single reason why the economy developed so rapidly in those years." And by 1895, Robert William Fogel noted, the railroad, all 181,000 miles of it, was now "an indispensable part, and a major catalyst for, the nation's economy." Granted, it is difficult to overestimate the importance of the railroad. Its network of trunk and feeder lines enveloped the country in a giant web that broke down the barriers of regionalism and gave all but the most remote villages access to markets previously unavailable. But these railroads crisscrossed the country on rails of Bessemer steel beginning in the 1880s. Iron, both forged and cast, and steel went into the creation of each railroad engine and the thousands of passenger cars and freight cars they pulled. Increasingly, iron and steel replaced wood in the many railway bridges that traversed American rivers and canyons. During the last years of the century, railroads found they needed to replace their worn out track, much of it iron or Bessemer steel, with rails made of more durable open hearth steel. In the end, abundant supplies of Lake Superior iron ore alone were capable of satisfying the needs of steel manufacturers struggling to meet these demands. And the availability of an efficient, proven system that included Lake freighters ensured that the ore would be delivered as inexpensively as possible and in an adequate volume.[4]

Kenneth Warren's 1973 *The American Steel Industry, 1850–1970: A Geographic Interpretation* considered the importance of transportation costs in steel production. At one point the author spent 20 pages discussing Andrew Carnegie's battle with railroads over lower fares for transporting ore from the ports on Lake Erie to his Pittsburgh mills. Eventually he acknowledged that Lake freight rates were cheaper than rail fares, but relegated this conclusion to one sentence. He later referred to a "superb system of Lake transportation" and briefly discussed the growth in capacity of Lake carriers. But this single-paragraph summary assumed too much and explained too little. The development of Great Lakes bulk carriers involved more than simply making them larger. It required the introduction of improved assembly techniques, better construction materials, and design refinements, not to mention improvements to docks, canals, and river channels.[5]

Warren's abbreviated acknowledgement of the contributions made by those involved with Lake transportation is all too common. Numerous scholars have been quick to acknowledge the value of "rich Lake Superior ore" in the growth of the Pittsburgh iron and steel business. And some, like Warren, even make a passing reference to Lake carriers. Others seem to take the existence of the ore for granted. In his 1995 *A Nation of Steel*, Thomas J. Misa studied the importance of steel in "the making of modern America." It is an outstanding investigation of development and consolidation of the nation's steel industry. The author, however, provided no information about the transportation of the Lake Superior iron ore, which was the foundation of this industry. The failure to appreciate contributions made by the Great Lakes maritime industry to American economic growth, not surprisingly, extends beyond the work of academics. As part of the Federal Art Project (FAP) in the 1930s, the Department of Transportation commissioned Carl Rakeman to create a series of paintings tracing the "Historic Roads" of America's past. The guidelines of the project were broad enough for Rakeman to illustrate 93 incidents deemed important in the development of transportation in the country. While featuring such "milestones" as the U. S. Army's ill-fated attempt to use camels in the Southwest and several paintings depicting the evolution of the bicycle, Rakeman did not render a single illustration of transportation on the Great Lakes. Nor did he depict any notable improvements that eased travel on the Lakes, such as the building of the locks at Sault Ste. Marie. Such oversights are difficult to understand in light of the volume of commerce that had coursed over those waters during the preceding 60 years.[6]

Unfortunately, even many marine historians ignore the evolution of Great Lakes shipping. In 1948, F. G. Fassett edited *The Shipbuilding Business in the*

United States of America. In chapter two, John G. B. Hutchins contributed an essay with the sweeping title "History and Development of Shipbuilding, 1776–1944." It was a painstakingly detailed summary of the technological evolution of United States shipping. But Hutchins made no mention of Great Lakes ships or shipping. Like the Rakeman paintings, this was a serious oversight considering the contributions Lake shipbuilders had made in the decades leading up to the publication of this essay.[7]

This book, then, is an effort to remedy the limited scope or the omissions from previous studies of the importance of events on and around the Great Lakes during the late 19th century to American economic development. Specifically, it is an attempt to better understand the evolution of a system to transport Great Lakes iron ore. It was fortunate for many living near the Great Lakes that the quality of iron ore needed at the time could be found in great abundance in their region. But it was located in a remote and isolated area, forcing them to expend considerable skill, money, creativity, and energy to successfully exploit these natural riches. Their contributions were generally recognized by Americans at the time, who were exposed regularly to stories in national periodicals concerning developments on the Lakes. But a decline in industrial activity in the United States in general, and the loss of heavy industry in the Midwest in particular, has left most people indifferent about the development of those activities. Mining iron ore seldom conjures up nostalgic images, like, say, the "49'er miner" striking out to seek his fortune in the California Gold Rush. The process of making steel lacks the compelling aura surrounding events like the Civil War. And working a Great Lakes ore carrier will never compare to the romance associated with a tall-masted Clipper Ship bound for Asian ports. Working with iron ore is a dirty, unglamorous business. But it was the foundation of American economic development in the late 19th and much of the 20th centuries. The wealth it brought to the nation provided the financial foundation for the innovation and changes that followed.

No doubt some, after reading what follows, will find areas that seem very familiar to them and question what new ground has been broken. Others might wonder why there was not more depth regarding a topic that is of paramount interest to them. My goal has been less focused on updating the reader on, say, the latest shipwreck discovery and more on how changes occurring on the Lakes in the 19th century interacted with one another to produce a remarkably efficient and unique system to deliver iron ore. Once this system had been established by 1900, people worked to refine it but never drastically altered it.

  I faced, as many know who have studied the early 19th century, an uneven, often contradictory, sometimes non-existent set of records and artifacts that both assisted and frustrated me. In certain cases, one is forced to employ seasoned judgment where nothing else exists. Fortunately, the amount and variety of useful information improved after the Civil War, increasing appreciably by the end of the century. This will account for the abundance of statistical information that appears in the later chapters versus the agonizingly scanty amount, much based on reminiscenes of events by participants years later in life, found in earlier chapters.

1

A "sterile region on the shores of Lake Superior"

(Beginnings)

On the morning of September 19, 1844, the men of William Burt's surveying team, camping near Teal Lake in Michigan's Upper Peninsula, awoke to brisk winds and an ominous, overcast sky. Winter comes early to the southern shores of Lake Superior and the weather on this morning made it apparent that this year's surveying efforts were nearing an end. It had been a trying season. The terrain in the heavily forested Upper Peninsula was hilly and the low lying areas were mosquito-infested, conditions less than ideal for the precise calculations demanded of surveying operations. Also, the supplies they had brought with them from their base camp were running low. In fact, the men this morning breakfasted on the meat of three porcupines that they had killed the day before. Still they knew that Burt would insist that the range and township lines be true and that their field notes be accurate. He had a reputation for accuracy, and even late in the year and under these trying circumstances Burt could be expected to maintain his exacting standards.[1]

Burt, who had been a deputy surveyor for the federal government for eleven years, was well suited for this demanding task. Born in Petersham, Massachusetts, in 1792, he had left school at an early age to help support his family. Yet, he retained a keen intellectual curiosity throughout his adolescence. In 1810 he had purchased a used surveyor's compass, repaired it himself, and taught himself how to use it by undertaking surveys near his home in East Aurora, New York. Following service in the army during the War of 1812, Burt moved west, settling in the Michigan Territory in 1824. Here he took an active role in regional affairs, most notably by participating in the surveying of the Northwest Territory as mandated by the Ordinance of 1785.

During the 1830s, while serving as the United States deputy surveyor in northwest Ohio, Burt invented a solar compass. He was able to field test his invention on surveying assignments in Iowa in the late 1830s and early 1840s. Patented in 1836, it won several international prizes over the next decades. The prestige Burt gained with his compass resulted in his promotion to deputy surveyor for Michigan in 1844.[2]

As the men broke camp near Teal Lake and headed south to begin the day's surveying, they worked with diligence, hoping to complete operations before the weather conditions became even worse. Shortly after they got underway, however, they began to experience interruptions. The compass man, who was using a traditional magnetic compass, began to notice fluctuations in his readings, and as the morning progressed they grew more exaggerated. As Burt recorded, "The variation high and fluctuating, on the first mile, section one. On sections 12 and 13, variations of all kinds, from south 87 degrees east, to 87 degrees west. At some places the north end of the needle would dip to the bottom of the box, and would not settle anywhere." Assuming that nearby ferrous rock caused this, Burt told his party, "Boys, look around and see what you can find." They collected samples of rock, which Burt immediately recognized as iron. Dutifully, Burt recorded in his field notes that they had found spathic and hermatite ores in great abundance along the eastern boundary of township 47 north-range 27 west. He then employed his solar compass in the iron fields to overcome the shortcomings of the magnetic compass and complete the survey. According to Jacob Houghton, who served as Burt's barometer man, Burt was delighted to have his invention available under the circumstances they faced on September 19. "How could they survey this country without my compass? What could be done here without my compass?" Houghton recalled the usually reserved Burt exclaiming at the time.[3]

Most of the men picked up samples, which they took with them. This event, which at the time served as little more than a diversion from the otherwise mundane routine of surveying, eventually altered the nation's history in ways that neither they nor anyone at the time could have imagined.[4]

Americans in the 1840s generally considered the land that Burt was surveying as a remote, unwelcoming wilderness. For centuries it had been the home of the Chippewa and Ottawa tribes. In the 16th century French traders, trappers, and priests began to appear in the area, living among the native peoples and often, the clergy excepted, intermarrying with them. While they brought Christianity and trade goods, nothing they did radically altered the rhythm of life in the region. Like Spain and Portugal, their counterparts in the Southern Hemisphere, France had come to the New World solely to exploit its wealth. True, the French had encouraged settlement along the St. Lawrence River, but the harsh living conditions and a limited growing season there discouraged all but the hardiest Frenchmen. The British, who colonized to the south, were different. Handicapped by a shortage of arable land and a burgeoning population that threatened to overwhelm her cities, particularly London, they were considerably more successful in developing permanent settlements along the eastern coast of North America. Although the colonies grew steadily, even rapidly, the Crown, seeking to avoid confrontations with the tribes, actively discouraged westward expansion after replacing the French in the Great Lakes and Mississippi River basin at the end of the French and Indian War in 1763. Once freed from British rule following the American Revolution in 1783, Americans flooded into the virgin Trans-Appalachian west.

Not surprisingly, friction grew between these settlers and the indigenous tribes. In the Old Northwest, organized resistance ended temporarily with the Indian defeat at the Battle of Fallen Timbers near the Maumee River in 1794 and the Treaty of Greenville a year later. Although the Shawnees under Tecumseh sought to revive Indian fortunes in the early 1800s, the death of Tecumseh and the defeat in 1815 of the British, who had provided the Indians with material and moral support, left Americans nominally in control of the region. While a few tribes remained obdurate in their relations with Americans, many tribes at that point either moved further west or signed treaties that allowed them to remain. But the inability of the federal and state governments to control Americans' lust for land in the west, regardless of treaty arrangements, and the parallel, if contradictory, need to establish forts in the region to provide for the settlers' protection, created considerable volatility in the region. By 1830, Congress instituted a national policy of removal, which sought to open these tribal lands to settlement by removing the tribes across the Mississippi River. Even the far reaches of the Upper Peninsula were not immune to this inexorable drive for land. Fueled by reports of copper and silver in the area, the federal government concluded a treaty with the Chippewa in 1842 for lands that included the Upper Peninsula as far east as present-day Marquette. It was these lands that soon revealed substantial deposits of remarkably pure copper and where Burt's surveying party discovered iron. But they did not end up near Teal Lake on that overcast September morning only as the result of those treaties. A series of events that began during the last days of the United States under the Articles of Confederation also conspired to deliver them there.[5]

Hamstrung by its lack of authority under the Articles, the Continental Congress unsuccessfully struggled to govern the unruly 13 states in the years immediately following the Revolutionary War. In the summer of 1787, as delegates from the states were meeting in Philadelphia to create a new constitution, Congress labored over the final draft of a bill that addressed unresolved concerns about the status of new states admitted to the union. Combined with the earlier 1785 ordinance that ordered scientific surveys of the region, the Northwest Ordinance of 1787 dealt directly with the territory north of the Ohio and east of the Mississippi rivers. In a clear break with British colonial policy, it guaranteed that the new states carved out of this Northwest Territory would enjoy the same political rights and guarantees as the current states. Article five of the document established guidelines for creating these new states, providing for no fewer than three, but no more than five states. Moreover, it fixed two meridians dividing the lands south of Lakes Michigan and Erie and a parallel of latitude separating the northern and southern tiers of the territory.[6]

This line of latitude led to considerable confusion and a growing rancor between Ohio and the Michigan Territory starting in the early 1800s. The terminology of the ordinance was quite clear: the line would run directly east and west from the southern most point of Lake Michigan. But maps of the territory in 1787 were inaccurate and placed the lake further north than it actually was. Therefore, when Ohio petitioned to join the union, the area around Maumee Bay was accepted as being part of the state, a conclusion incorporated into the 1802 Enabling Act that federally authorized the establishment of the state. Two years later, when the Michigan Territory was established, many of its inhabitants argued that, based on the language of the Northwest Ordinance, Ohio's original boundary line was too far north. In 1817, Congress authorized a survey of the disputed area. But, at the insistence of the Survey General of the United States (and former Ohio governor) Edward Tiffin, the surveyor was instructed to adhere to the provisions of the Ohio constitution of 1803, not the guidelines established in the Northwest Ordinance. Apprised of this duplicity, Michigan territorial governor Lewis Cass immediately ordered a second survey, this time following the guidelines set out in the ordinance.[7]

Not surprisingly, the surveys arrived at different boundary lines, creating a "no-man's land" eight miles wide in the east and five mile wide in the west. Encompassing 468 square miles, it became known as the "Toledo Strip" after the fledgling city at the mouth of the Maumee River. Although unresolved, the issue remained dormant until the 1830s. By then the economic boom resulting from the success of the Erie Canal in 1825 had spurred similar canal projects in Ohio, one of which, the Miami and Erie Canal, planned to connect the Ohio River with Lake Erie at Toledo. High economic expectations not only set off a wave of land speculation in the Toledo area but also reinvigorated the Toledo Strip debate. By this time too, Michigan was actively seeking statehood, making the resolution of the boundary line issue imperative. Any attempt to influence the Toledo strip question at the federal level in favor of Michigan, however, ran into strong and effective opposition from well-entrenched Ohio congressmen. By 1836 Ohio had two senators and 19 representatives; the Michigan Territory had only one non-voting delegate in Washington. Growing frustration in the state prompted young Michigan Governor Stevens Mason to call out the territorial militia and lead it into the strip, intent upon expelling any "trespassers" from Ohio. At one point, the militia fired over the heads of some surveyors from Ohio, sending them fleeing south. Ohio responded by also calling up its militia. President Andrew Jackson, fearing that this might escalate into an inter-state war, pressured both states into a deal. The details, presented in the Northern Ohio Boundary Bill in 1836, seemed to favor Ohio. The politically astute Jackson clearly wanted to encourage Ohio's important votes in the elections that year be cast in favor of the Democrats.[8]

The bill gave Ohio the strip, including Toledo. Michigan received the western portion of the Upper Peninsula as compensation. Although the territory's voters had to agree to this boundary if they expected to become a state, their initial reaction was almost universally unfavorable. The *Detroit Free Press* referred to Upper Peninsula as "a region of perpetual snows — the *Ultima Thule* of our national domain in the north." The territorial legislature in a resolution adopted in March 1838 characterized the region as a "sterile region on the shores of Lake Superior, destined by soil and climate to remain forever a wilderness." In what many in Michigan took as a final insult, slave-holding Arkansas was admitted to the Union without conditions on the same day as Michigan was offered her deal of statehood in return for giving up claims on the Toledo Strip. To make matters worse, many on the geographically isolated Upper Peninsula opposed becoming a part of Michigan, seeking instead to create the Huron Territory. Ultimately, however, Michigan saw more benefits in statehood than in the possession of the Toledo Strip and accepted the congressional offer. The Upper Peninsula remained largely ignored until the early 1840s when reports of copper, lead, and even silver deposits along the southern shore of Lake Superior began to circulate. These reports lent urgency to the 1785 requirement that the area be surveyed. Such potential riches could generate serious disputes regarding land claims.[9]

When Burt's party finally returned to their base camp late in 1844, they shared the story of seemingly abundant and easily accessible iron deposits scattered around Teal Lake with locals and travelers in the region. Burt, of course, included an account of these events in his final report to the government. Clearly indifferent, neither Burt nor any of his team made a claim on this apparently rich deposit. With a growing interest in the region's copper, such an attitude to an obviously rich iron discovery seems surprising. But their reaction was mirrored in the lack of interest shown by others who had seen the mineral riches of the region before them.

Although accounts of Burt's find was the first indication most Americans had that iron existed in the Upper Peninsula, Europeans had written of its existence centuries before. In the early 1600s, French Catholic missionaries began proselytizing in the upper Great Lakes, scouring the rivers and shorelines as aggressively for Indian souls as their fellow French *coureurs de bois* and *voyageurs* sought the indigenous fur-bearing animals. Although the land around the Great Lakes was claimed by the French crown and was part of what was referred to officially as New France, it was largely unknown. Eager to learn more about their vast colonial holdings, French authorities turned to the Jesuits, who, unlike the trappers and traders active in the region, were highly educated. Dutifully, often enthusiastically, they recorded their observations in regular reports back home, including information not only on their efforts to convert the natives but also on the region's flora and fauna, geography, and the tribal customs of the locals. In his 1653 report, Father Bressani, a Jesuit Friar, commented on the purity of the copper and iron located in the Lake Superior region. But he also observed that they were found "in places far distant and hard to reach, which render its transportation almost impossible." More than a century and one-half later, while accompanying Michigan Territorial Governor Louis Cass's party, naturalist Henry Schoolcraft recorded that "an Indian brought me a number of specimens of iron ore, procured at Point Keweena ... where he represents it to exist in large quantity ... on the Iron River, which enters the lake fifteen miles west of the Ontonagon [River]." As recently as 1840 — shortly before Burt's discovery — John T. Blois noted that "the large quantities of iron sand upon the coast of [Lake] Superior, and the iron pyrites and specimens of lead ore found on the banks of the rivers [of the region], presuppose the more extensive existence of those metals."[10]

Some, oblivious to, or ignorant of, Bressani's admonitions, actually sought to extract the mineral wealth of the region. In 1770, British fur trader Alexander Henry convinced a number of investors, including the Duke of Gloucester, to join him in underwriting a mining venture on the Ontonagon River on the southwestern coastline of Lake Superior. Although they were organized to extract silver thought to be plentiful in the region, they later sought to mine the more accessible copper found there. But, as Bressani had warned, the cost to extract and ship the minerals from this area was too costly.[11] Still, by the early 1840s, reports of mineral wealth — particularly copper — "got to a fever pitch" after a report by a Professor Jackson of Boston, who had spent time exploring the shores of Lake Superior, supported Schoolcraft's earlier claims. By the middle of the decade, fortune hunters began making their way to the Keweenaw Peninsula eager to cash in on the copper, and even silver, deposits reported in the region.[12]

Reaching the area, however, was no easy matter. While new technologies were beginning to improve travel in other parts of the country in 1844, they had yet to make an impact on the remote Lake Superior region. The 1845 journey of Philo Everett, one of those attempting to exploit the area's mineral deposits, detailed the difficulties faced by those simply trying to reach the area. Everett was part of a group of fortune hunters that organized The Jackson Mining Company during the winter of 1845 in Jackson, Michigan. They planned to search for copper in the Keweenaw that year once the weather was favorable. Departing from Jackson aboard the Michigan Central Railroad in June of 1845, the party traveled west on a strap-rail track to the terminus of the line at Marshall, Michigan, in one day at the then breakneck speed of 15 miles per hour. From there, they journeyed northwest to the Straits of Mackinac, first by stagecoach to Grand Rapids, and then by buckboard the rest of the way. At the Straits, several Indians ferried them to Mackinac Island, probably by canoe. Here they booked passage aboard the steamboat *General Scott,* which took the party up the St. Mary's River as far as the falls at Sault Ste. Marie. There they hired a newly constructed bateau, a flat-bottomed river boat, for the final leg of the journey to Carp River (present-day Marquette, Michigan). The boat was piloted by Ma-dosh, a Chippewa chief who had built the boat, and was manned by the two mixed-breeds who had helped him construct it. The journey of around 400 miles ultimately took the group 21 days to complete.[13]

The area where Burt located iron ore lay roughly 20 miles inland from the spot where Everett's group landed on the Upper Peninsula of Michigan. Here only occasionally did the remnants of narrow Indian trails penetrate the dense forests. Hacking a useful road through the region's foliage and across the stony hills to support a working mining camp would have been time-consuming and expensive.[14] Using railroads, in their infancy even in the most economically advanced parts of the country at the time, to reach inland from Lake Superior seemed nothing short of impossible. As copper miners in the Keweenaw were learning, those interested in exploiting the region's resources had to also solve the problem of transportation from the inland mines across the rugged country to ships moored on the shores of Lake Superior.[15]

Assuming there was an efficient way for the iron to reach the lake shore — which Schoolcraft noted was "very elevated ... even mountainous," there were no dock facilities to efficiently load the bulky, heavy ore aboard a waiting ship. Human muscle power, time consuming and arduous, would have had to supply the energy for this. Even if this problem could be overcome, only a few small vessels then sailed Lake Superior waters, and they had too little capacity to accommodate an increased volume of cargo. Furthermore, once loaded, the ships would have to negotiate a rocky shoreline that Schoolcraft remembered as "subject to storms and sudden transitions of temperature, and to fogs and mists, which are so dense as to obscure objects as at short distance." In his autobiography, Great Lakes captain and shipbuilder Alexander McDougall recalled that no truly reliable charts of Lake Superior existed until the 1870s. Like most sailors of the period, he navigated the lake with little more than experience, intuition, and nerve to guide him. Also, there were no lighthouses to offer warnings of navigable hazards or ports for escape during severe weather. In fact, McDougall recalled that even in 1874 there were "only a few huts on 175 miles of [Lake Superior's] shoreline." Twelve years later in a letter to the U. S. Army Corps of Engineers, E. T. Evans, the manager of a shipping company, voiced support of the federal government's takeover of the Lake Superior Ship Canal through the Keweenaw Peninsula. The canal, he argued, would offer refuge from the unpredictable weather of the region. And, he noted, "There is no available harbor of refuge anywhere in the south shore [of Lake Superior]."[16]

Should a ship survive the travails of this passage and reach Whitefish Bay and then the mouth of the St. Mary's River, the only outlet for Lake Superior, the rapids at Sault Ste. Marie prevented it from carrying its cargo uninterrupted through to the lower lakes. Although only about a half mile in length, the rapids dropped the water level 18 feet. This unfortunate quirk of nature kept ships north of the rapids virtual prisoners of the lake. The only way to move cargo south from this point was to off-load it, move it by cart around the falls, and reload it on another vessel. To characterize this process as time-consuming and expensive, given the technology of the day, is an understatement.

Burt and his team were acutely aware of these challenges to any enterprise that sought to exploit the iron ore deposit they had discovered near Teal Lake. But there were other impediments of a broader scope that no doubt also influenced their decision not to attempt to profit from their discovery. They were, of course, part of the larger national experience. The United States in the 1840s was a country of spirited growth, but also one uncertain what path it should follow. Many southerners, who passionately favored personal independence and strong state governments, found themselves at odds with others, particularly in the North, persuaded that the federal government needed to insert itself into debates with interstate or national implications. Furthermore, while the nation proudly trumpeted itself as the world's first democracy, southerners fervently maintained a rigid socio-economic system that relied on a huge slave population. The elite in these states fervently believed that the region's prosperity, even survival, rested on their ability to resist any interference from outsiders seeking to alter this feudal arrangement. Many in the North, alternately puzzled and aggravated by this intransigence, embraced technological innovation, supported the expansion of capital, and encouraged the entrepreneurial spirit, anything that promoted economic growth. By 1844, a growing number of Abolitionists, particularly in New England, raised the stakes in this sectional rivalry by questioning the morality of the human bondage practiced in the slave-holding states. These regional issues, particularly slavery, increasingly influenced events and decisions in the first half of the 19th century, interjecting sectionalism into every debate.

While few in 1844 took notice of Burt's discovery, other events that year generated considerably more national interest. In New England, the Transcendentalist movement had been urging individuals to be spiritually and intellectually independent and to avoid organized religion by communicating directly with God. Ralph Waldo Emerson, whose publications and lectures spearheaded the movement, published *Essays: Second Series* in 1844.[17] That same year Samuel F. B. Morse transmitted the first message by telegraph over a line running from Baltimore to Washington, D. C. For the first time, people could communicate instantaneously miles apart. This ability transformed the way people thought and worked, and served in many ways to draw the country closer in the coming years.

In the presidential campaign that year, Democrat and Andrew Jackson protégé James K. Polk, the first "dark horse" candidate nominated by a major party, defeated Whig Henry Clay, who had been forced to split his votes with Liberty Party candidate and anti-slavery advocate James Gillispie Birney. Although generally remembered for aggressively pursuing border issues involving the Oregon Territory and Texas, Polk, a southerner, founded his domestic policies on the fervent belief that the Constitution should be interpreted literally. Guided by this philosophy, he used the Democratic majority in Congress to reduce both tariffs and funding for internal improvements, issues that more liberal interpreters of the Constitution, particularly in the West, had championed to promote business interests.[18] He also urged his countrymen to keep slavery an issue for individual states to decide. These three issues, particularly slavery, grew increasingly contentious, fanning the fires of sectionalism that consumed the country for the next 16 years and led inexorably to civil war.

Only three states existed west of the Mississippi River when Polk took office. Yet, it had been clear for some time that the nation would continue to push westward, although there was "no unanimity regarding either the area into which the United States should expand or whether it should expand at all." Here once again the conflicting interests of the North and South were played out. While northerners saw opportunity in places like the Oregon Territory, critics in the South viewed its settlement as a villainous plot hatched by abolitionists. The area was north of the boundary line created by the Missouri Compromise (1820) that divided states seeking admission to the Union into free and slave-holding. Southerners feared that any new state(s) emerging from this territory threatened to disrupt the delicate balance in Congress and give an advantage to supporters of tariffs, internal improvements, and abolition. Instead, expansionists in the South looked to Texas, Mexico, and even the Caribbean, where the climate could support cotton production, the cornerstone of the southern economy. The expansion of slave states in this area caused consternation in the North, where concerns over potential southern majorities in Congress likewise weighed heavily.[19]

The Deep South in the 1840s remained an anachronism, having changed very little since the Colonial period. Here an oligarchy of elite southern families controlled state and local governments. Generally, they owned considerable property dedicated to agricultural production, which they operated as independent, self-sufficient feudal domains. These plantations functioned under a rigidly enforced social structure, where white owners and overseers performed the role of medieval nobility and African slaves performed the manual labor. The South looked to New England and Europe as markets for their output, which by this time was overwhelmingly dedicated to the production of cotton. In return they imported a variety of manufactured items. This reliance on foreign trade made them acutely aware of tariff issues. Tariffs, along with the sale of federal lands, were the major sources of government revenue at the time. But they also artificially raised the costs of imported items in an effort to protect fledgling United States industries, mostly in the North. In addition, Congress appropriated some of the revenue generated by these tariffs to improve rivers, harbors, and roads — again usually in the North and West — in an effort to stimulate internal economic growth. And while taxes on imports forced southerners to pay more for their imports, tariffs also cost them money when European countries retaliated with tariffs on southern exports. Not surprisingly, the use of tariffs to benefit other sections of the country infuriated southerners. Why, they asked, should taxes disproportionately levied against them be used to support economic development in the North or West?[20]

Cotton had grown in importance during the Industrial Revolution, which began in the textile mills of England, but had an evolving counterpart in the American northeast after 1815. Because these mechanized mills could produce a prodigious amount of cotton fiber, they had an insatiable appetite for raw cotton. With the invention of the cotton gin in 1793, the once tedious and expensive process of removing seeds from the raw cotton was streamlined. Now that cotton could be produced profitably, anyone in the Deep South who could began to plant it. Although it brought wealth to growers, middlemen, and shippers, it made the region economically dependent upon the European and, to a degree, New England mills.

Nonetheless, some southerners, acutely aware that they were losing economic and politic influence, questioned the wisdom of carrying on business as usual. Beginning with an October 1837 convention in Augusta, Georgia, a group of far-sighted southern business leaders began to meet regularly to consider commercial ventures that might allow the South to compete with, even overtake, the North's growing dominance in transportation, manufacturing, and finance, and its control of international trade. This latter issue was particularly galling because the bulk of the agricultural items exported came from the South, and a substantial amount of the imported items went to southern buyers. Most of this trade passed through the Port of New York, where tariff duties were assessed. And, these buyers noted, the tariff money collected tended to be allocated to the region that collected it. Although sectional friction with the North increasingly diverted their attention, conventions, such as the one held at Atlanta, continued to be held around the South until 1859. Some attendees, realizing that their success depended on upgrading the region's waterways, even advocated federal funding for at least some river and harbor improvements. Why, they argued, should they too not receive a share of the federal funds generated in part from the South's heavy tariff burden? This thinking was controversial because it deviated considerably from the traditional southern view, which held that the federal government's role in the internal affairs of the nation should be limited to those powers specifically granted to it by the Constitution. Only the most liberal reading of that document granted the national government any authority to fund improvements that should be the responsibility of the individual states.[21]

If southern leadership in the 1840s sought to retain the region's rigid social traditions while expanding its cotton production, many in the North at the time eagerly embraced technology innovation and commercial growth, believing they offered the best opportunity for creating personal wealth. After all, it was Eli Whitney, a northerner, who designed the cotton gin while traveling in the South in 1793. In a letter to his brother written shortly after his arrival in New York City in 1831, Tocqueville noted that "political passions here are only on the surface. The profound passion, the only one which profoundly stirs the human heart, the passion of all the days, is the acquisition of riches; and there are a thousand ways of acquiring them without troubling the state."[22] Although a recession in 1837 slowed the pace of entrepreneurial activity for several years, the energy had returned by the mid–1840s. Manufacturing, once limited to small New England textile factories, had become more widespread and diverse. Unlike their British counterparts, who tended to concentrate in manufacturing districts, Americans scattered their factories throughout the country along the streams and rivers from which they derived their power. One observer in 1829 noted that the businesses were so dispersed that it was difficult to accurately "estimate the extent of manufacturing operations" in the United States.[23] With a growing population dispersed across a rapidly expanding country, coupled with the lack of anything resembling an integrated transportation system, manufacturers tended to produce items for local consumption. At times their efforts received support from congressmen eager to encourage this capitalist spirit by erecting protective tariffs and, when possible, using this revenue to fund improvements for bridges, harbors, and roads.

Among these new enterprises, the evolution of iron production is central to this narrative and warrants further explanation. Iron masters had been active in New England and the Middle Atlantic region since early colonial times. Their operations were generally small and located near iron ore deposits, although nearby forests necessary for the production of the charcoal used for fuel and rivers required to transport raw materials in and finished products out also played an important role in choosing a site. There were, however, a few "iron plantations" that combined puddling furnaces, foundries, a firebrick yard, workers' houses, company stores, even iron and coal mines under a patriarchal system of ownership that one author characterized as almost "feudal."[24]

With transportation costs high, iron manufacturers, like most other businesses, generally served a local market. Railroads did not exist, river boats were small, and even the largest freight wagons of the day carried fewer than two tons. Consequently, the distance between the mill and the market often dictated the survival or failure of an iron maker. As they burned their way through the once-abundant forests near their facilities making charcoal, iron makers had to face some serious questions. Should they allow their operations to remain where they were and charge more for their finished product to offset the increased costs associated with transporting the fuel to their plants? Or, should they relocate closer to the timber and charge more to transport the finished iron to market? On the other hand, was there an alternative fuel source available that would render those issues irrelevant? American iron makers, however, had been able to survive the threat of cheaper European imports in part because of a series of protective tariffs beginning in 1816 that allowed them to produce iron in an artificial marketplace that did not require them to be innovative or efficient. Thus removed from competition with cheaper British imported iron, the answers to these questions became less important.[25]

Living amidst rich iron reserves and conveniently close to their markets, some Eastern producers, who enjoyed the luxury of generally competing only among themselves, only slowly moved to seek a new fuel source. During the War of 1812, Philadelphia iron maker Joshua Malin had produced some pig iron castings using anthracite coal. A few other local producers, noting his success, also began to use it. Known as "stone coal" by colonial iron makers, it was easily located in nearby fields throughout the Lehigh and Schuylkill Valleys of Pennsylvania. Its small but growing popularity led iron makers in the Philadelphia area to urge local authorities to improve nearby river navigation to allow them to transport this coal more economically to their plants. By the 1830s a number of producers regularly produced wrought iron with anthracite coal because it was cheaper. To make one ton of pig iron, for example, they required 200 bushels of charcoal ($10) or two tons of anthracite coal ($5). But traditions died hard, and it was not until the mid–1850s that the use of anthracite exceeded charcoal, and then primarily only along the East Coast.[26]

As the impact of the Panic of 1837 wore off in the mid–1840s, iron makers in western Pennsylvania turned to the extensive reserves of bituminous coal found in the nearby Appalachians. Having experienced increasing costs for charcoal fuel as their forest had also become reduced, they simply used what they had available. Unfortunatley, bituminous coal when heated emitted sulfur in addition to other gases. Since the fuel came in direct contact with the ore during the production process, the iron tended to absorb the gases from the fuel. Pig iron that absorbed sulfur became brittle, rendering it useless. To avoid this, western producers used bituminous coal only in puddling operations where the fuel and iron never came in contact.[27]

In the 1830s experimentation with coking began in Pennsylvania. Coke, which is made from bituminous coal heated to around 2400 degrees but not burned, eliminates the gaseous elements in the coal, leaving it almost pure carbon. Besides being free of sulfur, coke could also create a higher oven temperature. But its adoption was slow and uneven, particularly during the first half of the century. The regional nature of the iron industry, aggravated by inadequate transportation systems, found the isolated iron makers working independently. Each region continued to rely on local sources for its raw materials. Still, some producers did experiment with coking, much of their inspiration coming from the work of British iron makers who began using coke in the 1730s. Their forests long ago depleted for houses, ships, and fuel, most iron producers in England had adopted the process by the 1750s.[28]

As noted, most colonial iron makers had been reluctant to try coke as long as they had access to plentiful supplies of wood for their charcoal needs. In addition, transportation to and from the few known sites of bituminous coal were poor or non-existent. Moreover, few of them understood the coking process. American iron makers, safe under the mantle of tariff protection, remained complacent and continued to rely on charcoal. Historian George Rogers Taylor offers another explanation for their continuing use of charcoal. Since charcoal iron was easier to weld into such items as plows and hardware, it was better suited to the needs of the country at the time. Isaac Meason, who built the first rolling mill west of the Allegheny Mountains in Fayette County, Pennsylvania, used coke in 1817 to puddle iron and roll iron bars. But few western producers explored its possibilities before the 1830s when British cokers began arriving in the states looking for work, and even then coke tended to be used in combination with charcoal rather than alone to make iron. In the early 1840s, transportation costs remained an obstacle for the region's iron makers desiring to use coal, either by itself or for coking. Eventually iron makers grudgingly began to consider using coke when experimentation revealed that it had three distinct advantages over anthracite: it increased the rate of smelting by 30 percent, it required a less powerful "blast" of hot air, and its castings were softer.[29]

By the 1840s exploitation of the Connelsville coal fields south of Pittsburgh was under way. Reflecting on this forty years later, Joseph D. Weeks concluded that the development of these coal fields contributed immeasurably to the production of coke in the United States and to its use as a blast-furnace fuel. It had many advantages, not the least of which was the ease with which miners could extract it. Weeks demonstrated this by recounting the results of a wager made between miners there. He reported that one man and one boy loaded 23 wagons with 57,684 pounds of coal in less than 10 hours. The two spent a small fraction of the time actually mining the coal; rather, they simply scooped up the naturally loose coal into the wagons. On average, he concluded, one man could load between eight and ten wagons in one day at a cost of $.25 per ton.[30]

Connelsville coal had other favorable properties. The coal field itself was extensive. Also, the coal found there had a low volume of impurities, particularly sulfur. In addition, unlike fragile charcoal, it could withstand a heavy burden in the furnace without collapsing. It did have one troublesome drawback; it was "tender" and "ill adapted for shipping." Most coal was bulkier than iron ore and deteriorated quickly. Following the tradition of charcoal smelters earlier in the century, 19th century coal and coke ironmasters attempted to construct their plants as close to plentiful coal supplies, and the traditionally nearby coking facilities, as possible.[31]

The fragile nature of coal became a significant factor in the rise of Pittsburgh as the iron capital of the United States during the last decades of the 19th century. The Connelsville coal fields south of the city, once connected by rail lines to Pittsburgh in the 1850s, ensured iron producers of an abundant supply of coke for their furnaces. Nonetheless, Pittsburgh was "considerably later than some other western Pennsylvania points in getting its iron industry definitely established," concluded city historian Frank C. Harper. When Alsace emigrant George Anshutz built the first blast furnace in the locale of present-day Pittsburgh in 1792, he believed that the area had usable iron deposits. It did not, and he went bankrupt relying on iron brought 25 miles by boat down the Allegheny River. This lack of a large, accessible iron field continued to plague western Pennsylvania iron masters for more than half a century. At one point they even contracted to have ore laboriously transported to their furnaces from the Missouri ore fields. Their salvation came in the last decades of the century when efficient Lake transportation allowed them to pair high grade iron with an equally high grade coal supply located nearby.[32]

If iron production had yet to show signs of its future importance, transportation was experiencing a revolution by the 1840s. At the heart of this drastic change was steam. It was revolutionary because it used an inanimate source of power to provide consistent and relatively reliable energy. Civilizations historically had relied on animate, or natural, sources of power to accomplish their work. Horses carried messengers and pulled wagons, while wind drove ships across open waters or turned stone wheels to grind grain. Water propelled vessels downstream or spun large wheels that caused factory machinery to run. Men and women manually planted and harvested crops. But people and animals became tired, required food, and were temperamental; water and wind were fickle. Rivers flooded, but they could also dry up. Winds could gust, turn damaging, or simply cease. By harnessing the energy of heated water (steam), mankind could avoid the uncertainty and inconvenience of animate power sources. As long as fuel was maintained to fire the boiler, the steam engine produced power. Moreover, if properly regulated and serviced, these engines could keep producing that power night and day.

The first experiments with steam can be traced back to the ancient Greeks, who viewed it primarily as a novelty and failed to develop any useful applications for it. In the 1600s, European scientists, invigorated by a natural curiosity born of the Renaissance, again theorized about its possibilities. In 1712 Englishman Thomas Newcomen actually created a large, low-pressure steam engine that became popular for pumping water out of coal mines around England and on the continent. But the real revolution occurred when steam began to be adapted to transportation, beginning with movement on water. The mists of history obscure much of the early experimentation with steam navigation. While Thomas Savery may have constructed the first steam-powered vessel in 1698, it apparently exploded. Jonathon Hulls proposed a plan for navigating a towboat by a stern-wheel worked by steam in 1730, but no evidence exists that Hulls ever followed through by building a prototype. In France, Count Auxiron carried out some experiments on the Seine River in 1774. And in 1782, Marquis De Jouffroy, a fellow countryman, actually moved a boat 140 feet down the Saone River with a steam engine that drove paddlewheels on the vessel's sides.[33]

While Europeans continued to struggle with the problem, several American inventors independently began to consider using steam power in transportation as a way to overcome a vexing problem that perplexed the young nation's business interests. With only a few primitive roads, the nation's commerce tended to travel by water, driven by wind or carried by the currents. While trade between seaports like Charleston and Boston was accomplished with relative efficiency by ocean-going sailing ships, the movement of goods inland posed a greater problem. Anyone referring to a map would conclude that the most direct routes between settlements often involved using the various river systems in the country. And this was usually true, if you only planned to follow the current downstream. Returning home against the currents, however, was another matter. Americans had developed the practice of building flatboats, loading them with cargo, and floating downstream to market. Farmers living in the Ohio River basin, for example, often used this method to transport goods south to New Orleans via the Mississippi River. Once they arrived, they sold their cargo and broke up the flatboat, which they sold as lumber. They then walked home. Although terribly inefficient, they had no other choice if they wanted to sell their produce to East Coast market, which paid the best price.[34]

In the 1780s, James Rumsey of Virginia and John Fitch of Pennsylvania separately began working on the problem of steam navigation. Both embodied an exuberant optimism then common in the young country. As Fitch wrote about himself early in his quest to develop the steamboat, "What cannot you do if you will get yourself about it." Both aggressively sought the patronage of George Washington, Benjamin Franklin, Thomas Jefferson, and other state and national leaders; they also petitioned several state legislatures for money, as well as for exclusive rights to operate in the rivers of those states. After a "long war of pamphlets" arguing "the merits of their invention and claims to priority," Fitch won exclusive rights to experiment with steam navigation from the legislatures of Pennsylvania, Delaware, New York, and Virginia. With a small group of investors to support him, he installed a steam engine with a three-inch cylinder on a skiff in 1786. It did not generate much speed running against the current, so the following year he built a second boat with a 12-inch cylinder. This vessel, which used an awkward-looking arrangement of six paddles on each side that alternately paddled and recovered with each cycle of the engine, actually made several successful trips between Philadelphia and Burlington, New Jersey, at about four miles per hour. At one point, several members of the Constitutional Convention, then meeting in Philadelphia, witnessed Fitch's boat under steam. In common with most Americans at the time, they generally viewed it as the amusing work of an eccentric that had little practical application. Still, Fitch persevered, launching a third boat in 1790, this time employing an 18-inch cylinder. It ran regularly along the same route as its predecessor, carrying passengers at seven and a half miles per hour. Even though it traveled over 2,000 miles that season, Fitch's boat did not make a profit and most of his investors withdrew their support. After a final failed attempt to interest investors in Kentucky,

Fitch ended his frustration with an overdose of opium in 1798. Rumsey, prevented from experimenting in the United States by Fitch's patents, worked abroad. He died in 1793, one day before the first trial run of his steamboat in London.[35]

Plagued by a lack of funds, education, primitive technology, and simply bad timing, neither Fitch nor Rumsey achieved the success that they had envisioned for themselves. Yet their efforts spurred other inventors. Robert Fulton, who had originally studied in London as an artist, was a relative latecomer to steam navigation when he piloted his *North River* steamboat, later renamed the more familiar *Clermont*, comfortably both with and against the Hudson River current in 1807. It offered nothing new either in technology or in design. But Fulton's engineering skill in combining various elements of steam navigation into a commercially successful design made it unique. Others failed, wrote Fulton, because of their "ignorance of proportions, speeds, powers and probably mechanical combinations. All these things being governed by the laws of nature, the real invention is to find them." Fulton's success "marked the final acceptance by [Americans] of the principle that steam could be made of practical use in travel and transportation." With steam propulsion, wind, current, even to a degree storms, did not influence navigation as they once did. Bolstered by his success with the *Clermont*, Fulton formed a company to build additional boats, often with classically inspired names such as the *Car of Neptune* and the *Vesuvius*. He and his partner, New York state chancellor Robert R. Livingston, then set out to create a monopoly by gaining exclusive rights to license his operations in the various states.[36]

By 1811, the pair had received exclusive rights to the waters of New York State and New Orleans, the two most active waterways in the country. Their first venture in the West was the *Enterprise* (later renamed the *New Orleans*), originally a keelboat built at Marietta, Ohio, but later fitted out with an engine and stern paddle wheel in Pittsburgh. It was sailed down the Ohio and Mississippi Rivers to New Orleans in late 1811, where it ran between New Orleans and Natchez until it was wrecked in 1814. Although a number of attempts to break this monopoly were undertaken, Livingston and Fulton initially fended them off. Some states enacted retaliatory measures by closing their waters to ships licensed in New York, while others issued monopolies of their own. Not surprisingly, confusion and enmity came to characterize commercial activity involving waterborne trade throughout the country. The issue finally reached the United States Supreme Court in 1824 with Gibbons v Ogden. Although the two plaintiffs were partners, they operated steamboats under two different licenses: Ogden had acquired rights from the Livingston-Fulton monopoly, while Gibbons held a federal permit under the 1793 Coastal Licensing Act. When Gibbons began sending his boats to New York, Ogden sued to protect his monopoly rights. While the New York courts predictably ordered Gibbons to honor the Livingston-Fulton monopoly and cease operating his ships in New York waters, Gibbons appealed to the United States Supreme Court. He argued that his federal license should take precedence over Ogden's state issued monopoly license. The Marshall Court agreed, holding that the federal government may regulate commerce among states under the commerce clause of the Constitution. This effectively broke the Livingston-Fulton state-issued monopolies on steamship operations in the country, opening up opportunities for others. But the following year the Court placed a limitation on government intervention in waterborne commerce. In the case of the steamboat *Thomas Jefferson*, it ruled that federal jurisdiction applied only to waters where the tide ebbs and flows, thereby excluding all inland waterways and lakes. Responding to this limitation, the Senate in 1845 finally passed a bill that extended federal jurisdiction to "certain cases upon the lakes and navigable waters leading to and connecting with the same."[37]

In 1816, some local investors launched the *Ontario*, the first American steamship on the Great Lakes, at Sackett's Harbor, New York. It went into service in April the following year. The *Frontenac* was launched about the same time on the Canadian side of the lake, although Canadians had been employing steamers on the St. Lawrence River since 1809. The *Ontario* traversed the waters of Lake Ontario, but could not travel into the western (upper) lakes because of the falls on the Niagara River. Sensing a business opportunity, Dr. J. B. Stewart of New York City obtained rights from the Livingston-Fulton Company to build the first steamer above the falls in 1817. Built in the village of Black Rock, New York, and launched on May 28, 1818, she was christened *Walk-in-the-Water* after a local Wyandot Indian chief who died shortly before her maiden voyage. *Walk-in-the-Water* was 240 tons with a length of 135 feet and a beam of 32 feet. Building this vessel was no easy task. Her engine, for example, had to be brought from the East Coast, first up the Hudson River by sloop and then west by wagon. Black Rock was so primitive, and the engines of the boat so weak, that ten pairs of oxen had to help move her down the Niagara River to the lake by what locals came to call the "horned breeze." Even before her appearance, it was standard for all sailing ships to lie off Buffalo because the city had no harbor. Passengers and cargo had to be lightered between the city and ships moored out in Lake Erie. *Walk-in-the-Water* had a unique method for signaling, a four-pound cannon on board was fired one-half hour before she departed and within one mile of Buffalo upon her return. Not surprisingly, Stewart, convinced that no one living in such a remote wilderness would know how to run the steamer properly, sent officers from New York City to manage and sail her. Her first commander, Captain Job Fish, had, in fact, been an engineer for Fulton, Livingston & Company on the North River. That year *Walk-in-the-Water* carried 100 passengers at $20 each the 300 miles from Black Rock to Detroit in 48 hours. The time required to make the same trip under sail, running against the prevailing westerlies and sailing against the current in the Detroit River, varied from five to seven days. *The Bethel Magazine* recorded the "novelty of the sight, as she made her first trip through lake." It "excited a great degree of interest and curiosity among the people who live upon the shores, especially among the native Indians. They stood gazing with astonishment to see such 'a thing of life' moving through the water without the aid of oars or sail."[38]

The *Walk-in-the-Water* at anchor. She was able to make eight miles-per-hour on smooth water. On her maiden voyage in 1818 she transported 100 passengers between Buffalo (New York) and Detroit (Michigan Territory) in 48 hours. (From *American Steam Vessels, 1895*, reprinted in J. B. Mansfield, ed., *History of the Great Lakes*, 1899.)

While the ability of steamships to travel upstream was an advantage on the nation's rivers, this made less difference on open water. Besides, steam technology was expensive and, at the time, was considered primitive and unreliable. Therefore, Great Lakes shipbuilders were slower to accept this new technology. Steamships operating on the Great Lakes, for example, usually installed functioning masts and rigging until late in the 19th century. While this equipment often helped with loading and unloading, and allowed the ships to conserve fuel by sailing with the wind, it also suggests that some wanted an alternative power source in the event of mechanical breakdowns. In 1820 the Great Lakes sailing ships had no problem sharing the shipping lanes with the four steamers (at collectively a little over 900 tons) operating there. During that same year, 52 steamboats (10,564 tons) operated along the East Coast and 71 (14,207 tons) traveled the western rivers. By 1836, however, 38 steam vessels had operated on Lake Erie alone, and only three boats and one life had been lost. And, unlike the "dreadful disasters which have been so common upon other waters," reported the *Bethel Magazine* in 1836, "resulting from the bursting of boilers, are altogether unknown upon this lake." The article concluded that in 1836 "the engines in use are of both kinds, high pressure and low pressure — about equal in proportion."[39]

Steamers, nonetheless, remained a distinct minority on the Great Lakes, as sailing vessels dominated the horizons and harbors. But even their numbers remained small during the early days of the Republic. The Treaty of Paris (1815) ending the War of 1812 reduced international tensions around the Great Lakes and made the southern shore of Lake Erie available for settlement. But it was not until the completion of the Erie Canal in 1825 that immigrants began to pour into the region. Soon the white-canvassed brigantines, barks, and schooners became a familiar, and welcome, sight to the settlers of Cleveland, Portland (now Sandusky, Ohio), and other settlements established along the Erie shoreline. They also became increasingly active in Lakes Huron and Michigan, delivering passengers and supplies, and providing an early communications network for the region. Because they were better suited to the lakes, schooners eventually superseded the barks and brigantines, dominating shipping on the Great Lakes for a good portion of the 19th century.[40]

Brigantines were two-masted, having a fore-mast with yardarms supporting square sails and a main-mast with fore and aft rigging. Barks had three masts, the first two being square-rigged and the third rigged fore and aft. Square-rigged masts recalled the early sailing ships on the lakes and served a military role. This design divided the sail area among a large number of spars, reducing the chance that enemy cannon fire could render the ship inoperable by destroying its sails. Square sails also operated very efficiently when running with the prevailing winds. But square-rigged vessels responded too slowly in the narrow channels and the quickly changing winds of the lakes. Moreover, they required more rigging — a problem when loading and unloading — and not surprisingly more sailors to operate than schooners.[41]

Schooners, on the other hand, had from two to four masts, all rigged with a boom and a gaff. This gave schooners greater maneuverability. There was one important and unique exception, however, in the Great Lakes schooner. At some point mariners on the lakes adapted a square top sail or a triangular "Raffe" for the foremast. These variation on the lakes were unique in the country, a compromise that permitted these ships to take the greatest advantage of the winds and geography of the region. While under way, sailors also could employ a variety of auxiliary sails — jibs, staysails, studding sails — depending on the wind and weather conditions.[42]

The grace and beauty of these ships as they moved silently but deliberately across the lakes belied the complexity involved in their operation. Understanding the workings of the myriad lines, masts, booms, and sails was simply unfathomable to the uninitiated. Each played an integral role in the overall operation of an efficient sailing ship, but they also shrouded the vessel like a web, which could become a considerable inconvenience when cargo was being moved on and off the ship. Spare sails, cordage, and other tackle also took up valuable cargo space, but had to be kept on hand to deal with the frequent repairs resulting from weather or simply wear and tear.

Sailing ships faced other problems as well. They operated at the mercy of the weather conditions, making it all but impossible for them to maintain any kind of schedule. If forced to sail against the wind, ships employed a zig-zag maneuver called tacking; this obviously took more time and extended the length of their voyages. When winds were light, ships moved slowly or not at all. When caught in a gale, sailors could usually do little more than furl their sails and pray. Trying to enter the often narrow breakwaters of harbors, challenging under ideal conditions, was virtually impossible during unfavorable weather conditions. The *Cleveland Leader* reported in its September 19, 1865, edition that "the schooner *Beard* was towed into port after having been anchored off the west pier all night, unable to get into port due to the gale." Finally, the day-to-day operation of these vessels was an extremely labor-intensive activity. Even small sailing ships required crews of three to five men to help set and furl sails, to keep up with the constant maintenance associated with wooden hulled ships, and to assist with loading and unloading.[43]

These sailing ships transported a variety of cargo, including bulk items,

Great Lakes schooners in the harbor at Frankfort, Michigan, circa 1890. The vessel in the center of this group has been refitted with a steam engine, a sign of the changing times.

to and from ports around the lakes. For instance, ship captains found that they could fill their holds with locally caught fish and find a ready market for them at most lower lake ports, where rapid immigration into the region had created a large and growing demand for inexpensive food. Grain, however, became the most important bulk commodity carried on the lakes after the late 1830s. Before that time, ships sailing from Lake Erie ports like Buffalo carried cargo and immigrants westward, often returning with furs or in ballast. By the late 1830s immigrants who had settled in the Midwest sought passage for their agricultural production destined for eastern markets. Brought from small inland farms by canalers, river barges, or wagons to the small ports along Lakes Erie and Michigan, the grain was painstakingly loaded for shipment to Buffalo, the terminus of the Erie Canal, and eventually by the canal to New York City. As early as 1831 *William's New York Register* reported that Cleveland, the northern terminus of the Ohio-Erie Canal on Lake Erie, recorded that a total of 176,689 bushels of wheat, 32,000 barrels of flour, and 2,442 barrels of whiskey arrived in the city in 1830 on the canal. Most of it was then loaded on lake ships for Buffalo and the Erie Canal.[44]

As the demand for grain and other commodities increased around the lower lakes, many along the lakes' shores realized that ship ownership could be a lucrative enterprise. Communities of all sizes on or near the water supported an active shipbuilding business. The only requirements were an abundant supply of timber and a good launching way. Financing for nearly all these early ships came from local sources, including merchants, prosperous farmers, and others who owned shares in the ships. It was not unusual for a captain to have personally raised the capital to build his ship, to oversee its construction, and to sail it over its entire career. Shipbuilding provided employment for the thousands immigrating into the Great Lakes during the period. Even farmers found they could make a profit by selling the timber removed after clearing their fields to shipbuilders. Many of these same farmers enjoyed additional income during the slow winter months by serving as

Schooners load and unload cargo along the Cuyahoga River in 1874. The serpentine shape of the river made movement in and out of the port of Cleveland particularly challenging.

laborers in the construction of the ships themselves. As the Erie Canal, and later the Ohio canal systems, brought immigrants and increased trade, some port cities, such as Cleveland, located at the mouth of the Cuyahoga River, became increasingly important centers for ship construction. Here shipbuilders began launching boats that went beyond the limited needs of local communities and could satisfy the more demanding requirements of shippers who sailed throughout the lakes.[45]

Once launched, sailing ships became a source of pride for their owners and the communities from which they sailed. But wooden vessels, whether sail or steam, possessed inherent weaknesses. One of the most troublesome was the constant maintenance and repair necessary to keep them operational. "I have heard old timers say," recalled Great Lakes shipbuilder H. C. Inches, "that after 15 years, repairs [on wooden ships] were a constant source of trouble and expense." Some early shipbuilding facilities learned that they

Canal boats pick up and drop off cargo along Water Street in Chillicothe, Ohio, circa 1870. Chillicothe was located on the Ohio-Erie Canal, which meant some of the boats pictured here eventually made their way north to Cleveland. There they unloaded cargo from Ohio's interior destined for the East Coast via the Erie Canal and picked up manufactured goods for transport to towns south along the canal.

could augment their revenue by building drydocks where ships could come for repairs. Submerged rocks and shoals, forced groundings, severe weather, fires, and other ships also damaged or destroyed a large number of these vessels. Although the number of losses before the 1840s is sketchy at best, better records in the following years show just how precarious navigating the Great Lakes could be. In the fall of 1869, for example, 66 ships were lost for a variety of reasons on the lakes during a single two-month period.[46]

By the early 1840s, despite the predominance of sailing vessels in lake traffic, steamships were becoming more common. A congressional committee on commerce reported that in 1841 there were more than 50 steamers on Lake Erie and the upper lakes. Although their aggregate cost of construction — estimated to be between $2 and $3 million — was considerably more than for the region's sailing ships ($1.250 million), the revenue from both was about the same ($750,000). These figures should be viewed only as rough estimates, but they suggest that steamships, although more expensive to build, could produce comparable revenues but with the added benefit of being able to maintain a schedule. Moreover, as an epitome of the new steam technology, they generated considerable enthusiasm and wonder. Gustave Beaumont, Tocqueville's traveling companion during his 1831–1832 tour of the United States, remarked that "even to a European these great vessels propelled by steam are without gainsaying one of the marvels of modern industry."[47]

Lake steamships were punctual, making them a favorite of the passenger trade; less expeditious, schooners, barks, and brigs remained the workhorses that hauled cargo. People were itchy to get where they wanted to go; cargo, for the most part, arrived when it got there. This division of services was also a function of design. For stability of a ship and for its own protection, cargo, especially bulk items, was generally carried in the hold. The technology of the day required that the engines that drove large paddlewheels on each side of the ship be placed directly between these paddlewheels in the center of the ship, with their boilers forward and the fuel bunker located in close proximity. This left little room for cargo below decks, with the result that most package freight was carried on deck.[48]

Passengers, on the other hand, could be comfortably housed in cabins rising from the main deck above the engine. Steamship owners, in addition to transporting immigrants and businessmen from port to port, began promoting pleasure trips round the lakes to help assure an optimum return on their investment. Beaumont recorded a daily notice that appeared in the July

21, 1831, *Detroit Courier* encouraging the "traveling public" to book passage aboard the "superb" steamboat *Superior* so they could view "the splendid scenery of the Upper Lakes, the intention of the trip being to accommodate *Parties of Pleasure* at a season of the year when the voyage through the lakes is both agreeable and healthful." Earlier steamers did provide space for those unable to afford cabins, which was more likely than not a spot on the open deck. They also paid extra for their meals. From Cleveland to Detroit, for example, a deck passenger might pay $2.50. Those with cabins and meals paid $6.00.[49]

These boats were constructed somewhat differently than the steamers that plied the nation's river systems. Since they ran most of the time on open water, it was necessary for them to have a deeper draft to ensure stability in rough seas. But their draft could not be so deep that it prevented them from navigating the frequently treacherous rivers, shoals, and channels they also encountered around the lakes. Likewise, the uncertainty of weather and a variety of formidable underwater obstacles led builders on the lakes to make these vessels stronger and more durable. While steamboats on the western rivers ran almost exclusively with high-pressure engines, the lake steamers were larger and generally operated with low-pressure engines. Clearly, the construction of steamships required specialized shipyards, skilled artisans, and experienced mechanics. The expenses associated with the production of steam vessels usually necessitated the formation of companies and willing investors to raise enough capital. Profits, of course, were distributed according to the proportion of capital raised.[50]

By the 1830s, despite the concerns of some, the speed and dependability of steamships had increased their popularity and their numbers grew. Following the completion of the Erie Canal in 1825, New Englanders and New Yorkers joined immigrants from across northwest Europe on canal boats to Buffalo. Where they boarded steamboats to take them west. By 1830, on average 300 people a week passed through Buffalo on their way to Detroit and points west. John Mullett, writing Sylvester Sibley in April of 1834, could hardly contain his enthusiasm: "There are Steamboats now running on the waters of Lake Erie almost without number." He later speculated that the number would reach 30. Hyperbole aside, it was clear that steamships were certainly becoming a familiar sight, at least on the lower lakes, by the 1840s.[51]

During this decade, truly large and often quite elegant steam ships began appearing on the lakes. For example, the 1,140 ton *Empire*, launched at Cleveland in 1844, was the first vessel in the United States to measure over 1,000 tons; in fact, she was 200 tons larger than any other vessel in the world at the time. Her dining cabin on the upper deck was 230 feet in length with state-rooms located on either side. Paddlewheels 30 feet in diameter, powered by a 600 horsepower, low-pressure engine, propelled her swiftly over the water. She made the passage from Buffalo to Detroit in 20 hours and 25 minutes, after her engine was replaced in 1846 with a new one that generated 1,400 horsepower. This was less than half the 48 hours required by *Walk-in-the-Water* on its maiden voyage. Without question, she was then the fastest boat on the lakes.[52]

Traditional wooden ship designs and construction methods, however, proved inadequate for these large steam vessels. Specifically, builders ran into problems trying to reinforce the steamers amidships as the bows and sterns grew further apart. With the engine and machinery — by far the heaviest component on the ship — located at its center, the considerable pressure at that point threatened to buckle the vessel. George Washington Jones, the Cleveland shipbuilder responsible for the *Empire*, devised an ingenious method to

The harbor at Buffalo (New York) circa 1860. The canal boats at the left and the hogback, side-wheel paddleboat on the right symbolize Buffalo's location as an important link between the Erie Canal and the East Coast, and the Upper Lakes and the West.

address this problem, thus allowing wooden steamboats to stretch much further than previously thought possible. He installed an arch on either side of the vessel running nearly bow to stern. It peaked directly above the weakest point — amidships — at the height of the uppermost deck. This "Bishop's Arch" applied downward pressure at the extreme ends of the ship, thereby preventing it from buckling in the center. Most builders on the lakes adopted Jones's invention, making it a standard part of the Great Lakes steamers, whose humped appearance inspired the name "hogback." But, of course, this additional reinforcement added more weight to the vessel, reducing its efficiency.[53]

The British too faced structural problems with their steamships, but they had the added burden of having long ago depleted their timber supply. Therefore, they were the first to begin experimenting with iron hulls. In 1818 the iron lighter *Vulcan* was launched near Glasgow. As steam engines became more popular, so did iron shipbuilding. This was encouraged by the British government, which began to subsidize steamship construction in 1836. Unfettered by debates concerning constitutional limitations, Parliament viewed such support as necessary for the infant steam-shipping industry to prosper. In addition, the demands of a far-flung, global empire would benefit from improved communications available with more reliable ships. They also concluded that the subsidies would support improvements that could very well have important military applications.[54]

The first iron ships in the United States were probably the steamboats *John Randolph* (122 tons), the *Chatham* (198 tons), and the *Lamar* (196 tons) launched at Savannah between 1834 and 1838. Each used imported British iron because there were inadequate supplies of iron in coastal Georgia. The tariff on iron proved to be too costly for these ships to turn a profit. By the 1840s, local iron deposits in Delaware made it advantageous to begin building iron ships there, and this was where most iron ships were built over that decade. But even here an underdeveloped machine-tool industry meant that the manufacturers of iron ships, marine engines, and related components were unable to produce that equipment at the technical level required. Meanwhile, the first iron-hulled vessel on the lakes was fabricated at Pittsburgh and assembled in Buffalo for the U. S. government in 1844. Aptly named, the *Surveyor* conducted surveys of the Upper Lakes from 1844 until 1878, when she was sold by the government and became an excursion boat renamed *Julia*. Still, most in the shipping business, whether involved with coastal or fresh water commerce, continued to question the wisdom of iron. In an 1869 letter to the Senate from John Codman, an advocate of iron ships, itemized some of the concerns he had heard. Some feared that metal ships were in a greater danger from lightning. Others believed they would sink because iron was not buoyant. Wood, still others argued, was more durable. Shipyards, traditionally used to working on wooden boats, were incapable of cleaning and repairing iron ships. Furthermore, how were magnetic compasses supposed to operate on an iron ship? Finally, a United States tariff on imported iron made iron vessels more expensive, especially where timber remained plentiful ... such as along the shores of the Great Lakes.[55]

Therefore, wooden paddle-wheelers continued to transport passengers throughout the lakes into the 1870s. While their ability to maintain a schedule gave them an advantage over sailing ships, they did exhibit a number of shortcomings. First, their equipment was heavy, as well as expensive to both build and operate. In addition, the boiler and machinery took up potential cargo space below decks. Finally, the side wheels themselves were a problem. They not only made maneuverability more difficult, they also added width to the vessel, making it a challenge for steamships to negotiate the frequently narrow channels, canals, and harbors around the lakes. And while paddle-wheelers performed particularly well in shallow waters, such as rivers, they were at a distinct disadvantage in open water during rough seas. As the vessel rolled under such weather conditions, the wheel on one side often came out of the water while the opposite wheel dug deeper into the water, creating a severe strain on the engine.[56]

As steam power grew more popular in the United States in the 1800s, there were bound to be other problems of a more general nature as well. Undoubtedly the most serious were the dangers of fire and boiler explosion. From 1816, when eleven people died from steamship fires and explosions around the country, the losses rose steadily as the ships became more common and they grew in size. With more passengers crowding onto these ships, the number of deaths reached 682 in 1837. Loss of life through explosions on lake steamers by comparison was considerably lower. The bursting of a steam pipe aboard the *Wm. Peacock* in 1827 left sixteen dead and a similar accident on the *Commodore Perry* in 1835 killed four others. The practice of using low-pressure boilers on lake vessels no doubt accounted for the considerably fewer deaths from explosion. But fires plagued steam vessels everywhere, including on the Great Lakes. In November of 1847, for example, the propeller *Phoenix* burned off Sheboygan, Michigan, taking over 200 lives, including 150 immigrants from Holland. Reports concluded that the fire began under the deck near the back of the boiler. The large steam boilers necessary to run the engines tended to generate a tremendous amount of heat, which posed considerable dangers to the wooden hulls universally used. At this time, the regulation of steamships was still the responsibility of the states and was, not surprisingly, generally inadequate and woefully inconsistent.[57]

In an effort to mitigate the maneuverability problems of Great Lakes sidewheelers, investors in Oswego, New York, decided to incorporate a propeller on the small schooner *Vandalia* they were converting to steam in 1841. This principle can be traced back to the third century B.C. when Archimedes constructed a screw device to raise water for irrigation purposes. But limited technology prevented it from being used for propulsion until the 19th century. Then, following the pattern established with the steam engine, much of the original work on the propeller originated in Europe. Englishman Bennet Woodcraft patented a propeller design in 1832. John Ericsson, a former Swedish naval officer living in London, developed his own design, for which he received a patent four years later. In 1837 he demonstrated his invention on the Thames for representatives of the British Navy on the *Francis B. Ogden*, a 45-foot vessel named for the American Consul in London who had encouraged Ericsson's efforts. While the British doubted that a helmsman could properly steer a ship equipped with a propeller, Captain Robert F. Stockton, an American naval officer who also witnessed the test, immediately recognized its potential. Taking the initiative, and without prior authorization, he ordered two propeller-driven vessels from the Laird shipyard in England. Outfitted as two-masted schooners after their arrival in the states, the propellers, when employed, performed favorably. By 1839, there were 150 ships driven by propellers in the country.[58]

With a 91-foot length and a 20-foot beam, the 138 ton *Vandalia* was small. It used a 25 horsepower engine to drive twin propellers that straddled the rudder. Following several short trips on Lake Ontario, her optimistic owners sent her on a 660-mile trip to Chicago with 30 passengers on April 10, 1842. She made the round trip in about 30 days, burning an average of only six chords of wood every 24 hours. The average steamboat making the shorter round trip between Buffalo and Detroit at the time, although of greater tonnage, could consume as much as 200 chords of wood at an average cost of $1.75 each. Of course, at opportune times the *Vandalia* did unfurl her sails to take advantage of the wind, which, free from the drag of two motionless paddlewheels, allowed her to perform with great economy on her first voyage.[59]

Since side-wheelers employed their sails less frequently because of the drag caused by the paddlewheels, builders began to discontinue rigging them altogether. Propeller-driven ships, however, sported masts and sails, some as late as the 1890s. Although propellers caused comparatively little drag, they had another advantages as well. They were less expensive to build, enjoyed more powerful propulsion, and proved to be more maneuverable. Propellers also reduced the width of the ships, making it easier for them to negotiate narrow passages, such as canals and locks. And, as the March 17, 1841, *Oswego County Whig* noted, the machinery associated with propellers was considerably lighter than that of side-wheelers, allowing them to operate more efficiently. Also, ship designers could now move the machinery and boiler, no longer required amidships, to the stern. This, of course, made it possible to transport cargo, including bulk items, in the holds below deck. The holds were enlarged further when lake ships moved away from the more traditional hull shapes to flat, shallow bottoms in an effort to avoid running aground in the unpredictable depths of channels, locks, and harbors around the lakes.[60]

Unfortunately, these types of hulls presented a problem on the open water. Ocean-going vessels, whether sail or steam, could maintain their stability with deep, or standing, keels. Prevented from doing so by the unpredictable channel depths and hidden shoals, shallow hulled lake boats became vulnerable in rough seas. Originally, builders of Great Lakes sailing ships designed their hulls in such a way that the sterns were deeper and the bows upthrust. This gave them additional stability by putting more of the hull in the water. By the 1840s, however, lake sailors found that centerboards assisted in maintaining stability while underway, but they could be retracted in shallow water. The centerboard allowed for sailing vessels on the lakes to grow in size without compromising stability. Such equipment and design variations, necessitated by the peculiar features of the lakes, contributed to the uniqueness of Great Lakes ships.[61]

If ships on the lakes were beginning to evolve, methods for handling cargo there remained unchanged and resembled the process found in contemporary ports around the world. In the earliest days of sailing on the lakes, ships carried a variety of cargo to and from the small, often isolated villages. Between April 9, 1830, and July 12, 1831, for example, the sloop *Forester* carried the following between Detroit and various Lake Erie ports: lumber, shingles, bushels of potatoes, pork, barrels of whiskey, barrels of fish, and "sundry goods." Shippers usually consigned bulk items during this period to barrels. In design and operation, sailing ships were not suited to hauling such items any other way. Barrels were reasonably watertight, easy to handle, made the accounting of loads easier, and reduced cleanup time. Equally important, if the crew stored them properly in the holds, there was little chance that the cargo would shift while underway, a serious problem that could affect a vessel's stability.

Finally, depending on the cargo, barrels could be reused. The crew of each vessel generally loaded and unloaded the cargo manually, often using the spars and rigging as makeshift block and tackle. The relaxed pace of commerce and the variety of goods carried on the lakes during the Antebellum period placed little pressure on shippers to improve this method of handling cargo.[62]

Whether a cargo-carrying schooner or a passenger steamer, a Great Lakes ship in the 1840s faced a variety of natural obstacles in the course of its travels. Falls on the St. Mary's and the Niagara Rivers effectively isolated Lakes Superior and Ontario from the other lakes, although the Canadian Welland Canal in 1829 permitted some traffic in and out of Lake Ontario. There also was the St. Clair Flats in the northern part of Lake St. Clair, where the volume of water passing from the upper lakes through the St. Clair River caused sediment to build up on the flats. Lime Kiln Crossing in the Detroit River presented a particularly shallow, stony bottom, which became a major concern as ships grew bigger over the course of the 19th century. Islands, reefs, and shoals greeted sailors in western Lake Erie and at various other spots around the lakes. Since nearly all ports on the Great Lakes were located at the mouths of rivers, sediment was continuously being deposited in these harbors and became a chronic problem for vessels seeking to enter or leave port. Underwater obstructions were constantly being discovered scattered along the shoreline around the lakes, more often than not when unsuspecting ships smashed into them.[63]

The uncertainty of severe weather on the lakes made the lack of harbors for refuge a particularly serious concern. "While violent gales are frequent and the storms rival those of the ocean itself," an 1882 Army Corps of Engineer's report stated, "a vessel is never more than a few hours run from shore, and cannot, as is generally the case at sea, drift before the wind until the storm is over, but in a long-continued gale must be thrown upon the shore, unless a port or harbor of refuge can be entered." In 1841, the report continued, a ship leaving Chicago would be unable to find a harbor or shelter from storms until it reached Manitou or the Beaver Islands in northern Lake Michigan. And after passing the Straits of Mackinac, it was at the mercy of the elements on Lake Huron, except in the vicinity of Presque Isle (Michigan), until it reached the mouth of the St. Clair River. As bad as travel on the lower lakes could be, Lake Superior was even more dangerous. In late 1847, for example, the steamer *Julia Palmer* ran into a series of nasty storms running between Copper Harbor and Sault Ste. Marie. Feared lost, she finally limped into harbor badly damaged. It had taken her 16 days to cover the roughly 160 miles, a trip that should have taken a little over a half a day. With no harbors of refuge,

Traditionally, Great Lakes vessels were laid up from mid–November to late March because of unpredictable, and frequently adverse, weather conditions. The schooner *Parana* in the port at Milwaukee in 1871 shows the effects of a December blizzard.

she had been forced to ride out the storms that repeatedly battered her. On June 13, 1870, Representative O. D. Conger (Michigan) reminded his fellow congressmen just how dangerous travel was on the lakes earlier that century. "There are gentlemen now on this floor," he recalled, "who remember that the emigrant from the Atlantic states to Ohio, or Michigan, or Illinois, parted from his friends and departed with his family amid tears and prayers and sorrowful farewells, as if he and his family were going down through the valley of the shadow of death."[64]

Consider the account given by a woman in 1872 about her trip aboard the steamer *Superior* from Buffalo to Huron, Ohio, 50 years earlier. In order to reach the *Superior* in the first place, she and her party took a ferry from Buffalo out into the lake where the ship lay anchored because the city's harbor was inadequate. Upon arriving at Huron, which also had no harbor or docks, her party took a rowboat ashore. From there, a sailor carried her on his shoulders across the surf to the dry beach. Even during favorable weather conditions, boarding or disembarking passengers under such circumstances could be difficult, even dangerous. Clearly those who ventured on the Great Lakes during the early decades of the 19th century did so knowing that it could be a perilous undertaking.[65]

In addition to the lack of ports, the design and layout of the harbors that did exist also posed a problem, particularly in the positioning of the breakwater. This was a special concern for sailing ships. While breakwaters could assist ships entering harbors in rough weather, they could also serve as the final resting place for those vessels that, battling wind and water, took a wrong position as they tried to enter. Barks and schooners, unlike steamships, had no power to make corrections in heavy seas. To compound the problem, there were few good harbor lights or fog signal stations on the lakes.[66]

Other problems, while not life threatening, were nonetheless time consuming and aggravating. Horace Greeley traveled to the 1847 Chicago Rivers and Harbors Convention by boat on the lakes. Leaving Buffalo, which by then had a harbor, of sorts, Greeley recalled, "After the tedious process of working her [the *Empire*] way out of Buffalo harbor — which is a burning shame to leave hardly wide enough for half-a-dozen watersnakes, while the vast and rapidly increasing commerce of half a continent seeks passage through it — she was a little more than twenty-four hours reaching [Detroit]." Later, he described the difficulty his ship encountered on Lake St. Clair. "Passing out of the [Detroit] River and through the comparatively small Lake St. Clair, we found a steamboat [*Wisconsin*] and several sail vessels hard aground on the St. Clair Flats, where, as I am informed, it is usual to find a far larger num-

Sailing vessels, although economical to operate, were often at the mercy of weather. On November 15, 1893, the Canadian schooner *Flora Emma* became endangered during a heavy west gale on Lake Ontario. As the tug *Eliza J. Redford* attempted to tow her into the safety of the harbor at Oswego (New York), they struck the east pier. Both were total losses. Much of the lumber that the *Flora Emma* had been carrying on her deck washed overboard during the accident and lies scattered at the water's edge.

ber of steamboats and other vessels in the same interesting predicament." Later that year, the *Milwaukee Sentinel* also reported on the problems encountered on Lake St. Clair. The paper quoted Captain Billings of the brig *Giddings*, who stated that every time he crossed the Flats "he had to light from 3(000) to 5,000 bushels (that is off-load part of his cargo of grain to lighten his ship), at a cost of about $150, and lose nearly a week's time." The editors, reflecting a growing rancor among inhabitants of the region over the unwillingness of Washington to provide more assistance, added, "For this tax upon Western commerce we may thank James K. Polk and his Mexican War."[67]

In the early decades of the 19th century, local businessmen and government officials around the lakes generally shouldered the responsibility for any improvements that needed to be done, sometimes with the assistance of state governments. While some far-sighted federal officials, such as Secretary of the Treasury Albert Gallatin (1802–1814), supported the use of federal funds to improve roads and canals around the country, an ongoing debate over the constitutionality of such initiatives rendered federal support sporadic throughout much of the century. In 1817, Congress did appropriate $17,000 for two lighthouses on Lake Erie, one at Erie (completed in 1818) and another at Buffalo (completed in 1820). In 1824, Congress earmarked $20,000 to deepen the harbor at Presque Isle (Pennsylvania) near Erie, the first federal money given to improve any lake harbors. One year later, Congress enacted the General Survey Act as part of Henry Clay's program known as the American System. This was a surprisingly aggressive federal plan that included a second national bank, a protective tariff, and improved internal transportation designed to foster commercial development in all sections of the country. During the years that followed, improvements to navigation on the lakes, particularly harbors, was generously funded annually by Congress. The loss of the presidency by John Quincy Adams in 1828 and Clay's failed presidential bid in 1832, however, ended this vision of an integrated national economic system coordinated and supported by the federal government. But annual funding for projects on the lakes continued uninterrupted until 1838. From then until 1860, while Congress passed 8 bills for improvements to lake navigation, seven were vetoed. Only an appropriation bill for harbor improvements on the lakes was signed by Whig Millard Fillmore on August 30, 1852. Congress was eventually able to override three of the vetoes.[68]

While cities around the lakes and private investors attempted to fund necessary navigational improvements, the costs of most of these projects exceeded their resources. Moreover, large corporations or investment bankers, which dominated funding in the post–Civil War economic boom, did not exist at that time to supply the needed capital. And most improvement projects on the Lakes and elsewhere at this time were developmental in nature, meaning that returns on investment were too uncertain for all but the most adventuresome speculator. Many, particularly in the West, sought assistance from government to undertake such risky projects. While various levels of government — local, state, and federal — sporadically assisted in internal improvements in the 19th century, they did so in a variety of ways, but generally in combination with, and in support of, private enterprise. The least common was outright construction. More likely, they purchased private stock from the companies doing the work, or granted builders loans or guaranteed their bonds. Another option was subsidies of money, credit, or, as was frequently the case with the federal government, land. An important federal contribution to the commercial development of the Great Lakes began with authorization of the U. S. Army Corps of Engineers to begin assisting in improvements to Lake harbors with the March 3, 1823, congressional appropriation of funds to survey ports at Presque Isle and Erie. For the balance of the 19th century, the Corps planned and supervised each harbor improvement regardless of the source of funding. These improvements usually corresponded with the advance of the steamboat on the western rivers and lakes in the years before the Civil War.[69]

By 1838, the appropriations for the annual rivers and harbors acts, which funded navigational improvements around the country, were coming under increasing criticism from strict-constructionists and states' rights advocates, particularly in the South, who opposed federal support for what they saw as a local responsibility. The Survey Act was repealed in 1838, and discussions about federal aid for transportation grew increasingly heated regardless of the region seeking assistance. Western States, newer and often the recipients of federal money for internal improvements, were less concerned about constitutionality of such assistance than those in the original 13 states. Still, Congress stopped appropriations for improvements on the Lakes altogether until 1844, when President John Tyler, a Whig, began to advocate the renewal of funding for improvements, including the lakes. "It is as much the duty of the Government to construct good harbors, without reference to the location or interests of cities, for the shelter of the extensive commerce of the Lakes as to build breakwaters on the Atlantic coast." The Great Lakes experience "destructive storms," he continued, "and the annual loss of ships and cargoes, and consequently of revenue to the Government, is immense." But Tyler was adamant that any such bill had to meet a strict constitutional test: it must be necessary for the safety of interstate and foreign commerce. As a result, only requests that Tyler had read and approved before their passage were ever submitted to him for his signature. By 1845 Democrat James K. Polk was in the White House; a year later, with the Mexican War (1846–1848) distracting both Congress and the president, no new river and harbor bills were passed for some time.[70]

The indifference of William Burt and his party to their discovery makes it clear that they understood that political, technological, and geographical limitations made the profitable mining of iron ore from the area around Teal Lake unlikely at the time. This changed in the coming decades as the nation began to move westward on rails of iron and later steel, broke the concrete-hard soil of the Great Plains with steel plows, and watched awe-struck as steel-framed buildings grew skyward within its expanding cities. The demands of the mid and late 19th century eventually made Burt's discovery important and initiated changes in and around the Great Lakes that made its exploitation possible. Iron mined from the Teal Lake region and shipped out of the new port of Marquette, Michigan, after 1845 accounted for virtually all of the ore shipped from the Lake Superior region over the next three decades. As iron eclipsed copper as their focus of interest, prospectors worked to uncover and exploit other iron ranges along the lake's southern and western shores. By 1900, Lake Superior iron shipped to the various southern Lakes' ports totaled 19,059,393 tons, nearly 66 percent of all the iron mined in the United States. Only five years later the combined volume shipped from these ranges grew to 34,252,115 tons, roughly 80 percent of the iron mined domestically that year.[71]

A number of important changes, however, would be necessary before this could take place. The growing national demand for iron, beginning with the construction of the Transcontinental Railroad in the 1860s, led entrepreneurs to search out other deposits around Lake Superior. But locating the iron ore was only the beginning of their challenge. Compelling questions faced those seeking to exploit the iron deposits. Could iron be manufactured near the mines, or would the ore have to be shipped to existing centers of production? Regardless of whether the ore was converted to blooms or simply shipped out in bulk, how could it be hauled from the remote inland mines to the shores of Lake Superior for shipment? If that was accomplished, how could the bulky ore efficiently be loaded into the waiting ships? What could be done about the lack of natural harbors in the region? Could the motley collection of small sailing vessels or the smaller fleet of steamers, which were primarily designed to haul passengers, accommodate the volume of iron ore necessary to make this enterprise profitable? Assuming these challenges could be met, how would the vessels negotiate the myriad of natural obstacles, the most formidable being the Falls of St. Mary's, that faced them in their voyage south to the mills? Moreover, when these vessels arrived at the ports on Lakes Erie and Michigan, would they be able to unload their bulk cargo in a timely fashion? Finally, even if plans could be formulated to address these serious obstacles, who was going to finance them?

Answers to these questions became more pressing as the demand for iron grew in the decades following the Civil War. In the end, the solutions to these problems, and many others, were found independently. But the resolution of one issue generally created a challenge elsewhere. For example, introducing a new ship design that permitted ships to carry a larger volume of ore often meant that the dimensions of harbors, channels, and locks would necessarily have to be upgraded to accommodate this change. But who was going to pay for these navigational improvements? And, once larger ships were able to operate freely throughout the lakes, how would they be able to load and unload their cargo quickly enough to make them cost-effective? Ultimately, the process that made the transportation of ore between the mines and the smelters more efficient was the result of a synergistic relationship that developed among the various fields of capital investment, technological innovation and creative engineering, constitutional interpretation, and organizational sophistication.

2

"The right to demand equal and exact justice"

(1845–1865)

"At an early hour the streets were thronged with strangers ... flags were flying from every steamer and sail-vessel in port, blasts of martial music swelled ever and anon upon the air, and the deep notes of artillery boomed over the prairie and lake. Joyous faces were everywhere, and heaven itself smiled upon the scene." Thus the *Chicago Daily Journal* described the excitement surrounding the opening of the River and Harbor Convention in that city on July 5, 1847. In fact, this town of 16,000 had postponed its Fourth of July celebration for one day to coincide with the event. Over 10,000 visitors from 19 states, including delegates from as far away as Florida and South Carolina, had made the trip. Not surprisingly, they overwhelmed the limited facilities of this energetic, young port city on the southern shore of Lake Michigan. Still, Horace Greeley, who had arrived only the day before, could write enthusiastically about the "cordial and bounteous hospitality" he witnessed by residents who "had already thrown open their dwellings, welcoming strangers in [the] thousands." Even the steamboats that had delivered many of the delegates "proffered their spacious accommodations and generous fare to their passengers during their stay." But the festive mood belied the purpose of this gathering. These thousands of visitors, including 2,315 who were enrolled delegates, had come to address serious matters. Over the next three days they met on the city's courthouse square to hear speeches and pass resolutions seeking to influence a change in federal government's parsimonious attitude toward navigational improvements for harbors and channels on the Great Lakes. "The proponents of the convention," Mentor L. Williams concluded, "believed that this kind of pressure would work a major revolution in political circles and permanently guarantee the welfare of the North and West."[1]

The catalyst for this gathering was President James K. Polk's veto of the 1846 River and Harbor bill. A Democrat from Tennessee, Polk voiced the sentiments of many in his party, and particularly those from the South, when he wrote in his veto message that congressional funding of internal improvements led "to a consolidation of power in the Federal Government at the expense of the rightful authority of the states" and embraced "objects for the expenditure of the public money which are local in their character, benefiting but few at the expense of the common Treasury of the whole." And even worse, such legislation would "engender sectional feelings and prejudices calculated to disturb the harmony of the Union." To those gathered in Chicago, Polk's veto of funds to improve harbors and to keep navigational channels open around the lakes did indeed engender a feeling of sectional inequity. But it was their region, they argued, that had experienced the prejudicial treatment. One speaker reminded the delegates that an estimate of commerce on the lakes in 1845 was roughly $100 million dollars, almost equal to the nation's total exports in 1846. Furthermore, the federal government had readily funded many improvements for ocean ports and channels to the open sea. But, the speaker went on to note, federal expenditures for improvements on the lakes amounted to only one-sixth of the total federal expenditure for internal improvements between 1806 and 1846.[2]

Predictably, the political differences growing out of Polk's veto added to the sectional debate between the "slavocracy" and the abolitionists. To the latter, Polk's miserliness toward the commercial interests of the Great Lakes seemed blatantly hypocritical for a president who had unashamedly led the country into a war with Mexico for the sole purpose of extending slavery. Not surprisingly, therefore, newspaper accounts of the convention followed partisan lines, the Democratic papers generally disapproving of the proceedings while Whig papers applauded the resolutions calling for renewed federal support for navigational improvements on the lakes. The convention itself, although beginning as a non-partisan protest, soon evolved into a Whig-dominated affair. Horace Greeley estimated that two-thirds of his fellow delegates were Whigs. Acting on the precedent established by the 1845 Memphis Convention, arguably one of the most important of the southern commercial conventions, a memorial of the proceedings, including the convention's 15 resolutions, was presented to Congress. The zeal and unanimity of the delegates inspired their supporters in Congress to press forward. This initiative renewed debates over the constitutionality of federal support of internal improvements, as had the resolutions forwarded by the delegates of the Memphis convention. But unlike the Memphis memorial, the resolutions adopted in Chicago prompted Congress to act. True to his convictions, Polk also vetoed this second River and Harbor bill in 1847. Undeterred, Congress passed a third bill, for which the president was preparing a veto in 1848 when his term ended. While the issue of slavery tended to dominate rehetoric contributing to the growing friction between the North and South, it is clear that enmity generated by the question of federal subsidies for internal improvements likewise added to the unrelenting and increasingly acrimonious sectional strife. But if the convention exacerbated these regional tensions, it also served to clarify issues and reinforce the beliefs of northern and western Whigs, "welding them into a unified, coordinated group" eager "to see justice done to their cause." In addition, it brought together eastern investors, now aware of the business opportunities of the region, and local businessmen eager to attract their capital.[3]

This conference, occurring just three years after Burt's discovery of iron in Michigan's Upper Peninsula, suggests that there was a spirited economy in place along the southern shores of the lakes aggressively seeking opportunities to expand. Rapid population growth in the area beginning a decade earlier helped to spur this growing commercial activity. During the entire year of 1833, for example, only two brigs and two schooners arrived in Chicago from the lower lakes; just three years later 456 vessels visited the burgeoning town. Milwaukee grew from two families to 1,300 inhabitants between 1834 and 1836. The population along the lake coasts of New York, Pennsylvania, and Ohio doubled between 1829 and 1837. Other lake cities, such as Buffalo, Cleveland, Detroit, Toledo, and Sandusky also expanded as settlers, many of them European immigrants, poured in and agricultural production from the region passed through these Lake ports on its way to East Coast markets via the Erie Canal. But throughout the 1830s and 1840s, Lake Superior remained on the sidelines, cut off and isolated from all but essential commercial activity. The region's economic potential, particularly in fish and minerals, was tantalizing. There, however, would have to be a considerable infusion of investment capital, a change in economic priorities, an adaptation of innovative technology, and a reassessment of the federal government's role in support of business before its exploitation was possible.[4]

This chapter will trace developments on the waters and along the shorelines of the Great Lakes between 1845 and 1865. There was some experimentation in ship construction, design, and power during this period. Several entrepreneurs, captivated by the potential they saw in the mineral deposits being uncovered along the southern shores of Lake Superior, undertook a bold, if ill-fated, experiment with iron smelting on the Upper Peninsula. Their lack of success made it clear that the ore would have to be transported elsewhere for production if the Lake Superior iron deposits were to be profitable. Sensing commercial possibilities in the region, the State of Michigan, relying on private investors and some indirect federal support, neutralized the Falls of St. Mary's with a short canal and lock system. Although small and quickly rendered inadequate, this lock succeeded in opening the Lake Superior region to limited development. Also during the period, the United States Supreme Court addressed the constitutional issue of congressional responsibility for inland waterways. Their decision permitted increased congressional authority in the region and, to many, justified a broader role for the federal government in aiding improvements on the lakes. Numerous tariffs kept the cost of imported iron and other items high, at the same time effectively, if unintentionally, discouraging innovation in the United States industries, including shipbuilding. During the Civil War, activity on the lakes focused primarily on moving as much grain as possible to the East to feed both northern armies and civilians, as well as the populations of Britain's industrial cities, temporarily curtailing most other entrepreneurial activities in the region.

If Burt and members of his surveying group had been reluctant to exploit the iron deposits around Teal Lake, others were not. But it was only by accident that this happened. The discovery of Teal Lake iron, which members of Burt's party undoubtedly shared with the inhabitants of Sault Ste. Marie, generated little excitement among most locals. It did, however, make an impression on a local mixed-breed, Louis Nolan, and Madjigijig, an old Indian living near the shore of Lake Superior where the Carp River, which flowed through the Teal Lake region, emptied into the lake. When Philo Everett led a party to Lake Superior in the spring of 1845, motivated by stories of copper and silver on the Keweenaw Peninsula, they, by necessity, passed through Sault Ste. Marie. Here they heard the story of Burt's find from Louis Nolan for the first time. Intrigued, Everett hired Nolan to lead them to iron deposits at Teal Lake. With the eventual help of Madjigijig, they located the iron on two small mountains, later named Jackson and Cleveland. Having in their possession permits issued by the Secretary of War to preempt any mineral deposits they found, presumably for copper or silver on the Keweenaw, the party decided to use one of the permits to claim a mile square area on Jackson Mountain.[5]

Gathering some samples, the party returned to Jackson, Michigan. Everett, in a letter notifying the Army of their claim, commented on the quality of the ore. "The ore looks as bright as a bar of iron just broken. Since coming home we had some of it smelted and find it produced iron and something resembling gold — some say it is gold and copper." Encouraged, Everett and his partners formed the Jackson Mining Company and returned to their claim the following spring. After constructing a house, they mined about 300 pounds of ore and hauled it on their backs overland along the Carp River to Lake Superior. It must have struck them immediately that such a primitive method of transporting the ore over this unforgiving terrain would make it difficult for their company to profitably exploit their claim. Nonetheless, while the rest remained at the Jackson site to retain possession, A. V. Berry departed for Jackson with the ore to run further tests. While awaiting passage down the St. Mary's River, he met and fell into conversation with J. Lang Cassels, a noted mineralogist in the area representing Cleveland businessmen eager to capitalize on the mineral resources of the area. Berry's mission and the details about his company's find eventually made their way into the conversation. Before providing Cassels with information about the location of the iron deposits, Berry wisely got him to agree that the two groups of investors would share the costs of constructing and maintaining roads between the deposits and the lake, a matter that Berry and his partners now knew had to be addressed. Cassels immediately went by canoe to inspect the iron deposits and secured a section of the Cleveland Mountain by permit. In the meantime, Berry returned to Jackson, where, after several unsuccessful attempts, he found a smelter who was able to convert the ore he brought back with him into iron, the first substantial amount of iron produced from Lake Superior ore.[6]

By 1848, the Jackson Company had constructed a forge near the mines and was producing blooms, the first of which were sold to Detroit shipper Eber B. Ward, who used them in the walking beam for the steamer *Ocean*. Although the Jackson Company could forge six tons of blooms a day, the ten-mile trip between the Teal Lake operations and fledgling village of Marquette, along the Lake Superior shore where the blooms were shipped out, was proving to be a major challenge. Two teams of six horses carried the daily production down a primitive road through country described by one author as "jagged, broken and mountainous, densely wooded and thick with underbrush." Each trip was dangerous and breakdowns were common. They faced the same challenges hauling supplies back to the forge. After mining the iron ore and hauling it to the forges, processing the charcoal and moving it to the furnaces to forge the blooms, hauling the finished blooms to the Marquette docks and loading them on ships, negotiating the St. Mary's River rapids and the unpredictable St. Clair Flats, and finally sailing to the southern shores of Lake Erie, the Jackson Company had to sell their product for $200 per ton. On average, their competition in the rest of the United States during the early 1850s could sell their iron for around $80 per ton. Such a price disadvantage, despite any claims of improved quality, must have been discouraging. Some subsequent mining companies, such as the Marquette Iron Company, hoped to cut costs by hauling the ore to Marquette and manufacturing the blooms on the shores of Lake Superior. Not surprisingly, they faced most of the same obstacles that hampered the Jackson Mining Company and their efforts had only a minimal effect on the final cost of the blooms.[7]

This helps explain why the discovery of new iron ranges in the Lake Superior region — the Gogebic in 1844 and the Vermilion in 1850 — received such little attention at the time. It took entrepreneurs 25 years before they began to invest in mining those deposits. Furthermore, at the same time and hundreds of miles to the southwest, the Pilot Knob and Iron Mountain mines in Missouri were beginning to ship iron ore to St. Louis smelters. To contemporary observers, these mines, with easier access to the ore and developed systems of transport, held greater promise than those near Lake Superior, which faced not only transportation problems inland but also major delays associated with the navigational bottleneck created by the Falls of St. Marys. Yet, reports of the volume and quality of the Lake Superior ore continued to intrigue many. In 1852, for example, Edward Brewster visited the Carp River district where he inspected iron works under construction. He confided in his diary that during a tour of the area miners showed him a mountain of iron 300 feet in height and several miles in circumference that was "of a quality superior to any yet known."[8]

By 1849 the mining companies around Teal Lake concluded that the horrible condition, or total absence, of roads to the forges at Marquette made delivery of ore too risky during any time other than winter when sleds could be employed. Even using this method, each trip from the mines to Marquette took all day and delivered less than 1½ tons; consequently, the forges rarely received more than 1,000 tons in any one winter. To make matters worse, during the winter of 1849 there was so much snow that the Jackson mine could send only a small amount, and the Cleveland mine, two miles further inland, sent none. Consequently, when the lake waters opened to ships in the spring of 1850, there were only a few blooms ready to be transported out.[9]

Transportation of the ore from the mines to the city was not the Marquette iron makers' only problem. They also faced a chronic shortage of char-coal. Brick or stone kilns, commonly used to produce charcoal in other parts of the country, were too expensive and sophisticated for the Marquette pro-ducers to construct. Instead, they were forced to manufacture charcoal in open pits, which was time-consuming and inefficient. Coal, which was gain-ing acceptance in iron producing regions in Ohio and Pennsylvania, was not found naturally in the region. And shipping coal from Ohio and Pennsylva-nia mines to Lake Superior at this time was impractical. Not only were the costs prohibitive, especially moving it around the falls on the St Mary's River, but coal was also "tender" and "ill adapted for shipping." Quite simply, it progressively deteriorated during prolonged travel aboard sailing ships. While coal occasionally might be carried as ballast on upbound ships, at this time it was not brought north in any great quantity. Other than its generally acknowledged high quality, about the only thing that recommended Lake Superior iron ore was its easy accessibility. Centuries of seasonal frost had bro-ken up the iron-bearing rock into loose piles of ore that required no drilling equipment or dynamite. While workers sometimes broke up larger pieces with sledgehammers to make them easier to handle, often they only had to scoop it up into wagons or onto sleighs. These two characteristics explain why, despite all the other challenges, some persevered in their efforts to suc-cessfully mine the iron from this region.[10]

While some smelters continued to search for ways to make iron produc-tion profitable near the Lake Superior mines, it was becoming evident to many that the successful exploitation of the region's iron ore must involve shipping it to larger, better equipped smelters elsewhere rather than trying to manu-facture blooms at or near the iron mines. This would require, among other things, major improvements in the way the ore was delivered to Marquette for shipment, as well as better dock and port facilities from which the ore could be shipped out. Late in 1851, an enterprising entrepreneur, Heman P. Ely, offered a solution to the first problem. He convinced both the Jackson and Cleveland mine owners to sign an agreement that allowed him to build a railroad from the mines to Marquette. To many this seemed like an idea ahead of its time, and investors, viewing the undertaking as being too risky, were initially slow to materialize. Frustrated by the delay, the mining com-panies agreed to construct a plank road instead the following year, to be jointly funded by both.[11]

In 1852 six barrels of bulk iron ore were shipped from Marquette aboard the steamer *Baltimore*. Off loaded at Sault Ste. Marie, it was hauled around the falls and reloaded on another vessel, which delivered the ore to Detroit.

It was the first commercial shipment of iron ore sent from the Lake Superior mines south. The following year the first substantial quantity of ore, 152 tons, was shipped in four vessels to Sault Ste. Marie. After being portaged around the falls, it was reloaded on another vessel and delivered to Erie, Pennsylvania. Here it had to be transferred to canal barges for the final trip to the Sharon Iron Works (Sharon, Pennsylvania), where it was "converted into bar iron and nails of very superior quality." While a question regarding the purity of the ore led to some controversy among smelters, improvements to furnaces at those plants having problems processing the ore eventually resolved the issue. The positive reports were encouraging, but it was now unclear whether the proposed plank road from the Cleveland and Jackson mines would be able to keep pace with the expected demand from the generally enthusiastic Pennsylvania and Ohio smelters. Plans for the plank road were therefore scrapped in favor of a strap railroad, with the iron straps sent from Sharon. Mule-drawn rail cars could now carry ore from the mines to the docks. But the steep terrain and curvy rail line led to a high mortality rate for the mules, which cost $1,400 per team to replace. The hay to feed them, shipped from southern lake ports since none was grown locally, was expensive, averaging $50 per ton. And it still took one team an entire day to pull eight cars of ore, totaling only 35 tons, from the mines to the docks. This method of transporting iron did little to improve efficiency or reduce production costs.[12]

In late 1853, no doubt influenced both by the loss of their forge to fire and their inability to turn a profit, the Cleveland Iron Mining Company gave up efforts to manufacture iron in Marquette; henceforth, they concentrated on mining and shipping iron ore only. Unfortunately another bad winter once again interfered with transporting the ore from the mines and only about 1,000 tons sat on the docks at the opening of the 1854 shipping season. Purchased by the Forest City Iron Company, the entire amount was carried onboard the propellers *Sam Ward, Napoleon,* and *Peninsula* by wheelbarrows, where it was dumped on the open deck. Once the vessels reached Sault Ste. Marie, the bulk ore had to be shoveled onto carts, portaged around the falls, and once again painstakingly loaded on other ships for its final trip to Cleveland. It had become apparent that, whether the ore was converted to iron in Marquette or hauled to the docks and shipped out, transportation at all stages of the operations was woefully inadequate. The fact that easily mined, high grade ore lay in great abundance in Michigan's Upper Peninsula had to be balanced with the reality that it resided in a remote, nearly inaccessible area. Developing more efficient ways to deliver this ore to where it could be processed was critical to the successful exploitation of the Teal Lake reserves.[13]

Of paramount importance in this effort to make the exploitation of Lake Superior iron ore, as well as the rich copper and fish resources, profitable was neutralizing the falls on the St. Mary's River. It dropped the water level approximately 18 feet, running nearly a half mile through a rock-strewn area that resembled a rapids more than a falls. This geological anomaly was the result of severe natural disruptions that had altered the region over the previous millennia. Beginning about 1 million years ago, five different large glaciers advanced and receded over what is now the Great Lakes area. Each time they moved, they picked up abrasive material that scraped the earth beneath, much as sandpaper does wood. This left the banks of earlier shallow seas that once covered the region much deeper and wider. When the last glacier retreated nearly 10,000 years ago, the meltwater filled in these gouged pockets in the earth's surface. With the weight of the glaciers gone, the surface area began to rise throughout the Great Lakes region. During this process, a gradual shifting and tilting of the earth's surface made the wide, but shallow, St. Mary's River the only outlet for Lake Superior.[14]

The Native American canoe, which displaced very little water, could travel over all but the most shallow or treacherous rapids. Consequently, the St. Mary's falls did little to slow down Indians, and later European trappers

Native American fish from a canoe amidst the rapids of the St. Mary's River. This shallow, rock-strewn stretch of the river had to be neutralized by a series of locks before boats larger than a canoe could pass in and out of Lake Superior.

who had adopted the canoe, from moving through the river. In fact, the Chippewa had maintained residence near the rapids since anyone could remember. They relied heavily on the plentiful whitefish for food, which they harvested at the base of the falls from their canoes. The French, who had established a fort, a trading post, and a Jesuit mission at the falls sometime before 1720, realized immediately its strategic importance. Henry Schoolcraft, although he first observed the site a century later, also quickly grasped its importance. "By this place," he wrote, "all the fur trade of the northwest is compelled to pass, and it is the grand thoroughfare of Indian communications for the upper countries, as far as the Arctic Circle." Later, the larger canoes of French *voyageurs* often struggled with the rapids when traveling north to collect furs along the Lake Superior shoreline. In 1797, the Montreal-based North West Company responded by constructing a small lock on the north (Canadian) side of the rapids. It consisted of a water runway and a lock 38 feet long and eight feet, nine inches wide. A towpath along the runway allowed oxen to pull the bateaux and canoes through the upper part of the system. Schoolcraft, who visited Sault Ste. Marie in June of 1820, found the lock still in operation.[15]

Six years later Thomas McKenny of the Indian Department, traveling with Michigan Territorial Governor Lewis Cass on a treaty mission, stopped at Sault Ste. Marie. By this time, the U. S. Army had built Fort Brady there and garrisoned it with 200 soldiers. He found the nearby village of 152 buildings itself "unoccupied and going to decay." Although the boom of the fur trade was long past, the American Fur Company had built a tram road around the falls that passed through the village in 1823. The few remaining inhabitants contented themselves with supplying the needs of the nearby soldiers and looking to their own subsistence. By every appearance, Sault Ste. Marie had receded into commercial oblivion.[16]

Michigan's admission to the Union in 1837, however, found the falls on the St. Mary's River receiving renewed attention. Encouraged by the potential of a lucrative fishing industry in Lake Superior, the state made plans for a canal around the falls. It was, after all, the age of canals. Spurred by the commercial success of New York State's 363-mile Erie Canal, which opened in 1825, Ohio, for example, began construction of two major canals that same year linking Lake Erie with the Ohio River. Surely, Michigan engineers concluded, a canal around the short one-half mile Falls of St. Mary's should be easy enough to complete. Accordingly, the state had the river surveyed and authorized the construction of a canal 75 feet wide and 10 feet deep. There were to be two locks 100 feet in length and 32 feet wide. The state appropriated

$112,544 for the project and hired a Buffalo construction firm to complete it. In their enthusiasm, the surveyors either ignored or failed to notice that the proposed canal crossed an earlier millrace, which had been dug in 1823 by the U. S. government to power a sawmill that had provided lumber for the construction of nearby Fort Brady. Since that time, the sawmill had burned down and there were no plans to replace it. Despite the obvious uselessness of the millrace under these circumstances, the War Department ordered the fort's commander, Captain Johnson, to prevent the State of Michigan from interfering "with improvements made by the United States at your post, amongst which the millrace is regarded as one of the greatest importance." Armed with this order, Johnson on a May morning in 1839 led a "company of thirty regulars ... fifes playing, muskets and bayonets shining, in a rapid and orderly march" to the spot where fifty workers were beginning work on Michigan's new canal. Ignoring Johnson's order to disperse his workers, the foreman confronted the captain. Johnson then "engaged in a hand-to-hand battle with the foreman wresting his spade from him." This bizarre "Battle of the Millrace" ended with the workmen being driven from the field.[17]

Eventually, Michigan and the federal government agreed to allow a canal to be constructed, but the contractor refused to continue, stating that the state owed him money for the work completed to date. Furthermore, he argued, the contract was about to expire and it seemed pointless to begin the canal under such circumstances. A change in state government, from Democrat to Whig, found the legislature now placing blame for the incident on the military rather than the contractor. Accordingly, the Michigan legislature passed a joint resolution on March 27, 1840, protesting federal interference with the project. Members also sent a memorial to Congress conveying their ire. But by this time the bank failures of 1837 had deflated the bubble of optimism that had accompanied statehood. Furthermore, efforts by the state to promote internal improvements, including the canal, generally failed. When Michigan rewrote its constitution in 1850, the new document specifically prohibited the state from sponsoring any improvements. There was an exception; the state could undertake such projects if funds or property were donated to finance the work. While the state did not give up the idea of the canal, officials realized that the project would require the blessing, and probably the assistance, of Washington. Advocates in Congress, in fact, had begun advocating for funding as early as 1839. They could find support for a canal in articles like the one in the November 11, 1838, issue of the *Michigan State Journal* that reported that shippers sent nearly 7,000 barrels of fish worth $108,000 south from Lake Superior that year. Two months later the same publication again called for federal government assistance for a canal to facilitate the transportation of the vast resources of timber, copper, and — no doubt speculatively — iron one located in the Lake Superior region. Although bills throughout the 1840s were introduced in Congress to grant land to the state to assist in construction of a canal, they failed to pass. Ironically, it was Henry Clay, whose American System had encouraged aggressive government support of internal improvements following the War of 1812, who spoke for many when he opposed the measure in 1840 because, "it contemplated a work beyond the remotest settlement in the United States, if not in the moon." But the reports of valuable copper finds on the Keweenaw Peninsula were attracting prospectors by the mid–1840s and Sault Ste. Marie began to gain a renewed importance.[18]

This rebirth, in large part, resulted from the need to provide transportation around the falls. Each upbound or downbound ship that arrived at Sault Ste. Marie could go no further. Regardless of the cargo, it had to be offloaded, placed onto horse-drawn carts or trams, and carried through the center of the village. Workers then reloaded it onboard another vessel, which carried it to its final destination. The ships above the falls were sometimes built along the shoreline. But others, such as the first steam vessel on Lake Superior, the *Independence* launched in Chicago in the spring of 1845, had to be laboriously moved around the falls on rollers. Lewis Marvill, a member of the crew of the *Independence*, recalled years later that "no mishaps occurring the progress of hauling progressed slowly but surely, and in about seven weeks we were again launched in the river at the head of the falls." The following year, he continued, two more steamers were operating on Lake Superior, the *Baltimore* and the *Napoleon*, a sailing ship that had been fitted with engines over that winter. But they too had to be painstakingly hauled around the falls in the manner of the *Independence*. Such time-consuming, labor-intensive activity was also expensive. H. G. Kingston, an Englishman, wrote in his memoirs after a visit to the falls in 1853 that the costs associated with moving the steamer *Sam Ward* around the falls nearly matched the cost to build her. The lack of a canal here wrote Horace Greeley, who had visited the falls on his way to the Chicago Convention in 1847, "has hitherto practically shut the Superior region against emigration and settlement, now greatly embarrasses the development of the mineral wealth of the region, nearly doubles the cost of transportation, while it greatly delays and renders irregular all travel and communication."[19]

Pressure for a canal increased as frustrations with the falls grew. John N. Ingersall, publisher of the *Lake Superior News and Mining Journal*, no doubt encouraged by the optimism growing out of the Chicago River and Harbor Convention the previous year, launched a campaign for a canal in 1848 from his office in Copper Harbor, Michigan. Detroit businessmen met in December of 1851 to plan how to pressure the government for a canal at the falls. And they were not alone; other lake cities also petitioned Congress to support the canal. In 1851, *The Lake Superior Journal* reported that over one-half of the total cargo capacity of the Superior fleet had become incapacitated by accidents in less than three months. Without a canal, replacement ships could not reach the lake quickly enough. The *Journal* estimated that this situation left 18,000 barrels of supplies stranded at the end of the season.[20]

In Congress, Michigan Senator Lewis Cass, a Democrat whose presidential ambitions had been dashed in the election of 1848, threw his still considerable political weight behind the effort to construct the canal in an August 6, 1850, debate. He played on fears of another war with Britain by reminding his colleagues that "if such a canal is not constructed, we should be compelled to build and equip a double fleet, one to defend Lakes Huron, Michigan and Erie, and the other to defend the upper lakes." Later that month he admonished his fellow senators to treat the federally held lands in Michigan much as a responsible private landowner. "The government should not sit still and hold on to their lands, and yet perform none of the great functions of a land owner. They should not," he argued, "see their land improved by the progress of settlement, by the industry and by capital of their citizens, and remain inactive; expecting their property to be improved without their cooperation." And such improvement could only be realized if a canal existed around the Falls of St. Mary's, opening the government lands in northern Michigan to trade and settlement.[21]

Cass found an ally in Stephen Douglas, and the Democratic senator from Illinois offered a funding suggestion. He observed in the same August 30th debate over the canal that numerous canals and improvements to rivers in the Old Northwest had all been made possible because Congress had donated public lands to subsidize the work. Before the grants, however, there were "lands of great fertility, but [they] were inaccessible." Improvements to navigation opened up these areas to settlement, bringing timber to build towns and providing an avenue for the produce of the area to reach market. Granting federal land to Michigan for the canal, he added, would also make the 50,000,000 acres of government land bordering Lake Superior more valuable. "Unless you do this, your lands there, as they have elsewhere, will remain unsold for forty years." In fact, by September 30, 1851, a total of 500,000 acres of public land already had been donated to Michigan for other internal improvement projects. Nearly 20 million more acres of public land remained in the state, more than enough to satisfy the financing requirements for building the canal.[22]

With Whig Millard Fillmore in the White House and the economic fortunes of the lake states continuing to show steady improvement, representatives from the region renewed their efforts to win congressional support for a canal. Finally, with the surprising help of congressmen from the lower Mississippi River states, Congress enacted and Fillmore signed Public Law XLVI in 1852. It gave Michigan 750,000 acres of federal land that they could sell to finance the canal "around the falls of the St. Mary's." If the federal government was not ready to build the canal, it was willing to support its construction indirectly by donating what it had in abundance — land. To avoid any more confrontations between the federal government and the state, the law also donated a strip of land 400 feet wide within the military reservation through which the canal would pass. The law also required that "said canal shall be at least 100 feet wide, with a depth of water of at least twelve feet, and the locks shall be at least 250 feet long and sixty feet wide." It further stipulated that, while the federal government should have free use of the canal, the state could assess a toll on other traffic, but only in an amount necessary for maintenance of the canal.[23]

The state of Michigan planned to serve as supervising agent in building the canal, but decided to let the actual construction out to bids. Charles G. Harvey, an agent for the E. and T. Fairbanks Company of Vermont, was in Sault Ste. Marie recovering from an attack of typhoid fever when news of Public Law XLVI reached the village. He had used his several months of recuperation to assess the potential of the nearby copper and iron operations for his employers, who sought investments in the region. Impressed by what he had observed on these trips, he immediately sensed a business opportunity when news of the land grant to Michigan reached Sault Ste. Marie. Accordingly, he contacted his employer, Joseph P. Fairbanks, who quickly organized six other capitalists eager to fund the project. Their unguarded enthusiasm for the project was based on the prodigious Erie Canal, which stretched 363 miles over the Appalachian Mountains by connecting existent rivers and lakes with a series of canals and locks. During its first year of operation alone, the Erie Canal had generated $1 million in tolls, one-seventh of its total cost of construction. The investors, mirroring the confidence of the Michigan legislature in 1837, concluded that building a canal and lock system around the half-mile falls on the St. Mary's, with its relatively minor 18-foot drop, would pose relatively few problems. And, with the economic potential of the mineral deposits Harvey reported clustered along the southern shores of Lake Superior, it should produce considerable profits.[24]

Authorized by the investors to oversee the project, Harvey contracted the services of L. L. Nichols, an engineer for the Erie Canal, to estimate the cost of constructing locks and a canal around the falls as soon as they were awarded the contract. Harvey, wise beyond his 24 years, insisted that the lock be 350 feet in length and 70 feet wide to accommodate the larger steamers that he was convinced would be needed to haul the wealth of the Lake Superior region south. This would make the lock the largest in the country, if not the world. The recommendation was duly incorporated into the Michigan legislature's bill authorizing the construction of the canal. But Harvey's decision to enlarge the lock generated a strong protest from Detroit ship owner Eber B. Ward, whose fleet made him the largest vessel owner on the lakes. While Ward supported building the canal, he feared that Harvey's grandiose plans would discourage potential investors and postpone completion of the project. He argued further that the St. Mary's River south of the falls was crooked in many spots and filled with shallow, rocky channels, making it impossible for the large ships Harvey envisioned to even reach the locks. Called before a legislative committee in Lansing to respond to Ward's criticism, Harvey successfully convinced them that the dimensions were appropriate and necessary. Accordingly, Nichols incorporated Harvey's specifications in his survey. Based on his initial survey, he estimated that the project would cost $403,500. But, he freely admitted, this figure relied upon a considerable amount of guesswork.[25]

Since the Michigan State constitution forbade special charters, the investors, through Harvey, secured a charter from the New York legislature under the name of the St. Mary's Falls Ship Canal Company. And since each had originally bid the job as an individual, they now all assigned their contracts to the company, whose officers and directors represented a number of the better known investors from around New York State and New England. Meanwhile, the ubiquitous Harvey, now back in Michigan, was again hard at work obtaining an appointment from the governor of Michigan to select the federal government land in the Upper Peninsula to be donated to the state to fund the canal. His familiarity with the region proved invaluable, as he carefully selected nearly 140,000 acres of land that turned out to be rich in mineral deposits. By late spring, Harvey was rewarded with the position of general agent for the Canal Company in return for his considerable efforts in helping them win the canal contract. He immediately began rounding up about 400 men and the necessary supplies in Detroit and loaded everything aboard the steamer *Illinois* for the trip north, arriving at the falls on June 1, 1853.[26]

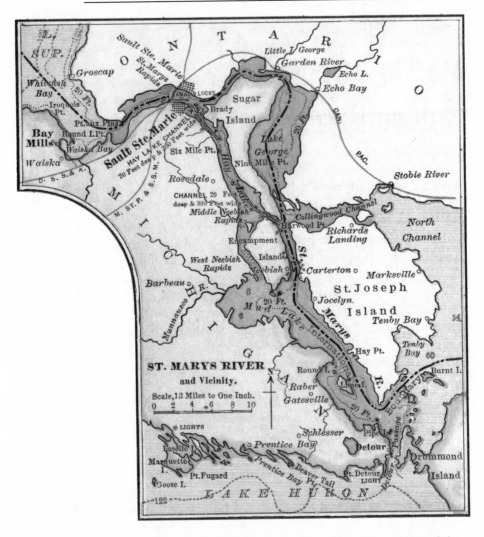

The St. Mary's River. The Sault Locks are located on the northern bend of the river at Sault Ste. Marie. Note the distance saved and the safety gained by traffic using the Hay Lake Channel verses the older route through Lake George.

Construction commenced on June 4, with the workers experiencing difficulties from the start. It quickly became clear that Nichols had underestimated the volume of rock workers would encounter in excavating the canal and locks. This delayed construction throughout most of September as Harvey tried to locate workers knowledgeable in blasting rock and bring them to the site. Nichols had also counted on being able to use limestone from Lime

Island, which lay only 40 miles below the work site, for the walls of the lock. But that stone turned out to be unsuitable and Harvey was forced to rely on stone shipped from a quarry near Fort Malden on the Canadian side of the Detroit River and from others on Marblehead Peninsula on the southern shores of Lake Erie. And there were other frustrations. Even though the region frequently experienced brutal winters, Nichols had planned on the work season lasting nine months. It turned out that seasonal conditions limited the workers to, at best, only seven months. The project lost even more time because 450 miles separated the canal from the nearest telegraph, which meant delays lasting up to six weeks waiting for supplies. Events taking place in other parts of the country, namely the rush to the California gold fields and a boom in railroad construction, siphoned off potential workers. Even the local inhabitants added to Harvey's woes. Many of them had worked as laborers carrying cargo around the falls. Since the lock threatened their livelihood, they resented it. Accordingly, some vandalized the construction site when they could.[27]

Workers who signed on suffered through bitterly cold winters, blistering summer heat, and a cholera epidemic in 1854 that claimed one man in ten. With few diversions to occupy their free time, most frequented the local grog shops. Despite these hardships, the work never stopped during the favorable months. Not surprisingly, all these challenges found the cost estimates being revised upwards. Nichols's $403,500 estimate soon grew to $557,739; the final cost for the lock and canal came in just under $1 million. These spiraling expenses placed a great burden on the investors, who could begin selling off the government land to offset their costs only after the work had been completed. The Canal Company's money problems became so bad in 1854 that they petitioned for early release of the land for sale based on the work completed to date. Canal historian John Dickinson notes that funds from the owners' other investments, like Michigan Central Railroad profits, also were appropriated by the company to help complete the work.[28]

Despite the hardships, Harvey completed the work by the spring of 1855. Water was run into the canal on April 19, but it did not officially open until June 18 when the *Illinois*, the same ship that had first brought workers and supplies to begin work on the canal two years earlier, passed through upbound with cargo and passengers. She traveled down a canal one and one-twelfth miles long, 64 feet wide at the bottom sloping to 100 feet wide at the surface. The two locks were placed back-to-back, each 350 feet long by 75 feet wide and with a lift of about nine feet. The depth of the canal was nearly 13 feet and the locks about 11½ feet. U. S. Army Corps of Engineers General

1885

The Michigan State Locks as they appeared shortly after they opened in 1855. (In Ralph D. Williams, *The Honorable Peter White*, 1907.)

Orlando M. Poe, the engineer in charge of expanding the canal system later in the century, wrote that "[Harvey's] canal was a remarkable work for its time and purpose. The construction of the locks especially bore evidence of a master's hand in their design and execution. These locks are now being torn out to make room for a new one," he continued, "and every step in their destruction reveals the excellence of the workmanship, the honest character of the materials employed, and the faithful compliance with the conditions under which they were built, not merely in its letter but in its spirit." Considering the youth and limited experience of Harvey, the remoteness of the site, and the numerous obstacles that had to be overcome, the quality of the finished product was remarkable indeed.[29]

A grand celebration marking the opening was organized at Sault Ste. Marie was planned to coincide with the village's annual Fourth of July festivities. Interestingly, the speakers invited to participate that day represented iron, not copper, mining concerns in the area. Heman Ely, who had just months before begun work on the Iron Mountain Railroad between the mines and Marquette, paid for the festivities, which included fireworks and refreshments for the entire village. Many of the residents of Sault Ste. Marie, however, were no doubt less than enthusiastic. "The completion of the canal," recalled resident John H. Forster, "seemed to be fatal to the growth and prosperity of the place. The golden harvest reaped from the trans-shipment of merchandise and minerals across the portage, as well as that derived from the money expended in canal construction, ceased to enrich the inhabitants and furnish them employment." The more traditional industries — fishing, trapping, and the fur trade — had been too long neglected by the residents for them to be resuscitated. Moreover, the war with Mexico had taken away the troops stationed at nearby Fort Brady and no one was certain when, or if, they would return. "A large number of the inhabitants," Forster remembered, "emigrated, many of them in time becoming leading pioneers in the iron and copper fields further west. In short, the Sault fell from its ideal and boasted position as the metropolis of Lake Superior, to a very dull village, with grass-grown streets and rotting wharves and warehouses. The pleasantly situated village of the Falls," he concluded, "was given up to lounging Indians and contented Frenchmen, who could laugh and grow fat on a diet of fish and potatoes; cheering their evenings with the violin and dancing."[30]

If the inhabitants of the town suffered, shippers and miners were pleased with the canal, which now permitted unfettered commercial activity between the Lake Superior region and the lower lakes. Although by agreement federal vessels could use the locks without a fee, all commercial boats paid a fee to the State of Michigan for maintenance of the canal and locks. The initial charge per ship was six and one-half cents per registered ton, but the state later reduced the toll to two and one-half cents. John Dickenson noted that basing the charge on registered tonnage of ships penalized steamships because they had to forfeit potential cargo space for boilers, machinery, and fuel. This situation was ironic because sailing ships, which always had difficulty operating in confined spaces, caused more problems passing through the canal and locks than steamers, which could use their engines to maneuver.[31]

Even before the canal was opened, however, it had become clear that the dangers inherent in the shallow channels south of the canal needed to be addressed, just as Eber Ward had forecasted earlier. Accordingly, in an 1854 appropriations bill Congress set aside funds for a survey of the area. Based on the results, Congress voted two years later to provide $100,000 to deepen the St. Mary's River through the west channel of Lake George. A year later, after the project had consumed over a quarter of the funds allocated, a new survey revealed that the money would be better spent on deepening the middle channel of Lake George (see illustration "The St. Mary's River"). The remaining funds ended up being used on both channels, as well as on a channel further south on the river at East Neebish between 1858 and 1860. Even the demands of the Civil War failed to delay further surveys of the river in 1863 and 1864 designed to locate other spots in need of improvement.[32]

The impact of the locks and canal on shipping in the region was almost immediate. During its first year of operation, 1,447 tons of iron ore, and a nearly identical amount of manufactured and pig iron, passed through the locks; by 1860 the annual tonnage of downbound ore through the locks had reached 120,000, while that of pig iron had changed little. Copper shipments through the canal during that period, on the other hand, showed only slight growth. The improved iron ore tonnage benefited from the completion of the Iron Mountain Railroad in 1857. Unfortunately, the Iron Mountain's guiding light, Heman Ely, did not live to see his railroad completed; he died suddenly in his home at Marquette in October of 1856, shortly after the arrival of his first locomotive, the *Sebastopol*. As the 25-ton locomotive was making its initial trial runs on the newly completed track, the August 15, 1857, *Lake Superior Journal* observed an unfamiliar dilemma facing those in the Marquette iron trade. "There are now twelve sail vessels and one propeller loading and waiting to load with ore, and there is not a pound on the dock except that which comes down from day to day." The opening of the canal on the St. Mary's quite suddenly made Marquette accessible to virtually any ship then operating on the Great Lakes. The pace with which the ore was being delivered to the docks was proving inadequate to meet the demands of the growing number of ships in the village harbor, each capable of carrying the ore straight through to southern lake ports. But, the *Journal* continued, "'It is always darkest just before the dawn,' so now, our companies are having their greatest difficulty in supplying their vessels, just before the time when the ore can be brought down like an avalanche." Even though the trials had only begun, the arrival of a second locomotive, the *Dockersley*, emboldened railroad officials to promise the delivery of 1,200 tons of ore to the docks per day. Their optimism, while exaggerated, was not unfounded. The tonnage shipped out of Marquette in 1858 increased a modest 20 percent; yet the following year it more than doubled. It nearly doubled again the following year. At the same time, railroad freight rates on a ton of iron ore delivered from the mines to the Marquette docks plummeted from $3 in 1855 to $.87 in 1859. Throughout the Civil War the rate remained steady at $1.09. Still, as late as 1863, one observer noted that 50 ships waited in the harbor for ore from the mines, which still could not be brought to the docks quickly enough. Even with the several engines used to haul the ore the 14 miles to Marquette, the terrain remained a challenge. He characterized it "as wild as one could wish, mountainous and dreary in the extreme." And, he continued, "this road has an average rising grade of seventy-five feet to the mile, and in many places the grade is much heavier than that."[33]

If the locks on the St. Mary's brought more ships to Marquette and the Iron Mountain Railroad brought more ore to the city's docks, the primitive process of transferring that ore to the ships had changed little by 1857. Each of the three iron mining companies — the Jackson, the Lake Superior, and the Cleveland — had built and maintained its own dock. Building a dock in the 1850s on the shores of Lake Superior was no mean feat. Peter White, who helped found the city of Marquette in 1849, recalled for his biographer the settlers' first attempt to construct a dock. "The trees were carried into the water whole and piled lengthwise and crosswise until the structure was even with the surface of the water. Then they wheeled sand and gravel upon it and by the end of the second week the dock seemed both capacious and substantial." For added protection against the lake waters, the settlers built a wall of stone on the side of the dock facing the lake. One morning during the fourth week of construction, White arose to find that the dock had simply disappeared, carried off by the lake waters during the night. "Not a trace remained. The sand of the beach was as clean, smooth, and packed as it had been for centuries." It was some time before anyone in the community attempted to build another dock.[34]

While the three iron companies eventually managed to construct permanent docks, loading remained slow and labor-intensive. In the beginning, ships' crews loaded their vessels manually, for which each crewman received an additional $.25 per hour. Loaders used wheelbarrows and a series of planks to haul the ore aboard, all the time choking on the red dust that accompanied any attempt to move the ore. Loading in rainy weather of the region added to the men's misery as the already heavy ore became almost impossible to move with hand tools when wet. Under such conditions, it frequently took four days to load 300 tons of ore. Many captains were leery about transporting iron ore because it was so dirty, causing considerable time cleaning up, and heavy with jagged edges, which invariably damaged the ship. Moreover, unloading the ore from within the hold took more time. To avoid such problems, some captains simply refused to haul the ore. Others chose to carry it, but loaded the ore directly onto the decks of their ships, often in barrels. But after a few trips, they learned that this method made the vessel top-heavy, adversely affecting its balance and maneuverability. Moeover, sailors found that the ore stored on deck interfered with their responsibilities in operating the ship while underway. Lake water washing over the gunwales also turned the deck-loaded ore into a muddy, red mess. Soon most ships departed Marquette with the ore placed in their holds. Of course this required another step in the loading process, trimming the ore not carried in barrels. This shifting and leveling of the ore in the hold was necessary for the ship to ride properly and respond quickly while underway. Since side-wheel steamers carried passengers, most avoided the bulk ore trade. They generally had little cargo room below decks and knew that transporting the dirty ore on the decks would not be popular with the ship's passengers. Some steam propellers, however, did carry iron ore southbound. Often these ships left Lake Superior carrying, besides the iron ore, a combination of other cargo, such as copper and fish.[35]

In an effort to reduce the loading time, the Lake Superior Iron Company, acting on a suggestion from a vessel captain, built a trestle 25-feet tall on its dock in 1857. It contained 75 pockets (bins) for holding the ore, each with a gate at the bottom. Once the bin was loaded with ore, the gate could be opened and gravity carried the ore down a chute and into the hold of the waiting ship below. Some captains objected, believing that the falling ore would damage their ships, maybe even sink them. Despite their concerns, the trestle was a success, both simplifying and speeding up the loading operation. The Cleveland Iron Mining Company, noting the advantages of this new design, added a 30-foot trestle with 100 pockets to their existing dock in 1858. The additional five feet in elevation allowed for deeper bins, thereby increasing the efficiency of their loading system. When schooners arrived for a cargo of ore, however, their lines and rigging often interfered with the loading process. Still, the idea proved to be a practical one, especially when wooden propellers received the ore. The surrounding cliffs above the lake were connected to an expanded trestle system at Marquette after the Civil War. At that point much larger bins could load ships with thousands of tons in mere hours, although the vessels employed to carry the ore in the late 1850s had only a fraction of that capacity. The amount of ore shipped out of Marquette for the week ending August 14, 1857, for example, by the Cleveland Iron Mining Company was 254 gross tons aboard the schooner *Consuello* and 106½ gross tons on the propeller *Mineral Rock*.[36]

While the *Consuello* had a larger cargo capacity, its trip south to the Lake Erie docks was less predictable. Powered only by wind, she often had to adjust to unfavorable winds or survive sudden and sometimes violent storms. The *Mineral Rock*, whose steam power allowed it to make her way regardless of weather conditions, was subject to mechanical breakdowns. Either ship also

This 1858 photograph shows the first ore dock at Marquette (Michigan) to use gravity pockets for loading ships. Note the ore cars lined up on the left of the dock. They have arrived by rail directly from the mines and are waiting to deposit their loads. Since only a few ships could load at the same time, others are anchored to the north and west of the dock awaiting their turns.

could have been slowed by traffic congestion at the Sault locks, ending up stranded at the always-troublesome St. Clair Flats, or run aground during periods of low water levels on the lakes. The latter, which occur from time to time in the Great Lakes basin, made some shallow channels more dangerous by exposing vessels to otherwise harmless underwater obstructions.

Regardless of the challenges they experienced on the waters of the lakes, the ore-laden boats arriving at southern lake docks now faced the unpleasant task of unloading. Here an innovative technology, comparable to the one employed to ease the loading operation, eluded them during the first decades of ore hauling. Unloading vessels in 1857 was crude and time-consuming. It reversed the methods first used to load ships at Marquette, but was even more laborious and inefficient because much of the process worked against the forces of gravity. For those ships carrying bulk cargo unloading began with the construction of temporary staging halfway up the hold. The workers, who again often included the ship's crew, shoveled the ore onto this stage. They then climbed onto this platform and repeated the operation onto the ship's deck.

Here dockworkers loaded the ore into wheelbarrows and muscled it down a gangplank to storage locations near the docks. Longshoremen of the period, including those engaged in unloading iron ore, often labored under conditions that could best be characterized as Draconian. During the height of the shipping season, it was not uncommon for them to work to the "limit of physical endurance." One account recalled that a single shift shoveled coal for 42 hours straight at a Lake Erie dock in the late 19th century. The stevedore system controlled virtually all labor on the lake docks until the early 1890s. Under this system, highly competitive labor contractors furnished men to ships' captains or owners, commonly using physical force to win a contract. "A stevedore backed by a strapping band of fighters would drive away the stevedore with the weaker followers, and ultimately secure a monopoly of the business. These men were forced to become brutes or be kicked off the docks and kicked to pieces." In return for the employment, the men were expected to perform favors for their contractor. Since many contractors owned saloons near the docks, they often required the workers to spend virtually everything they earned in their establishments. Many men even lived in the saloons to be available for work when a boat arrived.[37]

At some point, someone began to harness the power of horses or mules to assist in unloading bulk commodities like iron ore. Jacob Cox, founder of the Cleveland Twist Drill Company in the 1880s, began his career in 1869 on the docks of the Cleveland Iron Company weighing iron ore unloaded from schooners arriving from Lake Superior. His autobiography included details of unloading procedures employing horses and mules:

> When a boat was ready to be unloaded, a block was suspended by ropes from the mastheads over each of the two hatches. A rope passed over this block and down into the hold, and on the end was suspended a wooden bucket, holding from 500 to 1,000 pounds. The other end of the rope passed under a snatch block attached to the edge of the dock. To this end of the rope a horse was hitched. A boy led the horse back and forth, up and down the dock, lifting the bucket as he led the horse forward, and dropping it into the hold as he backed up. A staging was erected on the edge of the dock on which two men were stationed to dump the buckets into wheelbarrows. A runway of planks was built from the staging on the dock back to the ore dump, and two men with wheelbarrows operated on each runway. This arrangement entailed the labor of four men on each runway and a horse and boy on the dock, making ten men altogether. Besides the men in the hold who shoveled the ore into the buckets there were also two horses. All the men working in each hatchway were called a gang, and the two gangs working ten hours a day under favorable conditions could unload a 500-ton schooner in from five to six days.[38]

Such quaint methods might be tolerated by an iron industry whose practitioners generally served a limited local clientele. But in the case of large consumers of iron, such as railroads, iron companies struggled to broaden their operations. At that point, the technology and capital needed to undertake such expansion within the rapidly growing country was only beginning to emerge. Moreover, a series of tariffs favored iron producers by providing a wall of protection against imported iron. For example, after enacting a law in 1832 encouraging the construction of railroads throughout the country, Congress levied a temporary tariff of 100 percent on railroad iron in 1842. And, when a depression hit Europe following the Revolutions of 1848, English iron companies flooded the United States market, causing some American iron mills to close. Congress responded by continuing a 30 percent tariff enacted two years earlier. Although the rate had dropped to 24 percent by 1857, the Morrill Tariff three years later placed a 30 percent tax on imported steel railroad rails and a flat $12 on iron ones. By 1864 Congress increased the tax to 45 percent and $14 respectively. But instead of encouraging the domestic mills to become innovative and self-sufficient, the tariffs spawned complacency. "The duties simply taxed the community; they did not serve to stimulate the industry." While the national production of iron increased, much of it was manufactured for local consumption, and the demand of railroads accounted for only five percent of the increase in the 1840s. In 1849, for example, iron mills produced about twice as many nails as they did rails. The decades of lethargy fostered by the tariffs meant that domestic production had considerable ground to make up once iron manufacturers decided to compete for the burgeoning rail business after 1850.[39]

Through the 1850s, the combined mileage for all railroads in the United States grew from 9,021 to 30,626 miles. As a result, the railroads' demand for iron began exceeding supply, especially if all forms of railroad consumption, not just rails, are considered. As early as 1840 the majority of the locomotives used in the United States came from domestic mills. But interested domestic producers increasingly found themselves unable to attain the standard achieved by Britain's advanced iron making plants and rolling mills. Their superiority "conferred a price advantage on British rail makers great enough to overcome the additional costs of ocean shipping, commissions, etc." In 1851 domestic rail companies purchased 188,625 tons of imported railroad iron, which rose to more than 282,000 tons in 1854. On average, domestic iron producers met only about 40 percent of the nation's rail needs between 1840 and 1860; the balance was purchased from the more progressive British mills. Since domestic rail prices tended to float to the level of the taxed imports, railroad companies struggled financially regardless of which rails they used. These artificially inflated costs became particularly troublesome when several of the larger northern lines found themselves struggling to compete with the Erie Canal system during the 1850s. Cargo arriving in Buffalo from ports around the western lakes was shipped by the canal system to New York City, just like it had been since the route opened in 1825. It had become customary for the canal boats to also function as storehouses both in Buffalo and New York, making grain elevators and warehouses unnecessary. Without access to such temporary storage facilities, early railroads found themselves at a disadvantage. This was exacerbated by the fact that legislature in Albany had a long and successful association with the canal system. This relationship found the legislature imposing tolls on the railroads competing with the canal, an issue that generated considerable political interest in the state during the mid–1850s. Many at the time simply did not view the railroads as a serious threat to the canal. In 1852, for example, the combined tonnage (both eastbound and westbound) of the two lines seeking to compete with the canal, the Erie and Central railroads, was 78,134 tons; that year the Erie Canal hauled 1,151,978 tons (east only). Railroads of the period often expanded by purchasing smaller regional or local lines. Therefore, it was common for the lines to be fragmented rather than contiguous. When this occurred, railroads usually employed river, canal, or lake craft to fill in these gaps. For example, early railroad entrepreneur Erastus Corning and his associates purchased the moribund Michigan Central line in 1846 as a feeder for their Central (later New York Central) Railroad. After completing the Michigan Central, they had a route connecting Buffalo to Chicago in 1849, which included the steamer *Mayflower* between Buffalo and Detroit and a ferry for the final leg of the trip. By 1854, the persistent New York Central and the Erie Railroads combined to haul 385,047 tons of cargo (east only), while the Erie Canal carried 1,070,845, down 142,845 tons from the previous year.[40]

That same year, the Chicago & Rock Island Railroad reached the Mississippi River. Now produce from the farms of the region could travel by rail to Chicago (and from there by boat to Buffalo and the Erie Canal), eliminating the more costly trip to the East coast via New Orleans. Regional rail lines also connected several Mississippi River towns with other ports on Lake Michigan. This expansion, mirroring the growth of railroads around the country, emboldened rail executives to lobby Congress for removal of the tariff on imported iron and rails. Demand had driven the cost of rails from $45 per ton in 1852 to $75 in 1854. Furthermore, railroad lobbyists argued, the treasury now enjoyed a surplus, much of it generated by the tax on the imported iron. Unfortunately the panic of 1857 eliminated the surplus and slowed railroad expansion, effectively neutralizing the two arguments that favored eliminating the tariff. But railroads continued to enjoy success despite the panic. Even discussions about a transcontinental railroad, which had emerged in the early 1850s, continued. Unfortunately, wrangling over the route to be followed served to further inflame the already heightened sectional tensions of the decade. As a result, construction did not begin until the secession of the southern states encouraged Congress to support investors of a northern route between Omaha, Nebraska, and San Francisco. Well before that time, however, the increased speed, improving reliability, relative ease of construction, and year-round service of railroads made transportation by water, especially the canal systems, less desirable. These advantages become clear when one considers that the New York Central in 1857 was forced to charge an average of 3.187 cents per mile, while the Erie Canal assessed a rate of only .799 cents a mile but continued to lose business to the railroad nonetheless.[41]

Between 1840 and 1860, the federal government donated over 100 million acres of public land to state and local governments to assist in financing early railroads. Sales of these lands generated $280 million, roughly 30 percent of the railroads' capitalization needs. The first railroad lines in the United States ran through the South (The Baltimore and Ohio in 1828, the "South Carolina road" in 1833, and a short 20-mile line in Mississippi in 1832). And here, as later in every other part of the country, most people viewed these noisy, bewildering contraptions as novelties, and dangerous ones at that. Besides being expensive and slow moving, the sparks they threw off created grass fires along the tracks. Even railroad executives saw them as having limited usage, mostly serving as feeders for waterways. The skepticism and uncertainty surrounding these early railroads can be seen in an anecdote related by railroad historian Henry Poor in 1881. He wrote that in late 1829 a group of distinguished engineers was brought together to judge the best way to move the rail cars. They were presented with two options: using a locomotive or erecting a stationary power plant every three miles, each of which pulled the train by means of an endless rope. Reflecting their misgivings regarding mechanical technology at the time, they opted for the stationary power plants. But the potential advantages of railroads eventually became apparent, leading to improvements. Locomotives became more reliable, strap rails gave way to solid iron rails, and investors became easier to find. By 1850, then, there was rapid expansion, even in the South where lines linked industrial and market areas with trade centers. While on the eve of the Civil War southern lines accounted for only one-third of all the railroads nationally, their 10,386 miles represented a 500 percent increase from 1850. Like their northern counterparts, financing for the southern rail lines came from bonds sold both abroad and to northern capitalists. These lines also sought and received financial assistance from state and federal governments. But they differed from their northern counterparts in that they were organized to pay dividends, not to make speculative fortunes. Capitalization in the South came close to the actual cost of the lines and equipment. As a result, most southern lines felt little impact from the Panic of 1857, which found many northern lines forced into receivership.[42]

Problems were bound to occur during such rapid expansion. One of the most inconvenient had to be the lack of uniformity in rail gauges among the many railways of the period. In 1860 there were at least twelve different gauges in use by the various regional lines spreading across the country, from six feet on the Erie Railroad to four feet three inches on the short Delaware and Hudson Railroad. This meant that freight and passengers were often forced to transfer from one train to another when they connected with another line. The rails themselves proved to be troublesome as well. Iron rails, while certainly an improvement over the dangerous strap rails, wore down quickly. Old rails became scrap, which was then melted down and reused in new rails. This increasingly liberated the operations of the rolling mills from those of the blast furnaces. It became common for the management of the railroads to own their own iron manufacturing and sales operations. Erastus Corning, for example, received no salary as president of the New York Central Railroad, but eagerly took commissions from both his rolling mills and from his merchandizing of new rails sold to the railroad. Unfortunately, the rapid deterioration of the iron rails continued to cause problems. J. Edgar Thomas (Pennsylvania Railroad) reacted to the growing frustration with iron rails by ordering 100 tons of steel rails in 1862 from England, where they had enjoyed great success. The high carbon content of these rails, however, caused them to fail during the severe winters in the northeast. Although rails with reduced carbon were purchased later and performed well, most railroads remained apprehensive about the expensive steel rails.[43]

American iron producers in the 1840s had experienced a revival before the rail issues emerged, much of it based on the internal market for chain, cable, stoves, hardware, and the like. Most supplied nearby markets and were scattered across the landscape. These mills shipped bar iron to nearby blacksmiths who hammered it into items for local consumption. Although it was relatively easy to get into the business of iron producing, few manufacturers of iron goods were large enough to take advantage of the efficiency found in economies of scale. Furthermore, the iron industry lacked areas of concentration. Kenneth Warren noted that every state east of the Mississippi River — except Rhode Island, Delaware, and Mississippi — had at least one furnace plant by the 1850s. Not surprisingly, strong competition among them led to a high casualty rate. Their dispersion across the countryside also meant that transportation costs were expensive, both for receiving raw materials and for delivering the finished product to market. This was compounded by high labor costs, the result of large tracts of cheap farmland that provided an attractive alternative for potential mill workers. Although some producers had begun importing new ideas and methods from Britain as early as the 1830s, most American mills, enjoying various levels of tariff protection, lagged several decades behind technologically, particularly in the use of blast furnace techniques for smelting. The British, their timber supplies used up years earlier, had adapted coke, which burned longer and at a higher temperature than charcoal or coal. Once again, most American mills, surrounded by plentiful supplies of timber and comfortably ensconced behind their tariff wall, were slow to seek alternative fuels. As the demand for iron increased in the late antebellum period, the advanced production techniques employed by the British mills rendered the American efforts noncompetitive and the protective tariffs irrelevant. For example, between July 1, 1851, and June 30, 1852, United States mills exported roughly $52,000 of bar iron, mostly to Canada, and $31,600 of steel to Latin America. During the same period, American imports of British iron bar topped $8.5 million, and imports of British steel exceeded $1.7 million.[44]

The impact of the Lake Superior iron mines on national iron production, however, was infinitesimal. After the locks at Sault Ste. Marie opened in 1855, the volume of Lake Superior iron traveling south fluctuated through the remainder of the 1850s. While the mines sent 36,343 tons out of Marquette in 1856, the effects of the Depression of 1857 reduced shipments to only 15,876 tons in 1858. Reflecting the declining demand, the price of the ore at lower lake ports during the same period dropped from $8.00 per ton to $6.50. By 1860 shipments from Marquette rebounded to 114,401 tons, but prices of ore on the docks continued to decline, dropping to $5.25 that year. Despite a precipitous drop to just under 50,000 tons shipped out amidst the uncertainty and disruption that accompanied the beginning of the Civil War in 1861, the movement of Lake Superior ore rose dramatically during the war years. It peaked at 243,127 tons in 1864; the price of ore on the docks on

Lake Erie also rebounded, reaching $8.50 that year. More than half of the ore shipped out of Marquette entered the port of Cleveland. The end of the war initially brought about a reduction in demand as the country adjusted to a peacetime economy. Local plants, noted the June 1, 1865, *Cleveland Leader*, were operating at only one-half capacity, mirroring a situation common throughout the country following the end of the Civil War.[45]

Iron ore was only one of many commodities carried on the lakes in the pre-war years, and certainly not the most important. Grain from western farms near the lower lakes remained the staple cargo for lake boats. In the first week of June 1847, for example, over 282,000 bushels of wheat left the port of Cleveland. This grain had been brought to Cleveland on the small boats operating on the northern part of the Ohio and Erie Canal, one of two canals within the state connecting the Ohio River and Lake Erie. Farm production from the southern part of the state tended to follow the canal south onto the Ohio and Mississippi Rivers, and eventually to New Orleans. But by the 1850s the canals, whether hauling goods north or south, began losing business to the railroads, which could carry Ohio's produce year-round to the East Coast. Other parts of the Old Northwest contributed to the grain production heading to the East Coast. Minnesota, for example, produced a surplus of wheat during its first year of statehood (1858) and began shipping it "eastward." While some was sent to St. Louis, where it was milled into flour, railroads also brought it to Milwaukee, where it was loaded onto ships for transport to Buffalo.[46]

The Civil War drastically altered the normal flow of commerce, much to the benefit of lake carriers. In June of 1861, Union forces blockaded the Mississippi River at Cairo, Illinois; the Confederates responded with their own blockade near Memphis, Tennessee. The shipments of grain and other commercial goods, once destined for New Orleans or St. Louis, now moved by railroad to Chicago. Further east, Confederate concerns about the rapid redeployment of Union troops from the West to Virginia led to numerous raids on the Baltimore and Ohio Railroad, which carried considerable commerce between the upper Ohio River and the Chesapeake Bay region. They began by destroying several bridges, but eventually took control of about 100 miles of track following the First Battle of Bull Run. The *Cincinnati Gazette* (quoted in the October 9, 1861, *Wheeling Intelligenser*) reported that the situation had idled 2,000 of the company's freight cars, as well as 200 of its locomotives. To make matters worse for those accustomed to shipping produce by railroad, the federal government increasingly requisitioned trains to move troops and supplies. The Pennsylvania Central, observed the *Cincin-*

nati Gazette (this time quoted in the October 4, 1861, Baltimore Sun), "is largely occupied in government business." The article further noted that, compared with 1860, railroad facilities have been reduced by half at the same time that there is an increase in business as a result of these events. Desperate to move production from the west to the east, "managers have put prices up fifty percent, while the canal and lakes are navigable, without being able to move all the property that is offered." When winter closes the canals and lakes, the article concluded, "it is probable that the freight on flour to New York will advance to two dollars per barrel by the first of January."[47]

With the Mississippi River effectively shut down and many east-west railroads likewise closed or otherwise engaged, it fell to ships to move the grain through the Great Lakes to Buffalo, where the Erie Canal could deliver it to New York. In 1859, for example, 250,872 tons of grain traveled on the canal east. Two years later, during the first year of the war, 1,054,295 tons reached New York via the canal. Commercial interests around the lakes petitioned Congress in 1864 for funds to construct two ship canals — one from the Mississippi River to Lake Michigan, the other connecting Lake Ontario with the New York Canal system — to further enhance trade in the region. Faced with the costs of a long war, the federal government declined. Not surprisingly, this rapid expansion in commerce placed a considerable burden on ships and grain facilities around the lakes. "The grain carrying trade of the past three years," noted the Cleveland Leader on January 3, 1863, "has given great impetus to vessel and steamship construction at all the lake ports. Our own shipyards have reaped substantial benefits for it." Many local shipbuilders, the article continued, had to turn down contracts because there were too few artisans and laborers available to do the work. Not surprisingly, those involved in the grain trade were rewarded with substantial profits. "Storage rates have gone up," the January 15, 1863, Cleveland Leader reported, "with some warehouse men making $1,000 to $2,000 profit a day." Within a year, however, much of the prosperity along the lakes had vanished. The fall of Vicksburg in July 1863 had reopened the Mississippi River to western farmers. The Cleveland Leader, reflecting on the shipping business, reported that the stagnation in shipbuilding experienced by the city in 1864 was the result of growing costs associated with labor and materials, as more men and supplies were diverted toward the war effort, and low freight rates. The paper noted that only 58 ships had been built on the Great Lakes that year, down from 81 in 1863. And only nine of those vessels, it lamented, had been launched at Cleveland.[48]

In the early years of the war, established ties between the South and

Great Britain had many in the North concerned that the Crown might intervene in the war in support of the Confederacy. This was particularly disconcerting to northerners living along the Great Lakes because Canada remained a British possession at the time, giving rise to fears of invasion from the north. In fact, confederate agents operated with considerable freedom in Canada, going so far as to plan and launch several inconsequential, if unnerving, raids into the United States from there during the war. By 1863, though, it had become clear that the British were not about to actively aid the South. Certainly Lincoln's Emancipation Proclamation, which abolished slavery in the rebellious states on January 1, played a key role in discouraging the British. Having abolished slavery themselves in 1833, they would be hard pressed to actively support any country whose economic foundations rested on enslaved workers. And certainly the unqualified Union victory over Lee at Gettysburg and the surrender of Vicksburg, the latter effectively divided the South by reopening the Mississippi River, called into question the South's long term prospects for victory by mid 1863.

It seems that the British themselves were divided over which side to support. Early in 1863, the *Buffalo Commercial Advertiser* published an editorial and several articles on the topic. While the House of Commons and popular sentiment, even among the laboring classes, generally sided with the North, the Queen, the House of Lords, and the aristocracy tended to favor the South. (Labor's support of the Union is especially surprising, considering that the war had adversely affected the British economy and cost many workers their jobs.) Interest in these matters was of particular concern for Americans living along the Great Lakes not only because they worried about being attacked. Many also had a stake in the growing, transporting, and storing of grain, which an industrializing Great Britain needed to feed its large urban population. In fact, an article in the October 26, 1861, *Detroit Tribune* encouraged direct grain sales with British ports, "as it will eventually lead to large orders being sent here direct from the European market." In 1863, stevedores in Cleveland alone loaded over 155,000 bushels of wheat on British ships for transport back to Europe, a trip made easier by enlargements made to the Welland Canal that year. Some concluded that the British reliance on American grains, much of it from the Midwest, also discourage the Crown from taking an active role in the war. "They [French and British governments] begin to realize the great truth," trumpeted the March 3, 1865, *Buffalo Commercial Advertiser*, "that we hold a power, both North and South, through bread and cotton, more potent than armies and navies."[49]

Despite concerns about British intervention early in the war, American ships remained prominent on the lakes throughout the period. In 1861, there were 350 steamships (147 sidewheelers and 203 propellers) and 1,102 sailing ships (989 of which were schooners) operating in the lakes. Their combined total tonnage was 383,309 (nearly 250,000 tons was under canvas) and their aggregate value was $11,862,450 (with sailing ships accounting for over $7,200,000). Without question, sails rather than smokestacks dominated the horizons. The growth in the number of ships, of course, provided Great Lakes shipbuilders the opportunity for experimentation. In 1862, eighteen years after the iron hulls *Surveyor* and *Michigan* were launched for the federal government, David Bell of Buffalo built the *Merchant,* the first commercial iron propeller on the lakes. Designed for hauling passengers and freight between Chicago and Buffalo, its hold was 13½' in height and contained five watertight compartments. But since iron inherently possessed greater strength, the ship required fewer frames. This gave the *Merchant* an increased carrying capacity of 715 tons, about 160 tons more than a wooden ship with the same dimensions. The need to use numerous stanchions and braces to reinforce wooden steamships, where engines, boilers, and other machinery placed a tremendous strain on the hull, meant that the vessels were often as heavy as their cargo. The *Merchant* was built at Buffalo because it had a pool of skilled iron fabricators in its established boiler and machinery works. Furthermore, its ample wooden shipbuilding yards could accommodate the larger iron hulls.[50]

But the launching of the *Merchant* did not flood Buffalo shipyards with orders for more iron ships. On the contrary, wooden steamships retained their popularity in many quarters, although there were nagging problems associated with their engines and boilers. Marine engineering in the antebellum United States struggled with an underdeveloped machine-tool industry. Consequently, engines remained simple, the walking-beam design being the most popular. In addition, cylinders tended to be poorly bored because shipyards lacked sophisticated drilling equipment. The boilers, hand-punched and riveted, were more likely to explode. Moreover, very few trained and skilled machinists were available. But the advantage of steam power was simply too important to curtail production of engines. The machining process, therefore, continued to be refined and wooden steamships continued to be built. Those desiring to build iron ships, whether on the lakes or for deep water service, faced three daunting challenges. First, iron was terribly expensive for the reasons detailed above, namely the lack of sophisticated iron production methods domestically and the impact of tariffs on imported iron. Second, Americans, particularly around the lakes, saw no compelling reason to abandon wooden hulls since the region still had great stands of white oak available. Finally, as with steam engine construction, there was a shortage of the advanced industrial organization and technical skills necessary for such an undertaking.[51]

Britain, whose shipyards on the Clyde River (near Glasgow) and the Mersey River (in Liverpool) were located quite near abundant supplies of iron ore and coal, had begun experimenting with iron hulls earlier in the 19th century. They employed the new technique of rolling wrought iron plates. By 1838, the first iron, ocean-going steamer, aptly named the *Ironsides*, had been launched at Liverpool. Six years later, ships like the *Great Britain* employed double bottoms for greater strength and watertight bulkheads to contain flooding in case the hull ruptured. Any lingering concerns about the reliability of iron hulls were removed in 1846 when the *Great Britain*, which had been stranded, was removed without damage. But the costs of these early iron vessels were nearly as steep for British shippers as for their American counterparts. As a result, many still preferred wooden hulls. Unlike American shippers who were prohibited by a 1792 law from buying vessels abroad, the British were free to purchase ships anywhere. By the 1850s American coastal builders had transformed their plentiful supply of natural timber into the best deep water sailing ships in the world. Fast and durable, they commanded the highest freight rates and enjoyed the lowest insurance rates. Since they were wooden, they also could be easily converted to warships if needed. As American wooden hulls attracted British buyers during the decade, British yards were left free to experiment and developed increasingly more sophisticated, and less costly, iron ships. At the same time, whether on the lakes or along the coast, American shipyards felt little pressure to change, even if the technology and resources had been available. Most shipbuilders on the lakes, therefore, viewed efforts like the *Merchant* with only passing interest.[52]

But, as the British were discovering, iron hulls had demonstrable advantages over wood. Besides their greater carrying capacity, the increased strength of iron meant that ships could be made longer and wider, and, offering less resistance, they traveled faster. Iron plates could be more securely fastened than wooden planking, which tended to become loosened on wooden steamers as a result of vibrations from those employing a screw propeller. Since iron could be fabricated to order, builders did not need to spend time and money searching through forests for appropriate timber for a given ship design. As a result, "(iron) shipbuilding became an assembly operation instead of a craft industry." This, in turn, allowed iron shipbuilding to experiment with new designs and assembly techniques. By the early 1860s,

British builders even tried to interest shippers in steel hulls. But this was an idea ahead of its time since the cost was roughly twice the cost of the already expensive iron hulled vessels. Clyde shipbuilder John Elder, seeking to make seagoing steam engines more efficient — thus reducing fuel costs and opening up more space below decks for cargo — employed the principle of compounding, first patented by fellow-countryman John Hornblower in 1781. Instead of allowing steam to escape after driving the engine, it was recaptured and returned to power the engine a second time. In 1859 a British ship employed an expansion engine at sea for the first time. Without question, the British were at the forefront of ship building technology by the mid–1860s. American builders remained aloof amidst their plentiful supplies of timber, protected by tariff laws, and comforted by the longstanding requirement that all hulls under the American flag be of domestic manufacture.[53]

In the midst of this paralyzing complacency in American shipbuilding, the federal government took notice of the growing interstate commerce within the country and the compelling need to begin assuming some of the regulatory responsibility with the states. Although *Gibbons v. Ogden* (1824) had provided an opportunity for the federal government to extend its influence within the Commerce Clause of the Constitution, Congress was slow to act. Predictably in the years before the Civil War, the debate became absorbed into the states' rights issue and it remained unresolved. The Taney Court (1836–1864) also found it impossible to maintain any consistency regarding exclusive federal power over commerce verses shared regulation with the states. The cumbersome "Selective Exclusiveness Doctrine," which emerged out of *Cooley v. Port Wardens of Philadelphia* (1852), found the court making determinations on a case-by-case basis.

Although *Gibbons* had ruled that navigation fell under the meaning of commerce, *The Steamboat Thomas Jefferson* ruling a year later restricted federal maritime jurisdiction to waters that "ebb and flow," that is, the oceans. This effectively eliminated inland rivers and the Great Lakes, where "commerce was in its infancy and of little importance," from federal regulation. Within a generation this argument had become an anachronism. In February of 1845 Congress, acknowledging the growing commercial activity along the southern shores of the Great Lakes, enacted legislation extending the jurisdiction of District Courts to certain cases on the lakes and their connecting waters. The court upheld this legislation in *The Propeller Genesee Chief v. Fitzhugh* (1852), ruling that the Admiralty Courts had jurisdiction over public navigable lakes and rivers of the country regardless of the issue of tidewater. Delivering the majority opinion, Chief Justice Roger Taney was unequivocal. "These lakes are in truth inland seas. A great and growing commerce is carried on upon them between different States and a foreign nation which is subject to all the incidents and hazards that attend commerce on the ocean. Hostile fleets have encountered on them, and prizes been made, and every reason which existed for the grant of admiralty jurisdiction to the General Government on the Atlantic Seas applies with equal force to the lakes."[54]

The Chief Justice's observations were clearly on the mark. Commercial expansion on the lakes by the end of the Civil War had made it an important part of the nation's economic system. This prominent role stimulated increased, if tentative, government interest. There had been limited and inconsistent federal aid to the area for navigational aids (lighthouses), harbor improvements, and surveys since the 1820s. The amounts spent, however, paled in comparison with federal monies spent on other river and harbor projects around the country. This disparity was not lost on congressmen from the lake states. Graham Chapin (New York) was particularly passionate in a February 27, 1837, speech delivered before the Committee of the Whole on the State of the Union. "This unequal state of things should no longer exist — a speedy remedy ought to be provided. The people of the West," he complained, "have the right to demand that equal and exact justice should be done alike to all portions of the Union presenting substantial claims for the consideration of Congress."[55]

By the 1850s, Congress had agreed to assist Michigan in its canal-building efforts at Sault St. Marie with the donation of 500,000 acres of federal land, a method it had employed to assist other projects around the country previously. Now the Supreme Court too had reversed itself, stating that the lakes, in fact, did possess a vibrant commerce in need of federal supervision. Still, President Franklin Pierce, a New Hampshire Democrat who sought to reestablish unity by coddling the party's southern wing, vetoed a bill that included funds to open the St. Clair Flats. Pierce, following Polk's lead, argued that the federal government should confine its appropriations "to works necessary to the execution of its undoubted powers and [to leave] all others to individual enterprise or to the separate states, to be provided for out of their own resources." His veto triggered another convention of region's business interests, this time at Buffalo in 1855, to address their frustrations over Washington's inertia. They did not enjoy the luxury of endless debates over what many of them considered the nuanced meaning of the Constitution. Shipping interests on the Lakes had pressing problems that needed to be addressed. For example, in an effort to once again clear a shipping lane through the shifting bottom of northern Lake St. Clair, several lake cities donated money to dredge the Flats. But even here they had to rely on the five dredges owned by the Army Corps of Engineers, since no private ones existed on the lakes. And the Corps itself often had proven less than helpful in other situations. At one point, the Board of Trade of Chicago actually seized one of the dredges for work on the city's harbor when the Corps refused to comply with their request to borrow it. By 1860 none of the dredges was operational because the federal government refused to pass appropriations to keep them maintained. And, the ability of cities to occasionally raise money for projects around the lakes simply reinforced the contention of critics of funding for internal improvements, such as Pierce, that local interest can and should deal with their own problems. Only appeals for funds to help offset shipping losses on the lakes caused by natural disasters like storms won general sympathy in Washington.[56]

Obviously, then, it would be premature to conclude that the federal government had "seen the light" and was now prepared to assume a major role in the region. But it would be fair to say that the unmistakable commercial importance of the lakes had forced the federal government to take notice. But the bitter sectionalism that festered throughout the decade continued to insert itself into nearly every debate, crippling efforts to accomplish anything constructive. The exuberant optimism regarding the potential of the lakes expressed by the participants at the 1847 Chicago Convention continued to resonate throughout the lakes. But local commercial interests and governments generally remained on their own until the cataclysm of civil war more clearly defined the relationship between the federal government and the states.

In the years following the war, as the country moved into the Great Plains and consolidated its hold on the continent, the lakes played an increasingly greater part in the development of the nation. The country began evolving from distinct regions with unique characteristics and regional economies into a more homogeneous nation with an integrated commercial network. Large, national corporations provided the bedrock for this transformation. And their needs were insatiable. Those charged with keeping these industries adequately supplied themselves grew into formidable entities. The motley collection of lake craft, the quaint methods of loading and unloading bulk cargo, and the unpredictable and dangerous waterways around the lakes were likewise on the threshold of change. The unrelenting demands placed on Great Lakes transportation eventually transformed it, its ancillary services, and the regional waterways into an integrated system designed to achieve more efficiency, speed, and safety. And the catalyst for these changes centered on the growing need for a large volume of high quality iron ore, the kind found along the southern coast of Lake Superior.

3

"The War changed everything"

(1865–1880)

The opening of the shipping season in 1867 found the Cleveland firm of Bothwell and Ferris, under contract to the New York, Pennsylvania, and Ohio (Nypano) Railroad to unload iron ore from ships from Marquette, beginning operations on the Nypano docks along the Cuyahoga River. Sailing ships arriving from Lake Superior waited offshore for a tug to tow them into the harbor and up the winding river to the various docks scattered along its shore. The confines of Cleveland's harbor made it impossible for sailing vessels to maneuver on their own without creating congestion, in part because they were often required to mingle with barges arriving on the Ohio-Erie Canal. On the Nypano docks, Bothwell and Ferris employed 40 horses and many times that number of men to remove the ore. It took them at least two days, and usually more, to unload 400 tons, an average cargo for a lake schooner. Relying on manual labor and horse power to remove the dirty, bulky cargo from the hold onto the decks, the stevedores found the work slow, wearisome, and, at times, dangerous. But with a drop in grain revenues after the war, lake shippers saw the iron ore trade as a way to keep their ships working. This was certainly no surprise to dock workers in Cleveland, like those at Bothwell and Ferris, as they watched ore arriving with increasing frequency from the Lake Superior mines. The peak year for ore shipments during the war had been 1864 when 243,127 tons left the Marquette docks. By the end of the shipping season only three years later that figure nearly doubled to 475,567 tons. In 1870 shipments reached 830,940 tons. As a result of this considerable increase in ore shipments, most of which was destined for Cleveland, traditional methods of unloading had become one of the more troublesome bottlenecks in the journey of the ore from the mines to the smelters.[1]

One of the firm's partners, J. D. Bothwell, supervising operations on the Nypano dock that spring, noted workmen making improvements along the river. Watching a small steam engine they used to help drive pilings into the riverbed, he became particularly intrigued by the action of the machine as it lifted each timber into the air before driving it into the riverbed below. Might this same action, he wondered, be utilized to lift ore from the hold of a ship, thereby eliminating the need for the horses he now used? Bothwell theorized that such a machine, which could operate for hours without food or rest, might reduce unloading time, thereby improving the firm's profitability. He discussed his idea with Robert Wallace of the local Wallace, Pankhurst and Company, who proceeded to design and build a small steam-powered engine that reproduced the lifting movement that Bothwell envisioned. Wallace also placed the unit on wheels so workers could move this "donkey engine" to service ships anywhere along the Nypano dock. The first vessel unloaded by the new device was the *Massillon*, despite the animated objections of her skipper who raged that this contraption would have his ore laden schooner in port for at least a week. In fact, the ship's 400 tons were completely unloaded before the end of the day. This engine was the first mechanical innovation introduced for unloading since ore had been carried on the lakes. Its success paid great dividends to Bothwell and Ferris since their contract gave them a flat percentage for each ton unloaded. The more quickly they unloaded each vessel, the more vessels they could handle. Wallace, Pankhurst, and Company also benefited immediately with orders for nine more engines.[2]

While the "donkey engine" did little more than hoist the tubs filled with ore from a ship's hold, it was unquestionably more efficient than horses. Workers were still necessary to load the ore into the tubs in the ship's hold; other workers had to dump the tubs the engine lifted out of the hold into wheelbarrows and muscle it down the gangplanks to the docks. Here they dumped it onto large piles of iron ore awaiting rail shipment to smelters. Still other workers had to load this ore, in a separate step, into the rail cars later. Despite the "donkey engine's" obvious advantages, more traditional unloading companies steadfastly continued to use horses. While the engine unquestioningly improved unloading operations and remained in use until the 1880s, it was only the first small step in refining the unloading process. Time eventually exposed the engine's woeful inadequacies as the flow of ore arriving along the southern lakes' shores in the coming years grew into a torrent.[3]

Americans in the years following the Civil War, particularly those living in the North and Midwest, saw a future that held great economic promise. During the war years, the United States Congress, freed from the paralyzing sectional bickering that had dominated the antebellum period with the exodus of southern congressmen, quickly enacted a number of important bills that proved helpful in stimulating the nation's post-war economy. A protective tariff passed in 1861 continued support for the nation's manufacturing interests, thereby encouraging investors and stimulating growth. The following year the Land-Grant College Act donated federal land to states to help them fund public universities. Here engineers could be trained, ways to improve agricultural output could be studied, and professionals needed to supervise the growth could be educated. That same year Congress enacted the Homestead Act to encourage economic growth through the distribution of federal land in the Upper Midwest. This act eventually attracted tens of thousands of farmers, many of whom were immigrants, to the region. They contributed to the nation's growing agricultural output, providing food to feed the factory workers swelling the populations that flocked to the country's urban areas following the war. Congress also enacted the Pacific Railway Act that same year. Thus, after years of pre-war sectional debate over which route the proposed transcontinental railroad should take, the nation was ready to embark on the final phase linking the East Coast with San Francisco on the Pacific by rail, thereby forging the foundation of a true national economy.

If congressional legislation helped spark economic growth in the post-war years, the Civil War itself had forced manufacturers to expand their operations, as well as coordinate with the federal government to meet the needs of the Union Army. Those engaged in iron production, for example, not only had to provide armaments but, after 1862, they also had to prepare to fill orders for rails, engines, and cars expected by the Union Pacific and Central Pacific Railroads, which together began construction of the transcontinental railroad in that year. In fact, the production of iron rails, despite the demands of the military for ordinance during the war, increased 250 percent between 1855 (when 138,674 were produced) and 1865 (which saw 430,778 rails manufactured). The war also stimulated growth and innovation in a variety of other industries, which further increased expectations for the post-war economy. "The war changed everything," concluded Peter Hall. It forced financial and transportation interests, for example, to coordinate their efforts in order to win the war. This, noted Hall, "even if impelled by civil war — at last [led] Americans towards the achievement of functional nationality." The years immediately following the war, however, found many regions returning to a pre-war sectional emphasis, with the depression of 1873 exacerbating this fragmentation. Still, the experience of the war years provided a model for cooperation and held the promise of a strong national economy in the future.[4]

Business expansion, however, required more workers. Many eventually came from the nation's farms. Here expanded acreage under cultivation, innovative farm machinery, and new methods improved harvests, which drove down prices. This agricultural bounty successfully fed growing urban populations, but it also made farming less appealing for many, especially the young. Increasingly, they saw their future in the blossoming industrial cities. Here they competed with immigrants from poor, overcrowded regions around Europe. Although immigrants, mostly from western Europe, had continued to arrive during the war, the 50 years following 1865 witnessed the largest influx of immigrants in the nation's history, many now from eastern and southern Europe. Even these large numbers of native and foreign workers often proved inadequate to meet the demands of an economy expanding at a prodigious rate by the last decades of the century. The wives, and frequently the children, of the transplanted farmers and hopeful immigrants were also hired to meet the demands of an insatiable American industry.

Industrial growth required vast amounts of capital. While overseas investors, particularly the British, continued to find investments in the United States appealing after the war, American financiers and entrepreneurs became increasingly important. This process culminated in the expansion of investment banking, as personified by John Pierpont Morgan in the late 1870s. The sale of stocks also grew and became formalized by mid-century, generating more operating capital.

The post-war economic growth took many forms: railroad expansion, increasingly sophisticated production of textiles and food, architectural and engineering innovation, the harnessing of electricity, and petroleum production, to name a few. And as the March 1880 *Scientific American* observed, "There is scarcely a mechanical occupation that does not depend for its tools, machinery, or raw material upon iron and steel." As a result, "The demand for iron is far in advance of the means of supply." Unquestionably, "The condition of the iron industry is in some measure at least indicative of the state of other interests." Consequently, the costs associated with the production of iron and steel played an important role in the depth and breadth of the nation's economic growth, and would do so for the rest of the century. While economies of scale, cheap labor, a rapidly expanding railroad network, available financing, and improved production and managerial techniques helped spur profits and growth by driving costs lower, numerous maritime improvements made on the lakes helped to reduce the delivery costs for iron ore and contributed considerably to this economic expansion.[5]

This chapter presents the important events occurring between 1865 and 1880 in the evolution of ore transportation on the lakes. Now freed from the uncertainty, inconsistency, and conflict that had frustrated antebellum efforts by lake interests to secure federal funds, the federal government renewed subsidies for improvements on the lakes in 1866. This generosity resulted in the construction of a ship canal through St. Clair Flats and the funding for a second lock at Sault Ste. Marie, this one owned by the federal government. In addition, the Army Corps of Engineers, heeding the demands of shippers, cooperated by deepening and improving selected channels, rivers, and harbors around the lakes.

Great Lakes shipping, reflecting the economic optimism common throughout much of the country, underwent change as well. For the first time, a shipyard in Cleveland launched a ship, the *R. J. Hackett*, designed specifically for the iron ore trade. A few years later an even larger vessel of the same design, the *V.H. Ketchum*, was launched. Some at the time characterized it as a "monster," awed by its imposing 233 foot length, its 40 foot beam, and its 23 foot depth. But the ship fell victim to a persistent problem that plagued many seeking to improve the carrying capacity of Great Lakes ships. Despite its larger hold, the *Ketchum* rarely traveled fully loaded. To do so, she would have run too deep to clear many of the channels, locks, and rivers around the lakes, which lacked uniformity in depth. As demands for larger cargoes, particularly iron ore, grew, shipbuilders continued to experiment with stronger materials and innovative designs to increase their ships' hauling capacity. But the lack of parallel innovation in loading and unloading equipment, as well as the inadequate and inconsistent depths of the region's waterways, often nullified their efforts.

As larger propellers like the *Ketchum* appeared, the number of sailing ships on the lakes, which peaked in 1869, began to decline. In what must have been vexing to their owners and crews, many of these once proud vessels ended their days with masts and rigging removed, towed as barges, known as consorts, behind tugs or steamers.

In the early 1870s, a shipyard in Buffalo launched three iron propellers for the passenger trade. By then the production of wooden side-wheelers, the subject of much fascination in the early days of the passenger trade on the lakes, had dropped off dramatically. Consequently, the hog-back construction so closely associated with many of those early ships disappeared from lake vessel design. In keeping with technological improvements elsewhere, electric lights began appearing on lake ships in 1879.

As noted above, "donkey engines" made their appearance on the ore docks at Cleveland in 1867. They were revolutionary because they were the first effort to mechanize unloading operations, and they proved to be successful in reducing the time required to off-load the ore. But, surprisingly, there were few improvements made to them, nor was there any competition from other manufacturers. The abundance of cheap labor — predominately Irish in the early days, but later including most European nationalities — made any demands for labor-saving devices unnecessary. But by the late 1870s pressure grew to consider further mechanical improvements in unloading capabilities. A second Michigan iron range, the Menominee, had opened. But instead of using Marquette, mine owners there transported their ore to Escanaba, on Lake Michigan, for shipment south. By the end of the decade, the Lake Superior iron ore downbound from both ports was approaching 2 million tons annually, roughly four times the volume in 1867.

Events away from the lakes also influenced activity in the basin. Supreme Court decisions continued to expand federal authority to regulate lake commerce. The economic panic of 1873 all but shut down commercial activity on the lakes for much of the decade, as it did throughout the rest of the country. In 1875, the Edgar Thomson plant revolutionized the production of steel using the Bessemer process. The desirable properties of the ore required for successfully manufacturing this product helped place Lake Superior iron in high demand and presented those in the region's ore business with tremendous opportunities.

Ships traveling south out of Lake Huron must pass through the St. Clair River. Only about half a mile wide, the river, running in a nearly straight channel slightly toward the southwest, carries all the water flowing out of the upper lakes — Superior, Michigan, and Huron — along its 30-mile length. As with most rivers, it also carries a variety of detritus. The river eventually flows into Lake St. Clair through any number of channels formed over the years by the deposition of this debris where the river's velocity decreases as it enters the lake. The area is known as the St. Clair Flats. Although less direct and "very crooked," the North Channel, which branched off to the west, was the swiftest and deepest. From LaSalle's first voyage to the upper lakes 1679, it remained the choice of mariners traveling between Lake St. Clair and the St. Clair River. The South Channel, which followed the international boundary line between Canada and the United States established in 1821, was more direct. Most of this channel had a depth of between 30 and 40 feet, but an extremely shallow sand bar averaging 8 feet in depth stretched back roughly 6,000 feet across this approach to Lake St. Clair, effectively limiting passage to boats with a shallow draft.[6]

As the number of vessels operating on the lakes grew in the 1850s, there were repeated appeals from maritime interests to the federal government seeking aid to prevent groundings of ships on the Flats. Fluctuating lake water levels and the ongoing build up of silt and debris continually altered the depth of the North Channel. In addition, the increase in mechanized ship traffic disturbed the bottom, shifting the sediment and further changing the depth and course of the channel. E.C. Martin recalled during a trip in 1847 that "after much twisting and turning, [we] successfully passed the flats, but stirred up mud pretty thoroughly." Taken together, these problems increased the chance of ships running aground. But requests for federal support in the antebellum period repeatedly confronted entrenched Democrats unflinching in their opposition to such funding. As a matter of doctrine, Kenneth Stampp noted, Democrats from the Southeast "denied the constitutionality of any form of federal aid for internal improvements." Following the Pierce veto of an appropriations bill for improving the Flats, maritime interests around the lakes convened at Buffalo in 1855 to organize a response, much as their predecessors had done at Chicago less than a decade earlier. Appeals to those attending the convention for funds to dredge the North Channel found a variety of commercial interests in Chicago, Milwaukee, Detroit, and Buffalo eager to contribute. Their unhesitating response spoke to the urgency of the problems at the St. Clair Flats. Unfortunately, their willingness to fund this project themselves unwittingly played into the hands of the Democrats in Washington, who could now argue that funding for the improvements was being successfully undertaken by those living in the region where the improvements were made, the position they had been arguing all along.[7]

On July 8, 1856, however, Congress overrode a presidential veto and appropriated $45,000 for the Army Corps of Engineers to dredge the sand bar in the South Channel. The project was completed in 1858 with a channel 275 feet wide cutting through the bar. The depth varied from 12 to 15½ feet, making it possible for any ship then on the lakes to make comfortable passage through the South Channel. That same year the Canadian government donated $20,000 to the Buffalo Board of Trade, which it used to further deepen and widen this shared channel. Shippers also had benefited from a general rise in lake levels, up four feet since 1841. Fears, however, that continued silting and the possibility that the lakes could return to earlier lower levels prompted the Corps of Engineers to request that Congress appropriate funds for renewed dredging in 1859 so that the channel would not "become an obstruction to navigation." The Corps proposed that the funds be used to ensure that the depth between the river and the lake should be a uniform 18 feet (during high water) or 12 feet (during lower water). Only one year after the 1858 dredging had been completed, they noted, the dredged sediment was sifting back into the channel. This added to the natural ongoing buildup of silt in the waterways. Boats were leaving Marquette without full loads, in part, to clear the Flats, which translated into reduced revenues for the shippers. Congress passed legislation to address the problems, but President James Buchanan remained unconvinced. In a veto message on February 1, 1860, echoing the earlier sentiments of fellow Democrats Andrew Jackson and James K. Polk, he concluded that, while the intentions of the bill were worthwhile, such appropriations exceeded the constitutional limitations of congressional authority. "The truth is," he wrote in his veto, "that most of these improvements are in a great degree local in their character and for the especial benefit of corporations or individuals in their vicinity." Therefore, "it would be unjust to impose upon the people of the United States the entire burden, which ought to be borne jointly by the parties having an equal interest in the work." The veto stood and efforts to improve the channel, as so much else that year, became lost in the relentless march toward civil war.[8]

Sectional tensions, and later the demands of the war, dried up federal funding for all maritime improvements between 1857 and 1865. By 1866, neglected maintenance of the South Channel made passage into and out of the mouth of the St. Clair River unpredictable. But the Corps decided against dredging the existing "tortuous" South Channel. Instead, they proposed making "a direct cut from [the river's] mouth proper to deep water in Lake St. Clair." A compliant Congress approved the funding and the project began on August 20, 1867. Completed in the autumn of 1871, the St. Clair Flats Ship Canal stretched almost one and a half miles in a straight line. With a width of 300 feet and a low water depth of 13 feet, it seemed capable of accommodating any fully loaded ship currently plying waters of the lakes. It also matched the depth of Michigan State Locks at Sault Ste. Marie. To prevent the canal from quickly refilling with the dredged sand, a revetment consisting of two rows of piling 13 feet apart were driven into the floor of the river on both sides. The dredged sand was then thrown between the two rows of piling to form what engineers hoped would be a permanent barrier against currents that might otherwise fill in the canal. A single row of sheath piling was added to the interior walls of the revetment to help stop the flow of the dredged sand back into the canal. To prevent deterioration of the wooden timbers, each piling was carbolized. Finally, to make the canal more easily visible to ships, the engineers planted willow trees along the top of the revetment.[9]

Post-war congresses, when funding projects like this one, proved to be considerably more generous than their antebellum counterparts. In the 41 years before 1865, federal appropriations for navigational improvements throughout the country totaled $11,985,125.22. Yet, in just the four years following the war Congress funded maritime projects amounting to $14,711,829.31. Up to 1870, a full year before the St. Clair Flats Ship Canal opened, the total spent by the federal government to make the Flats more navigable was $720,150, a figure that far exceeded expenditures for improvements at any other location around the lakes up to that time. It almost exactly doubled, for example, the $320,692 spent to improve the St. Mary's River and the canal at Sault Ste. Marie. In fact, other than improvements made along the Hudson River, at the mouth of the Mississippi River, and three other spots, the appropriations for the Flats exceeded the amount spent on any other river or harbor project in the country during that time. By 1870, only the state of New York had received more federal aid for river and harbor improvement than Michigan during the period beginning in 1824.[10]

By the end of the decade, increased traffic through the new canal and the ravages of nature had allowed the sand piled behind the revetment to reenter the canal and caused serious damage to the pilings. At the opening of navigation in 1877 "an extraordinary and continuous flow of ruining ice pouring down the St. Clair river day after day" prevented ships from moving north into the river. Consequently, the vessels began to use the canal as a harbor of refuge, a purpose for which it was never intended. Since there were no mooring facilities, the ships, many of them steamers towing consorts, had to keep moving within the canal waiting for the ice flows to subside. As a result, "both dikes were badly damaged by tugs and propellers, injuring the willow growth or plank revetment, or working their wheels violently in close proximity to the timber revetment, thereby sucking out through the meagre sheath piling the loose sand filling amounting in the aggregate to about 4,000 cubic yards in volume." But of greater concern, the carbolizing of the pilings had been applied unevenly. As a result, "the timbers thus treated [were] as a general rule at this date [June 1879] a mere shell with a core of dry rot." Additionally, the sheath piling had proven to be inadequate for holding the sand in. The Corps tried a variety of remedies to reinforce the sheath piling, including clay, willow cuttings, fagots, fascines, and marsh hay. Still, the interior walls required another layer of sheathing to truly hold, but such an improvement "would cost more than could be expected to be afforded." The 1879

The wooden steamer *Arizona* leaves the St. Clair Flats canal.

Corps of Engineers report concerning the canal concluded that an annual appropriation of $3,000 to $5,000 would be required from Congress just to keep up with repairs on the revetment.[11]

By late in the decade, government-sponsored projects on the lakes, as elsewhere around the country, confirmed the commitment of the federal government in the support of economic development. Much of this came in the form of government land grants and appropriations for internal improvements designed to encourage transportation facilities necessary to sustain economic growth. Although slowed by the depression of 1873, the country renewed its expansion late in the decade. Congress sought to remove any roadblocks that might slow this process down, helping to smooth the way to what many saw as the nation's destiny as a world economic power.

Another canal on the Lakes came about as a result of this government largess. In 1860 the Portage Lake Ship Canal had begun operations for the benefit of the copper miners working on the Keweenaw Peninsula west of Marquette. It connected Keweenaw Bay on the eastern side of the peninsula with Portage Lake further inland. Constructed by private investors involved in the copper business, it provided water access into the interior of the peninsula and simplified the movement of copper ore out and supplies into the region. Four years later, the Portage Lake and Lake Superior Ship Canal Company was formed with the goal of providing a western access to Portage Lake from Lake Superior. This would effectively create a ship canal across the entire peninsula, thereby shortening east-west navigation on the Lake by 170 miles. Appeals for support to Congress by the Canal Company resulted in a government land grant of nearly 400,000 acres to the State of Michigan. Mirroring the process used a decade earlier to build the Michigan State Locks, the State then gave this land to the company to sell to acquire funding for the project. Work on the canal was begun in 1868, but financial problems three years later led to the breakup of the company. Following litigation, the canal was finally completed in 1873. The Lake Superior Ship Canal, Railroad, and Iron Company was created to oversee operations and was granted the right to levy tolls.[12]

The completed canal was 100 feet wide at its narrowest point and at least 14 feet deep throughout, with most depths at 16 feet. The sides of the canal were constructed of sheet-piling, with two rows of piles about seven feet apart. The outer row had four-inch planking behind it to prevent sand from spilling into the canal from the sides. Piers made of cribs 30 feet wide extended 1,000 out into Lake Superior, forming an excellent harbor. Not only did the canal eliminate 170 miles for boats traveling on Lake Superior, it also offered a harbor of refuge in the event of bad weather on Superior. With few natural harbors anywhere along the southern shore of the Lake, such a harbor was of no small significance. Even in fair weather, some compared passage around the Keweenaw to "rounding the Horn," at the tip of South America. Congressman Byron M. Cutcheon, in fact, referred to it as "the Cape Horn of the North" and called it "the most dangerous point on the great chain of lakes." The opportunity to take advantage of a safe harbor during threatening weather took on even greater importance with the development of the Gogebic, Vermilion, and Mesabi iron ranges in the coming years, as well as with the continued growth of grain shipments out of Duluth.[13]

Land grants and appropriations for improvements created the expectation of continuing government support. This was true not only for new projects but also for periodic subsidies to maintain existing ones. As they have always done, the forces of nature continually conspire to undermine the efforts of marine engineers. This inevitability was compounded by an increase in lake traffic during the period, leading to a serious deterioration of facilities and improvements around the lakes. In 1874, the gross tonnage of all ships operating on the Great Lakes (excluding canal boats) reached 581,246, up 28 percent since 1868. This included 1,696 sailing ships (down 10 percent), 876 steamers (up 40 percent), and 216 barges (up 238 percent). By 1875 the effects of the depression two years earlier, which had dramatically slowed down lake commerce, reached the region's shipyards. In that year, lake shipbuilders launched only 177 new vessels, a considerable decline from 417 the year before. But, with some ships being built with larger dimensions, the total tonnage of documented steam vessels on the lakes remained steady throughout the remainder of the decade, while that of ships under sail declined slightly. While steamers could maneuver with considerably more precision than sailing ships, their means of propulsion by paddlewheel or propeller stirred up sediment and their increased power caused considerable damage when they struck pilings or canal revetments. Sailing ships were terribly difficult to control in tight spaces or during foul weather, causing these vessels to repeatedly pound the sides of locks as they passed through or docks as they attempted to tie up. This damage was simply compounded as the number and tonnage of lake vessels grew.[14]

The increase in the volume of ship tonnage on the lakes after the Civil War was spurred, in large part, by the demands of the iron trade. The postwar years found iron ore shipments from the Marquette Range growing at a remarkable rate. The 278,796 tons of ore shipped out of the Marquette mines in 1866 grew to 617,444 tons only three years later. Much of this ore found its way to northeastern Ohio and western Pennsylvania, particularly Pittsburgh, where the demand for railroad rails for the Transcontinental Railroad had made that city an important iron producer. In 1867 the city boasted 46 iron foundries, 31 rolling mills, and seven steel "manufactures," which accounted for one-third of Pittsburgh's $100 million revenue from manufacturing. The fuel to run these operations came from the Connelsville bituminous coal fields to the south, which one source described as the "greatest storehouse [of coal] in the United States, if not the world." Of course, the coal first had to be converted to coke to remove impurities and to make it burn hotter. But, concluded Joseph D. Weeks in a *Special Report* for the 1880 Census, the development of these coal fields contributed immeasurably to the production of coke in the United States and to its use as a blast-furnace fuel. While iron producers in eastern Pennsylvania continued to rely on anthracite coal, which remained abundant in the area, western producers were finding the coke to be a more efficient fuel. An article in the *New York Times* (April 6, 1875) reported that, while the cost of coke and anthracite was about the same, it took one and one quarter tons of coke, verses one and three quarter tons of anthracite, to produce a ton of iron.[15]

Besides the size of Connelsville fields and efficiency of the coke derived from them, this coal had other advantages. Foremost was the ease with which miners could extract it. Weeks demonstrated this by relating the result of a wager in which one man and one boy loaded 23 wagons with 57,684 pounds of Connelsville coal in less than ten hours. The two workers, Weeks observed, spent very little time mining the coal; rather, they concentrated most of their efforts on scooping it into the wagons. On average, one man could load between eight and ten wagons in a single day at a cost of $.25 per ton. In addition, Connelsville coal had relatively few impurities, particularly sulfur. Moreover, this coal, unlike the more fragile charcoal, could withstand a heavy burden in the furnace without collapsing. But, the coal was "tender," which caused it to deteriorate during shipping. Therefore, following the tradition of charcoal smelters earlier in the century, coal and coke ironmasters tried to build their plants as near plentiful supplies of coal as possible. Coking facilities were usually built near the coal fields, and both preferably as near as possible to smelting operations.[16]

The fragile nature of the coal became a significant factor in the rise of Pittsburgh as the iron and steel capital of the United States during the last decades of the 19th century. The location of the Connelsville coal fields southeast of the city, when connected by rail lines, ensured Pittsburgh producers of an abundant supply of coke for their furnaces. Nonetheless, Pittsburgh was "considerably later than some other western Pennsylvania points in getting its iron industry definitely established," concluded historian Frank C. Harper. When Alsace emigrant George Anshutz built the first blast furnace in the locale of present-day Pittsburgh in 1792, he believed that the area had usable iron deposits. It did not, and he went bankrupt relying on iron brought 25 miles by boat down the Allegheny River. This lack of a large, easily accessible iron ore field continued to plague western Pennsylvania iron masters for more than half a century. At one point, they even contracted to have ore laboriously transported to their furnaces from Missouri ore fields. Access to plentiful Lake Superior ore changed everything.[17]

The city's iron producers had benefited, as had others around the country, from a federal mandate that only domestic rails be used in the construction of land-grant railroads. Thomas Misa noted that "in the one year of 1869 the nation had laid more miles of rails than ever before, nearly five thousand." The frenzy of railroad building after the war resulted in an increase of nearly 23,000 miles of new track laid between 1860 and 1870. Not surprisingly, demand exceeded production. New lines, free of the domestic-only requirements of the land grant railroads, took advantage of imported rails. By 1872 imports, both iron and steel, accounted for one-third of the 6,000 miles of track laid that year. Still, domestic producers did their best to keep up, which meant increased demands for iron ore. By 1872, the Marquette loading docks sent 900,901 [long] tons of ore south, almost half again as much as left the port just three years earlier.[18]

In that year, the number of imported steel rails exceeded the number produced domestically. Domestic producers continued focusing instead on iron rails. In fact, their total output of 809,000 gross tons of iron rails made 1872 the peak year for iron rail production in the United States. Nonetheless, steel rail production was on the ascent, with domestic production jumping 50,000 gross tons over the previous year to 84,000. The advantages of steel had been evident for centuries. It provided considerably more strength per pound than iron and was much more malleable. In addition, it held up better under conditions of unexpected stress, such as in armaments and armor. The problem was that it cost too much to produce to be commercially profitable. The first crucible steel produced in the United States was poured in Cincinnati in 1832, but it generally lacked consistency. Moreover, the pots used to produce this steel held around 100 pounds, frustrating efforts to make the large batches necessary for rails. This crucible steel instead went for tools, dies, saws, fine springs, and cutlery.[19]

The shortages experienced by the nation during the War of 1812 had exposed the flaws in the Jeffersonian belief that a simple agrarian economy could trade its surplus to Europe to meet its limited needs for manufactured items. The appearance of small factories scattered along rivers and streams in the East even before the war ended testified to an emerging industrial self-reliance. Still, the production of these mills generally remained limited, designed primarily for local consumption. While this method seemed to work with the production of things like textiles, by mid-century some in the United States were growing impatient with the inability of iron and steel producers to keep up. While the Civil War generated increased iron production for armaments and rails, the need to import the more desirable steel rails during and after the war for the rapidly expanding railroads considerably inflated prices. There was tremendous opportunity for anyone able to increase domestic steel production.

Iron manufacture, of course, remained important in the post-war years, with the production of pig iron continuing to be scattered around the country to meet local or regional needs. By the early 1870s, Marquette could boast over 16 smelters turning out blooms, which were then shipped south on Lake boats for use in the manufacture of iron products. Hardwood charcoal, manufactured from nearby forests, continued to provide the fuel, making it unnecessary for ships to back haul coal from the southern Lakes. This was just as well since coal tended to break up during long distances aboard ships, which rendered it useless. There were later discussions about producing steel in the region using alternate fuels — coke, and even natural gas — but, for the reasons discussed below, this never materialized.[20]

Fayette Brown, the inspired general manager of the Jackson Iron Mining Company, also struggled with a way to make the company's operations more profitable. Like Peter White and other pig iron manufacturers in Marquette, he realized that as much as 40 percent of the content of the ore shipped to foundries near Lake Erie was waste. Manufacturing blooms locally was a way to make the company more efficient because ships would be hauling pure iron. In addition, the locks at Sault Ste. Marie, while greatly appreciated, could also prove to be a bottleneck during peak shipping months. Instead of building another pig iron furnace in Marquette, Brown chose to build his operation at the tip of the Garden Peninsula near the Escanaba ore docks on Lake Michigan. Ore coming by rail to Escanaba, which began receiving ore for shipment south from the Marquette area mines in 1866, could be shipped the short distance to his new facilities. Here it was transformed into pig iron and shipped south without having to travel through the locks and tortuous St. Mary's River. The company created an entire town, aptly named Fayette, around the deep Snail Shell harbor, putting the first furnace into blast on December 25, 1867. Eventually, the community had a school, stores, homes, and even a theater. The company added a second furnace in 1870.[21]

Although pig iron manufacture at Fayette and around Marquette helped make Michigan a leader in production nationally, inherent problems festered just below the surface. The producers remained small, were located a considerable distance from industrial centers, and lacked telegraph communications. Long winters meant that operations had to be slowed down or ceased all together because there was no way to transport manufactured blooms when the Lakes were frozen. Capital for expansion was unavailable locally, requiring dependency on either New York or Chicago. Furthermore, charcoal necessary for the furnaces would last only as long as the hardwood forests in the region remained, and they were becoming quickly depleted. But fate also intervened to help undermine iron production in the Lake Superior region. The Panic of 1873, for example, had a severe impact. The bankruptcy of Chicago industrialist Albert Meeker, a major purchaser of Lake Superior pig iron, in 1877 forced all but four Marquette furnaces out of business. Those who remained in business faced a serious drop in demand, which glutted the

Marquette Harbor, 1873. The ore dock has been extended in order to handle more ships.

market with iron and forced prices to decline dramatically. As if all this was not enough, a fire in 1868 destroyed much of downtown Marquette, drying up investment funds for a proposed rolling mill to be fueled by coke. A growing demand for steel forced larger mills along the southern Lakes to seek out newer, richer iron ranges to the west of Marquette beginning in the late 1870s. Gradually that city no longer seemed as unique or valuable as it once had. Even Michigan state law conspired against iron (and steel) manufacture in the Upper Peninsula. Investors planned a steel mill there during the 1870s and put together the necessary $4 million to see it completed, only to learn of a law that limited capitalization in the state to $500,000 per industry. For the plant to be built according to the law, the investors would have had to create eight separate companies. They quickly concluded that this was unnecessarily clumsy and took their investment to another state.[22]

While iron production remained the focus in the United States after the war, the British had already begun experimenting with ways to make inexpensive steel. The success of British steel production initially rested on the drive, creativity, and personal and political contacts of the French émigré Henry Bessemer. While only one of "at least five English or American inventors [who eventually] devised processes for making steel by blowing steam or air through molten iron," he was unmatched in self-promotion and establishing connections with the "right people," particularly the military. By the mid–1850s Bessemer's experimentation with methods to refine iron by means of introducing air into the molten iron in a converter furnace had caused considerable interest in Britain, as well as generating a number of eager investors. His Sheffield plant, after several unprofitable years in which Bessemer further refined his production methods and equipment, showed healthy profits by 1860. During these early years, Bessemer also realized that some ores worked better than others. In particular, ore with higher levels of phosphorus tended to be too brittle to roll or forge. Since most ores in Britain contained elevated levels of phosphorus, Bessemer eventually imported Swedish iron ore, which was more pure with reduced phosphorus levels.[23]

Thomas J. Misa concluded that the reasons for Bessemer's continued success included the zealous protection of his patent rights and a decidedly aggressive stance toward his competition. But he gladly shared his process with those willing to pay for a license. One of the first Americans to seek out Bessemer was Alexander Holley, who shared Bessemer's talents for self-promotion and innovation. After concluding a licensing arrangement with Bessemer, he opened his first plant at Troy, New York, in 1867. But Holley was not content and introduced so many innovations to the process that Bessemer might

This illustration from the April 10, 1886, *Harper's Weekly* captures the somewhat surrealistic interior of a Pittsburgh Bessemer steel plant in operation.

have had difficulty recognizing it. He went on to design 12 other steel mills for the production of rails. In 1879, Holley devised a heat exchanger for Pittsburgh's Edgar Thomson iron works. It created a "continuous feedback loop of heat" that transformed the mill from batch to continuous production. In these heady days of unrestrained railway expansion, improved production techniques, rather than attention to issues of quality, inspired iron producers. By the 1870s Holley and other American licensees had formed a pool known as the Bessemer Association. By controlling the number of licenses awarded, and thereby access to the technology, they effectively dictated the price of steel rails in the United States into the 20th century. Many railroads, in an effort to control their costs, established special relationships with their rail suppliers. Andrew Carnegie, for example, began his career with the Pennsylvania Railroad in 1853. When he left in 1865 to enter the steel business, he maintained strong ties with, and enjoyed the financial backing of, the company's leadership. This cozy relationship ensured that Carnegie would remain their exclusive rail supplier.[24]

Holley and other Americans involved with manufacturing Bessemer steel had learned early on that the process required a high grade of iron ore with a low phosphorus content for them to be successful. There were at the time various mining locations around the country, some established and some new, seeking to meet the growing demand for iron ore. It soon became apparent that the ore most compatible with the production of Bessemer steel was from the Lake Superior region. As late as 1886, for example, Pennsylvania led the nation in iron ore production with 2,185,675 tons, but only 20 percent of the ore could be used to make Bessemer steel. Michigan, on the other hand, mined a respectable 1,837,712 tons, but sent 43 percent of it to Bessemer steel plants. Ore from the Upper Peninsula had the highest average percent of metallic iron (almost 60) of any ore mined in the country, besides having generally low percentages of phosphorus. As the country grew increasingly more reliant on steel, the expanding production of the Lake Superior mines quickly became the favored choice of steel manufacturers driven to meet this demand.[25]

In the early stages of this prodigious increase in the mining and transportation of iron ore, which had served as a catalyst for Bothwell's innovative design for unloading ore on the Nypano docks in 1867, a fellow Clevelander, Elihu M. Peck, was motivated to reconsider the design of lake steamers themselves. Born in Otsego County, New York, in 1822, Peck had been employed as a ship carpenter by early Cleveland shipbuilder Philo Moses while still in his teens. He built his first vessel, the schooner *Jenny Lind*, in 1848. Peck later captained his own ship, the *Fountain City*, before joining with Irvine U. Masters in a shipbuilding partnership that lasted until the early 1870s. In 1869 the firm launched a ship based on Peck's revolutionary design, the *R.J. Hackett*. The changes Peck introduced forever altered the look of bulk carriers on the lakes.[26]

The *Hackett*, 208 feet in length with a beam of 32.4 feet and a depth of 12.5 feet, was a wooden propeller with a gross tonnage of 1,129. It certainly must have turned heads as it came off the ways in Cleveland. Peck's first-hand experience piloting ships had exposed him to the unique challenges faced by ships on the lakes. Hidden shoals, narrow channels, and oncoming ship traffic in narrow confines made it crucial that ships' masters be able to react quickly. As ships grew in length, commanding from the stern became more difficult and dangerous. Peck, therefore, placed the pilothouse over a cabin forward at the bow, giving the *Hackett's* captain better vision and the opportunity to respond to sudden crises quickly. The helmsman, who obviously came forward with the pilothouse, had to adjust his steering techniques to respond to this change. The machinery remained aft beneath a two-story cabin. Between

The revolutionary *R. J. Hackett* was launched at Cleveland in 1869. In this silhouette, the pilothouse is forward (left) and the crew's quarters and machinery are aft. This opened up the area between for cargo

the bow and stern lay a continuous, open cargo hold with hatches on 24-foot centers. Peck was aware that ore loading docks had spouts every 12 feet. His design meant that loading could be accomplished by using alternate spouts without moving the ship. In addition, the spar deck between the pilothouse and the aft cabin, with the exception of rigging directly behind the pilothouse and in front of the aft cabin, was clear. This made the loading and unloading of the vessel more efficient. It seems clear that Peck designed this vessel specifically to address the needs of the iron ore trade. The following year Peck and Masters launched the barge *Forest City*, a vessel of nearly the same dimensions, which the *Hackett* towed as a consort in the iron trade. This consort system revolutionized the movement of bulk cargo by increasing the volume that could be transported and the consistency with which it was delivered. It was an important transition in lake bulk delivery and represented the culmination of wooden cargo carrier design. While logic suggests that constructing a single vessel with larger dimensions would be more practical and less expensive, the shallowness of some channels — and particularly the 12-foot depth of the Michigan State Locks — prevented builders from exercising this option. In addition, the design of progressively larger wooden ships required additional bracing and stanchions for longitudinal strengthening, which not only added weight but also complicated loading and unloading operations. Later builders were able to enlarge the ships by replacing wood with metal, while retaining the basic design created by Peck. Other builders soon began to adapt Peck's design for their new vessels. Still, the captain of the *Hackett* operated in an environment where sailing ships continued to outnumber steamships nearly three to one.[27]

When the *Hackett* first touched water in Cleveland, she did so in a unique way. Traditionally ships were launched kneel first, sliding into the water perpendicular to the shoreline. But shipbuilding on the lakes was often carried on, as in Cleveland, at the mouth of a river. These rivers are frequently narrow and, in the case of the Cuyahoga River, serpentine. Osborne Howes, in an 1889 article on Great Lakes shipbuilding, characterized the Cuyahoga as "little more than an enlarged canal." How then could these larger vessels be launched? After all, machinery was not incorporated into the vessel until it was in the water. The momentum generated by a stern-first launch would quickly find the ship run aground on the far shore without an engine to help slow it down. Beginning in Cleveland, builders introduced sideways launches. "She rubs down the ways," observed Howes, "maintained in an upright position by props and wedges, and then drops into water with a sudden splash." But the vessel had only traveled "a few score feet from the place where the keel was laid." Soon shipyards around the lakes patterned launches on this method.[28]

During the winter of 1870–1871, the Anchor Line of Buffalo, New York, which had been incorporated as the Erie & Western Transportation Company in 1867 as the lake connection for the Pennsylvania Railroad, commissioned three unique package ships for their line: the *India, China,* and *Japan.* Package vessels carried freight, other than bulk items, and often passengers. They provided an important service around the lakes in the years even after railroads reached lake towns. Unlike their predecessors, these vessels were made of iron. Despite the general lack of any enthusiasm associated with the launch of the iron hull *Merchant* in 1862, Buffalo shipbuilders had continued to experiment with iron during the 1860s, working on tugs and small harbor craft. According to Alexander McDougall, who helped build and later captained the *Japan,* each of these identical vessels cost $180,000 and was capable of carrying 150 passengers and 1,200 tons of cargo on 12 feet of water. The iron for all three came from Philadelphia, "then the seat of the iron industry." With a reputation for clean, fast service and unique decorations that included hand-made, life-size statues atop their pilothouses, these vessels enjoyed great popularity over the 30 years they operated. But once again, most lake shipbuilders failed to embrace the concept of iron hulls. In light of future events, this may seem provincial and shortsighted, but these men had reasons that, to them, made their choice obvious. First, an abundance of white oak, long the favored material for the hulls of lake ships, remained readily available around the lakes. Second, the Panic of 1873 brought Lake commerce to a standstill, and at the same time grossly deflated vessel values. Although ship construction continued on pace over the next two years, these new ships had no doubt been ordered before the downturn. During such gloomy times businesses typically forego experimentation. In any case, the depression curtailed economic activity, including shipbuilding, until the early 1880s. Third, the cost of iron and the labor to work it were too high. For example, in the late 1870s shipbuilder John Roach paid between three-fourths and seven-eighths of a cent more per pound for ship plate than his English counter parts. This — coupled with the fact that British builders had more experience; access to a pool of skilled workers; and a short distances between the country's mines, smelters, and shipyards — meant British shipbuilders could produce iron ships between 20 and 35 percent cheaper. Although Americans by law could not purchase foreign-made vessels, they could import the cheaper British iron. But a tariff on British iron still made the cost unacceptable to most seeking to purchase an iron ship.[29]

By the end of the decade, United States shipbuilders on the East Coast were beginning to compete with their British counterparts in the production of iron vessels. This, according to an article in the 1877 *New York Daily Tribune*, was the result of a reduction of labor costs, which amounted to roughly 80 percent of the total cost of a ship. American shipbuilders could compete because they used labor-saving machinery that the British yards did not employ and because of an equalization of the price of labor. The firm of Roach and Sons as a result was able to launch 33 iron steamers between 1872 and 1877, more than any builder in Britain. While these ships tended to be smaller than their British counterparts, nearly half were in the foreign trade. This meant that the ships were "of a good size," meaning more than a coaster or tug. The article, quoting from the Registry of the Treasury, found 251 iron vessels operating in the United States in 1877, with an average of 30 new iron boats launched each year. But, unlike the British shipping industry, which enjoyed large contracts from their government, the United States government, the article concluded, "has shown no disposition to aid this interest further than to maintain our Registry laws." But, if iron boat production was growing in the foreign and coastal trade, it remained a novelty around the lakes.[30]

In the years immediately preceding the depression, the increase in the number and size of vessels that prompted improvements in the South Channel and elsewhere on the St. Clair Flats was having a similar impact on traffic through the Michigan State Locks at Sault Ste. Marie. Even the optimistic dimensions insisted upon by Charles Harvey in 1853, which were generally accepted as being large enough to meet all commercial needs well into the future, were proving inadequate. In an 1880 article entitled "Deeper Water" in the *Chicago Inter Ocean*, the author reported that "each season since [1874] has witnessed the commissioning of vessels and steamers of dimensions larger than any craft that was afloat the previous season, until now we have what we allude to as 'monster' propellers, 'great' steambarges and tows, and the 'big fellows' among sail ships." The increasing flow of commerce out of Lake Superior, particularly iron ore, also meant an ever-larger number of ships arrived at Sault Ste. Marie, resulting in delays as they waited their turn to lock through. The beams of some of the ships were now too large to allow them to share a passage through the locks with another ship. Thus, instead of being able to send several vessels through the locks at the same time, a growing number had to lock through separately. This added to the delays. As a result, both upbound and downbound ships were backed up for hours waiting to pass through the canal. Such delays were aggravating, raised safety issues, and cost shippers money. In addition, larger ships were sometimes forced to arrive without full loads in order to clear the locks' 12-feet depth. Harvey's sloped canal walls further compounded the problems because larger ships or those hauling barges struggled to fit into the locks, often scraping the walls and causing damage to their hulls just below the waterline.[31]

Besides delays at the locks, the St. Mary's River approaching the locks from the south presented another set of concerns. The St. Mary's, in fact, is not so much a river as a series of lakes connected by channels, some of which are often quite tortuous. Numerous islands dotted the waterway, and underwater obstructions provided additional challenges for ships' captains. By the late 1860s, buoys had been set out to help ships navigate the tricky waterway. But as W. H. Gorrill observed during a trip through the North Channel in 1868, "The buoys barely wide enough apart to permit two vessels to pass, indicate a narrow and very crooked channel, which may be passed only in daytime." He gave an indication of the potential danger if one strayed outside the buoys when he observed, "On each side may be seen rocks above the surface, against which the water is always dashing, showing a very rapid current." Such conditions made passage at night nothing short of foolhardy. As a result, ships did not venture into the river late in the day for fear of being caught in route when the sun went down. Conditions in the St. Mary's River, then, simply added to the frustrations of shippers passing between Lakes Superior and Huron.[32]

After the war, Congress, using information developed by lake surveys completed in 1863 and 1864, appropriated $110,692 (allotted in 1866, 1867, and 1869) for improvements to the St. Mary's River. Most of it was spent to construct a 14-foot channel through the Lake George section of the river. After consulting a map, one might conclude that these funds were ill spent. The 35-mile Lake George route is less direct and much more crooked than the alternate 15 miles through Middle Nebbish Channel into Hay Lake. But three shoals along that route discouraged, at least temporarily, improvements in that area of the river.[33]

The major concern when traveling between Lake Superior and Huron remained the outdated dimensions of the canal and locks at the falls. And it was clear that the State of Michigan was not keen on undertaking any improvements. Faced with increasing pressure to address problems there, the Michigan legislature passed a joint resolution on April 3, 1869, authorizing transfer of the canal to the United States, if Congress would indemnify the state against any losses arising from canal bonds they had already issued. Congress, aware of the canal's growing national importance, approved of the transfer in an act passed on July 11, 1870. A provision in that bill appropriated $150,000 to begin improvements, which centered on three areas: enlargement of the canal and existing lock, the construction of a second lock, and continued improvements to the river. Ultimately, these improvements, culminating with the opening of the new second (Weitzel) lock in 1881, cost an additional $2,255,000 and were made in eleven different appropriations. The canal, which now led to two locks, was widened from its uniform 100 feet to as much as 500 feet (270 feet directly in front of the locks). Instead of sloping, paved sides reaching a depth of only 12 feet, the new canal boasted vertical timber revetments and a depth of 16 feet. A curve, built in the 1850s where the river flowed out of Lake Superior from White Fish Bay to deflect spring ice flows, proved a hardship for mariners, particularly those towing barges, approaching the canal from the lake. The curve was straightened out and a coffer dam was placed there, much of the work being done after the lock closed on November 15, 1880, and "the coldest, severest, and most enduring spell of freezing weather ever known at that season" had set in. The new lock, placed to the north and parallel to the Michigan State Locks, was 515 feet long and 80 feet wide; its depth allowed ships to overcome the fall of 18 feet in one lift. In addition, hydraulic machinery was introduced to operate the lock gates and the coffer dam.[34]

At the same time, work progressed on deepening the St. Mary's River through the longer Lake George section to 16 feet. The Corps of Engineers also initiated a campaign to win congressional support for improving the shorter American Channel through Hay Lake. As the officer in charge of these operations, Major G. Weitzel, reported that the advantages to be gained by pursuing this route were compelling. First, this "new and comparatively straight channel would permit navigation by night with the assistance of a few lights." It would also shorten the distance between the lakes by at least 11 miles. In addition, this route "would in a few years amply repay the cost [of construction] in the saving of loss if time." But additional funding would also be needed to deepen the East Neebish channel further south on the river. Although the Canadians had earlier begun excavating a deeper passage there, they had concluded by 1881 that a better route would fall on the American side of the Channel and had halted operations.[35]

By the mid–1870s increased commerce on the lakes had forced Canadians and Americans to address shippers' concerns at another location along the shared waterway, the Detroit River. The problems centered on two locations: shoals at Limekiln Crossing near Fort Malden and at the mouth, where the river flows into Lake Erie. The former, named for a former lime kiln on the Canadian side of the river at that point, offered the greater challenge. At this point, where ships were forced to change channels to follow the deepest water that snaked among numerous islands, the river's current was particularly swift. This difficulty was compounded by the existence of a rocky ledge, known as Ballard's Reef, with natural depth ranging from 12½ to 15 feet over a bottom of solid rock. Moreover, as a report from the Chief of the Corps of Engineers noted, "the water surface, usually changing slowly, may rise or fall from a few inches during many days of calm weather to about four feet during severe storms and to about six feet during short, severe hurricanes. The monthly mean," the report continued, "may change as much as 2 feet in one year, or 4 feet in forty years." Such unpredictability posed considerable risks for "monsters" like the *V.H. Ketchum*, but caused concerns for smaller vessels as well, especially if they attempted passage through the river fully loaded. Most ships, regardless of their flag, preferred a course through the Canadian side of the river at Limekiln. Diplomatic efforts led to mutual funding of the project in 1874, much of it earmarked for improvements to the popular channel on the Canadian side. Although the project provided for a channel that was a uniform 20 feet in depth and 300 feet in width, it remained a winding — and therefore still dangerous — passage.[36]

The problems at the mouth of the river were different. A course existed, but ships had to carefully follow buoys around "partially obstructed" shoals, which made their passage dangerous. In a February 10, 1874, letter, C. B. Comstock, Major of Engineers, reported that "the commerce passing this point is so large and increasing so rapidly that it seems advisable to dredge off this shoal, and thus obtain a straight channel." As at Limekiln, he added, "Part of this dredging would be in Canadian waters." Whether or not this project was funded, Comstock concluded that a light-ship, which could work in conjunction with the existing Bois Blanc Island lighthouse, was also needed to ensure safe passage around the "22-feet curve at the south end of the channel." Comstock closed his letter with a request that the international boundary line be ignored. "As it would inure almost exclusively to the benefit of American commerce, would be in a better location, and would cost much less, the question of jurisdiction should not be considered in these inland seas further than to obtain the consent of the Canadian government."[37]

Comstock's justification for funding this project was simple and direct, but it again reflected the changing mood of the post-war federal government regarding improvements. "The justification for such an expenditure is," he wrote, "the same as for the surveys of islands or coasts of the Pacific, not belonging to the United States, namely, the imperative of commerce." It was clear to Comstock that the federal government had an obligation to facilitate economic growth. This mood was evident also in Congress's willingness to accept ownership of the Michigan State Locks in 1870, and with its promise to add a second lock to handle the increased traffic through the St. Mary's River. Congressional funding of the canal through the St. Clair Flats was yet another example of strong government support of business. Grants of land common before the war were now paired with direct appropriations. This funding in the Great Lakes came to play a significant role in the growth of commerce around the lakes, but particularly in the movement of iron ore.[38]

Paralleling increased congressional appropriations for internal improvements was an acknowledgment by the federal courts that Congress had control over maritime activity on the inland waters of the United States, including the Great Lakes. In *Gilman v City of Philadelphia* (1866) the Supreme Court reaffirmed *Gibbons v Ogden* (1824), ruling that Congress had complete control over navigable waters "which are accessible from a State other than those in which they lie." Five years later in *The Daniel Ball*, the high court extended federal regulation to include vessels that transport goods in interstate commerce even though the boat operated solely on waters entirely within one state. These rulings removed any remaining concerns around the lakes that individual state actions could frustrate the expanding commercial activity in the region. The Court further clarified the issue by ruling in *The Lottawanna* (1875) that congressional control over maritime law exclusive of the states originated not with the commercial clause of the Constitution (Article I, Section 8) but with Article III, Section 2, that is, "to all cases of admiralty and maritime jurisdiction." Its control, the court added, was supplemented by the "necessary and proper clause" of the Constitution (Article I, Section 8). As iron ore transported out of the Lake Superior region entered Illinois, Ohio, or Pennsylvania waters, those with an interest in the ore were now assured that maritime regulations and laws would be uniformly controlled out of Washington.[39]

Although in the years immediately following the Civil War the nation's commercial interests had begun blossoming, the impact of the Credit Mobilier scandal, which broke in 1872, quickly cooled down the economy in the form of a depression the following year. Maritime operations on the lakes were particularly hard hit. By the late 1870s, the production of new ships had been cut back. Innovations in design and construction were, as a result, slowed considerably. Still, the volume of commerce on the lakes grew, placing demands on the Army Corps of Engineers to neutralize the increasingly frustrating myriad of obstacles that challenged shippers at a number of critical locations around the lakes. An indication of the growth in commercial activity, particularly involved in the delivery of iron ore, was the awareness in the late 1860s that the Michigan State Canal had become inadequate to comfortably handle the flow of traffic moving in and out of Lake Superior. In fact, the size and design of the canal and locks had ceased being an aid to shipping and had instead become an irritating bottleneck.

By the 1870s sailing vessels were beginning their decline in favor of steam vessels. The latter moved faster and more predictably. This increased efficiency translated into more passages per season and contributed to the increased flow of traffic. The power of these vessels, however, could cause more damage to docks, channels, locks, and canals, especially if mishandled. The damage they did to the St. Clair Flats ship canal during the early spring of 1877 provides an excellent example. Although the gridlock that prevented government support of improvements before the war was gone, Congress was beginning to learn that appropriations did not end with the completion of a project. Quite the contrary, improvements — especially in an area of extreme seasonal changes and fickle weather patterns like the Great Lakes — brought with it the expectation that maintenance and repair costs had to be built into each annual budget.

If the national economy in general, and the lake economy in particular, did not perform as many had anticipated when the 1870s began, the decades that followed surely must have exceeded their expectations. On the Great Lakes the flood of iron ore that flowed out of the Michigan mines traveled south to smelters capable of handling all the ore they could get. New techniques in steel production required a pure ore, one low in phosphorus. No iron ore on the planet could match the composition of the Lake Superior ore for the requirements of this new Bessemer process. The demand for this ore placed tremendous pressure on miners, shippers, dock workers, and railroads to improve not only the speed of delivery but also the volume of each load. Innovations of shipbuilders that could address these requirements eventually met with great approval and lucrative contracts. New unloading equipment also came on the market to try to handle the onslaught of ore reaching the docks along the southern lake shores.

The 1880s witnessed a remarkable increase in innovation and production in the region. It was the direct result of new technologies in iron and steel production that sought to meet the expectations of entrepreneurs eager to take advantage of undreamed-of opportunities in the dynamic economy of the country at the time. The role played by the shipbuilders, inventors, engineers, miners, seamen, and dock men around the Great Lakes was an indispensable component in the march of the United States economy toward a position of world leadership.

4

"The ore fleet will have to be increased largely to get all the ore"

(1880–1890)

In September of 1884, the Wyandotte Iron Ship Building Company, a division of the Detroit Dry Dock Company located along the Detroit River, sent a new steamship down the ways. Named the *Albany*, it was followed the next month by a second vessel of identical design and dimensions, the *Syracuse*. Both were built for The Western Transportation Company of Buffalo. They were modeled after Western's iron propeller *Boston*, a "most successful business boat" built in 1880 also by the Detroit Dry Dock Company at its Wyandotte yards. Although the *Albany* sank in 1893 following a collision with the *Philadelphia*, the *Syracuse* remained active into the mid–20th century. None of this seems particularly noteworthy considering the similar histories of dozens of other commercial vessels launched on the lakes during this time. But the *Albany* and *Syracuse* were, in fact, unique. Unlike the *Boston*, which had been built of iron, or the numerous wooden ships constructed by the parent Detroit Dry Dock Company, the *Albany* and *Syracuse* were constructed entirely of mild steel.[1]

There had been a tradition of innovation at the Wyandotte yard. In 1872, Great Lakes entrepreneur E.B. Ward became the first on the lakes to attempt the construction of iron ships on a regular basis there. He failed, as did early iron shipbuilding efforts on the Atlantic seaboard, because labor costs were too high and laborsaving machinery was not available. In addition, pig iron for the steel plates was expensive, while abundant supplies of cheap lumber from nearby forests remained plentiful, providing all the necessary materials for traditional wooden hulls. Moreover, the Depression of 1873 curtailed ship production of all kinds on the lakes until the end of the decade.[2]

Facing such odds, it is not surprising that Ward sold out to the Detroit Dry Dock Company in 1879. The Wyandotte division immediately took advantage of a recovering economy and new labor-saving equipment to begin producing iron ships, such as the *Boston*. The ability of the Wyandotte yard to upgrade its facilities directly related to the protection afforded shipbuilders in general, and the Lake Superior iron ore industry specifically, by the laws of the United States. But, unlike East Coast builders who seemed content with iron hulls, some lake builders were more willing to experiment with different construction materials. While several tinkered with composite hulls, yards at Wyandotte and Cleveland developed an interest in steel ships.[3]

Forced to seek new construction materials because native timber had been depleted, British shipbuilders had begun launching iron ships much earlier. Later, they flirted with the idea of steel hulls but had little success because they were forced to use indigenous supplies of phosphorous-rich iron ore, which made the production of steel suitable for the demands of ocean-going vessels prohibitively expensive. The Thomas Basic process, introduced in 1879, allowed British steel manufacturers to economically remove the troublesome phosphorus; consequently steel costs there soon dropped dramatically. Encouraged, the Denny Yard at Dumbarton, Scotland, launched the first steel steamship, the *Rotomahana* later that year. In 1881 the Cunard Line purchased its first steel ship, the 7,392 gross ton *Servia*. According to maritime historian John G. B. Hutchins, "In England, the shift to steel construction subsequently proceeded rapidly, being practically completed in a dozen years." In the United States, steel shipbuilding began with the long overdue plans of the Navy to upgrade its fleet beginning in 1882. *Harper's Weekly* had warned that the Navy's current fleet, much of it comprised of wooden steamers that had fought in the Civil War, would be "simply helpless before any fourth-rate power with whom complications may arise." Accordingly, some shipyards on both coasts refitted and bought new equipment to meet this demand. Yet, blue water commercial shippers were reluctant to replace their iron ships with steel ones. The clear advantages of steel over iron and wood found the lake vessel owners, however, increasingly eager to place orders for steel hulls over the remainder of the decade. This demand stimulated steel shipbuilding on the lakes, fostering the construction of shipyards for that purpose that by 1891 ranked as the largest in the country.[4]

In this chapter, the elements of ship design and propulsion, iron and steel production, iron ore loading and unloading, and governmental support of commercial activities on the lakes, which heretofore existed and evolved with considerable independence, began inextricably to weave together into a fabric of mutual interdependence. The impetus behind the creation of this new tapestry was the growing demand for an adequate supply of iron ore to meet the needs of the iron and steel industries, which had become "so vast as to almost control the industrial and financial conditions of [the nation's] life." High-grade ore, one low in phosphorous, was also an important consideration when producing steel using the popular Bessemer process. No purer ore existed than that found along the shores of Lake Superior. While Lake Superior ore accounted for 25 percent of all the domestic iron mined in the early 1870s, that percentage doubled to 50 percent by 1881. Between 1880 and 1890, tens of thousands of laborers, entrepreneurs, financiers, miners, engineers, builders, and sailors combined their energy and creativity to deliver this precious ore with increased efficiency to steel plants in western Pennsylvania, northeastern Ohio, and northern Illinois, as well as to smelters in other parts of the country. The system they created played an integral role in the nation's industrial maturation in the late 19th and early 20th centuries. It made possible the altered skylines rising over the nation's metropolitan areas and contributed to improving the standard of living that a growing number of Americans began to enjoy in the late 19th century. It made the country's rise to industrial prominence possible in the 20th century and was indispensable in the production of war materiel vital for the success of United States and her allies in World War I and World War II.[5]

This chapter begins with the changes introduced in unloading iron ore. While the gravity method of loading ore changed little, the 1880s witnessed some revolutionary improvements in the unloading process. The first, known as a "Tom Collins," began operations late in 1880 along the iron ore docks at Cleveland. Two years later the "champion" hoist was introduced at Chicago. By shortening the amount of time spent unloading, ships spent more time on the open water hauling cargo, which translated into higher profits.

Mirroring similar activity in urban-industrial centers around the country, efforts to unionize dock workers and seamen began. Countermeasures, particularly by vessel owners, emerged during the early part of the period. These initiatives frequently grew out of pressures associated with an increased demand for Lake Superior iron ore.

Of course, smelters appreciated the increased flow of ore as the steel they produced began to replace iron in structural applications. And for the first time lake ore was in high demand by East Coast smelters, causing even more competition for the ore. Consequently, by the end of the late 1880s, with the newly opened Gogebic iron range adding to the stream of ore moving southward, iron ore for the first time became the leading commodity carried on the lakes.

The decade witnessed the beginning of mergers in the iron industry. Pickands, Mather, and Company of Cleveland, formed in 1883, used vertical integration to eventually become the largest miner of iron ore in the country. Large, well-financed shipbuilding concerns, necessary for the more sophisticated construction requirements of larger metal ships, also began to incorporate in Cleveland, Buffalo, Detroit, and other locations around the lakes by the end of this period.

While the Bessemer process continued its dominance in steel production into the 1900s, other processes began to vie for consideration, namely the Open-Hearth method. The struggle between these two became intense after Congress in 1884 authorized the creation of a "new Navy" built of steel to catch up with the navies of the European powers.

Steel-hulled vessels proved their worth during the 1880s. No longer limited in size by wood, builders could produce vessels of virtually any length and depth, which gave carriers the opportunity to enjoy an economy of scale that heretofore was unimaginable. These larger boats also benefited from compound engines that were able to recapture spent steam for reuse, which improved efficiency and reduced operating expenses.

The U. S. Government ceased to fund surveys of the lakes in 1882, arguing that all the lakes had been thoroughly surveyed and charted. Later in the decade, water levels around the lakes dropped by four to five feet, a problem that continued into the early 20th century. This, along with the increased size of the newer steel ships, revealed new underwater hazards that forced the government to renew the survey the lakes. The second lock at Sault Ste. Marie, the Weitzel, opened early in the decade. But it was considered inadequate by 1886 and the Corps of Engineers began planning a new lock the following year.

On May 24, 1880, Captain Henry Wallace guided the schooner *Thomas Gawn* into the loading dock at Escanaba and "commenced loading" iron ore at 7 P.M. By 10 P.M. he had taken on 1,027 tons of ore and was headed out with a "wind very light from [the] east." The ship was under sail constantly over the next five days, aided only by tugs through the Straits of Mackinac and the Detroit River. Attesting to the prodigious volume of lake traffic at the time, Wallace recorded in several entries "a large fleet bound down with us." The *Thomas Gawn* arrived off Cleveland in mid-afternoon on Saturday the 29th, where a tug took the ship under tow and delivered her to an ore dock along the Cuyahoga River at 4 P.M. Since there were laws that prevented unloading on Sundays, the ship and cargo sat idle until Monday morning. It took until 2 P.M. on Tuesday for the ore to be unloaded, at which point a tug took the *Gawn* to the coal dock to be reloaded for Milwaukee. After nearly five days sailing time, the schooner had traveled from northern Lake Michigan to the south-central shores of Lake Erie, roughly 580 miles. At times winds from the southwest or east slowed her progress; at other times the "wind all died away." More favorable, steady winds might have reduced the trip to less than four days. Forced to rely on the unpredictability of wind and weather, there was simply no way to anticipate the sailing time for schooners between ports. Discounting the loss of Sunday, unloading took nearly two additional days. If the demand for ore continued to increase in the coming years, as it appeared likely to do, how could the current system, which relied on a large number of assorted vessel types, but especially schooners, and inadequate, overworked unloading procedures, meet the challenge?[6]

Despite the repercussions of the Panic of 1873, a second Lake Superior mining range, the Menominee, had begun shipping ore south from the Lake Michigan port of Escanaba in 1877. The *Gawn's* late May cargo contributed to the total of 1,908,745 tons of Lake Superior iron ore, whether shipped out of Marquette or Escanaba, arriving at southern lake ports in 1880. This was

nearly twice the volume of the previous record established in 1873. More to the point, it was roughly four times the volume of ore shipped to Lake Erie ports in 1867, the year Bothwell and Ferris had introduced the donkey engine. In addition, new ship designs, popularized by the wooden steamer *R. J. Hackett*, had not only improved the transport of bulk commodities, particularly iron ore, they had also done away with much of the rigging associated with schooners like the *Gawn*, particularly amidships. By reducing the likelihood of becoming entangled in the rigging, it now became possible — and desirable in light of the

Alexander Brown.

increased volume of ore arriving — to consider more innovative unloading techniques.[7]

Alexander E. Brown, the first to exploit the commercial opportunity of this situation, was the son of Fayette Brown, who had been instrumental in the creation of the iron processing town of Fayette, Michigan, in the late 1860s. Supported and encouraged by his father, Brown received a degree in civil and mining engineering from Brooklyn Polytechnic Institute in 1872. He worked briefly for the United States Geological Survey, but was soon attracted to the Great Lakes to design bridges and superintend mines in the expanding Lake Superior iron ore region. When he returned to Cleveland at the end of the decade, Brown was quick to observe the limitations of current unloading practices, which became clear as the pall of the depression lifted and the volume of iron ore entering Cleveland rose dramatically. Combining his engineering expertise with an intimate knowledge of the iron business, he responded by designing an unloading system that, like its predecessors, relied on a mechanized bucket lowered into the hold. But once filled, it was raised up vertically and then traveled over the dock on a cable running between two vertical pairs of legs. The contents of the bucket were then unloaded at the back of the dock. The legs nearest to the dock were movable, allowing the rig to work directly over a ship's hatches without forcing the captain to move the vessel for the convenience of the hoist operator during the unloading process.[8]

In 1880 Brown's revolutionary design, nicknamed the "Tom Collins," went into operation on the same NYPANO docks that had witnessed the introduction of the donkey engines 13 years earlier. But, as Brown related a few years later, the new apparatus initially caused considerable resentment. As he began to assemble his tramway on the docks, word leaked out to those whose livelihood depended on unloading ships in the more traditional manner. "The stevedores found me out and broke my machine as often as I put it up. Thus for one whole year I did nothing more than rebuild my apparatus as fast as someone wrecked it." After the season ended and there was no need for the workers to continue to disrupt his operations, Brown was able to convince several of them to help him "shovel the ore into the hoister, for that must still be done by man power." Once the stevedores learned that the savings came "in time and men [needed] to wheel the ore" off the ships, they were converted. In fact, since the "Tom Collins" removed a ship's load more quickly, they were able to earn more for a day's work. "After that I was not molested," he recalled. Iron merchants were equally pleased since unloading costs dropped from $.25 per ton to $.076, while simultaneously reducing

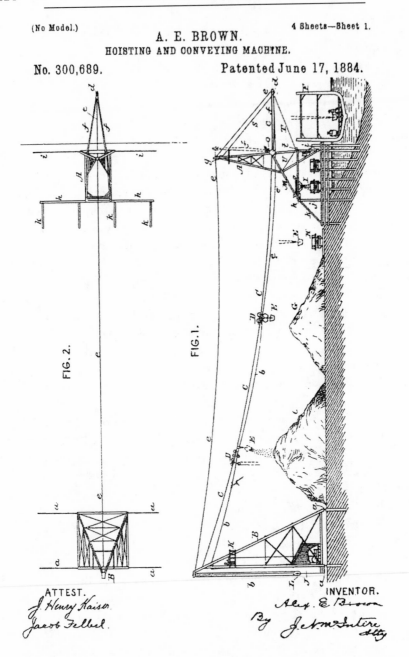

An Alexander Brown Rig. This drawing of one of Alexander Brown's early iron ore unloaders accompanied his application for a patent. (From *Specifications of Patents*, Vol. 145, 1884.)

unloading time from days to hours. In a November 3, 1884, article, *The Cleveland Herald* reported that a gang of 18 men using a Brown Unloader could remove "one hundred tons an hour from a vessel working at three hatches, and this rate has been kept up for a full working day." This, the article concluded, was "at least 150 tons more a day than could be taken out by wheelbarrows, even under the most favorable circumstances."[9]

Brown's device could lift nearly a ton of ore out of a ship's hold and carry it over the docks, a distance of about 350 feet. Operators generally stored the ore in piles between the front and rear legs, using a trip wire to release the contents of each tub. Brown also designed the operating system for optimum efficiency. A single steam-powered engine house was capable of driving five of these units simultaneously. But Brown discovered almost immediately that the "Tom Collins" had troubling shortcomings. First, the cable supporting the tub tended to sag under a heavy load, often preventing the moving tub from clearing the previously unloaded ore piled on the dock below. Brown responded by suspending the tubs from a rigid bridge structure rather than a cable. To cover more dock space, he made the rear legs movable like those in the front. Such flexibility permitted as many as twelve rigs to operate on one dock simultaneously, where they could unload up to three ships at the same time. A second problem centered on the need for the stevedores in the hold to fill each tub manually. Here Brown, no doubt angering the stevedores he had only recently won over, designed and built a larger grab bucket that filled itself. It operated on the same principle as a clamshell, a name that it soon took on. The huge "clam" dropped into a ship's hold open; when the operator closed the jaws, he was able to extract up to three tons of ore from a ship's hold. The remaining stevedores, their ranks thinned considerably as a result of the clamshell buckets, were relegated to moving ore lying along the edges of the hold to the center where the bucket could remove it.[10]

"Tom Collins" continued to unload vessels, even schooners, on the wide NYPANO docks at Cleveland for decades after their introduction. But even with Brown's system, the Cleveland docks were incapable of handling the volume of ore arriving during the 1880s. As a result, Brown noted, new ore docks at "Ashtabula, Lorain, and Fairport sprang up and got ore which would have otherwise been unloaded at Cleveland." Speaking at the Civil Engineers Club of Cleveland in 1882, he acknowledged that "more than 100,000 tons were sent away from here this season which the docks would not accommodate." These smaller harbors lacked the space for the sophisticated Tom Collins unloaders. In response, the McMyler Manufacturing Company of Cleveland introduced a variation of the donkey engine that improved unloading of the smaller ore vessels that frequented these ports. Known as "whirleys" because each was capable of spinning 180 degrees, they rode on wide tracks set as close to the edge of the docks as possible. A small steam boiler mounted inside the wooden cab worked the hoisting mechanism that raised and lowered a tub attached to a cable. Workers still had to load the tubs by hand, but some of the tubs were equipped with a tripping device attached to the bottom to facilitate dumping the ore. Unfortunately, these small cranes only had the ability to deposit their loads within the radius of the tracks. This slowed unloading by forcing a second operation to move the ore off the docks either onto railroad cars or into storage.[11]

While McMyler's creation was popular at smaller Lake Erie docks in the 1880s, the "whirleys" alone were never intended to keep up with the onslaught of iron ore arriving daily along the southern shores of Lake Erie on its way to iron manufacturers in Cleveland, Youngstown, and Pittsburgh. The future of unloading was to be found with more economical systems, like Brown's, capable of handling high volumes of iron ore efficiently. Brown's monopoly on large unloading rigs, however, did not last long. In fact, the November 3, 1884, *Cleveland Herald* noted that the Cleveland & Pittsburg (sic) Railroad Company ore docks had "two sets of patent hoisting machines erected by Messrs. Fleming and Stovering of this city. They are of the same general style as the Brown Machine, though operating on an entirely different principle." The same article recorded that the "new docks of Andrews, Hitchcock & Company" have installed "four cranes of the Pound patent and [they] are in constant use." Brown's hoist also had competition from the Champion Ore Hoist on the southern Lake Michigan docks where inventor Robert Aspin installed the first one in 1882. In the 1880s the Illinois Steel Company in south Chicago had begun diverting some of the ore shipments from Lake Superior ports south into Lake Michigan for its steel production. Word of Brown's unloading system inspired the enterprising Aspin, a Newfoundlander who had been a lake sailor in the 1860s but was now a dock foreman for Illinois Steel, to design his Champion hoist as a way to speed up unloading, thus making Illinois Steel more competitive. When it went into operation during the 1883 shipping season, the Champion hoist revolutionized ore handling on Lake Michigan, much as Brown's system had at Cleveland.[12]

The Champion system employed a series of fixed timber structures along dockside, each one supporting a tilting, vertical boom shaped like an "A." A bucket on a knotted rope hung from the apex of the boom. When a steam-powered windlass tilted the boom forward, it suspended the bucket over a loaded vessel. The operator then lowered the bucket into the hold where

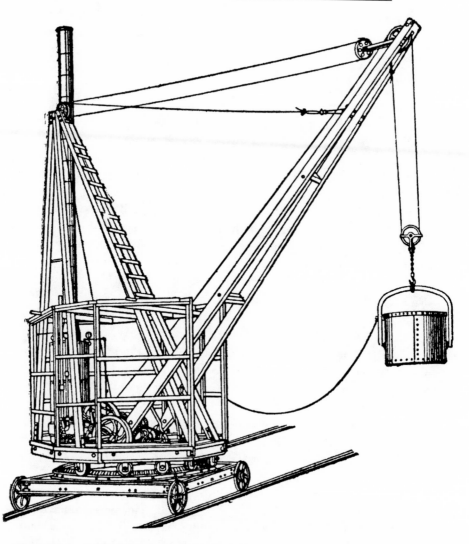

The "whirley." This illustration accompanied the story of the McMyler Manufacturing Company in the 1888 edition of *Industries of Cleveland.*

workers hand-loaded it. In the hoisting process, the knotted stop on the rope
caught on the boom as it was lifted out of the hold, causing the boom to return
to vertical. This brought the bucket over the dock and above an elevated platform. At this point, a worker pulled a trip line that dumped the contents of
the bucket into a large hopper that directed the ore through chutes into railroad ore cars waiting below. Although the Champion hoists remained in oper-

ation on a number of south Chicago docks until 1908, they had several weaknesses. First, since Aspin had designed the system to deposit the ore directly into railcars, it could not be used in dock storage operations. Dock storage had become important as a way to ensure that there was an adequate supply of ore for steel production during the winter months when freezing conditions brought an end to the shipping season. Second, Champion hoists were stationary, unable to move laterally along the docks like Brown's tramway. This added to unloading time by forcing ships' captains to reposition their ships periodically during the process. Finally, it was labor-intensive. Aspin never adopted clam buckets, making it necessary for laborers in the holds to fill each bucket by hand.[13]

No doubt driven by all his competition, Alexander Brown continued to modify the Brown hoist. Although the steam-powered model had been a success, he was quick to adopt the recently harnessed power of electricity in his new Brown Fastplant, which was a fundamental departure from all previous onloading systems. Instead of traditional bridges, the Fastplant employed box-shaped structures that supported a fixed, overhead rail tramway. A bucket on an electrically powered windlass was attached to the trolley that carried the operator. He moved back and forth between the ship and the back of the dock, first lowering the bucket directly into the ship's hold to retrieve a scoop of ore then moving back across the dock to deposit it either in a waiting rail car or on the dock for storage. Besides being the fastest unloading machine of its day, the Fastplants were versatile and easily assembled or repaired. In fact, they were so successful that many of the original ones remained in continuous operation into the 1930s. Mechanical engineer John A. Burke observed that ore unloading rigs found at many ocean ports in the 1970s were larger versions of Brown's Fastplant.[14]

Back in Chicago, the Hoover and Mason Company introduced a newly designed grab bucket that dramatically improved unloading. Unlike earlier versions of clam-shell buckets that had trouble handling heavier grades of ore, the considerable weight and larger opening (18 feet) allowed it to deal with virtually any grade of ore. Moreover, its unique closing action — a downward bite to penetrate the ore pile followed by a horizontal scraping to closure — reduced much of the cleanup in a ship's hold. In addition, the Hoover-Mason bucket rode on hoisting drums that could rotate. This further facilitated cleanup since the buckets could reach ore lying between the hatch openings.[15]

The labor saving innovations introduced by Brown, Aspin, Hoover and Mason, and others were designed specifically to reduce unloading time. The issue had emerged as one of particular importance to those in the iron trade.

A Brown Fast Plant unloads an iron freighter at Conneaut, Ohio. (From Ralph D. Williams, *The Honorable Peter White*, 1907.)

An article in the April 13, 1889, *Harper's Weekly* attributes much of the success of Great Lakes transportation to improved cargo handling. "The saving of time to the ship-owner is a factor of even greater importance [than savings in unloading costs], since it gives to his vessel a much greater freight-earning ability than she would otherwise possess." Transportation historian Henry Penton concurred, noting that lake voyages were relatively short compared with those of ocean transport. Therefore, any reduction in port time was crucial, even more so than increased vessel speed, since it allowed ships to make more trips during the season. Still, to those intimately involved with the process, it was clear that there was room for improvement. An August 5, 1889, letter from William Livingston, general manager of The Michigan Navigation Company, to Harvey Brown, managing owner of the Brown Hoisting and Conveying Machine Company, finds Livingston venting his frustration over long unloading times in lower lake ports of Cleveland and Ashtabula. He offered no explanation for the delays, but bemoaned the fact that larger boats — which stood to make more profit because they could benefit from economies of scale — spent too much time in port waiting to be unloaded. He concluded that longer trips to Lake Superior (Marquette) were more advantageous than shorter ones (Escanaba) because boats spent less time in port.[16]

While the Tom Collins and the Champion Hoist cut unloading costs and ultimately made the production of iron and steel cheaper, they also radically and permanently altered the work patterns of manual labor on the docks. Traditional workers — fatigued by long hours, mercilessly manipulated by the stevedore system, and facing pressure from increasing numbers of European workers eager for any type of employment — looked on the growing mechanization as yet another challenge. While some gangs of workers continued to unload ore and other bulk items as they always had, increasingly throughout the 1880s others were reduced to acting as cleanup gangs for rigs equipped with grab buckets. Still, they were paid on an hourly basis for the entire time the automatic equipment operated. Although this resulted in less money per man, it did provide some job security.[17]

Historian John Garraty concluded that workers of the period "did not generally object to the introduction of machinery, recognizing the relationship between increased output and higher wages." Such an attitude was probably more common among American-born workers on the ore docks. Fewer of them worked in the dusty, dark holds where immigrants — Irish, German, Finnish, Southern European, and Slavic — labored. Promotions to operating hoisting equipment came from the dock and nearly always went to English-speaking workers. Instead of earning $500 to $600 a year as shovelers, hoist operators could make $950 or more annually. Regardless of the nature of their work, dock workers on the lower lakes, mirroring efforts by workers in other industries, attempted to unionize several times in the late 19th century. Most of the early unions were local and sought to organize workers based on occupation. Lumber handlers in the cities of Bay City and Saginaw, which served as important ports for Michigan's timber industry, set up a local as early as 1870. Dan Keefe, a tugboatman, established the first truly effective union in his native Chicago in 1877. Although information is sketchy, there is evidence to suggest that Terrance Powderly's Knights of Labor actively sought to unionize dock workers and sailors in some port cities around the lakes. The Knights, for example, established a local in Escanaba in 1885, replacing a local "laboring men's union" that had been active over the previous two years. It is unclear which groups, such as the feisty ore trimmers, joined the Knights and which formed their own association. But Keefe remained indomitable and his energetic efforts in promoting "the labor gospel" at ports around the lakes throughout the 1880s culminated in the formation of the National Longshoreman's Association of the United States during a meeting of delegates from eleven lake ports in Detroit in 1892.[18]

By the 1870s, sailors too began to investigate the benefits of unionization. The life of sailors, while often conjuring images of romance and adventure, especially onboard sailing vessels, involved long hours, was actually quite dangerous at times, and employment was anything but steady. By federal statute, all sailors had to sign labor contracts, known as "articles of agreement," before each voyage. They stipulated a rate of pay (usually a fixed amount per day) and the general details of the voyage. Additionally, they required the crew to obey "each and every lawful command of the master and officers of [the] vessel, attending with the strictest fidelity and attention to any ship's duty which may be required of [them]." Further, the master could "enforce discipline with any means, and he [was] entitled to respectful behavior and obedience, and he may use deadly weapons if mutiny is threatened and is justified, though subsequent events prove that less severe means would have been sufficient." But crewmen could not expect many reciprocal protections. The obligations of the captain to his crew, in fact, were often limited to seeing "that the crew [had] sufficient provisions and to protect them from illegal violence, and to quell an affray between the mate and crew." Another issue served to make matters worse. Throughout much of the 19th century on the Lakes, sailors, and even mates, were expected to assist in the loading and unloading of vessels. This not only added to the hours they were expected to work, it often found their responsibilities as sailors competing with the demands of loading or unloading. For example, labor historian John Beck observed that sailors working topside often did not have the time to guide the chutes loading bulk cargo and simultaneously trim the load as it filled the ship's hold. The speed with which the holds could be filled meant that both speed and knowledge were critical in loading a ship. Conflicts such as these eventually led to the popularity of trimmers and the reduction in the use of sailors in loading iron ore.[19]

The surge in immigration in the decades following the Civil War, accompanied by a growing exodus of young adults from the nation's agricultural regions, had generated a seemingly limitless pool of eager, if not desperate, laborers seeking employment in the surging industrial cities, but at inland port towns as well. The 1870 Census reported that 67 percent of Americans worked for someone else. "Self-employment," labor historian Eric Arnesen concluded, "was the exception, not the rule." In the resulting competition for work, sailors, like other workers, were rarely in a position to negotiate conditions or wages. Those who worked for a wage labored at the mercy of their employers, who themselves struggled to survive in a highly competitive marketplace where bankruptcies were common and sudden shifts in demand frequently forced them to lay-off employees. Moreover, with little government regulation or oversight, the economy itself was unpredictable, leading to periodic panics and several severe depressions, especially in 1873 and 1893. Since sailors were only hired for one trip at a time, those dissatisfied with their current position could, at least in theory, search for a better ship once they had fulfilled their contractual obligations. But this also meant that seamen who were happy with their current ship were not guaranteed continued employment once they reached port. Demographics, economic conditions, and the articles of agreement, then, clearly favored the shipmaster.[20]

The proliferation of steamships on the inland waters only increased sailors' employment anxiety since steamers required fewer, but often more skilled, crewmembers than labor-intensive sailing ships. This, of course, further exacerbated the competition for jobs aboard ships and drove wages for non-skilled seamen lower. Not surprisingly, some sailors, finding these conditions too harsh and uncertain, sought relief in unionization. Many of these early unions began as beneficial organizations, or "friendly societies" that traced their origins back to mutual aid societies in 16th century England and Scotland. Such societies were common throughout the country as industrialization developed after the Civil War, but they were especially popular in industries associated with transportation because of a higher potential for injury. The Cleveland Ship Carpenters and Caulkers, for example, formed an association in 1861. Members paid a $1 initiation fee and $.12 dues a month. After a 12-month waiting period, members were eligible for benefits, which included a payment of $3 per week for time off as a result of injury or illness. The Chicago Seaman's Union was formed in Chicago in August 1863 and reorganized ten years later. By 1884 it had a membership, which included Canadian as well as American sailors, of roughly 6,000. The Union's objectives were simple and direct: "the mental, moral, and financial improvement of seamen navigating the Lakes." They also sought to "establish a uniform rate of wages at the different ports" as well as "a sick and death benefit fund" and see to "the mutual protection of members." Another, the Marine Engineers Beneficial Association (MEBA), was created shortly after the Civil War to provide for the families of members disabled or killed while serving as engineers aboard lake steamers. By 1875, while the Association continued its service to members' families, it had begun to represent its members in contracts with employers regarding wages, benefits, and working conditions. Thus, by assuming the role of representative for the engineers in negotiations with shipmasters and shipowners, they had effectively begun to function as a union.[21]

Emboldened by union membership, some sailors began to defy, even threaten, shipmasters. But an even greater concern for ship owners was the potential loss of profitability as a result of collective action by sailors seeking higher wages. Cleveland ship owners were the first to respond to this new challenge. They gathered in the city's Board of Trade offices on September 1, 1880, to create the Cleveland Vessel Owners' Association. Their objective, as explained in their articles of association, was to protect the interests of its members and "especially to guard and protect its members against the hostility of sailors and to resist assaults and demands of the sailors' union." The association's strategy was to form similar organizations at other lake ports where they would hire sailors at reasonable wages, thereby forcing the good seamen to desert the union. Charges leveled at the union by the association included seeking to fix seamens' wages, dictating the number of sailors each vessel should carry, and mandating that union men alone could work on the ships. The association argued that such issues should be based on market variables, such as supply and demand. Hinting at a much wider role in the future, the association at its first meeting also resolved to request that the U. S. Army Corps of Engineers alter its proposed plans for harbor improvements in Cleveland.[22]

The following February the Association joined smaller groups of ship owners from around the lakes in Chicago to implement its strategy. In addition to trying to blunt the union initiatives, they agreed to share information concerning navigational hazards amongst themselves. The delegates also designated lobbyists to travel to Washington to voice their concerns. At their March 28, 1881, meeting the Cleveland association announced their first suggested (monthly) wages, specifically for mates and cooks. Most of the members, it should be noted, owned larger vessels and were involved with bulk cargo, namely iron ore, coal, and wheat. Increasingly, their meetings became dominated by the passage of resolutions designed to encourage the federal government to support issues favorable to lake maritime interests. An executive meeting on December 17, 1884, for example, unanimously condemned a treaty relaxing trade restrictions with Spain concluded a month earlier and sent a resolution to Congress asking that the Senate not ratify it. Their concern centered on the threat of imported iron ore. Two years earlier, George Ely, writing for the National Iron Ore Producers, had reported that the bulk of the country's iron ore imports came from Spain and the Mediterranean, and they were increasing dramatically. Foreign imports, he concluded, had effectively shut out domestic ore at Bethlehem, Pennsylvania, firms; of the 400,000 tons used at Johnstown, Pennsylvania, mills, only 75,000 came from domestic mines. On December 20, 1886, they passed a resolution in opposition to a railroad bridge over the St. Mary's River, mirroring their efforts to stop construction of a similar bridge over the Detroit River on April 4, 1886. Both of these bridges, they feared, would cause an interruption of ship traffic at those points. In their January 1888 meeting, the Association hired Col. R. C. Parsons as a full-time lobbyist in Washington, a position he had held with the Buffalo Lake Carriers' Association the year before. A newspaper article attached to the minutes of that meeting lists the many improvements recommended by the Association and passed by Congress, testifying to the influence the group enjoyed.[23]

In 1885, Buffalo ship owners formed the Lake Carriers' Association, dedicated to furthering the interests of vessel owners who operated out of the port of Buffalo. It eventually became apparent that Buffalo and Cleveland associations were duplicating their efforts. By 1892, when the Cleveland and Buffalo groups merged under the title of the Lake Carriers' Association (LCA), the organization's members had agreed to pursue four major objectives. Each represented challenges facing vessel owners at the time. First, the LCA planned to create shipping offices in order to locate and hire compliant seamen, presumably at "reasonable" wages, for their ships. Once they hired their crews, they next sought "to establish and maintain, by contract or otherwise ... amicable relations between employers and employed." In addition, the vessel owners wanted to "establish, maintain, and secure ... aids to navigation." This meant continued lobbying efforts, particularly with Congress, to improve and expand channels, canals, and harbors. Finally, the LCA promised to "provide for the prompt and amicable adjustment of matters affecting shipping and the interests of vessel owners on the Great Lakes." One of the LCA's first presidents, Franklin J. Firth, exuberantly proclaimed that the newly formed association was "the most powerful association of vessel owners in the United States."[24]

But this "powerful" organization represented only a fraction of the vessel owners on the lakes. Great Lakes historian Jerome K. Laurent calculated that members of the LCA owned or operated only 21 percent of the vessels in 1892. How, then, were they able to establish such a formidable presence in maritime matters on the lakes? Improvements in design, construction, and power of lake ships begun in the 1880s (discussed below) permitted builders to construct ships capable of transporting an increasingly larger volume of bulk cargo. The generally well financed LCA members understood that an enlarged cargo capacity was an important component in increasing a ship's profitability and, thus, favored the truly big ships of the lakes. Therefore, LCA member ships, while comprising only a small percentage of registered lake vessels, made up 66.5 percent of the gross tonnage on the "northern lakes." In the coming years, while the percentage of ships owned or operated by LCA members declined, their portion of the gross registered tonnage on the lakes continued to increase to nearly 80 percent. While originally formed by those aggressively seeking to maximize profits, the LCA also took the initiative, at least nominally, in efforts to improve employee-employer relations, an action that appears almost enlightened when compared with most contemporary business practices. In addition, sharing information concerning navigational hazards that posed a potential danger to all members contradicts the image of predatory capitalists of the period seeking to destroy their competition at every turn. Finally, LCA's lobbying efforts in Washington to improve conditions around the lakes provided a formidable and, for the first time, consistent voice for maritime interests in the region.[25]

The drive for efficiency seen in the actions of the LCA mirrored several mergers in the region's iron ore trade in the 1880s, a phenomenon that reached full bloom around the country in the following decade. Following the pattern established by railroads in the 1870s, these consolidation efforts could take the form of horizontal integration, which occurred when firms bought out or otherwise eliminated fellow competitors; vertical integration, where a company sought to control all phases of supply, production, and distribution; or a combination of both. Such behavior generally went unchecked. The federal government throughout the 19th century, especially when led by Whigs and Republicans, had championed private enterprise by enacting a number of tariff laws, by consistently protecting native shipbuilding, and by, if grudgingly at times, underwriting internal improvements. At the same time, they shied away from enacting any meaningful regulatory measures to deal with the excesses of what had grown to become "Big Business." In the particularly volatile climate that characterized the nation's economy after the war, many large firms engaged in ruthless competition or consolidation in order to survive. Smaller companies and ancillary firms faced an increasingly bleak future in such a climate.

Government support remained strong in 1880 when Congress sought to stimulate domestic iron and steel production by enacting a new tariff to protect American producers from foreign competition. The following year a new lock with a 16-foot channel, this one built with public funds under the supervision of the U. S. Army Corps of Engineers, opened at Sault Ste. Marie to help accommodate the flow of ship traffic in and out of Lake Superior. To emphasize its dedication to economic growth, Congress that same year agreed to abolish all canal fees at the locks. Initiatives such as these by the federal government fostered optimism in the iron mining districts and stimulated further investment there. This led to not only aggressive exploration along the southern shores of Lake Superior in search of new iron deposits. It also now justified investment in improved technology to facilitate existing operations. Early miners in the Marquette iron fields, for example, could literally shovel loose ore scattered on the surface into wagons for transport to the lakefront. By the 1860s, however, the surface ore was gone and they had to follow the rich veins deeper underground. The December 23, 1867, *Toledo Blade* reported, "Generally speaking, the deposits of ore in these mines enlarge as they worked downward, giving promises of an unfailing supply for the future." Such high expectations found investors anxiously underwriting the cost of more expensive machinery and deep mining techniques as mines tunneled into the iron-rich hillsides. By the 1880s owners had introduced steam-powered drills in the mines. This equipment also aided in the exploration of new deposits. Cornish pumps, used for years in British mines to remove the inevitable buildup of water as miners dug deeper, were installed in the region's mines. As the mine operators went deeper, they increasingly relied on innovative new hoisting equipment to help raise the ore to the surface. By 1882 there were 56 iron mines in the Lake Superior region connecting to one of three ports by rail: Marquette (via the Marquette, Houghton, & Ontonagon Railroad), Escanaba (via the Chicago & Northwestern Railroad), or St. Ignace (via the Detroit, Mackinaw, & Marquette Railroad). All this made the region, increasingly rich with possibility, crackle with energy. "During the 1880s," wrote Great Lakes historian Walter Havighurst, "Lake Superior was one of the most exciting regions in America, with discovery on discovery and men hurrying from one boom district to another."[26]

Two prominent figures in the region's bustling iron business, Jay C. Morse and Col. James Pickands, had arrived shortly after the war. They eventually married sisters, daughters of John Outhwaite, who, along with Samuel Livingston Mather, had founded the Cleveland Iron Mining Company and, along with Mather, remained one of its largest shareholders. Morse, in particular, sought out investment opportunities in mining, but also became involved in some of the iron furnaces that had grown up nearby in the early years of mining. In addition, he had interests in banking and transportation in the area. Pickands, who earned his military rank during the Civil War while serving with the 124th Ohio Volunteers, opened a store after arriving in Marquette shortly after the war ended. Following the entrepreneurial spirit that pervaded the region, he likewise pursued a variety of investments. For example, an advertisement in Polk's 1884 *Directory of the Marine Interests of the Great Lakes* for the Iron Bay Manufacturing Company listed him as secretary of the firm. Through their various enterprises, and Morse and Pickands' marriages, they came to know Samuel Mather, the son of Samuel L. Mather. Educated in the East, young Mather was then employed in Cleveland at his father's firm in the city's iron merchant district. Although he had actually spent a summer working at one of the company's mines in his late teens, an accident at the mine caused him serious injury and he was forced to return to Cleveland.[27]

Young Mather had been at Marquette long enough to realize that, despite the intense competition, innovative and aggressive investment in the region could bring great riches. In fact, it was Mather, working in his father's firm in Cleveland, who first proposed the idea of forming a new iron company to Morse and Pickands. Together their contacts in, and their collective knowledge of, the Lake Superior iron business made them, they believed, a formidable entity with a nearly unparalleled opportunity for success. Accordingly, in the spring of 1883, each resigned most of their current positions and together announced the formation of Pickands, Mather & Company, "dealers in pig iron and iron ore." But their approach was to be much broader than their name suggested. They set out from the start to control all phases of iron production — from the mines to the blast furnaces. This made them unique innovators. It was Mather who realized that the traditional methods of relying on an independent firm to mine the ore, another to move it to the docks, a third to ship it, and so forth, were terribly inefficient. With the competition to find, extract, and ship Lake Superior ore growing increasingly intense, success rested on a firm's skill at cutting costs. For Mather, this meant controlling all phases of production. During their first meetings, ironically in the parlor of the elder Mather's Cleveland Iron Mining Company offices, they began to devise a strategy to implement this goal. Their first mines near Marquette were small and soon played out. But a site on the newer Gogebic Range, located west of the Marquette Range and 20 miles from Lake Superior, proved more valuable, especially because it contained an abundance of low phosphorus ore ideal for the popular Bessemer process. By the late 1880s the Pickands Mather Company was exploring new mining opportunities in the Menominee Range and had formed the Minnesota Steamship Company to haul ore from their Minnesota Mining Company in the Vermilion Range.[28]

The firm's method of vertical integration involved purchasing shares in entities whose services they employed. At the end of their fiscal year (April 30) in 1889, the Annual Report of the Pickands, Mather & Company listed investments in a number of firms relating to the iron business. For example, they owned a 1/8 interest in the steamer *R.R. Rhodes*, and 1/48 control of the *Samuel Mather*. They also listed shares of stock in Penokee & Gogebic Development Company, the Struthers Furnace Company, the Minnesota Iron Company, the Union Iron Company, the Union Steel Company, the Minnesota Dock Company, the Minnesota Exploration Company, and the Sanford Coke Company. Two years later the firm had expanded to include stock in the Marine National Bank, 39/80ths ownership of the steamer *V.H. Ketcham*, and numerous other furnaces and mining companies. These investments, of course, were in addition to operations under their direct ownership, such as several mines and furnaces. In 1884, its first year of operation, the company shipped 90,071 tons of ore; five years later they sent 1,104,226 tons to furnaces in the southern lakes. Nearly 60 percent of this ore was Bessemer grade, underscoring the growing demand for steel late in the decade. In addition, the company shipped 116,019 tons of iron manufactured at their furnaces in the Lake Superior region; in 1884 the total had been 6,627 tons. Finally, they "back-hauled" 242,289 tons of coal from Ohio and Pennsylvania mines, up from 3,897 tons their first year.[29]

The growth of Pickands, Mather and Company reflects the general development of Lake Superior ore production during the decade. In 1884 the total shipments of iron ore from the four Lake Superior ranges amounted to 2,506,814 (long) tons, roughly one-third of the total national production that year of 7,718,129 tons. Five years later the Lake Superior ranges shipped 7,292,644 tons, which was nearly half of the national total of 14,518,041 tons. These increases were spurred by a fevered demand for Bessemer grade iron ore, but they were made possible by the new lock at Sault Ste. Marie and deepened channels around the lakes that provided uniform 16-foot depths. Prior to these changes, ship capacity was restricted to no more than 1,000 registered tons. This meant that a fleet of smaller, general-purpose schooners and steamers, often with one or more consorts in tow, had to make more trips in a futile effort to meet the demand. Freed to build larger vessels after these improvements, builders began launching vessels with registered tonnage of 1,500 to 1,900. These newer vessels, patterned after Elihu Peck's revolutionary *R. J. Hackett*, powered by steam, and constructed of steel, were more efficient and reliable than the motley collection of vessels that had preceded them, and with which they now shared shipping lanes. It is not surprising, then, that these enhancements to the Great Lakes maritime community, spurred by a seemingly insatiable need for the region's iron ore, enabled ore to become the "leading commodity of freight on the Great Lakes" by 1888.[30]

What drove this demand for iron ore, which inspired the improvements to waterways around the lakes, encouraged the production of larger vessels there, and drove entrepreneurs to search out new deposits of ore? "Through the 1880s, if not beyond," concludes steel historian Thomas J. Misa, "the mass production of steel in the United States was predicated on the mass consumption of steel rails. The demand for steel rails arose only with the impressive mileage that was laid down in the trans–Mississippi West after 1880." Historian Peter Temin observed that "the demand for rails was a major inducement for the introduction of steel, and in the railroad boom of the early 1880s the proportion of rolled steel products accounted for by rails was over 90 percent." The 1880s was indeed a period of unprecedented railroad expansion, with more miles of track laid than during any period before or since." Poor's *Manual of the Railroads of the United States for 1890* observed that the total mileage of railroads in the country in 1880 was 93,296; by 1889 it had grown to 161,396. This amounted to 44 percent of all the miles of railroad lines in the world.[31]

This expansion of the nation's railroads was made possible by American improvements to the Bessemer process that had "increased [mill] capacity at least fourfold." By 1886 U. S. mills turned out nearly 1 million tons of Bessemer steel, and dramatically reduced the cost per ton along the way. A ton of the product, which sold for $67 in 1880, cost $31 in 1884. The demand for steel rails was not limited to new lines in the West but also included replacement rails for the now fatigued iron rails that had been laid down earlier. This transformation of the nation's rail system from iron to steel had broad economic implications. It was "a revolution that reduced the average rate of freight per ton per mile on the roads in the State of New York from 1.7 cents in 1870 to 0.8 cents" in 1886. Since steel was stronger, the new rails had a greater carrying capacity. Cars operating on iron rails generally hauled a maximum of 20,000 pounds. Those using steel rails could be enlarged to accommodate 40,000 pounds or more. Heavier locomotives, capable of greater speed and more power, were built to haul these increased loads at a faster speed. This culminated in the development of "long 'through-line' traffic and of traffic on a large scale at small charges." The resulting economy of scale, noted the April 1886, *Harper's Weekly*, may be attributed "directly, and especially indirectly, to the Bessemer process," which allows "flour transported from the mills in the far West to New York at a lower cost than, as bread, it can be delivered by the baker from his shop to his patrons two blocks away."[32]

The 1880s also found the steel industry introducing new uses for their product. Steel nails, for example, were difficult to find in 1880 when iron nails, selling at $6 a keg, were common. Ten years later steel nails, selling at

$2.80 a keg, had virtually replaced their inferior predecessor. Makers of farm implements, aware of the strength of steel, took advantage of its falling cost and began to manufacture steel plows. Factories found steel castings had "a better record for durability and smoothness of wear than any equal number of forged pieces for the same uses." The July 17, 1880, *Scientific American* claimed that "nearly all the locomotive builders and makers of large steam engines are now using [steel] castings." Architects transformed the nation's urban skyline, beginning in Chicago and New York after 1885, when they introduced steel into building construction. Inspired by the possibilities inherent in the elevator, the electric light, and the telephone, all introduced in the 1870s, as well as rising land costs in the increasingly congested urban centers, they adopted plentiful Bessemer steel to allow them to drastically alter building design and construction. Traditionally, large structures had usually been built of stone, with the exterior walls expected to support the weight of the building. This meant that as an edifice grew in height the lower walls had to be increasingly thickened to accommodate the weight of the successive floors, reducing interior space and restricting access to natural light. Such limitations, even with the introduction of brittle iron support beams, restricted the tallest buildings to ten stories. Since steel possessed a much greater inherent strength, architects determined that they could rely on an interior frame of steel girders riveted together to take their structures as high as they liked. Exterior walls, freed from any structural responsibility, were composed of only a light skin, which opened limitless opportunity for aesthetic experimentation. The Home Insurance Company built the first building to use a steel skeleton in 1888.[33]

The new uses for steel were not confined to land. On the Great Lakes, but far less frequently on the coasts, the newer large bulk carriers increasingly were built of steel. Even crucible steel towlines imported from Great Britain found favor on the lakes because of their improved tensile strength. Despite the reluctance of commercial "blue water" shippers to embrace steel construction, the United States government embarked on a major rejuvenation of its naval fleet in the 1880s. Inspired by the growth of European navies, particularly Great Britain's, a number of critics argued that the country could not continue to rely on antiquated wooden warships, some dating back to the Civil War. The process began in the late 1870s with efforts to build an American version of the rifled, breech-loading guns being used by European navies. Unfortunately, the nation's steel industry at the time did not have the knowledge or capabilities to produce metal with the tolerance necessary for artillery. Reluctant to import European steel, the government worked with several companies to develop a suitable metal. By 1880, Midvale Steel had emerged to become the nation's leader of ordnance steel. A short time later, U. S. ordnance bureau chief Montgomery Sicard began planning a naval gun factory at the Washington Naval Yard, which broke ground in May of 1887. Prompted by the report of a naval board in 1883 calling for two steel warships, Congress appropriated funds for two steel cruisers in 1885, two battleships and a cruiser in 1886, two more cruisers in 1887, and seven cruisers and a gunboat in 1888. Competition for contracts to supply steel for the expanding fleet grew intense and remained so into the 1890s as the demand for steel rails dropped off.[34]

In short, it appeared to most observers at the time that "a strong tendency exists to substitute steel for wrought iron whenever possible." Surprisingly, noted the March 27, 1886, *Scientific American,* "the change is not the result of any demand on the part of consumers, nor in many cases is it due to any superiority of steel over iron. It is simply because it is easier and cheaper to make [Bessemer] steel than iron, and this being the case, the substitution must inevitably follow." But the popularity of Bessemer steel was not without its problems. First, as noted earlier, this process was "restricted by the quality of the crude materials it requires." An ore high in phosphorus produced weaker steel. This explains why the low phosphorus ore of the Lake Superior region was in such great demand at the time. Second, there was considerable cost associated with erecting and operating a Bessemer plant.[35]

But there was an even more troubling concern facing the manufacturers and consumers of Bessemer steel. "There is still a certain distrust," reported the May 15, 1880, *Scientific American,* "of the material in minds of many thoughtful men. This arises undoubtedly from some of the remarkable and seemingly inexplicable failures which have occurred in finished parts of steel." The problem first arose when Bessemer steel, incorporated into bridge construction to span the rivers and valleys confronted during the great railroad expansion of the 1880s, began to fail without warning. But the problems were not just related to structural weaknesses in bridges and buildings. An artillery piece, "carefully cast" by the Pittsburgh Cast Steel Company in 1888, "was broken from the trunnions to the butt in over twenty pieces" when test fired at the government proving grounds at Annapolis. One observer, Ensign Robert R. Dashell, concluded "the experiment proves that the Bessemer cast steel will not do for great guns." A number of experts offered explanations, such as the author of an article in the November 29, 1879, *Scientific America.* "The problem is not a simple one; and there are several difficulties to be surmounted, one of the greatest being the want of uniformity of production, the homogeneity of the material. It seems to be understood that high carbon steel, made at the same works from the same materials, differs materially, day by day, in strength and elasticity." Since it was impractical to test every bar produced in the Bessemer method, "there can be no certainty of just what strength the bridge will possess when the various bars are placed side by side." This uncertainty initiated in earnest the rivalry between the cheaper but unpredictable Bessemer and the slower, more expensive Open Hearth methods of making steel. Other variations of the Bessemer process were also introduced. The Clapp-Griffiths method, invented in England, was tried at Pittsburgh in 1885. It was designed to produce "good steel" with a high phosphorus content. By early 1886, there were eight Clapp-Griffith plants either in operation or newly completed. The Gilchrist-Thomas, or Basic Process, was another variation from Britain. It sought to make use of less desirable grades of iron ore by "dephosphorizing" it during the "after blow" phase of production. It will find application, concluded the July 24, 1886, *Scientific American*, "in the great valleys of Virginia [where] there are almost inexhaustible stores of limonite [highly phosphoric ore]." Despite these alternatives, Bessemer steel remained dominant through the 1890s. Its shortcomings, however, allowed Open Hearth steel to grow to the point where the latter accounted for more than a third of the nation's steel production by 1900.[36]

The controversy surrounding Bessemer steel had little impact on the demand for low-phosphorous iron ore in the 1880s. In fact, steel companies seemed capable of using all they could get. And supplies of Lake Superior ore, ideal for Bessemer steel, seemed limitless. But the delivery system that had been developed between the Lake Superior mines and smelters along the lower lakes struggled to meet the demand. Much of the problem was that the backbone of that system, the Great Lakes bulk carrier, was still evolving. Although the introduction of the *R. J. Hackett* in 1869 had revolutionized bulk carrier design, the economic collapse of 1873, reliance on traditional construction materials, inefficient steam engines, and navigational limitations stood in the way of further refinements, particularly increased capacity. That all changed in the 1880s. Writing in 1897, Walter Miller characterized the decade as "a transition period in Great Lakes Marine Engineering." More to the point, after a gradual increase in the combined gross tonnage of steam ships in the years following the Civil War, 1880 witnessed the beginning of remarkable growth in the combined tonnage of lake steamers. Between 1868 and 1880, the number of steamers rose from 624 to 931, while combined gross tonnage grew from 144,117 to 212,045. But between 1880 and 1897 the number of registered steamships on the lakes nearly doubled to 1,775. More importantly, the combined gross tonnage increased nearly 450 percent to 977,235.[37]

What accounts for this remarkable growth in ship capacity? Needless to say, increased demand from smelters prompted ship owners to seek ways to improve the efficiency of their vessels. If their ships could travel faster and carry larger loads, they could make more trips and haul more cargo on each passage. The new unloading equipment introduced by Brown, Aspin, and others in the early 1880s had reduced time in port. A second, larger lock at Sault Ste. Marie and increased depths at key channels around the lakes had opened the way for ships with greater capacity. Together, they encouraged builders to consider bold new ideas that would help meet the needs of the shippers.

But why wait on ships to evolve? Certainly the growth of railroads during the period suggests that laying track from the Lake Superior region to Chicago presented a logical alternative. With Chicago's growing importance as a rail center, iron ore arriving there easily could be routed east to Cleveland and Pittsburgh. Two issues undermined this option. First, shipping the ore through Chicago provided an opportunity for steel manufacturers in that city to gain an advantage over Pittsburgh-Cleveland producers, who dominated steel production at the time. The commitment made by eastern Ohio and western Pennsylvania producers to continue to control the expanding steel market, therefore, prevented them from supporting such an idea. But of even greater importance was the cheaper freight rates charged by the ore boats. In a December 5, 1890, memorial addressed to the Speaker of the House of Representatives, C. H. Keep, secretary of the Lake Carrier's Association, offered a cost comparison between Great Lakes ore carriers and railroads in the United States. Using statistics from 1889, he wrote that ore carriers traveled 5,540,646,352 ton-miles (average trip of 790.4 miles times the tonnage of ore carried) at a freight-cost of $8,634,246.63, or 1.5 mills per tonmile. Using information from the Interstate Commerce Commission for the year ending June 30, 1889, the average cost per ton-mile for railroads was 9.22 mills. If the ore carried by the vessels of the Great Lakes had been transported by rail, the cost would have been $54,772,759.36. Therefore, Keep concluded, Great Lakes bulk carriers saved the country $46,138,512.73 ($54,772,759.36 − 8,634,246.63). While there may be room here to question just how Keep selected and applied these statistics, it remains clear that there was a considerable disparity between lake and rail rates. This becomes even more striking when one considers that ships could only operate eight or nine months a year because of changing seasonal conditions.[38]

A transitional form of ship construction, called composite vessels because they combined iron and wood in their construction, was first attempted in Britain in the 1830s. The first ocean-going composite vessel, the 787-ton

Tubal Cain, launched in 1857, was designed as an answer to the American clipper ships in the China tea trade. This type of construction was less expensive than solid wood, considerably lighter, and provided increased internal capacity. Canadian shipbuilders at Hamilton, Ontario, launched the first composite vessel on the lakes, the *Acadia*, in 1867. The frames were built in Scotland then shipped to Hamilton, where workers connected the frames and attached native oak planking. There had been a number of iron hulls built around the lakes beginning in 1862, but insurance underwriters believed these hulls began to deteriorate after five years and, accordingly, assigned iron hulls a higher rate. Sheathing iron hulls with wood, however, assuaged the insurers. By the 1870s builders were launching vessels with charcoal iron frames and oak planking attached horizontally. Many then had iron or steel plates covering the planking from the waterline to the main deck, or above to the bulwarks. Still, composite construction failed to generate much interest in the United States because of the high cost of imported iron for the frames, which, in part, was the result of the tariff. The Detroit Drydock Company eventually became the center for composite ship building on the Great Lakes, launching nine such vessels between 1878 and 1890. One, the 2,132-ton *Manchester*, survived for 70 years in the rough bulk cargo trade. Few other vessels of any construction matched this record for longevity. But many, like John Codman, an advocate of iron ship construction, found fault with composite ships. Writing in 1869, he argued that oak, a favored wood for hull planks, contained pyroligneous acid that "eats" iron, which in turn made the wood "iron sick." The use of teak wood could prevent this chemical reaction, but since it was not indigenous, its importation would raise construction costs.[39]

Construction of iron ships also languished along the lakes through the 1870s. The punishing effects of the depression of 1873 lingered until late in the decade, seriously reducing the demand for new vessels of any kind and deflating any interest in experimentation in iron hulls inspired by the launching of the *China, India,* and *Japan* in 1871. Moreover, the cost of iron remained prohibitive and shipyards lacked the necessary equipment and expertise to build iron boats even without the depressed economy. But the economy was beginning to turn around by the late 1870s. By 1879 the gross cargo capacity of lake vessels had reached its limit, causing cargo rates to rise for the first time since the depression. In April of 1880 *The Detroit Free Press*, in an article discussing the shipment of iron ore on the lakes, noted that the 158 ships so engaged were incapable of hauling all the ore contracted from the Lake Superior mines that season. "If these figures are correct," it concluded, "the ore fleet will have to be increased largely to get all the ore delivered before the time when the shipments from Marquette and Escanaba cease altogether with the close of the season." The economic revival in the iron trade, but in other cargo as well, found the Great Lakes fleet of sailing ships, steamers, and barges growing from 3,127 to 3,403 vessels over the next three years. But, in a pattern that was to become familiar in the coming years, this 9 percent growth was less noteworthy than the 19½ percent increase in combined cargo capacity during the same period (605,102 gross tons to 723,911). Clearly, the new ships boasted larger dimensions and, accordingly, the ability to haul more cargo. It was no coincidence that a new, larger lock, the Weitzel, and a remodeled State Lock at Sault Ste. Marie opened in 1881. Unrestrained by the single, woefully inadequate State lock, builders were now free to construct boats capable of carrying more ore per load. While these new carriers also could, and did, haul wheat, coal, and other bulk cargo per load, it was the demand of the ore trade for greater capacity and speed that spurred the innovations in ship design along the lakes in the 1880s. And with few exceptions, these new vessels were steam-powered propellers; only the shipyards at Huron, Bay City, and Toledo continued to build sailing ships.[40]

The *Onoko*, which slid into the Cuyahoga River at Cleveland in 1882, manifested this new creativity during the early 1880s. Declining supplies of white oak after 1880 were driving up the costs associated with the production of wooden ships. This should not be surprising when considering how long shipbuilders and others had been depleting wood reserves around the lakes. As ships grew in size, they required more lumber. In 1878 a Cleveland builder, for example, used 250,000 feet of white oak and 20,000 feet of white pine to build a 1,300-ton vessel 220 feet in length. There were other problems too. Wooden steamers like the *R. J. Hackett*, with their machinery in the stern, rode with their bows out of the water when running empty, which reduced their maneuverability. Moreover, the vibrations caused by this equipment were detrimental to the structural integrity of a wooden vessel. Several lake shipyards responded by reorganizing to build iron hulls. The Globe Iron Works at Cleveland, which began as a partnership in 1853 to build engines and boilers for lake steamers, was one of those firms. With the launching of the *Onoko* they succeeded in creating a vessel that has been characterized as "a radical departure from anything then in service, the pioneer all-iron freight boat, and something of an experiment on the lakes at the time." At 2,164 gross tons, the *Onoko* had the largest carrying capacity of any ship on the lakes, a distinction she enjoyed for the next ten years. For most of her 16 years she carried the largest cargoes of any fresh water boat. These records attest to her durability as well as her considerable capacity. In what must seem surprising

The *Onoko* was the first iron-hull built for the iron ore trade. She was launched by the Globe Iron Works of Cleveland in 1882. Note the masts. Like most steamers of the time, the *Onoko* often used sails to reduce fuel costs or as backup in the event of engine failure.

in light of the *Onoko's* success, however, Globe Iron Works built only three more iron boats, a small sidewheeler and two tugs. Typifying the accelerated rate of change that came to characterize the Great Lakes maritime industry during the decade, in the space of two years steel superceded iron as the favored material for ship construction.[41]

Moving almost directly from wood to steel hull construction in the 1880s, shipbuilders on the lakes, in a manner of speaking, "leap-frogged" their counterparts on the coasts. An iron ship like the *Onoko*, while revolutionary for the lakes, was much more common along the coasts and on eastern rivers at the time. Builders there had been converting from wood to iron hulls during the 1870s. When the United States Navy announced that it planned to modernize its fleet with steel-hulled vessels, commercial shippers on the coast were reluctant to scrap their "new" iron ships in favor of steel hulls. Builders on the lakes, on the other hand, had only recently begun to experiment with iron and commercial interests and had not yet fully committed to it. In fact, there were "probably not more than fifteen [iron-hulled vessels] in the passenger and freight business [on the lakes] in 1882." Furthermore, many of the larger shipbuilders tended to be located in Cleveland or Chicago, amidst the emerging steel industry, theoretically making access to steel easier and less expensive. The growing demand for steel, not only by the Navy but also by railroads, manufacturers, and architects, was placing an incredible pressure on shippers to transport Bessemer-grade ore more efficiently from the Lake Superior mines. With new locks at Sault Ste. Marie and deeper channels at key points around the lakes, builders could apply the strength and design potential of steel to ore boats, giving them a better opportunity to meet that demand. Shipowners liked steel because ships had a longer life expectancy and a greater carrying capacity than iron ships of the same dimensions; moreover, repairs were easier, which found insurance underwriters awarding them a better rate than iron hulls.[42]

Between 1882 and 1886, larger Great Lakes shipyards began to install the equipment necessary to begin building and launching steel vessels. Certainly some yards continued to build wooden steamers, and even schooners. But for those wishing to supply ships to the bulk trade, and especially those dealing with iron ore, the message was clear: designing and building ships as large as the locks and channels around the lakes could accommodate guaranteed that shippers could achieve maximum efficiency. Such an insistence of improving the size of bulk carriers in the iron ore business was certainly not new. Henry Hall wrote in a special report for the Tenth Census in 1884 that as early as 1853 larger boats were needed for the "immense business [of] carrying iron ore from the Michigan mines to Cleveland and other ports." Later, he recalled, Canadians had tried to attract shippers into Lake Ontario with lumber and grain, but the demand for iron was so great that shipbuilders could not be troubled with building ships small enough to fit through the Welland Canal (around Niagara Falls). By the mid–1880s it was becoming increasingly clear that the best method to increase cargo capacity was to standardize ship design using steel construction techniques. When steel ships began coming down the ways in 1886, shipyards, like the recently incorporated Globe Iron Works, had expanded to include "shops equipped with a full complement of tools for the rapid construction of [steel] steamers." In fact, Globe Iron had the capability of building "six large steamers per year" by 1888. That year the company had ship contracts amounting to $2 million and, as a promotional piece for the firm stated, "especially worthy of note, are six steel vessels of 2,800 tons each, for the St. Paul, Minneapolis & Manitoba railway company." Given their aggressive commitment to steel boats, it should not be surprising that lake builders had a decided advantage over coastal yards, even though the latter were older and more well-established. This advantage continued into the 1890s. *Marine Review* reported in May 1891 that "on one contract for four light-ships that are to go to the coast the [federal] government saved over $70,000 by the presence of a shipbuilding industry on the lakes, and the average of the bids of all the lake builders was between $9,000 and $10,000 below the average bids of builders on the Atlantic."[43]

The commitment of lake shipyards to steel construction, however, created problems often accompanying the rapid adaptation of any new technology. Speaking before the International Engineering Congress in 1894, Joseph Oldham recounted how early steel ships on the Great Lakes faced problems because of "bad steel." Some of the steel, he observed, "was so bad that, after incorporation into the hull it had to be cut out. One experienced ship-builder has so little faith in the reliability of steel that he [made] all his flanged keel-plates and boss-plates of iron." Despite such concerns, shipyards producing steel ships, whether on the lakes or abroad, remained optimistic. For example, steel vessels launched at the Clyde River shipyards in Scotland, the largest concentration of ship building facilities in the world at the time, accounted for 48 percent of all the ships built there in 1885. Only six years before, they constituted less than 11 percent of the total.[44]

The reluctance of builders and shippers on the East Coast to join this rush to steel construction failed to dampen the enthusiasm of lake builders. The first lake bulk carrier built entirely of steel, the 1,741 gross-ton *Spokane*, was launched by the Globe Iron Works for the Thomas Wilson Fleet in July of 1886. Later that year, Buffalo's Union Dry Dock Company completed the steel-hulled package freighter *Susquehanna* at 2,780 tons. Larger than the *Spokane*, it was designed specifically to outperform the iron *Onoko*, testifying to the reputation and popularity of the latter. Globe Iron Works responded the next year by launching a second steel carrier, the *Ira H. Owen*. From this point, steel construction became the favored choice of those in the bulk trade, particularly those tasked with hauling iron ore. In the period between 1887 and 1890, the gross tonnage of new ships launched around the lakes exceeded the total that was then afloat: the 66,000 gross tons of all vessels in 1887 was dwarfed by a total gross tonnage of roughly 150,000 tons in 1890. Increasingly these vessels, at least on Lake Erie, were made of steel. Builders on Lake Michigan lagged behind, launching their first steel ship, the *Marina*, in March of 1891. There had been six steel vessels built in 1886; in 1890 68 were

The 265' *Spokane*, launched at Cleveland in 1886, was the first steel ship built on the Lakes. She proved to be a sturdy vessel, surviving at least one stranding in 1907. She was finally scrapped in Cleveland in 1935, a "stone's throw" away from where she had been built 49 years earlier.

launched. Encouraged by larger docks on Lakes Erie and Superior, and reflecting steel's design flexibility and improved tensile strength, the carrying capacity of these new ships grew increasingly larger. After 1886 2,000-ton vessels became common, while "large" 1,000-ton ships were rare only a few years before. Robert P. Porter, superintendent of the 11th Census, in an address before the Cleveland Board of Industry and Improvement in 1892, stated it simply. "The history of marine architecture does not furnish another instance of so rapid and complete a revolution in the material and structure of floating equipment as has taken place on the Great Lakes since 1886."[45]

The proliferation of steel vessels on the lakes was complemented by a new engine design that dramatically improved operating efficiency. Before 1880 the steam used in a Great Lakes low-pressure marine engine commonly expanded in a single cylinder. In the 1870s a few builders around the lakes began to install compound engines on their ships. These engines made use of exhaust steam from the first cylinder in a second cylinder, which simultaneously increased pressure per square inch and reduced the steam consumed per indicated horsepower. The *Spokane*, *Susquehanna*, and *Ira H. Owen* all operated with compound engines. Builders of the wooden steamer *Roumania*, launched at West Bay City, Michigan, in 1887, took the idea further by incorporating a triple-expansion engine, which reused the steam in a third cylinder, built by S. F. Hodge & Company of Detroit. Ships on the coast had used them for several years, but the *Roumania* was the first commercial boat on the lakes to employ one. The following year the *Corona*, built by Globe, became the first "modern type of team vessel, having [a] steel hull and [a] triple-expansion engine." To naval historian John Harrison Morrison, "this was the opening stage of the boom in shipbuilding on the lakes." While the economy of the compound engine over the low pressure system was an impressive 55 percent, the triple expansion engine showed a further improvement of 24 percent over the compound engine. A quadruple-expansion engine appeared in the early 1890s, but its results were not quite as dramatic as the compound and triple-expansion models. Still, in 1891, *Marine Review* considered the adoption of the triple and quadruple expansion engines one of the three "great developments of the previous ten years."[46]

Not surprisingly, the appearance of these larger vessels rendered the "new" Weitzel Lock at Sault Ste. Marie, which had opened with such promise in 1881, inadequate. The malleability of steel construction meant that the size and design possibilities of the new steel ships were boundless. The only impediments to their growth were the size of existing locks, channels, and harbors around the lakes. Length, it turns out, was not the major limiting factor. Most problem areas, such as the St. Clair Flats or the St. Mary's River, restricted the width and depth of boats. Since builders operated under "standard theoretic rule[s] in shipbuilding" based on a ratio of length to beam of nine to one and the ratio of length to depth of 14 to one, limitations in the depth and width of channels and locks necessarily influenced the length of vessels. Froggett concluded, however, that this standard was not always followed. In any case, by 1885 it was clear that changes were necessary at the Sault canal and original Michigan State locks to accommodate the size of the newer Great Lakes bulk carriers. Plans included deepening the canal leading to the locks to 20 feet and replacing the original Michigan States locks of 1855 with "a single [lock] having horizontal dimensions equivalent to the two, and a depth on the miter sills of 21 feet." The 1881 lock, 515 feet long and 80 feet in width, was universally considered "perfect" and its depth of 17 feet was determined to be adequate. Under the authority of Rivers and Harbors Act of August 1886, the Corps of Engineers began work on the replacement lock. Plans for the new lock, no doubt trying to anticipate future shipping needs, called for dimensions of 800 feet in length and 100 feet in width, with 21 feet on the sills. These improvements were matched with corresponding dredging projects in the Hay Lake Channel (south of the locks on the St. Mary's River), as well as improvements at Lime-Kiln Crossing (Detroit River) and the St. Clair Flats (Lake St. Clair). To place this in some perspective, the reader should remember that it took 30 years (1852–1882) of uncoordinated improvement projects for the minimum standard depth of the shipping lanes in the Great Lakes to increase from 9½ to 16 feet. Yet, in only eight years, the standard depth was increased 25 percent to 20 feet.[47]

Unfortunately, federal funds for the locks on the St. Mary's River did not always arrive regularly, which slowed down construction. Moreover, while the new lock replacing the original Michigan State Locks was under construction, the 1881 Weitzel Lock was forced to accommodate all the traffic in and out of Lake Superior. The older locks, granted, had only handled smaller steamers and sailing vessels, but during construction these boats had to share the Weitzel with larger ships. This came during the period of dramatic increase in traffic through the St. Mary's Falls Canal. The total tonnage through the locks in 1886, the year the old canal shut down and work on the new canal began, was 4,527,759 (registered) tons; by 1890 that number nearly doubled to 9,011,213 tons. Of even greater concern was the impact of a problem at the one remaining lock that might cause a delay or even a shut down. During mid-summer of 1890 the worst happened. A mechanical breakdown at the Weitzel suspended all traffic and created a monumental backup of hundreds of vessels both above and below the canal. A memorial dated August 2, 1890, probably from shipping interests in Chicago, pleaded with Congress to pass annual appropriations for the new lock that had been reported by both the Senate Commerce Committee and the River and Harbor Committee of the House in January. This appears to have been a recurring problem. Two years earlier, congressional inertia had also delayed funding until late in the year, stalling construction operations for that year. Even though work on the new lock had begun four years earlier, by the time of the 1890 memorial the foundation for the new lock had not yet been completed. "Real safety for [the] immense tonnage [of lake commerce] will not be secured until the new lock, but just begun, is completed. The engineers in charge of these great works are able and competent, but appropriations for completion should be given them at once through the special bill referred to." Despite such fevered concerns, the new lock did not open to navigation until August 3, 1896, a long six years later. Even then much remained unfinished: the canal and its approaches still had to be deepened, canal piers needed to be rebuilt and extended, and the canal grounds required grading and general improvement.

Considering the growing importance of iron ore, not to mention wheat and other grains, and coal, in the American economy at the time, seeming congressional indifference toward the efficient transport of these items through arguably the most important waterway in the country is puzzling.[48]

The dramatic increase in size of bulk carriers in the late 1880s raised another concern for those navigating the lakes. Confident that it had met its obligations set forth by Congress, the U.S. Lake Survey had ceased operations on July 1, 1882. It had issued a total of 76 charts detailing all the areas of interest to Great Lakes mariners and saw no need to continue operations. This cessation was predicated on two assumptions: first that the lakes never changed, and second that ship dimensions would vary little, their maximum depth remaining at 12 feet. Surely the canals and channels at 16 feet would be more than adequate. But time showed their decision to be premature. Only a few years later, steel construction spawned ships of dimensions unimaginable in 1882. This coincided with expanding mining operations and agricultural output in the area, which increased traffic on the shipping lanes. Again, Congress reacted slowly, only doling out $15,000 for new surveys beginning in 1889, increasing the annual appropriations by $10,000 four years later.[49]

Other events in the 1880s helped establish the period as pivotal in the creation of an integrated commercial network on the Great Lakes. In the 1889 decision *Butler v. Boston & S. Steamship Company* (130 U. S., 527), the Supreme Court supported and further explained its 1875 *Lottawanna* decision (21 Wall, 558), which had established federal authority over maritime law through the "admiralty" and "necessary and proper" clauses of the Constitution. This ruling, in conjunction with *Garnett* (141 U. S., 1) two years later, ended any lingering questions concerning the role of the federal government in maritime issues on the Lakes. New steamship companies also organized late in the decade. The Cleveland Shipbuilding Company (1886), The Chicago Shipbuilding Company (1889), F. Wheeler & Company (1889), and the American Steel Barge Company (1889) brought massive funding and innovative ideas to shipbuilding on the lakes in coming decades. The pressure to provide increasing amounts of iron ore to meet the voracious demands of smelters made that commodity the leading article carried by lake vessels in 1888. Steel companies were under increasing pressure because buyers of steel were becoming increasingly innovative. For example, the first building to incorporate steel into its structural skeleton, the Chicago's Home Insurance Company in 1885, demonstrated to architects that load-bearing walls were a thing of the past. Steel frames permitted them to experiment with revolutionary designs, which culminated in the introduction of the skyscraper that today dominates the urban skyline of cities around the world.

Changes to the Great Lakes maritime industry in the 1880s were critical in the emergence of the United States as a major industrial power in the decades that followed. The 1890s will see further refinements to the innovations that appeared during this crucial time. Writing in the September 1900 *Harper's Weekly*, Waldon Fawcett concluded that, if the 1880s was an innovative decade of change, the decade following appeared to be the culmination of all those changes. Ships grew even larger, companies stepped up consolidation efforts, and ore unloaders of undreamed proportions appeared. These and other topics will be the subject of the next chapter.[50]

5

"The wildest expectations of one year
seem absurdly tame the next"

(1890–1908)

In 1926, J. Bernard Walter, editor emeritus of the *Scientific American*, reflecting on the recent increase in productivity of the United States from $220 billion to $350 billion, wrote, "If the writer were asked to name the principal agent in [this] enormous growth in wealth during the past two decades, he would unhesitatingly name the vast iron ore deposits of the Lake Superior region and the consequent phenomenal growth of our steel industry." By the early 1890s, the five iron ranges that supplied this ore were located along the southern and western shores of Lake Superior: the Marquette (1855), the Menominee (1877), the Gogebic and Vermillion (1884), and the Mesabi (1892). While the development of the first four ranges had progressed steadily over the years, growth on the Mesabi Range was nothing short of meteoric. In their first year of operation, the Mesabi iron mines mined and shipped a mere 4,245 tons. In 1902, just ten years later, that range sent 13,342,840 tons to the ore docks along the shores of the southern lakes, nearly equaling the combined shipments of the other four ranges. Five years after that, mines in the Mesabi more than doubled their output to 27,495,708 tons. This figure came close to tripling the volume of ore shipped from the other four ranges.[1]

Not surprisingly, in the last decade of the 19th century iron and steel production in the United States also enjoyed a remarkable growth. The 16,264,478 (net) tons of product, valued at $478,687,519, produced in the country during 1890 almost doubled to 29,507,860 (net) tons ($804,034,918) in 1900. It was no coincidence that the three states leading in iron and steel production by 1900 were Pennsylvania (54 percent of the national total), Ohio (17 percent) and Illinois (7.5 percent), all located on the shores of the lower lakes. Correspondingly, plants for finished iron and steel products sprang up around the mills, especially in Pennsylvania where that state's firms manufactured over one-half of all the steel railroad rails produced in the country in 1900; Illinois was a distant second and Ohio fourth. The Keystone State also made more iron and steel bars and rods, as well as wire rods than any other state, while Ohio was second and Illinois third in these categories. The growing importance of structural steel for bridges, buildings, and railroad cars found Pennsylvania again in the dominant position, manufacturing over 89 percent of the nation's output. The state also led all other states in the production of locomotives, rolling out almost 50 percent of the national total in 1900.[2]

Despite the volatility of the late 19th century American economy, all phases of the iron and steel industry continued to attract eager entrepreneurs seeking new ways to gain a share of the wealth generated by its remarkable growth. Alexander McDougall, a shipbuilder and captain from Duluth, was such an individual. Born in Scotland in 1845, and raised near Collingwood, Ontario, on Lake Huron, he left home as an apprentice in the lake trade at 16. Although he lacked much formal education, McDougall had an innate ability that made him a quick study. He became a wheelsman aboard the cargo steamer *Edith* within a year and that ship's second mate in 1863 at age 18. After serving as mate and/or pilot on a number of vessels around the lakes, he was made captain of the *Japan*, whose construction he oversaw. This boat, launched in 1871 along with the identically designed *India* and *China*, was a revolutionary passenger-package steamer constructed entirely of iron. The 1873 depression, however, caused a drop in the number of people seeking passage on lake ships. He was soon bankrupt and struggled, as did so many around the lakes throughout the remainder of the decade, to survive.[3]

During 1879 and 1880, McDougall oversaw the construction of two of what promised to be the largest wooden boats on the lakes, the *Hiawatha* and its consort the *Minnehaha*. He later captained the *Hiawatha*, delivering railroad rails to the Lake Superior region and returning with iron ore or grain. "While captain of the *Hiawatha*, towing the *Minnehaha* and *Goshawk* [a second consort] through the difficult and dangerous channels of our rivers," he recalled in his autobiography, "I thought out a plan to build an iron boat cheaper than wooden vessels." But McDougall, unrestrained by traditional education and fearlessly independent, envisioned a ship design that was a radical departure from anything yet constructed. "I first made plans and models for a boat with a flat bottom designed to carry the greatest cargo on the least water, with rounded top so that water could not stay on board; with a spoon-shaped bow to best follow the line of strain with the least use of the rudder and with turrets on deck for passage into the interior." He shared his ideas with fellow members of the lake shipping community, but received little encouragement. "She has no flat deck and bulwarks to keep the waves off," he remembered one colleague remarking. Another dismissed his idea with, "You call that damn thing a boat — why it looks more like a pig."[4]

Undeterred, McDougall persisted, using his own funds to build the first boat incorporating his design in 1888. Intended as a consort, the steel hull held no machinery and was named simply *Barge 101.* Since steel ship building equipment was limited in Duluth at the time, McDougal had the bow and stern portions built under contract in Brooklyn, New York. Once they arrived in Duluth, he organized a group of stevedores to fabricate a center section. Barge *101* was built entirely of steel plates fastened to steel ribs by welded bolts, which gave the vessel considerable "strength and durability, and minimum resistance to the water." The design and construction of the vessel gave her an exceedingly light draught, making it possible to load her until she was nearly submerged. Moreover, she was self-trimming. "I brought her to Two Harbors [Minnesota] by the tug *Record,*" McDougall remembered; "there 1,200 tons of course ore were run into her many hatches without trimming, and she was towed to Cleveland." In an article in the July 17, 1888, *Toledo Blade,* entitled "The Big Cigar Ship," the reporter who inspected her in the Lake Erie port of Ashtabula resorted to science fiction in an attempt to explain the barge to his readers. "If Jules Verne could visit this city for a moment he would see a round steel, cigar shaped ship, resembling very largely what must have been in his mind when he conceived the Nautilus and wrote 'Twenty Thousand Leagues under the Sea.' The '101' may prove the germ from which an entire revolution in trans-ocean traffic will spring. Nothing," he concluded, "precisely like it has ever been launched before. It is yet a matter of conjecture whether this experiment will prove successful or be a valueless failure."[5]

Despite the interest swirling around the *101,* McDougall was unable to generate much interest in, or funding for, the construction of more vessels among the traditional lake community. Ever persistent, he sought out Colgate Hoyt in New York, an associate of John D. Rockefeller, "who had much lake ore to move." Hoyt clearly had no reservations about the design and quickly located seven other investors. Together with McDougall, they formed the American Steel Barge Company to produce vessels of this new design. Hoyt also served as the company's president. After launching two more barges, *102* and *103,* McDougall produced his first steamer in 1890, the 1252 gross ton vessel was appropriately named the *Colgate Hoyt* after his benefactor. By this time ships employing his design had been dubbed "whalebacks," owing to the appearance of their rounded, black hulls, particularly when fully loaded and riding low in the water. Other less enamored observers, noting the shape of the bow, which brought together the taper of the sides and bottom into the form of a snout, dismissed these ships as "pigboats." Regardless of the nomenclature, these whalebacks were designed and built with the express purpose of carrying iron ore. Charles L. Wetmore, writing Rockefeller in late 1893 regarding the extension of a railroad connecting the newly opened Mesabi mines with loading facilities on the Lake Superior shore, was clear on the matter. He stated that it had been done "simply to secure the transportation of the Missabe ores for the American Steel Barge Company." Wetmore, a director and investor in the Barge Company, added that "almost unlimited opportunities for profit lay open to the Barge Company if it maintained close relations with the Missabe Railway and the mines tributary to it."[6]

In June of 1891, the Barge Company launched the whaleback steamer *Charles W. Wetmore*. McDougall planned its maiden voyage to make his many

The whaleback *E. B. Barlett* and an unidentified whaleback, possibly its consort, leave the Poe Lock at Sault Ste. Marie downbound for the lower lakes around 1895. The creation and expansion of these locks on the St. Mary's River neutralized the 21' drop between Lakes Superior and Huron, opening up Lake Superior for commerce.

critics take notice. Although he had designed his ships for the ore industry, McDougall used the vessel's first voyage to demonstrate the adaptability of the whaleback. Accordingly, he had the *Wetmore* loaded with 90,000 bushels of wheat at Duluth and personally sailed her from Lake Superior through the lower lakes and the Welland Canal to Kingston, Ontario, where the grain was lightered ashore. By reducing the ship's weight, the flat-bottomed *Wetmore* was able to shoot the rapids of the upper St. Lawrence River, after which McDougall himself supervised the reloading of the wheat, "packing her as full as an egg." The *Wetmore* then continued to follow the river out to sea, crossed the Atlantic, and delivered her cargo to the docks at Liverpool, England. "Upon her way up the Mersey, at the end of her successful voyage, thousands of people thronged the shores for the news of the approach of the singular craft had preceded her." The ship's much touted stability was affirmed upon arrival in Liverpool; "When her hatches were opened, the footprints and shovel marks made by the [Canadian] grain-handlers were distinctly visible upon the surface of the cargo."[7]

Others now began to take notice. Edward Huntington Dwight, writing in the September 5, 1891, *Harper's Weekly,* was reduced to hyperbole. "Since the earliest day of the American merchant-marine probably no form of vessel — not even excepting Robert Fulton's first steam-propelled craft — has received more attention and excited more criticism, both favorable and unfavorable, in England as well as in this country, than the peculiarly shaped vessel known as the 'McDougall whaleback.'" After returning to Brooklyn, McDougall sought to take advantage of the publicity and announced plans for the *Wetmore* to sail to Puget Sound, a trip that would make her the first lake vessel to reach the Pacific Ocean. Prodded by McDougall's success, other shipbuilders began incorporating features of the whaleback into their designs. Back in Cleveland, the Globe Ship Building Company that year launched the *Grecian,* a "turtleback" design that clearly owed its appearance to the whaleback, as did another variation known as the "monitor." "Though ungainly and much ridiculed," observed noted Great Lakes ship authority Richard Wright, "the whaleback was the basis for most design changes that occurred between 1890 and 1895." As early as 1892 investors in the Barge Company enjoyed a 22 percent return on their investment. A year later McDougall's Barge Company had ten steel whalebacks under construction simultaneously at the firm's new Superior, Wisconsin, yards. He even designed a whaleback passenger ship, the *Christopher Columbus,* "the most wonderful ship contracted for and constructed up to that time," for the 1893 Chicago's World Fair. It seemed that McDougall's reputation — and fortune — had been made.[8]

McDougall went on to make 44 whalebacks in anticipation of cornering the Rockefeller ore business. Unfortunately, a shortage of investment funds delayed the opening of the nearby Mesabi Range, postponing McDougall's chance to fully exploit this opportunity. And then, as 20 years earlier, the country was rocked by a major depression in 1893, choking off commercial activity everywhere, including the lakes. As the economy began to recover in 1896, the new, considerably larger Poe Lock opened at Sault Ste. Marie. That year fully one-half of all new bulk carriers launched on the lakes exceeded 2,000 net registered tons, as shipbuilders sought to take advantage of the larger lock. Unfortunately, the whaleback's radical design prevented McDougall from enlarging his vessels to compete with the other builders. The arched frames originally designed for the whaleback required no additional supports in the hold, as long as the vessel's beam remained less than 45 feet. Anything wider required the addition of stanchions to maintain the hull's integrity. These vertical supports positioned throughout the hold interfered with loading and unloading, undermining one of the great advantages of the whaleback. In addition, the rounded deck, together with the fore and aft stringers, limited the size of the hatch covers. This became an insurmountable problem as new, larger unloading systems appeared in the late 1890s. Simply put,

Alexander McDougall's Superior, Wisconsin, shipyards in the early 1890s show at least eight whalebacks under construction. This was the peak of the whaleback's popularity; McDougall ceased production of the ship in 1898.

the whaleback was incapable of expanding without radical design alterations, which effectively neutralized the advantages of the design itself. While the existing whaleback barges and steamers carried a variety of bulk cargoes well into the next century, McDougall's ships could not match the expanding dimensions found on ships employing more conventional designs. Not surprisingly, iron ore companies increasingly sought out these larger, more efficient ships to reduce their per-ton carrying costs. McDougall's brainchild fell victim to a voracious steel industry that found his revolutionary design unable to meet its demands and relegated the "pigboat" to the backwater of marine architecture in less than ten years.[9]

The 1880s had witnessed the coming together of heretofore divergent patterns of evolution in ship design, navigational improvements, and unloading techniques The impetus for this synergism was a direct result of increased demand for Bessemer-quality Lake Superior iron ore brought about by the phenomenal growth of the nation's railroads and an increasing number of new applications for steel in the late 19th century. The market for charcoal pig iron had already begun declining in the 1880s. This doomed many smaller operations, such as the Jackson Mining Company's creation, Fayette, which saw the company shut down operations in 1890. The town was soon after abandoned. This chapter traces the deepening of the relationship among the various aspects associated with the transportation of iron ore on the Great Lakes, as well as the growing demands of steel companies driving innovation on the lakes. Ultimately, these developments served to further solidify the relationship between the Great Lakes maritime community and the steel industry.

The chapter opens with the discovery and exploitation of the incredibly rich Mesabi Range, which appeared capable of meeting all the iron ore needs of the Bessemer steel industry well into the future. The maneuvering and manipulation involved in establishing ownership of the mines, coupled with the 1893 depression, slowed development initially. By the end of the 1890s those obstacles had been overcome and the Mesabi figured prominently in the vertical and horizontal integration then under way in the nation's steel industry. This process culminated in the appearance of the country's first billion dollar corporation, United States Steel.

The growth of the steel industry spurred changes in the lake shipping industry, as it struggled to keep the smelters supplied. These efforts concentrated on enlarging the hauling capacity of the ships, although such growth was once again constrained by the dimensions of the locks and channels through which they passed and the harbors where they loaded and unloaded. Constructing vessels with increasingly larger dimensions, however, required large, more sophisticated, and heavily capitalized shipyards. The yards capable of designing and building the steel ships demanded by those in the bulk, particularly the iron ore, trades found themselves in intense competition with each other. Any innovations in labor-saving machinery or production techniques were quickly copied by the others. While this benefited those purchasing the new vessels, it jeopardized the profitability, even the survivability, of the builders. Mirroring the path taken by other industries in the 1890s, the major shipyards and dry docks around the Lakes consolidated under a corporate umbrella in 1899, forming the American Shipbuilding Company. By April of the following year they controlled all the steel shipbuilding firms on the Lakes except Toledo's Craig Company. That year also found the shipyards around the lakes launching four times the tonnage as did coastal yards building for the foreign trade. To give this some perspective, the January 30, 1902, *Marine Review* reported that, based on the tonnage launched in 1901, British Lloyd's declared the American Shipbuilding Company to be the third largest vessel producer in the world. During the company's first five years of operation alone, they launched 175 vessels. Innovation in ship design was as important as volume. New designs, particularly that of the *Augustus B. Wolvin* launched in 1904, created prototypes for the next 60 years of shipbuilding on the lakes.[10]

The extent to which these ships could be enlarged, of course, remained subject to the size and timing of improvements to harbors, channels, and locks around the lakes. Well before the end of the 19th century, Congress had come to acknowledge the importance of the Great Lakes as a critical conduit for badly needed iron ore, the chief component of America's industrial revolution, as well as other commercially important cargo like grain, coal, and timber. Accordingly, Washington funded improvement projects in the region more freely. In 1893, for example, the channel running through the St. Clair Flats was deepened to 18 feet to match the depth at other key channels. Three years later the new Poe Lock at Sault Ste. Marie opened. It had been designed to anticipate larger ships, which almost immediately began sliding down the ways at yards around the lakes. Clearly, government agencies a conscious effort to create and maintain uniformity in the dimensions of locks, channels, and passages around the lakes.

Larger ships by the end of the 19th century placed pressure on the unloading process, which once again had to be made more efficient to keep up with the greater volume of ore arriving along the southern shores of the lakes. Improved capacity and increasingly unencumbered passage through the lakes meant little if ships were stuck at the docks while outdated unloading equipment struggled to keep up. A new plateau in unloading efficiency was reached with the introduction of the awe-inspiring Hulett unloader unveiled in Cleveland in 1899. Its revolutionary design, which allowed for rapid yet precise movements, could remove ten tons of ore in a single bite. The Huletts immediately proved they could unload the largest ships in record time, and they continued to do so for the next 70 years. An alternative unloading method also emerged during the period, the self-unloader. This process employed an internal conveyor belt that continuously fed the contents of the ship's hold up to a moveable arm on deck that, when swung out over the dock, deposited cargo directly on shore. This process remains popular on the lakes today to unload a variety of items carried in bulk.

In the Chippewa language, "Mesabi" (originally "Missabe") means "giant" or "grandmother to all." It would be difficult to ascribe a more appropriate name for the last major Lake Superior iron range uncovered, for its reserves quickly dwarfed those of its four predecessors. Located about 60 miles north and west of present-day Duluth, the territory was part of the land encompassed by the Treaty of Prairie du Chien (1825). Governor Clark of Missouri and Michigan's Territorial Governor Lewis Cass had negotiated this treaty hoping to soothe tensions among the various tribes of the region competing, often violently, for hunting rights. Possibly inspired by Native American legends that valuable minerals existed in the region, a provision in the treaty gave the United States the right to exploit any such resources located there. Later, after the Treaty of LaPointe (1854) relegated local tribes to reservations, the area was thrown open to white settlement. Persistent tales of valuable deposits of precious metals in the region, coupled with stories of fortunes being made in the gold fields of California, created a "mining fever" in the region. While efforts to find precious metals bore little fruit, the region yielded a few iron samples as early as 1852. Repeated efforts by prospectors with wide-ranging levels of expertise and experience failed to find any deposits, other than the scattered Vermilion mines to the north near the Canadian border, worth mining. In the end, timber was the only resource that initially generated much of value.[11]

One group, seven brothers in fact, persevered in their quest to find iron ore. Growing up in the 1870s, their father, whose job led him to traverse the area as a "cruiser" in search of marketable timber, captivated the boys with stories of the pure iron ore he had seen. As adults, the Merritts repeatedly, almost obsessively, crisscrossed the region for over 15 years in a frustrating attempt to locate the elusive iron deposits they had come to believe were hidden there. They financed their efforts through the sale of timber lands, returning to the Mesabi year after year amid taunts that their frenzied search was foolish, even crazy. If these deposits truly existed, their neighbors argued, surely experienced mining firms like the Minnesota Iron Company, currently exploiting the range at nearby Lake Vermilion, would not have missed the opportunity to cash-in on such a valuable range. Experts had assured the Company's officials that the Mesabi was worthless and, consequently, Minnesota Iron showed no interest in the region. Finally, in 1888 or 1889, the exact year is in dispute since a fire destroyed many of the brothers' papers, Cassius Merritt by chance found a chunk of high-grade hematite while guiding engineers surveying a railroad line between Duluth and Winnipeg. Returning to the spot with his brothers, under the leadership of the indefatigable Leonidas, they once again took up their search. As they explored and dug, important evidence both teased and tantalized the brothers; ruts left by their wagon wheels, for example, revealed an abundance of red soil, a sure sign of iron. Encouraged, they brought in mining crews and purchased diamond drills, but still found little other than taconite, which at the time was viewed as too lean to mine. Undeterred, they persisted until, in a test pit dug on November 16, 1890, they at last discovered a large deposit of the soft hematite they had been pursuing.[12]

The brothers labored to consolidate much of the Mesabi under their control, as legions of competitors rushed in and opened mines. The appeal of the region's iron was in large measure based on the quality of the ore, soft hematites and limonites that one writer characterized as the richest deposit ever located in the history of the world. But the deposits had an additional advantage. The pockets of ore, recounted a writer for *Harper's Weekly* who visited the region in early 1895, were "parallel with the surface; and this, everyone could readily see, gave the range an advantage over sections where the mining must follow a vertical lead into the depths of the earth." This, he continued, "gave way on this new range to the easier and simpler process of surface excavation," a process enhanced by the introduction of "the great land-dredge called the steam-shovel." Companies in charge of the strip mining operations brought the shovels into the remote area on temporary tracks. Taking half-ton scoops, the shovels first removed the surface gravel and placed it into dump cars that ran on a separate track parallel to the one used by the shovel. Once filled, these cars were taken by locomotive to a dump site. After a seam of iron ore was encountered, however, the cars were loaded with ore and sent directly to the docks at either Two Harbors or Duluth where the ore was shipped south, usually to ports on Lake Erie. This process made it possible to extract an unprecedented volume of ore from a range that, while only two miles wide, ran 50 miles in length by 1895.[13]

Problems plagued Mesabi miners initially when it was discovered that the composition of the Mesabi ore required steel companies to make refinements to their furnaces before they could use this "blue ore." Once this was done, however, the ore proved to be extremely compatible with the production of Bessemer steel. Unfortunately, a larger problem plagued miners, like the Merritts, seeking to get their mines up and running. The depression of 1893 generated a loss of confidence in the industrial fortunes of the country and dried up investment funds. The national production of iron ore, the key component in industrialization, dropped by one-third in 1893 and did not return to pre-depression levels until 1896. With iron ore prices in decline, the Merritts found it increasingly difficult to raise the necessary capital for them to expand. This was particularly troublesome because in February of 1892 they, with the assistance of shipbuilder Alexander McDougall, had borrowed heavily to continue construction of a railroad they had begun a year earlier in a partnership with local railroad contractors Grant and Chase, the Duluth, Missabe & Northern. Such a line was crucial for moving the ore from the Minnesota backwoods to lake transportation on Lake Superior. Alexander McDougall, flush with the success of his whaleback and confident that he would find steady employment for his growing fleet, arranged for his Barge company to carry all the ore mined by the Merritts for the next 15 years. According to the agreement, McDougall would also "personally control ore docks on Lake Superior, Lake Huron, and Lake Erie." Charles W. Wetmore, an investor in the Barge Company and an attorney with considerable connections, was able to raise $2 million, including $500,000 from oil magnate John D. Rockefeller, to allow the Merritts to complete their railway to Duluth. The holding company that was formed for the mining property, railroad, and dock facilities, however, brought the brothers into a legal battle with their former partners, Grant and Chase. Another loan, even at less than favorable rates, was required if the Merritts expected to extricate themselves from these troubles. Despite these pressures, work on the railroad and docks continued. When payroll funds dried up, workers rioted. By July of 1893, the Merritts faced an accumulated debt of $3.2 million.[14]

While earlier appeals to Rockefeller interests for additional financial help went unanswered, Rockefeller by August realized the plight of the Merritts and that, as a result, his stock in the Duluth, Missabe & Northern was in jeopardy. Moreover, concluded his biographer Allan Nevins, Rockefeller was seeking to find diversified investments for his enormous income of approximately $10 million a year. In actions that have been called into question by his critics, Rockefeller used his considerable financial leverage to force the Merritts and Wetmore into a deal that kept the operation going, reorganized into the new Lake Superior Consolidated Iron Mines, in return for cash and the purchase of his stock for bonds. Although the Merritts owned 75 percent of the stock in Lake Superior Consolidated, Rockefeller's possession of the bonds meant that he, in fact, controlled the company. He did not seem interested in exercising that control initially; but, as the Merritts' fortunes continued to sink, Rockefeller bought the shares of Lake Superior Consolidated from the Merritts for $.10 on the dollar. The brothers, believing they had been defrauded by Rockefeller, sued in 1895. Their case was denied on appeal. Perpetually strapped for money, they later reconciled with Rockefeller, who relieved them of their debts, which amounted to $1 million. At that point Rockefeller took ownership of Lake Superior Consolidated outright.[15]

As the country emerged from the depression in 1897, three companies controlled the Mesabi ore reserves: the Oliver Iron Mining Company, the Minnesota Mining Company (with substantial funding from Pickands-Mather), and Rockefeller Consolidated Iron Mines. Henry W. Oliver, a plow and shovel manufacturer, had taken an option from the cash-desperate Merritts in 1892 and opened the Oliver Iron Mining Company, the first such company on the Mesabi. This provided him with a steady supply of high grade ore at a favorable price for his Pittsburgh-based firm. That year he was approached by Henry Clay Frick, chairman of Pittsburgh's Carnegie Brothers & Co., about forming a combination in the mining venture. Frick, acting on his own initiative, understood the advantages of controlling a source of Bessemer ore to feed the Carnegie steel operations. Oliver, realizing the potential for expansion with Carnegie capital, agreed. He gave Carnegie 50 percent of the Oliver Company stock in return for a $500,000 loan to develop the mines. But Carnegie, upon learning about Frick's deal while at Skibo Castle, his estate in Scotland, was less than enthusiastic. "Pioneering don't pay," he replied; "if there is any department of business which offers no inducement, it is ore. It never has been very profitable." He reiterated his objections on April 18, 1894, at a meeting of the Board of Managers of Carnegie Steel. "The Oliver bargain I do not regard as very valuable. You will find that this ore venture will result in more trouble and less profit than almost any branch of our business. I hope you will make note of this prophecy." But later that year he moderated his objections when it became clear that "Reckafellows" and his interests had established a presence in the region. His concerns about investing in mining operations were bested by his competitive nature as he sought to outflank Rockefeller, preventing the "Standard people" from "making ore a monopoly like oil." Still, Carnegie worked privately to discourage aggressive investment in the Oliver-Frick venture over the next two years, still not fully convinced that the high risk associated with mining operations was worth the expense.[16]

By 1896, now confident that the Mesabi reserves were genuine, Oliver and Frick arranged to lease Rockefeller properties for a royalty of $.25 per ton of iron ore extracted (the standard rate was $.65) with the guarantee of 600,000 tons of ore per year. Moreover, they agreed to ship the entire amount, plus an equal tonnage from the Oliver mines, via Rockefeller's railroad and steamship lines to Lake Erie ports. Oliver and Frick projected that the arrangement, which was set to run for 50 years, could generate an annual savings of $500,000 for their combination. With the boards of both firms in agreement, the only potential obstacle to the arrangement remained the unenthusiastic Andrew Carnegie. But concerns about his recalcitrance this time turned out to be ill-founded. Carnegie simply could not ignore such an advantageous business arrangement and he quickly endorsed the deal. Furthermore, he could hardly allow Rockefeller to challenge his leadership in steel, something Rockefeller might be able to do if he continued to acquire more of the now unquestionably valuable Mesabi ore fields. At this point, Carnegie demanded, and rather easily gained, control of the Oliver Iron Mining company, something that Oliver had anticipated and to which he was amenable. The reduced rates for Carnegie ore at the Lake Erie docks generated by this arrangement threw other mining companies into a panic. Unable to compete, investors tried unsuccessfully to unload their shares in Lake Superior mining stock, particularly those of the Mesabi. Once again, with prodding from Frick and Oliver, Carnegie picked up the options on these mines, thus providing his mills with all the Bessemer iron they could use at a steady and economical rate. "We are now secure in our ore supply; it was the only element," he noted in a letter to Frick later that year, "needed to give us an impregnable position." The initiative shown by Frick, in particular, and Oliver had given Carnegie control of two-thirds of the Mesabi Range, the world's most valuable iron ore deposit.[17]

Carnegie steel not only dominated the Mesabi, it also had preferred rates on Rockefeller's railroad from the mines to Duluth and on his fleet (the whalebacks of the American Steel Barge Company plus Rockefeller's own Bessemer Steamship Company). And by now he also owned the loading docks at Duluth and unloading facilities at various Lake Erie ports. One obstacle remained, the 200-mile trip between the Lake Erie docks and Carnegie's western Pennsylvania blast furnaces. Because the Pennsylvania Railroad had the only adequate lines traversing this stretch, they charged inflated rates on all the ore they carried. Furthermore, the railroad, which had enjoyed a long and intimate relationship with government officials, tended to provide less than optimum service, believing itself immune from state regulation or intervention. After years of tolerating this situation, the dramatically improved financial condition of Carnegie Steel in 1897 made it possible for the company to apply considerable pressure on the Pennsylvania Railroad, with Frick threatening to construct a parallel railroad if the steel company was not allowed to run its own trains over the Pennsylvania's tracks. In stark contrast to his negativity on mining issues, Carnegie here demonstrated considerable initiative and, without consulting Frick, quietly gained controlling interest in the old and largely ignored Pittsburgh, Shenango, and Lake Erie Railroad. Over the next 15 months, the railroad was renamed the Pittsburgh, Bessemer, and Lake Erie and totally rebuilt, including the addition of a new steel bridge two-thirds of a mile in length over the Allegheny River into Pittsburgh. "Thus was completed the thousand-mile chain," wrote George Harvey, "stretching from the bowels of the earth [west] of Lake Superior to the [furnaces] south of Lake Erie, which established the invulnerable preeminence of the Carnegie Steel Company." Carnegie Steel had become virtually self-sufficient in all phases of iron production. By the early 1880s, even coke produced at the nearby Connelsville coalfields had grown to the point that it accounted for 69 percent of total national production. It had been favored locally for its ease of mining, its purity, and its ability to sustain heavy weight in the furnace, all of which contributed to its popularity with Pittsburgh smelters after the Baltimore and Ohio Railroad connected the region with Pittsburgh in the late 1850s. Its quality combined with high-grade Lake Superior iron ore to most efficiently create the best Bessemer steel by the 1890s. Mirroring the pattern introduced on the lakes by Pickands-Mather in the 1880s, Carnegie had achieved complete vertical integration.[18]

Andrew Carnegie was a rarity in the late 1890s. Most large businesses had evolved from proprietary entities, where the responsibility for raising capital for growth and modernization fell upon the shoulders of the individual owner, into corporations where a pool of investors provided such funds. But these investors, of course, also expected to share in the profits. Carnegie had tenaciously fought to retain private ownership of his steel empire, maintaining close control over operations to ensure quality and profitability. Under his guidance, the company had made money even during the 1893 depression. Its dominance in the steel industry continued after the economy recovered, leading to revenues of $11 million by 1898. Profits nearly doubled to $21 million the following year and reached $40 million in 1900. Carnegie's ability to vertically integrate his business activities was directly responsible for these profits, much of which he reinvested in his operations. Such success, however, was bound to attract potential competitors. But taking on Andrew Carnegie in the rarified heights he occupied required investment capital beyond the reach of all but a few. J. Pierpont Morgan, the one investment banker of the time capable of attracting such monies, built his success on a formula of a healthy skepticism in his business dealings and the expectation of internal control of those interests in which he invested. He never gambled on business ventures; his firm thoroughly researched and scrutinized each prospective investment opportunity. Once the House of Morgan organized financing, he sought to protect his investment by mandating that Morgan executives serve on the boards of directors of the firms receiving its capital. His reputation for successfully orchestrating large financial deals over the decades, along with his ability to attract other experienced and wealthy investors, meant that he would be a critical part of any effort to challenge Carnegie Steel.[19]

Those looking to take on Carnegie knew that they also had to merge mining, transportation, and production operations into another equally powerful leviathan to entertain any hope of competing. Elbert Gary, general counsel of the Illinois Steel Company, presented just such an idea to J. P. Morgan in the fall of 1898. Not only had Gary organized his proposal well, but he had also impressed Morgan with his presentation. Gary possessed what Morgan biographer Frederick Lewis Allen characterized as the appearance of "a Methodist minister—benign, suave, cordial and earnest." Obviously won over by both Gary and his plan, Morgan agreed to organize funding for a vertically integrated firm known as Federal Steel. The company was capitalized with $200 million in preferred and common stock. Morgan's reputation for picking winners overcame concerns about the volatility of industrial firms that many investors initially voiced. Morgan's record remained untarnished; Federal Steel produced 15 percent of the steel ingots made in the United States and paid dividends to its stockholders in its first year of operation. It quickly became clear that Gary shared Morgan's philosophy of how to make a firm successful and, as a result, he was selected by Morgan as president of Federal Steel shortly after the deal was closed.[20]

Although he might have possessed the demeanor of a clergyman, Gary proved to be an aggressive entrepreneur. He envisioned a "steel republic," where Federal Steel would make basic steel but also expand into the production of finished steel products. Accordingly, he used Morgan capital to form National Tube, a consolidation of 14 large companies, and American Bridge, which brought together 25 firms under Federal's control. Unfortunately at this stage, Federal Steel alone could not supply all the raw steel required by these firms and Gary had to rely on Carnegie Steel for some of it. Looking to expand beyond the domestic market, sometime in early 1900 Gary suggested to Morgan they consider purchasing Carnegie Steel. Even the powerful Morgan hesitated; "I would not think of it. I don't believe I could raise the money." A market downturn later that year led Federal Steel to expand their operations in order to supply the raw steel themselves to National Tube and American Bridge, thereby reducing their costs of production. When Carnegie learned of the cancellation of orders to National Tube and others, he viewed it as an open attack on his domain, something he was not about to tolerate. "A struggle is inevitable," he wrote Charles M. Schwab, the new president of Carnegie Steel, "and it is a question of the survival of the fittest." Carnegie had been contemptuous of Federal Steel from its conception; it was now time to aggressively attack it.[21]

Carnegie began by directing Schwab to begin construction of their own steel tube company in Conneaut, Ohio. With Carnegie's vertically integrated organization, the two concluded that they could make a better product than Gary's National Tube and do so for $10 less a ton. Morgan rightly feared that this opening salvo could escalate into a highly competitive confrontation between the two steel giants, with disastrous consequences for both. Carnegie biographer Joseph Frazier Wall stated it more colorfully. "Carnegie was to Morgan what the Anabaptist had been to Calvin, the fanatical enthusiast who in an excess of fervor would destroy God's and Calvin's orderly plans for the universe." Furthermore, Morgan and Gary knew they could never hope to win this contest if they attempted to compete with the powerful Carnegie in the steel market alone. Morgan's strength rested in his ability to raise capital, vast amounts of it. This became the centerpiece of his strategy to better Carnegie. But how could he best allocate these funds? Pouring more cash into the Federal Steel conglomerate would only exacerbate the competition with Carnegie. Still, could he raise enough capital to buy out Carnegie? Furthermore, would Carnegie even entertain the idea?[22]

Carnegie, while still competitive, was in his mid-sixties and he increasingly valued the tranquility he found at Skibo. Raised in poverty, Carnegie also had become convinced that individuals, such as himself, who had accumulated large fortunes were morally obligated to improve the lives of those less fortunate. Carnegie's fortune was the result of hard work and he continued to see this as a requisite for a strong nation built on the capitalist system. Therefore, he did not view it as his philanthropic duty to simply dole out funds to the poor. Carnegie decided that he could make a lasting contribution by fostering education for those in rural areas, providing them with the opportunity to participate in the economic prosperity found in other parts of the nation. But, as always, he wanted to play a key role in this charitable work. And he could not do this and oversee the world's largest steel company simultaneously. His president Charles Schwab knew that Carnegie's interests were changing and believed his departure from the steel business was imminent. The interests and aspirations represented by these various individuals converged at a banquet honoring Carnegie's dynamic young president in New York City.[23]

On the evening of December 12, 1900, eighty leaders from the worlds of business and finance, including J. P. Morgan, met at the newly completed University Club at Fifth Avenue in Manhattan. At 37, Schwab was younger than most of the attendees gathered there to honor him. He had begun his career in steel at age 17 at Carnegie's Edgar Thomson plant carrying leveling rods, working his way up to president at 35. But, concludes Morgan biographer Jean Strousse, "He knew almost as much about the industry as Carnegie himself." Whether by design or through serendipity, Morgan found himself seated next to the guest of honor. Following coffee, Schwab rose to speak. During his speech, which lasted less than thirty minutes, Morgan must have found it difficult to contain himself. Schwab laid out a plan that envisioned nothing less than the complete consolidation of the nation's steel production. It sought to bring efficiency to all phases of the industry. "No wasteful spending," noted Carnegie biographer Joseph Wall summarizing Schwab's talk, "no unnecessary duplication among individual plants, no faulty planning in plant location, no inadequate transportation facilities." Here was someone who shared Morgan's — and Gary's — vision, but someone whose strong and trusted working relationship with Carnegie potentially made him an effective intermediary for the lengthy negotiations sure to follow. Schwab and Morgan spoke briefly after the speech, agreeing to meet soon to pursue the possibilities set forth in his talk.[24]

The two picked up the discussion in early January at Morgan's residence. The meeting lasted throughout the evening, ending around 3 A.M. Obviously pleased with their discussion, Morgan and Schwab agreed to move forward with a plan to consolidate the steel industry. Schwab promised to work out the details. A few days later, the two met again. After quickly reviewing

Schwab's list of companies that should be included, Morgan told Schwab, "Well, if you can get a price from Carnegie, I don't know but what I'll undertake it." They both were well aware that their plan rested on the ability to convince Carnegie, who controlled the bulk of the country's steel operations, to sell out to them. It was now up to Schwab to broach the issue with his boss. Uncertain how best to go about this, he put it off until early February when he stopped by the Carnegie residence to seek advice from his wife. She suggested approaching "Andy" over a game of golf, which always seemed to improve his temperament. Following her suggestion, Schwab discussed the sale of Carnegie's holdings with him over lunch after a round of golf, adding that Carnegie could name his price. The next day Carnegie met with Schwab and presented him with a handwritten note laying out his terms for the sale of Carnegie Steel and all its holdings. His asking price was $480 million, roughly twelve times annual earnings. Schwab met with Morgan later that day and showed him Carnegie's proposal. Without hesitation, Morgan responded, "I accept this price."[25]

On March 3, 1901, Morgan announced that he planned to organize the world's largest corporation, United States Steel, at $1.4 billion. At the time, this was a colossal amount, even for a man used to dealing in large numbers. To place this in perspective, the federal government at the time operated on a budget that was $130 million *less* than Carnegie's selling price. With Carnegie Steel as a base, Morgan began to buy up other firms related to steel production. In the end, a vertically integrated United States Steel controlled "nearly half of America's steelmaking capacity, and produce[d] more than half its total output — 7 million tons a year." As usual, control of the company remained firmly in Morgan's hands. He hand-picked the president (Charles Schwab) and chairman of the executive committee (Elbert Gary); Morgan and three of his partners sat on the 24-man board. Reaction to the creation of Morgan's gigantic holding company was broad and varied. "Pierpont Morgan is apparently trying to swallow the sun," exclaimed Henry Adams. *Cosmopolitan* concluded that "the world ceased to be ruled by statesmen" in favor of "those who control the concentrated portion of the money supply." Schwab, writing in the May 1901 *North American Review*, was unrepentant. "The iron business was kept back in this country for many years because there was no connection between the various industries on which it depended. It was not," he observed, "until the whole process was welded into a continuous chain under one management that the American iron industry began to make the giant strides which have now carried it into a position where it dominates the whole world." While controversy swirled around financing of United States Steel for years, its creation, concluded Jean Strousse, marked "the high tide of the turn-of-the-century merger movement." And it established the United States as the dominant steel producer in the world.[26]

Events culminating in the advent of United States Steel were paralleled by an important change in the manufacture of steel itself. Most of the steel produced in the 1880s, manufactured by the Bessemer process, was ordered by railroads rapidly expanding and consolidating across the country, particularly in vast expanses of the Trans-Mississippi west. But demand fell off once railroads had pretty well saturated the region and further expansion would have been counter-productive. At this point steel producers desperately sought new markets in the emerging urbanization of the country. Ironically, in a nation with seemingly limitless, inexpensive land, American architects were inspired to construct increasingly taller buildings within city centers rather than move the municipal boundaries outward. While iron had been employed early on, steel's malleability and relative cheapness made it more popular. Unfortunately, Bessemer steel proved to be unsuitable for structural applications. Much of the problem centered on a lack of consistency. First, the manufacture of Bessemer steel involves a short, 10-minute "blow" of air through the molten iron, which does not allow much time for workmen to ensure that the exact conditions exist to produce a quality product. Second, Bessemer manufacturers, no doubt reacting to the fevered demands of rail companies, focused on quantity over quality. Inconsistency could be tolerated more easily in rails, but the increased demands placed on steel in structural applications began to highlight the shortcomings.[27]

The answer lay in a refinement of the Bessemer process developed in England by Sidney Gilchrist Thomas and Percy C. Gilchrist known as the Open-Hearth method. Its most appealing advantage was its slower operation, which allowed "the melted mixture [to] be indefinitely kept in a state of fusion until experiments with small portions determine[d] the exact conditions necessary to produce a required quality of steel." In addition, the process could use wrought iron or scrap steel in addition to iron ore. Finally, it could remove phosphorus from lower grade ores during the process of manufacture. Rapid adaptation of open-hearth production was closely tied to the growth of modern cities. Thomas Misa concluded that "just as U. S. Bessemer output had surpassed British output because of the unprecedented demand of railroad building, U. S. Open-Hearth output also exceeded British output because of the unprecedented demand of city building." Despite Andrew Carnegie's reluctance to champion the process, the demand for structural steel grew during the 1890s, culminating in a decision by the American Society for Testing Materials to permit only open-hearth steel for structural applications.[28]

Events culminating in the formation of United States Steel Corporation were followed closely by those with shipping interests on the Great Lakes, where they sought to capture a piece of the ever-expanding iron ore trade. Their efforts to meet the accelerating demands of the steel industry fostered the development of an enlarged, yet more efficient, ship design in the early 1900s that became the prototype for lake ore carriers for the next 50 years. Foremost in the minds of these shippers was finding a way to increase the cargo capacity of each vessel, thereby improving its profitability because it could deliver more cargo in fewer trips than a smaller vessel. The introduction of steel construction in bulk carriers in the mid–1880s had permitted builders to not only build bulk carriers with an ever-increasing hauling capacity but it also gave them remarkable design flexibility. The growing dimensions of bulk carriers hardly went unnoticed. In a letter written in 1886 to Henry L. Abbott, colonel of the Army Corps of Engineers, E. T. Evans, general manager of the Lake Superior Transit Company, observed that Lake Superior ship traffic "has increased enormously and vessels are constantly getting larger and more valuable." Representative Theodore Burton (Ohio) reflected on this change in a speech delivered in the House on February 5, 1891. Citing a report of the Supervising Inspector General of Steam Vessels, he compared the growth in the size of ships on the lakes between 1886, when only 21 steamers exceeded 1,500 net registered tons, and 1890, when there were 110 such vessels. Making the connection between steel construction and increased ship size, he noted that only six steel steamers existed in 1886, while four years later there were 68.[29]

The growth in vessel size in the late 1880s, as dramatic as it was, proved to be a harbinger of the next decade and a half. Builders after 1890 continued to capitalize on the innovations of the previous decade, while developing new techniques and introducing revolutionary changes. One of the casualties of all this was the once ubiquitous Great Lakes lake sailing vessel. There had been 1,272 active sailing ships of varying designs and dimensions in 1890. Just ten years later, 832 remained in operation. Many of the original number had begun their careers carrying, at least occasionally, iron ore; those remaining ended the decade hauling whatever they could find, usually lumber, salt, or stone. They were simply too small, slow, and inefficient to be participating in the demanding iron ore, which now dominated lake commerce, or grain trades. Between 1880 and 1890, on the other hand, the number of steamers operating on the lakes increased moderately, from 1,527

Schooners, steamers, and other vessels struggle to maneuver in the busy port of Cleveland circa 1890. Cleveland was not only an important shipbuilding center and Lake port at the time, it also served as the terminus of the Ohio-Erie Canal.

to 1,732. But their average gross tonnage grew by nearly 50 percent, from 428 to 639, an indication of the considerable increase in the size and capacity of the newer bulk carriers. This trend continued through the 1890s. In an address before the Civil Engineers Club of Cleveland on March 3, 1898, R. L. Newman reported that "the demands are at present for boats of the largest practical dimensions, limited only by the tortuous channels of the connecting straits and the facilities obtainable at the ports of entry." In 1900 lake shipbuilders launched vessels totaling 111,241 gross tons, an unimpressive 16.2 percent of the national total. Yet, that same year the tonnage of cargo moved on the Great Lakes approached the total of imports *and* exports of the United States as a whole.[30]

At this juncture, where larger steam vessels had gained prominence over smaller sailing ships, as well as wooden steam vessels, on the lakes, a new kind of organization was created by necessity to finance their construction. When sailing vessels dominated the lakes, most were owned by small partnerships or by the captain and a few of his friends ashore in a very informal arrangement. In the 1870s, with the increased popularity of more costly wooden steam ships, firms had used their cash reserves for a down payment on a mortgage that tended to run the length of the expected life of the vessel. Considering the limited availability of investment funds at the time, they had little choice. By the mid–1880s, in what must have been considered a marked improvement, "Relatives, neighbors, and business acquaintances frequently went together," observed Jewell R. Dean, "put up a few thousand dollars and built a ship to be managed by a Wilson, Minch, or Tomlinson [owners of lake shipping companies]." The ledgers of the Wilson Fleet, for example, showed that stockholders varied from ship to ship, "with Captain Wilson, as manager and sizeable stockholder, being the only thread connecting a group of ships." By 1891, as *Marine Review* noted, it had become clear that the "transportation business of the Lakes is falling gradually into big hands." Some, like the innovative Alexander McDougall, living in the relatively isolated Duluth at the western end of Lake Superior, did not have access to the large amount of local capital required to make costly upgrades to shipyards for the production of steel vessels. Financing for such projects often came, as in McDougall's case, from centers of finance, particularly on the East Coast. Another option found large iron companies, like Cleveland's vertically integrated Pickands-Mather, financing their own fleets.[31]

Pickands-Mather Iron Company, under the creative leadership of Samuel Mather, had been the first Great Lakes iron firm to begin vertically integrating its operations in the 1880s, purchasing at least partial ownership in ore boats, docks, iron ore mines, and smelting facilities. One important component in this drive for efficiency was the creation of their own steamship line in the early 1880s. Mather's consolidation efforts proved so successful that he attracted the attention of a former Clevelander John D. Rockefeller shortly after he began investing in the Mesabi. In 1896 his admiration for Mather's skills and his reputation for honesty led Rockefeller to hire him, despite being a competitor in the iron trade, to arrange for the construction of what became the foundation of his Bessemer Fleet — twelve virtually identical ships of 475 feet each with a combined cost of nearly $3 million, certainly the largest single ship order ever placed on the Lakes up to that time. This undertaking was unusual not only because Mather supervised the construction of a competitor's ships but also because the money for this order came solely from Rockefeller corporate funds. When Rockefeller sold his interests in the Bessemer Fleet five years later with the formation of United States Steel, it had grown to 56 ships, which included the 25 whaleback steamers and 31 barges from McDougall's American Steel Barge Company purchased in 1900. Collectively, this fleet could haul 3,500,000 tons of ore in one voyage. "No other group of ore-carriers on the globe," concluded Rockefeller biographer Allen Nevins, "compared with it." Clearly, the capitalization necessary to control fleets like this had eliminated individuals and informal partnerships from the ownership of the new steel bulk carriers. The vertical integration pioneered on the lakes by Pickands-Mather was accelerating, with large ships increasingly owned by mining companies. And both, in turn, controlled by "the great steel-manufacturing interests."[32]

The shipyards too required huge infusions of capital to expand and upgrade their facilities to build these large boats. Alexander Smith, reporting on the state of the nation's shipbuilding industry in the Twelfth Census, observed that in 1890 there were eight firms on the lakes building iron and steel ships. Capitalized at a little over $3 million, they built 33 iron and steel ships, each averaging 1,113 gross tons. In 1900 there were still only eight companies, but they had nearly $12½ million in capital. And while they launched nine fewer vessels, the average gross tonnage of each had jumped to 4,014. In 1900, by way of contrast, there were 114 wooden shipbuilding facilities along the United States Great Lakes shoreline. They produced 57 wooden steamers with an average gross tonnage of 103 and 27 sailing vessels of 113 average gross tons each. The American Shipbuilding Company, incorporated in New Jersey on March 16, 1899, with an authorized capitalization of $30 million, provides a valuable insight into the changes under way in Great Lakes shipbuilding at the time. It was the peak year in a period characterized as the "great merger movement" in the United States (1895–1904). This consolidation, which brought together shipyards from around the lakes, gave American Shipbuilding better than half of the region's market share.[33]

The American Shipbuilding Company was formed through the consolidation of the Cleveland Ship Building Company, the Globe Iron Works Company (Cleveland), and the Ship Owners Dry Dock Company (Cleveland), as well as shipyards in Buffalo, Detroit, Milwaukee, West Superior, West Bay, and Chicago. Its general offices were in Cleveland. The dominance of Cleveland as the shipbuilding center on the lakes began to wane by the early 1900s as the confines of the serpentine Cuyahoga River prevented the construction of the larger vessels then in demand by lake shippers. Lorain (Ohio), Detroit, Chicago, Bay City (Michigan), and Superior (Wisconsin) had better facilities for these bigger boats and assumed responsibility for their construction. Corporate offices, however, remained in Cleveland. The impact of this merger was felt almost immediately with British Lloyd's declaring the American Shipbuilding Company the third largest in the world by 1901, based on the total tonnage launched that year.[34]

This consolidation and expansion coincided with an unparalleled demand for bulk carriers. The years around 1900 witnessed what marine historian Harry Myers called a "frenzy of shipbuilding unequalled until the two world wars and never surpassed for tonnage." Between 1896 and 1910, lake shipbuilders launched 300 bulk carriers, 176 between 1905 and 1910 alone. In fact, more than half of all U.S. merchant ship tonnage produced in 1908 was being built by a few corporations on the Great Lakes. The pace of construction was so intense that some yards could not acquire enough steel plates to complete vessels already under construction. The yards not only produced more bulk carriers, they also made them increasingly larger, from vessels of 504 feet in the late 1890s to 605 feet by 1910. Improved construction technology, replacing wood with steel in hull construction, and increased capitalization had allowed the American Shipbuilding Company and others around the lakes to make this possible. Consider the following comparison. A Cleveland shipbuilder named Radcliffe built a wooden propeller for roughly $75,000 in 1878. It had a 220-foot keel and was registered at 1,300 tons. Radcliffe reported that he used 250,000 feet of white oak and 20,000 feet of white pine in the vessel's construction. Each timber had to be cut, shaped, fitted, and assembled separately. The construction, considering the number of steps involved in building a wooden ship, took months and was, obviously, labor-intensive. By contrast, a typical 600 footer, although it cost $570,000 in 1907, had a cheaper per-ton cost. Writing in 1898, John Foord reported that a 5,000-ton steamer currently cost about $2 less per ton to build than a 2,500-ton vessel in 1885. And, since it was made entirely of steel, it could be completed in only 140 days. Moreover, it could carry 10,400 tons on each trip, eight times the amount carried by the 1878 wooden steamer. And steel ships lasted decades with a minimum of upkeep. But, lamented Great Lakes historian H. C. Inches, "even our good oak ships were at their best only for 15 years. After that it usually cost nearly all the ship could clear to keep it seaworthy. When decay started there was no stopping it." By way of example, he recalled that machinery was frequently transferred to as many as three different steamers as their wooden hulls gave out or were destroyed by fire. "Today [1951] some of our metal hulls are outliving two engines, just the reverse from the wooden-ship era." Myers concurred, noting that most of the 300 bulk carriers constructed between 1896 and 1910 were still in service in 1930.[35]

Important changes other than size were introduced in lake ship design during the period under investigation. For example, in 1892 the Anchor Line contracted with several shipyards around the lakes to build a new style of boat. A major feature of this new design was the elimination of sheer, making the vessel the same depth at bow and stern as amidships; the gunwales were also on a bevel line. This change promised construction savings of an estimated $12,000 to $15,000 per ship, making the cost of these 275-foot, 2,700-ton steamers about $178,000. The *James H. Hoyt*, launched in 1902, changed hatch spacing from the traditional 24 feet to 12-foot centers. Done to accommodate the iron ore business, this theoretically cut loading time by half. All iron ore loading spouts were mounted at 12-foot intervals, which required the typical bulk carrier with hatches on 24-foot centers to move once during the loading process. Twelve-foot centers meant that spouts could fill all hatches simultaneously. In another important innovation, electric lights first appeared in 1887 on a Great Lakes ship, the *Yakima,* which had been built for the Wilson Fleet. Unfortunately, although outdoor lighting had been available since the early 1880s, none could be found at any point along the 75-mile length of the St. Mary's River throughout the decade. This effectively shut down navigation along the river beginning at "4 o'clock in the afternoon [because ships] can not get through the river by daylight, and its tortuous character prevents navigation in the night." This forced downbound ships to anchor in Whitefish Bay and those upbound to stop at Sailors Encampment at the head of Mud Lake for the night. Beginning in 1894, however, the Lake Carriers' Association annually funded private lighting along many of the channels recently improved or expanded by the government, including the St. Mary's River. Allowing ships to pass at night certainly contributed to the increase in tonnage through the river during the decade, from 7,221,935 in 1889 to roughly 22,000,000 tons in 1899. Unfortunately, interdepartmental wrangling over funding responsibilities meant the government was unable to fulfill its initial promise to provide lighting for the improvements made earlier in the decade. Frustration with Washington's ineptitude led to the Lake Carriers lobbying influential Michigan senator James McMillan in 1899 for assistance in forcing the government to take responsibility for lighting the channels around the lakes and to reimburse the Lake Carriers for assuming these expenses over the previous five years.[36]

Certainly the most influential design change of the period occurred with the launching of the *Augustus B. Wolvin* in 1904. Named for the Duluth shipper who ordered her, the *Wolvin's* keel was laid on December 1, 1903, in Lorain, Ohio. The vessel's construction, in the midst of one of the most brutal winters ever recorded along the lakes, generated considerable anticipation throughout the lake shipping community because the word had spread that this boat would be special. Accordingly, the builders sent out 5,000 invitations and had posters announcing the early spring 1904 launching. In the days preceding the event, the population of Lorain grew by several thousand people as the invited guests and the simply curious gathered. A gala ball was held the night before, with the proceeds benefiting the community public library. On April 9, the *Wolvin* finally slid down the ways and into the Black River at around 1:00 P.M. The event was met with an outpouring of enthusiasm; factory whistles squealed, and the dense crowds along the river bank and peering from nearby rooftops erupted in cheering that lasted five minutes. What could possibly generate such curiosity and excitement about the *Wolvin*? One thing immediately set the boat apart from other bulk carriers. In fact, it was impossible to miss. The *Wolvin* was painted yellow. Henceforth, she became known as the "Yellow Monster." One cannot help wondering if William Dean Howells, in a letter to his brother Joseph in 1907 might have had the *Wolvin* in mind when he penned, "Lake craft are all interesting and strange — especially the big freighters."[37]

But more than color set the *Wolvin* apart from its contemporaries in 1904. Her length of 560 feet exceeded anything on the lakes by nearly 60 feet. With a beam of 56 feet and a depth of 32 feet, she was one of the 20 largest ships afloat in the world. New innovations were featured throughout the vessel. She had 33 hatches (on 12-foot centers, of course), each 33 by 9 feet, which were operated by a steam engine rather than manual labor. In fact, there were two steam engines, one always serving as a backup to ensure that not only the hatches but also the lights, capstan, and windlass had power. With a rather narrow smokestack and only her aft quarters and her (forward) pilot house rising above the deck, "the *Wolvin* resembled a barge more than a steamship." The ship's quadruple-expansion engine was capable of generating 2,000 horsepower to propel her at close to 12 miles per hour. But it was the revolutionary design of the *Wolvin's* hold that sparked considerable interest. There were no bulkheads that traditionally subdivided the holds of lakes ships; the entire 490-foot length remained open and free of all obstructions. In place of the traditional stanchions and beams, the builders had introduced heavy plate, arch girders under the spar deck between the hatches. In addition, the sides of the hold were sloped, a 43-foot width at the top tapering down to 24 feet at the bottom. The new design of the hold was introduced to eliminate anything that might interfere with unloading operations, as well as to concentrate the bulk cargo for the unloading machinery. The space between the hull and the hold was used for ballast. She made her maiden voyage on June 10, 1904, hauling coal from Lorain upbound for Duluth. After unloading her coal, she made for Two Harbors, Minnesota, on June 19. There, drawing 18 feet of water, she took on 10,894 tons of ore, far more than any other vessel had ever carried by a wide margin, and departed for Buffalo's Lack-awanna Steel Company docks. Her success spawned countless imitators, making the *Wolvin* the template for bulk carriers on the lakes for the next 50 years.[38]

If the *Wolvin* provided the standard design for lake carriers in the coming decades, the standard size was established in 1906 when seven 600-footers began operations. Each had a 60-foot beam with 32-feet molded depth. Their triple-expansion engines generated 2,000 horsepower, capable of propelling the vessels at nearly 12 miles per hour. A. F. Lindblad, writing in the 1924 *Marine Review*, demonstrated the economy of these larger vessels. He compared boats of 420 feet, 504 feet, and 580 feet at 16 trips (averaging ten miles per hour), 18 trips (averaging 11 miles per hour), 20 trips (averaging 12 miles per hour), and 22 trips (averaging 13 miles per hour). Despite proportionately higher costs in insurance, wages, and fuel, the larger ships showed a considerably higher percentage of return on investment than the smaller vessels. For example, a 580-foot boat making twenty-two trips at an average speed of thirteen miles per hour showed a profit of $45,493 (5.48 percent return on investment). A 504-foot vessel making the identical number of trips at the same speed generated a profit of $28,504 (a 4.30 percent return), while the 420-foot ship made $5,668 for its investors (1.13 percent return). Ivan Walton's studies 19 years later supported Lindblad's conclusions. He added that a 600-foot-class vessel could load nearly 960 additional tons of ore with each additional foot in length.[39]

Lawrence Pomeroy concluded that the economic advantages of these larger ships were the result of improved economies of scale. Using figures from the 1916–1920 shipping seasons, he observed that a vessel of 10,000 gross tons capacity had net earnings per mile of $2.08, while a ship between 5,000–5,500 gross ton capacity earned $.39 per mile. Pomeroy, quoting from a 1925 report by Fay, Spofford, and Thorndike, wrote: "It would appear that the earning capacity of bulk freight vessels in the Great Lakes trade increases more than twice as fast as the increase in cargo capacity; or, in other words, *doubling the cargo capacity multiplies the net earnings more than four fold.*" The captain of the 605-foot *J. Pierpont Morgan*, which was launched in 1906, implied the same more simply and succinctly. Responding to the size of the large vessel recently entrusted to his command, he observed that it would have required two and one-half years of round-trips for the steamer he commanded 28 years earlier to equal the amount of ore the *Morgan* planned to carry on its first trip out of Duluth.[40]

Production of Great Lakes bulk carriers, then, had settled on the 600-

foot/60-foot/32-foot size by the early 20th century. But problems emerged as builders sought to continue expanding the length of the ships, if ever so slightly. Frank Kirby and A. P. Rankin reported that in 1911 there was concern for two 617-foot boats then under construction. In order for a vessel to maintain its longitudinal integrity, its depth had to be expanded in proportion to its increased length. But these 617-footers, Kirby and Rankin observed, had retained the standard depth of the 1906 models because the channels and locks of the lakes remained at 20 feet. Writing in 1924, Lindblad echoed this concern with lengthening ore carriers without increasing the beam and molded depth proportionately. Kirby and Rankin also noted that there was additional concern in 1911 that the extreme width of the athwartship hatches, done to accommodate the sophisticated unloading equipment of the time, might further compromise the longitudinal strength. This led to a stabilizing of lake vessels at around 600 feet until additional improvements could be made on the waterways.[41]

Throughout much of the 19th century, the struggle to meet the demands for improved carrying capacity on lake ships had centered on the structural limitations of building materials available to shipbuilders as much as it did the lack of improvements to the region's waterways. This changed with the introduction of steel in ship construction, where that metal's malleability and strength eliminated most of the concerns about dimensions or design. From this point, any limitations to ship size tended to be a function of improvements to the channels, locks, and harbors round the lakes. "During the 40 odd years of continuous improvement of the lake channels," wrote John Foord in the 1898 *North American Review*, "the ship-builder has pressed close on the heels of the Government engineer. Steamers requiring when loaded a given draft of water have always been on the stocks while the corresponding depth of channel was being secured, and have often been afloat before it was forthcoming." Increasingly, the federal government assumed greater responsibility for the improvements, particularly in the 1890s and early 1900s. According to the Bureau of the Census Special Report, "Transportation by Water (1906)," aggregate congressional appropriations for the survey, improvement, and maintenance of the region's waterways through 1890 amounted to $37,522,937. Yet, between 1891 and 1907 alone, appropriations totaled $60,268,171, nearly 61 percent more than had been spent during the previous 70 years. The success of the *Spokane* in 1886 demonstrated the potential of steel and inspired the growth in steel hulls. Still, until 1890, most of these vessels were less than 300 feet, too small to guarantee profitability. The development of larger carriers, concluded the April 11, 1891, *Harper's Weekly*, was simply "the natural demand of capitalists for a fair return upon their investments." But the inconsistent and generally inadequate depths of lake waterways and harbors presented a serious challenge to these plans.[42]

Congressman Theodore Burton (Rep.-Ohio) voiced the frustrations of his lakeshore constituents on the House floor in August of 1891. He lamented to his colleagues that, although the total freight carried on the Great Lakes exceeded the aggregate tonnage of foreign commerce entering or leaving United States seaports, the Great Lakes had been neglected by congressional appropriations. He was arguing in favor of adopting the recommendations found in the report of Col. O. M. Poe, Chief of Engineers, submitted to the House in January of that year. The report had been prompted by Poe's suggestion in 1886 to consider deepening the lake ship channels. It provided detailed cost estimates for deepening the "ship-channel" connecting the ports of Chicago, Duluth, and Buffalo to 20 feet, thus effectively improving all the routes between the ore fields of Lake Superior and the southern lake ports. An alternative figure was included to make all the channels 21 feet deep to provide an adequate depth during rough seas. The width of the improved channels, except for the locks at Sault Ste. Marie, was calculated at 300 feet. Poe recounted the gradual improvements to the channels up to that point, noting that a depth of 9 feet had been adequate in 1852, but had to be increased to 16 feet by 1882. In his summary, Poe observed, "For nearly thirty-five years I have watched [Great Lakes ship commerce] increase, but neither I nor anyone else within my knowledge has been able to expand at the same rate. The wildest expectations of one year seem absurdly tame the next."[43]

The 20-foot dredging estimate of $2,379,085 was almost $1 million less than the 21-foot estimate, which probably explains why Congress selected the former for inclusion in the 1890 Rivers and Harbors bill. Although this choice proved to be an unfortunate one later in the decade, it is difficult to argue that these improvements failed to improve shipping capacity on the lakes, and by extension, dramatically improve the national economy. Alexander Smith's census report on United States shipbuilding in 1902 focused on improvements of rivers and harbors during the 1890s as the reason why shipbuilders were able to build larger boats, causing a drop in freight rates. This, he concluded, stimulated growth in domestic, water-borne commerce and was the salvation of shipbuilders. The Commissioner of Navigation, in his 1897 report to the Secretary of the Treasury, wrote that the two factors that accounted for the unprecedented growth in Great Lakes shipping were, first, the discovery and utilization of the region's mineral wealth and, second, congressional appropriations for navigational aids.[44]

An important provision of the 1890 River and Harbor Act set aside $350,000 to purchase the Lake Superior Ship Canal at Keweenaw Point, although opposition to this was strong early on in congressional debates. Opponents pointed to poor design and lack of maintenance as the principal reasons the company wanted to sell the canal, which they viewed as an irresponsible application of funds realized from the sale of public lands donated in 1865 and 1866. Proponents argued that such issues were of little relevance in light of the burgeoning commerce found on Lake Superior. Congressman John Farquhar, in a debate on the issue on May 22, 1890, was direct. "Any man who could, for any reason, vote against appropriating even $1,000,000 to secure on the iron-bound coast of Lake Superior two such good harbors of refuge as are found at the ends of that canal ought to leave this country, or at least this hall." He followed with this sobering observation, "There is no more dangerous spot in America than the point which this canal enables the lake navigators to avoid, and, independent of that, the canal cuts off the many additional miles of navigation which would be involved in going around Keweenaw Point." Purchase of the canal by the federal government, he concluded, "has met the approbation of every vessel-owner, of every merchant, of every board of trade in the whole Northwest." Such arguments, and the clear support of a considerable constituency, enabled this purchase to be included in the 1890 bill. Following the purchase, the government embarked on considerable improvements to the canal and the harbors of refuge.[45]

While congressional appropriations for navigational improvements on the lakes increased dramatically after 1890, they were inadequate to address all the necessary improvements. The April 18, 1898, *Sandusky Register*, although noting the recent alterations made to key channels and rivers around the lakes, argued that it was now time to have harbors deepened to correspond to the new depths now found in lake ship channels. Many cities, in fact, found it necessary to assume responsibility for funding such projects themselves. The July 21, 1898, *Marine Review* reported that the city of Lorain (Ohio) had appropriated $75,000 to dredge the Black River to a depth of 20 feet from the river's mouth to the Lorain Steel Company docks. In addition, the city announced that it planned to widen the river channel to 450 feet to enable "the longest boats" to turn around. Such allocations were necessary to ensure Lorain's continued prosperity, which relied heavily on an ore trade that increasingly depended on larger and larger vessels.[46]

But the discussion of improving lake depths now took on a new dimension. The April 14, 1898, *Sandusky Register* reported that "vessel men are becoming much alarmed over the continued lowering of the waters of Lake

Superior." The harbor at Duluth, Minnesota, was reported to be 30 inches lower than the year before. Ships could no longer leave Lake Superior ports fully loaded, which reduced their efficiency and, naturally, their profits. The mystery deepened, continued the article, because Lake Huron water levels had remained unchanged. Some experts concluded that there had to be a subterranean passage somewhere between the two lakes that accounted for the disappearance of such a large amount of water. But the problem of lower water levels soon became apparent on the other lakes. It was a topic of considerable concern at the 1899 Lake Carriers' annual meeting. It prompted discussions of building a dam upstream from Niagara Falls to control the flow of water out of the upper lakes. The Lake Carriers' Annual Report of 1904 quoted from a 1902 report of Major William H. Bixby, Corps of Engineers, that concluded that the water level of Lake Erie had dropped "at least 2 feet" since 1882. The problem festered over the coming years, prompting the Lake Carriers' Association to call again for a dam in 1910. But the International Waterways Commission, created the year before with the signing of the Boundary Waters Treaty between Canada and the United States, reported against the idea. Poe's alternate depth of 21 feet recommended in his 1890 report undoubtedly would have had a considerable impact on this issue had it been adopted.[47]

The problems associated with the drop in lake depths were made worse by the fact that the U. S. Lake Survey had ceased operations. Begun in 1841 to survey the lakes and issue charts for sailors, it had shut down operations on July 1, 1882. This decision was based on the assumption that ships had reached their maximum depth of 12 feet. But the launching of the *Spokane* four years later had demonstrated the feasibility of steel ship construction, which removed most of the previous limitations on ship size. This coincided with increased iron ore and grain production in the region that led to a demand for larger vessels. Numerous reports of water levels dropping around the lakes compounded the problems. In addition, obstacles uncharted during the earlier surveys were now making themselves known, often with serious consequences for ship owners and sailors. Unseen changes were also occurring naturally beneath the surface of the lake waters, and errors from the earlier surveys were likewise being discovered. Some of the charts sailors relied on dated back to the beginning of the survey. Two charts for the St. Mary's River still in use, for example, dated back to the 1850s. In another instance, a steamer with a 14-foot draught struck a shoal in northern Lake Michigan registered at 22 feet on the U. S. Survey charts. While Congress doled out some funds in the 1890s for piecemeal studies of the changes, these proved inadequate. By 1898, uncharted shoals and obstacles (even including old ship-wrecks), coupled with greater ship depths and reduced lake levels, forced the Secretary of War to recommend a new survey of the lakes. Accordingly, begin-ning in 1900, Congress appropriated an average of $110,000 per year to sup-port an ongoing survey of the lakes.[48]

Developments in ship design and carrying capacity, coupled with ongo-ing improvements in the lake channels and locks to accommodate these changes, allowed the volume of ore reaching the southern lake shores to grow rapidly during this period. In 1890 the shipments of iron ore from the Lake Superior mines totaled 9,003,701 tons. Ten years later, with the addition of ore from the Mesabi mines, that number reached 19,059,33 tons, doubling again to 38,421,173 (long) tons six years later. When Alexander Brown intro-duced his revolutionary unloading machine in 1880, the two ranges open at that time had sent 1,908,745 tons, less than five percent of the amount 26 years later. Brown's Fastplant and other unloaders of that generation, while invaluable in the 1880s, had become obsolete by the mid–1890s. They were simply inadequate to handle this flood of iron ore streaming into Chicago and the ports along the southern shore of Lake Erie in the holds of increas-ingly larger vessels.[49]

The problems with the existing equipment were numerous. The bucket used to lift the ore from the hold and deposit it on the dock, for example, held a maximum of one ton of ore and required laborers in the hold to move the ore from the sides and around stanchions to enable the clam bucket to retrieve it. As a result, boats had to remain too long in port to unload, cut-ting into efficiency and profits. "For years," observed Waldon Fawcett in the September 29, 1900, *Harper's Weekly*, "the vessel men have been chafing under [this] rather tedious system. Now comes this interesting new machine with its massive walking-beam and clam-shell bucket scooping up to ten tons of ore at a time, and with several of these employed on a vessel it will be possi-ble to remove the largest cargo in half a day." George Hulett, the mastermind behind this "interesting new machine," was born in Conneaut, Ohio, in 1846. He spent 25 years in the "produce and commission business" in Cleveland before he ventured into engineering coal and iron ore handling machines. The unloading machine he unveiled in 1899 remained, with only a few design changes, the premier dockside ore unloader at Lake ports into the 1960s.[50]

Hulett pioneered his new design as an engineer for the Wellman, Seaver Engineering Company of Cleveland, incorporating successful features of ear-lier rigs. With an appearance that marine historian Richard Wright described as a "mechanical praying mantis," the Hulett unloader consisted of a large,

This steam-powered version of the Hulett unloaded ore boats at Conneaut, Ohio, in the early 20th century.

tilting crane attached to a rail-mounted gantry that traveled parallel to the docks. The legs, or supports, were spaced in such a way that up to four railroad tracks could be run beneath the Hulett. They saved time by allowing the operator to unload either directly into railway cars waiting below or into a hopper car that ran out on a cantilevered frame to dump ore into railroad cars or in a pile for dock storage. An innovative design feature placed the device's operator in a cabin at the lower end of the vertical arm of the crane, giving him a clear view of the hold as he maneuvered the ten- (later 17-) -ton-capacity clamshell into position for the next bite of ore. This increased control dramatically reduced damage to the vessels being unloaded. Another important design feature kept the arm of the bucket in a constantly vertical position through the introduction of a lighter upper girder, resulting in a parallelogram motion.[51]

The Hulett, as the rig became known, worked faster and suffered fewer breakdowns than earlier unloaders. Additionally, its ability to weigh each scoop and selectively deposit it into a waiting railroad car was an important

The clam shell bucket of a Hulett unloading machine prepares to scoop ore from the hold of the *Augustus B. Wolvin.* Note the openings just above the clam shell that allow the Hulett's operator to observe the process. The innovative design of the *Wolvin's* hold, which employed arched steel beams, eliminated the need for stanchions. This, coupled with the slanted sides, streamlined unloading operations, especially when coupled with a Hulett. (From Ralph D. Williams, *The Honorable Peter White,* 1907)

feature that ensured that various grades of ore were not mixed. The clam bucket, which adopted the successful features of the Hoover-Mason bucket, continued to reduce the need for shovelers in the holds. "In ordinary boats," noted the August 3, 1905, *Engineering News,* "the [Huletts] can reach 90 percent of the ore [in the hold], and in some modern boats they have actually unloaded 97 percent without the aid of shovelers." Not surprisingly, it immediately drew the wrath of these workers who correctly saw in Hulett's invention their imminent unemployment. When coupled with advanced ship designs, such as the sloped sides and large, open hold of the *Augustus B. Wolvin,* the Hulett was remarkably effective. Brown fast plants continued in operation at various ports throughout much of the 20th century, but they tended to service older vessels. The newer ships, however, copied the advancements incorporated into the *Wolvin*. Marine Engineers introduced ships that expanded the traditional flush deck to accommodate up to 30 hatches. In the holds, they replaced the stanchions and beams traditionally used for support with heavy-plate arch girders beneath the spar deck. They also eliminated bulk heads, thereby opening up the hold and permitting the Huletts unobstructed operation during unloading. The perfectly matched engineering innovations of the Hulett and ship design were, at last, able to satisfy the demands of the iron industry.[52]

In some ports where unloading equipment was less sophisticated or non-existent, resourceful engineers, in the last major innovation in unloading technology, brought the unloading equipment on board the ship. These "self-unloaders" employed a moveable conveyor capable of swinging over the dock or shoreline. Many historians credit the *Wyandotte* with being the first ship to employ such a system in 1908, although the wooden steamer *Hennepin* introduced the technology in 1902. Ore was too heavy for these early conveyors so most early self-unloaders operated in the limestone trade. Following refinements later in the century, however, ore carriers too began to use self-unloading equipment.[53]

In May of 1893, Alexander McDougall's only whaleback designed for passenger service, the *Christopher Columbus*, began ferrying passengers to and from Chicago's Jackson Park, the site of the World's Columbian Exposition. Luxuriously appointed and capable of comfortably transporting 5,000 passengers each trip, the *Columbus* had been constructed in McDougall's Superior, Wisconsin, shipyards in less than three months and chartered to the World's Fair Steamship Company. Equipped with 5,000 horsepower engines and an 18-foot propeller, she could travel the six miles between the downtown docks at Randolph Street and Jackson Park at 18 miles per hour. Remarkably, the ship's design allowed all passengers to disembark within five minutes of their arrival. The *Columbus* safely carried over 1,700,000 passengers during its time of service at the exposition. After the fair closed, she was put on the Chicago-Milwaukee day run, operating successfully until she was dismantled at Manitowoc, Wisconsin, in 1936. Without question, over her lifetime she carried more passengers than any other passenger vessel in Lake history.[54]

The entrepreneurial spirit represented by McDougall's *Christopher Columbus* seems an appropriate metaphor for the exposition itself. Conceived to honor the 400th anniversary of Columbus's journey to the Americas, the

Fair featured large, palatial exposition halls celebrating the prowess of American commerce and technology. While exhibits for agriculture and the arts, as well as contributions from other nations, were also present, it seemed that they were ancillary to the success of American industry, which had made the country one of the wealthiest in the world by the last decade of the 19th century. And this was the result of the successful exploitation of Lake Superior iron ore, a process that had evolved in late 19th and early 20th centuries.

To be sure, the integrated system of efficient iron ore delivery to the steel mills along the southern Great Lakes shores was further refined after 1908. Mining operations, particularly on the Mesabi, expanded dramatically; ships carrying the ore grew still larger; newer locks and deeper channels appeared; and over 75 Huletts eventually worked ore docks on the lower lakes. But the integrated system of which each was a part came into its own in the late 1880s and, in particular, the 1890s. Economic activity on and around the Great Lakes during this period placed the region at the epicenter of national growth. The unrelenting demand for iron prompted much-needed improvements and innovation to the mining and shipping of ore that reduced production costs by improving efficiency. The process helped propel the nation onto the world stage, first as an economic power and later as a world military power. The final chapter will look at some of the new developments and assess the implications of these changes on the country during the 20th century.

6

"A swan song that will be a melancholy dirge"

(After 1908)

During the summer of 1942, unusually heavy ship traffic on the St. Mary's River proceeded at a steady, almost rhythmic pace along the river's roughly 60-mile length. These vessels passed by a shoreline where centuries before Native Americans and French Voyagers in birch bark canoes had fished and traded. The boats were larger now, many 600 feet, and constructed of steel. The robust songs of the Voyagers, which had helped relieve the tedium of long days of paddling, had been replaced by the dull throbbing of engines and machinery propelling these large vessels as they traversed the busy waters of the St. Mary's. It remained the only avenue for waterborne commerce between the ore fields of Lake Superior and the steel mills to the south. And all these vessels still had to pass through the locks at Sault Ste. Marie.

Those ships making their first passage through the locks in 1942 could not have failed to observe some startling changes. Paul T. Hurt, on a pleasure cruise to Duluth remembered "machine gun nests, anti-aircraft guns and barrage balloons," designed to interrupt attacks by hostile aircraft, floating overhead. Soldiers patrolled the river shore and no visitors were allowed at the locks; those passing through the locks were forbidden to take pictures there or anywhere else along the St. Mary's River. Some veteran sailors might have recalled that a few defensive positions had been set up around the locks shortly after war broke out in Europe in 1939, and that military guards had accompanied all non-commercial vessels locking through the Sault. No doubt many remembered the formal agreement in 1940 between the Canadian and United States governments that coordinated defensive operations for their respective locks on the St. Mary's. Few probably noticed a year later, however, when a company of infantry responsible for the security of the locks was quietly replaced by the 702nd Battalion, Military Police. With the country's declaration of war following the Japanese attack on United States military installations at Pearl Harbor late in 1941, the St. Mary's River, and particularly the locks at Sault Ste. Marie, suddenly took on a new importance.[1]

As a principal conduit for most of the iron ore consumed by the nation's steel mills, the locks at Sault Ste. Marie became a potential Achilles heel. With efforts under way to replace the horrendous losses of Allied merchant vessels to German U-boats in the ongoing Battle of the Atlantic, the Russians desperately seeking war materiel' to help halt the Wehrmacht pouring into their country along a 2,000-mile front, and American industry feverishly retooling to meet the requirements of a peace-time military transitioning to war, any disruption in the flow of iron ore would seriously undermine the Allies' war effort. Military intelligence experts, along with shipping interests and local residents, while dismissing the possibility of a large-scale German or Japanese attack on the Sault locks, feared other possible enemy actions there. For example, if the Germans decided to send either submarines or surface vessels into the isolated waters near the southern shores of Hudson Bay — a mere 400 miles from the Sault, they could use one of the remote islands in the area to reassemble bombers delivered in sections and launch an air attack against the locks. Should the Germans perfect a long-range bomber, they might also launch an attack from their bases in Norway. Considering the location's importance, it was even possible, they theorized, that the Germans would consider ordering paratroopers, again using their Norwegian bases, to undertake a suicide attack against the locks. U. S. Army engineers concluded that, after overwhelming the light, pre–1942 defense forces at the Locks, German demolition experts could destroy the gates and operating machinery at all three locks within a half an hour. Furthermore, they determined that it could require workers up to four months to reopen just one lock, and probably a year before all three were fully back in operation. After fielding numerous requests for additional protection from the iron industry, the Lake Carriers Association, and local newspapers, some dating back to months before Pearl Harbor, the Army, admittedly struggling with innumerable logistical problems in the opening stages of the war, finally agreed in February of 1942 to strengthen its forces around the locks.[2]

By the time the shipping season opened in 1942, it had to be obvious to even the most casual observer that the area around the locks, now designated as the Sault Military District, enjoyed an expanded military presence. Elements of the 131st Infantry, the 100th Coast Artillery for anti-aircraft protection, and the 39th Barrage Balloon Battalion, together totaling nearly 7,000 officers and men, had taken up positions there. In addition, the Canadian government organized an early warning system patterned after the Australian/New Zealand Coast Watchers operating among the scattered islands in the South Pacific. These ground observers occupied 266 strategically located posts stretching between Hudson Bay and the locks, where they could radio reports of approaching enemy aircraft. As a further precaution, Canada permitted the United States to set up five radar stations in northern Ontario in September of that year. The Canadian government also agreed to provide housing for American troops deployed on its side of the St. Mary's River. Appeals for fighter bases in the vicinity to intercept enemy planes, however, were rebuffed by the military, which had more immediate needs for planes and pilots on the many active war fronts around the world. But the United States and Canadian governments did agree to restrict air space in a 150-mile radius around the locks. Only planes that had received advance clearance could pass through this zone.[3]

By the end of 1942, however, concerns about enemy actions against the locks began to ease. The Germans seemed hopelessly bogged down in Russia and the Japanese were now on the defensive following their losses at the Battle of Midway in May. Moreover, spare lock gates and machinery parts were now stored at the Sault, greatly reducing repair time should sabotage occur, and a fourth lock, the MacArthur, was under construction and set to open soon. Therefore, orders were issued to reduce the garrison to 2,500 men by September 1, 1943. By the end of the year the joint early warning system had been abandoned and all anti-aircraft guns were removed. In January of 1944 one battalion of military police replaced the remaining troops, and this force was reduced to a single company by the end of the year.[4]

Although their understandable anxiety regarding the safety of the Sault Locks during the early, uncertain months of the war was short-lived, regional and national leaders were well aware that the system delivering iron ore from Lake Superior mines to steel mills along the southern lakes would play a crucial role in the upcoming struggle. The development of increasingly sophisticated mining operations and equipment; the construction and improvement of railroads to the ore docks; the creation of gravity loaders; the evolution of the lake bulk carrier; the ingenuity and perseverance of the designers and builders of the locks, harbors, and channels around lakes; the creativity of designers of ore unloaders; the intrepidity of the entrepreneurs who underwrote much of this growth, and the willingness of state and federal governments to support and encourage this expansion had combined to create a remarkably efficient system that effectively exploited the vast reserves of rich Lake Superior iron ore. By 1941 this system allowed Lake Superior mines to supply 90 percent of the iron ore consumed in the United States, but that system had changed very little since the early 1900s. The size and design of lake bulk carriers, for example, remained virtually unaltered. Granted the number of these large vessels had been increased to accommodate the volume of ore being transported, but the system itself created during the late 1800s, of which the ships were only a part, had been efficiently organized and was left alone to function.[5]

Important changes occurred during the 20th century, but most took place after the Second World War. The final chapter will briefly investigate key improvements to the system since 1907. In addition, it is important to understand some of the negative ramifications that resulted from the creation of this delivery system. While generating financial benefits to Americans at all socio-economic levels, as well as contributing to our nation's ability to successfully supply a substantial amount of the armaments necessary to defeat our country's enemies in two world wars, are undeniable, it is also clear that iron mining and movement of ore in support of the region's steel industry have had a profound impact on the ecosystem of the Great Lakes region. Were the benefits worth the cost? This is a particularly poignant question in light of the demise of much of the region's heavy industries in the late 20th century. While there have been efforts to redirect the economy of the region into a variety of other fields, such as technology, to offset the financial disruption, the scars and residue of over 150 years of virtually unrestrained commercial activity and navigational alterations remain.

Standardization of the Great Lakes bulk carrier had been achieved by the early 1900s. In 1941 John G. B. Hutchins argued in *The American Maritime Industries and Public Policy, 1789–1914* that Great Lakes shipbuilding "reached its greatest effectiveness because of the favorable material transport relations and of the standardization of [ship] design." In *End of an Era: the Last of the Great Lakes Steamboats*, David Plowden observed, "The shape of every steamboat — all vessels for that matter — is determined essentially by what it does and where it is used." This was never more so than "with the design of the Great Lakes bulk freighter — a type of vessel and a form of marine architecture found nowhere else in the world." Citing Eli Peck's *R. J. Hackett* as the template, Plowden reflected on the shape of the freighter that had evolved during the late 19th century and had become ubiquitous on the Lakes by the early 20th century. "The result was a boat that has been described as 'an island with a house at each end.'" Known as "straight-deckers," they "were characterized by a long, unbroken, sweeping hull, and a deck where hatches were placed from one end of it to the other. It was punctuated by a pilothouse at one end and an after house at the other, beneath which was the engine room and fire-hold." But design was not the only thing that remained unchanged. Speaking before the 1961 meeting of the Society of Naval Architects and Engineers about the early part of the century, Bernard E. Ericson noted that the size of the Great Lakes bulk carrier also had stabilized, awaiting further improvements to the region's waterways that would allow them to expand further. Following the launching of the 605-foot *J. P. Morgan* in 1906, vessels 600-feet in length, with a beam of 60 feet and a 32-foot depth, he concluded, "were almost universal."[6]

Even though the size and design of bulk carriers had become standardized, a few builders introduced some refinements. One change found builders integrating unloading operations into ship design. While Huletts, Brown Fast-plants, and other unloading systems designed and built in the previous century remained active on ore docks, the self-unloader, introduced in the early years of the 20th century, enjoyed a growing popularity among those hauling stone or coal. Its great advantage, of course, was the ability of a ship with this device to unload its cargo quickly at any location, whether or not a dockside unloader was available. Self-unloading systems embodied more than a conveyer on a deck boom that swung out from the boat over the dock. A series of interconnected conveyer belts within the hold brought the bulk cargo to the deck conveyor, which then deposited it on the dock. While initially it could not handle iron ore in its rough state, it proved to be ideal when iron ore began being transported in uniform taconite pellets after mid-century. In fact, all American bulk carriers built for the Lakes since 1960 have been equipped with a self-unloader as standard equipment. Many older boats were also converted to include one. While self-unloaders have improved bulk cargo removal over the years, the process required considerable coordination among crew members. For example, as in operations during the 19th century, ballast had to be added to the vessel as it dispensed its cargo in order to maintain stability. Self-unloaders required that the process be closely choreographed by the deck officer because the operation proceeded quickly, with some newer boats capable of disgorging nearly 70,000 tons of bulk cargo in four to six hours. According to veteran sailors, a shorter time spent unloading meant a faster turnaround time at the dock, which added to a more hectic pace to life aboard lake bulk carriers since the 1960s. In addition, relying on self-unloading systems meant "constant maintenance and cleaning during sailing to prevent grit from clogging the operations. The machinery must be ready to swing into action quickly when the boat reaches the next port." As one crewman working on a self-unloader commented, "If anything happens to the boom, the ship is useless."[7]

Mirroring the *status quo* in ore unloading procedures during the early 20th century, ships' power plants underwent limited change. The 600-footers on the Great Lakes remained steam driven with reciprocative engines, even as salt-water ships flirted with newer technologies. David Plowden observed, "Many an old laker built in the first half of the [twentieth] century continued to steam away through the years, seemingly immune to progress." Steam, he noted, "survived on the Great Lakes longer than anywhere else in America." By way of contrast, the British had begun to employ a steam turbine on some of their ships in the 1890s. Although it was able to generate far greater horsepower while taking up less room, early models could be temperamental and difficult to maintain. Still, its efficiency, which reduced fuel consumption by as much as half, found an increasing number of blue water shippers adopting it. In 1907, the (British) Cunard Line launched the *Lusitania* and *Mauretania*, both with steam turbines. The *Mauretania* was able to achieve a record of nearly 24 knots on her maiden voyage, and she remained the fastest ship in the world for 22 years. Meanwhile, Great Lakes shippers, less concerned with speed on the water, doggedly "clung to Scotch boilers and reciprocating engines with little change" during the first four decades of the 20th century. Although the *T. W. Robinson*, built for the Bradley Transportation Line in 1925, employed a 3,600 horsepower steam-turbo-electric engine, the first fleet of steam-turbine vessels did not appear on the lakes until the Pittsburgh Steamship Company launched the *John Hulst*, *William A. Irvin*, *Governor Miller*, and *Ralph H. Watson* in 1938. Another variation of the steam engine introduced at the time was known as the unaflow, which exhausted steam in such a manner that there was no back pressure. This made it ideal for smaller vessels, like tugs and ferries that had to change motion from forward to reverse rapidly. While a few old Lakers were repowered with the unaflow after the Second World War, most had adopted the diesel engine by that time. Pioneered in Germany during the 1890s, diesel engines were first introduced in American Lake vessels with the *Benson Ford* and *Henry Ford II* in 1924. Diesel engines had important advantages over steam: a shortened warming-up period, simplicity, and the fact that a large water supply was not required. At the time, a diesel could "extract more work out of each heat unit than any other engine in the world," making it highly efficient if the initial cost could be written off slowly enough so that operating costs could be influential.[8]

Clearly, the changes in iron ore unloading and ship propulsion on the

Lakes were initially limited and had a relatively minor impact until after World War II. A reduced expectation of innovation and the cookie-cutter approach to ship design and size implied a tacit satisfaction on the part of ship owners and clients that the 600-footer was adequate for their needs. But this complacency was also the result of two locks built early in the century at the Sault, the Davis (1914) and the Sabin (1919). Both were 1,350 feet in length and 80 feet wide, with a depth of 23.1 feet, a substantial improvement on the remaining 1881 Weitzel (515 feet × 80 feet × 17 feet) and 1896 Poe (800 feet × 100 feet × 21 feet) locks. The length and width of the new locks allowed each to accommodate two 600-footers vessels at a time comfortably, but there was only limited space available to handle ships any bigger. Consequently, builders were stuck launching 600-footers; shippers simply ordered more of them to absorb increased demand for bulk commodities, especially iron ore. Although the federal government authorized few new projects on the Lakes during the 1920s, the Great Depression found Congress authorizing funds to deepen

Ice dots the water surrounding ships waiting their turn to use the locks at Sault Ste. Marie, early spring 1905. Congestion such as this slowed down the movement of iron ore and other commerce, leading to appeals to Congress for additional locks. A third lock, the Davis, opened in 1914 and was followed by a fourth, the Sabin, in 1919.

downbound channels connecting the Lakes to 24 feet, a project that was completed by the mid–1930s. Encouraged, ships tried to fill to capacity, but this gave them a deeper draught and prevented many from passing through the locks at the Sault. Industrial demands for iron at the beginning of World War II, however, forced the government to scrap the woefully outdated Weitzel lock and replace it with the MacArthur, which opened in 1943. Its dimensions (800 feet × 80 feet × 31 feet) allowed ships to leave port fully loaded. It also inspired builders to begin thinking about bigger boats, although the demands of the war forced them to wait until the end of hostilities before seriously pursuing the idea. At 678 feet, the *Wilfred Sykes*, launched at Lorain, Ohio, in 1948, was the first to take advantage of the bigger lock, and six years later the *George M. Humphrey* became the first boat built on the Lakes to exceed 700 feet. Once again, builders pushed the limits of the existing channels and locks, pressuring Congress to undertake further improvements. Accordingly, funds were allocated to rebuild the Poe lock in the early 1960s. Begun in 1962, the lock was transformed into a formidable structure (1200 feet × 110 feet × 32 feet), which Washington no doubt hoped would satisfy shipping interests well into the future. But true to form, two days after the remodeled lock reopened in June of 1969, construction began on a new shipyard at Erie, Pennsylvania, designed to assemble the Lakes' first 1,000-foot vessel, the *Stewart J. Cort*. "With the launching of the *Cort*," wrote David Plowden, "the death knell had been sounded for all the old lakers."[9]

Stretching nearly one-fifth of a mile, "1,000-footers," with widths of 105 feet and 50-foot depths, transformed the maritime industry on the Lakes. Powered by two 14,000-horsepower diesel engines, the *Cort* traveled at 10.5 knots fully loaded. More importantly, she could unload 20,000 tons of taconite pellets an hour. As with all Lake bulk cargo boats, she was versatile, capable of hauling 1,830,000 bushels of wheat (the yield of 128 square miles of wheat fields) in one trip. Besides carrying the latest in navigational technology, ships the size of the *Cort* needed additional assistance negotiating narrow channels and the harbors around the Lakes. This came in the form of thrusters, propellers placed inside five-foot-diameter pipes under the bow. They were complemented by a similar pair of thrusters in the stern of the ship. By providing sideways thrust when needed, they give the pilot more maneuverability than possible with the rudder alone in narrow channels or confined harbor spaces. The *Cort,* the new pattern for Lake carriers, was owned by the Great Lakes Steamship Division of Bethlehem Steel Corporation. Even large corporations, however, found the cost for the 1,000-footers burdensome. Seeking relief, they turned to Washington. By the 1960s, the U.S.

Merchant Marine had fallen behind other ship building countries in the production of more modern commercial vessels, such as container ships, becoming popular with shipping companies operating on the world's oceans. Under pressure from the nation's Merchant Marine, including those representing Great Lakes shipping interests, Congress passed the Merchant Marine Act of 1970, which amended the 1936 Act. The act, for the first time, extended United States maritime areas — previously limited to the Atlantic, Pacific, and Gulf coasts — to include the Great Lakes. This made the Great Lakes maritime industries eligible for financial support from the federal government through Capital Construction Fund, part of the 1970 Act. This made domestic shipping on the Lakes eligible for tax deferrals and tax incentives, loan guarantees for ship construction, as well as operating and construction differential subsidies. Almost immediately, shipping companies on the Lakes began using these incentives to begin building super-ships. Concurrently, they began scrapping many of the 600-footers.[10]

Those boats, of course, had been the backbone of the system that hauled Lake Superior iron ore during much of the 20th century, and they had been busy. On the mining ranges, especially the Mesabi, operations during the first half of the 20th century had continued apace. The large, open-pit mines of the "endless" Mesabi iron range yielded tens of millions of tons of high-grade ore annually throughout the early decades of the 20th century. But by the early 1940s experts were beginning to issue warnings that these ore resources were, in fact, finite. With a war on, the demands for increased production of materiel' threatened to deplete the "nation's stockpile of iron ore." In May of 1942, E. W. Davis, Director of the Mines Experiment Station of the University of Minnesota, presented just such a conclusion to the War Production Board. Davis's report became the foundation of an article by Warner Olivier in the November 14, 1942, *Saturday Evening Post* entitled "The Coming Crisis in Iron." Olivier concluded, "This last heroic effort of the ranges [winning World War II] promises to be the swan song of the fine ore in great quantities over Lake Superior, a swan song that will be a melancholy dirge not only to the great steel cities of the lakes, from Duluth to Buffalo, but to our entire economy." While the time remaining before high grade ore disappeared depended on the length of the war, Olivier wrote that "after five years there is no question but that it will be extremely difficult to maintain present shipping [volume]." "It is shocking to realize," he wrote, quoting Davis, "that in a comparatively few years the great steel industry dependent on lake shipments will find itself short of the necessary ore to meet emergency steel requirements."[11]

But there was a solution to the impending shortage, reported Olivier: taconite. Taconite was a low-grade ore found among the deposits of the higher grades of ore on the Mesabi ranges, and, Olivier reported, between 5 and 10 billion tons of it was available. In 1942, however, there was little incentive to mine it. First, most of the mining companies were operating with 50-year leases, which encouraged them to mine as much high-grade ore as possible before their leases ran out. Second, taconite needed to be concentrated to remove impurities (slag) so it could be used in a blast furnace. This process was performed prior to shipping and it produced taconite pellets, "Small, round, artificial pebbles that look like dusty, black marbles." But the process was more costly than traditional mining operations. Olivier reported that "in taconite mining and concentration seven men would be employed to one man needed in open pits." Despite this, several mining companies, including Pickands, Mather & Company, concluded the purchase of land in the Mesabi in 1942 that contained only taconite. The demands of the war did, in fact, hasten the depletion of high-grade ore around the Lakes, which was further exacerbated by the Korean War (1950–1953), an expanded United States military during the Cold War, and a dynamic post–World War II economy. Having no alternative, the ore industry began to adapt. In 1956 the first load of taconite pellets left from Taconite Harbor, a new facility constructed by Pickands-Mather north of Two Harbors, Minnesota, on the western shore of Lake Superior. While more expensive to mine because of the processing, the uniform pellets proved to be easier to transport and finally allowed ore ships to begin employing self–unloaders.[12]

By mid–20th century, the "business-as-usual" operations of the iron ore industry, which had become standardized in the early part of the century, began to change. Harkening back to the early days of ore mining and Lake-borne transportation, challenges had once again prompted the industry to make necessary adjustments. But there was a difference. The innovations introduced after World War II served to enhance an existing, integrated process involving the movement of ore from inland mines to furnaces hundreds of miles away over both land and water. In contrast, the energy and creativity that occurred a century earlier on the Lakes had created that process itself.

Looking back, we sometimes forget that people had choices when making decisions in the past. The lack of familiarity with these alternatives tends to leave us with a sense of inevitability regarding historical events. We know, for example, that iron ore was shipped exclusively by bulk freighters from Lake Superior mines. Were there other transportation alternatives? If so, what were they and why were they ignored or avoided? Another pitfall awaits those studying the past. Tracing a single historical theme over time, to the exclusion of intersecting themes, provides a shallow, one-dimensional view of the past. All too often those studying Lake history have done so selectively, assuming only a limited correlation among developments that were clearly related. Someone who focuses on the history of the Jackson Mine, to the exclusion of all else, would have only a limited understanding of why and how that operation succeeded. Certainly such a student would learn that miners around Marquette conquered the distance between their mines and the shores of Lake Superior, first employing donkeys and later trains. But that was only the first step in the development of a system that made that iron ore valuable. How and why did the newer and larger ships, capable of handling the vast amounts of ore being mined and hauled to the Lake Superior port of Marquette, evolve? How were these increasingly larger vessels able to make unfettered passage across the Falls of St. Mary's and negotiate the St. Clair Flats? Why did mining interests around Marquette not simply manufacture the iron or steel near the mines and avoid shipping the ore altogether? What prompted improvements to the primitive unloading procedures common at Lake Erie ore docks in the 1860s, upgrading them to handle the growing flood of ore? Why did the federal government reverse its traditional reluctance to fund internal improvements and begin to actively support such projects in order to encourage growing economic activity in the region? And what motivated the private entrepreneurs who eagerly supplied the financing necessary for much of this growth? Too many Great Lakes scholars have investigated these and other aspects of the iron ore industry in isolation. Those concerned with Great Lakes boats, for example, frequently trace the evolution of hull design, construction techniques, propulsion, size, or ownership without fully appreciating how external forces, such as government support of internal improvements or design of new unloading equipment, influenced many of these changes.

For many, it simply seems fortunate or accidental that all these disparate pieces of history conveniently interacted together so well. But understanding these relationships, after all, has been the point of this manuscript. To focus only on the evolution of the lake bulk freighter or the contributions of the Corps of Engineers or genius of Alexander Brown loses sight of the interconnectedness of all the components that were necessary for iron ore to move from the isolated mines near Lake Superior to the smelters in the growing urban centers along the southern Lakes. Each component in the system was inspired or its evolution prodded by another component elsewhere in that system. Ships were limited in size initially by the construction materials available and by natural navigational obstacles. Repeated appeals to state and federal governments finally generated some support, which proved crucial in neutralizing several impediments in the connecting channels between the Lakes, erecting a few lighthouses, and beginning an ongoing survey of all the Lakes. Encouraged by these changes, shipbuilders began to experiment with new ship designs and construction materials. These new vessels, some now dedicated to carrying iron ore, benefited from docks designed to load the ore quickly through gravity chutes. But more importantly, improved procedures and equipment permitted the ore to be removed with less effort and much greater speed. Growing demand for iron, and later steel, by railroads, architects, and manufacturers attracted more investors into the iron ore business, all of whom expected progressively better returns. This began a drive for greater efficiency in handling and processing the ore, which included the construction of bigger vessels with greater hauling capacity, which, in turn, brought renewed pressure to bear on Washington to again improve the waterways to allow these larger vessels freedom of movement. Relieved of restraints imposed by strict-constructionists following the defeat of the South in the Civil War, bolstered by the expansion of federal maritime authority on inland waterways through a series of Supreme Court decisions, and pressured by various organizations (such as the Lake Carriers' Association) and port cities on the Lakes, Congress increasingly provided important financial assistance designed to support expanding commercial activities on the Lakes.

Congress indirectly encouraged the growth of the Great Lakes maritime industry by encouraging the development of the domestic iron and steel industry through a series of tariffs, primarily directed against imports from British mills. Under this protection, domestic iron producers, seeking to keep up with growing demand, particularly with the expansion of railroads after the Civil War, searched out new iron ore deposits. The coming of Bessemer steel, however, made ore quality as important as quantity, which quickly focused attention on the rich assets of the Lake Superior reserves. The desirability of coke in the production of Bessemer steel placed the steel manufacturers of western Pennsylvania and northeastern Ohio, surrounded by rich Appalachian bituminous coal reserves for coking, in an ideal position to exploit their situation. Now the stage was set. It became a matter of refining the process of transporting the unparalleled iron ore resources of Lake Superior to the expanding production facilities around Pittsburgh, as well as a growing steel industry in the Chicago area. In the expanding market for iron and steel during the late 19th century, corporations increasingly assumed responsibility for organizing and running the large firms necessary to respond to these demands. Their drive for profitability further increased pressure at all levels to improve efficiency, a goal often achieved through vertical integration of all phases of the iron business. This found its ultimate expression in the formation of United States Steel in 1901, which owned all the mines, mills, boats, and railroads associated with its production of steel. Inventors who could help speed up the movement of ore were rewarded with large contracts. Ship designers and builders of unloading equipment increasingly found it to their advantage to understand and complement each other's efforts. The federal government, aware of the growing importance of the Lakes in the national economy, grew even more sensitive to requests of the region for improvements. By the early 20th century, a fully integrated system had been developed that transported a seemingly limitless, very high grade of iron ore to ideally located steel manufacturers cheaply and in large volume. As a result, the United States entered the new century as the dominant industrial power in the world.

The development of this system did not, of course, evolve painlessly or without missteps along the way. Alexander McDougall's well-considered plans to revolutionize ship design and corner the Lake Superior ore business enjoyed a meteoric rise in popularity. But inherent limitations in his design soon became apparent as demands for larger ships increased. In fact, his last whaleback, ironically named *Alexander McDougall*, abandoned the distinctive "pig snout" bow for a more traditional form. Although it turned out to be his largest "whaleback," this was only made possible because he compromised his revolutionary design to do so.

Another dead end in the evolution of the iron ore delivery system was the ill-fated effort by numerous mining companies, primarily around the Marquette area, to manufacture blooms from the ore before shipping. Initially, there seemed to be a certain logic in this plan. Although unusually rich, the ore was not pure. Moreover, it was rough and bulky in its natural state. Producing blooms could eliminate waste, streamline hauling and unloading operations, and reduce damage to vessels, delivering only pure iron to southern lakes' mills. These iron producers, however, were without a local source of coal and had to rely on charcoal made from the surrounding forests, fully aware that charcoal production consumed an inordinate number of trees and, thus, limited their future prospects in the region. In addition, at least in the early years, many of the open pits for producing charcoal lacked the efficiency of the established pits in the eastern part of the country. Still, Michigan producers persevered and the state ranked second in the nation in wrought iron manufacture during much of the 1870s. The growing popularity of Bessemer steel in the 1880s,

however, effectively shut down iron manufacture in the Upper Peninsula. Charcoal contained impurities and did not burn hot enough to make steel. Since ore traveled better than coal or coke, and large bituminous coal fields could be found "at the backdoor" of manufacturers around Pittsburgh, investors concluded that operations already established in those areas were better suited for steel production. Therefore, the Lake system then evolving to deliver ore was supported and encouraged. Concurrently, searches for new mines in the region began. By the time the weaknesses of Bessemer steel gave way to Open Hearth steel after the turn of the century, as the country demanded more reliable structural steel, the system for delivering the ore had been firmly established. It was now a matter of expanding it to accommodate the increasing flow of ore from the new mines, especially the Mesabi Range.

Despite the proliferation of railroads throughout the country in the late 19th century, investors never seemed interested in adopting this form of transportation as an alternative to Great Lakes bulk freighters. Rail rates were simply too expensive. In correspondence dated May 11, 1888, General Orlando Poe, Detroit District Engineer for the Army Corps of Engineers, concluded that "it is not at all improbable that but for [the Great Lakes] water route, the [railroad] charges laid upon the freight carried [through the Sault locks] would have amounted to $50,000,000. If this estimate is not exaggerated, and I think it is not, then the actual benefit to the producer and consumer was fully $40,000,000." And, the February 6, 1902, *Marine Review* observed, since that time, "The cost of water carriage by the introduction of larger vessels, the deepening of channels, and the adoption of labor saving docking machinery has been greatly reduced, while that by rail has not been lessened materially. The savings is, therefore, greater than ever." Even without the geographic and logistical problems inherent in using railroads to transport Lake Superior ore, and despite the fact that Lake freighters could only operate eight months out of the year, the cost savings alone enjoyed by using Lake ships effectively eliminated any prospect of replacing them with rail transport.[13]

The many benefits that accrued to the nation as a result of the creation of this efficient delivery system, however, came at a considerable price to the ecosystem of the Great Lakes. This is a critical issue since the Lakes contain 20 percent of the world's fresh water, and they supply roughly 80 percent of the freshwater needs of North America. To be clear, those involved in the iron ore industry did not act alone in damaging the region's environment. Soil runoff, for example, from farms within the Great Lakes watershed, much of it containing chemical fertilizers and herbicides, built up at the mouths of rivers entering the Lakes altering, or curtailing, aquatic life there. Untreated sewage from lakeside communities, coupled with discharges from a growing number of pleasure boats using the Lakes, was so bad in some areas by the 1960s that public beaches had to be closed down. The use of high-phosphorous laundry detergents in the 1960s elevated the amount of this otherwise necessary chemical in the lifecycle of aquatic plant life, a process caused eutrophication. As a result, algae spread too rapidly and created blooms that discolored Lake water and choked out other marine life. Basically, the Great Lakes have suffered through an abusive past, which was only exaggerated as the population around the Lakes grew. Following a pattern going back centuries in human history, bodies of water were used as convenient dumping sites for those things that needed to be discarded. Since the Lakes were so large, people reasoned, how could this possibly cause any problems?

Beginning in the 1960s, public outcries led to both joint international and independent regional government actions designed to halt and then reverse the damage, as well as preventing the introduction of new pollutants. But the more studies undertaken on the problems, the worse scientists found conditions to be. Public and private efforts since that time have gone a long way in helping the Lakes to recover, but serious challenges remain.

Some of the disruption to the region's environment was directly related to efforts to develop the system that delivered iron ore. A case in point involved the manufacture of taconite pellets. Since natural taconite contains a low percentage of iron, it must undergo a process that eliminates the impurities, called slag, before it is concentrated into pellets for shipment. Companies involved in this process simply dumped the slag into Lake Superior. One of the components of slag turned out to be asbestos fibers, a carcinogen. The link between asbestos and cancer was not understood until the 1960s. By the time government action stopped the dumping of slag into the lake in 1980, "the floor of the entire western arm of Lake Superior [was] coated with a carpet of asbestos fibers." The fibers eventually found their way into the water intake pipes of Duluth, 60 miles south of Silver Bay, where they were dumped. Although expensive filtration equipment has been added to water intake pipes in the region, the asbestos continues to pose dangers for marine life. Since there is no way to clean up the asbestos, experts suggest that the effects "will continue to be felt for many years, perhaps even for millennia."[14]

The widening and deepening of channels and the construction of the locks at the Sault have opened up the Lakes for larger Canadian and American ships. And although international shipping using the St. Lawrence River and Canadian Welland Canal dates back to the mid–19th century, the completion of the St. Lawrence Seaway in 1959 permitted deep draft vessels from around the world to trade at Lake ports. A substantial amount of this international cargo is grain loaded at Duluth, Thunder Bay, Chicago, Toledo, and other Great Lakes ports located near farming centers. Tens of thousands of jobs are connected to this activity around the Lakes. Unfortunately, these foreign vessels enter the Lakes from all parts of the world carrying water in their ballast tanks often containing new species of aquatic life that threaten to alter the ecosystem of the Lakes. In 1985, for example, scientists began noticing small mussels (*Dreissena polymorpha*) in Lake St. Clair that were indigenous to western and central Europe. Called zebra mussels because of their distinctive striped shells, they reproduce at a prodigious rate (a mature female can produce over 30,000 eggs per season). The mussels eat plankton, which is ideally suited to the warm waters of Lakes St. Clair and Erie. They live their lives in large colonies attached to any hard, underwater surface, and to each other. While individually the size of a fingernail, these clusters can grow up to several inches thick. They have been found affixed to reefs, piers, shipwrecks, boat hulls, and engine outdrives. In addition, these colonies have clogged up thermal power plants and municipal water treatment plants. They have since spread throughout the Lakes, assisted in part by waterways improved for the movement of bulk cargoes, particularly iron ore.[15]

Ships themselves contributed to the environmental damage, which escalated as vessels became more sophisticated and larger. Inherently, canoes and sailing ships caused no such problems of a lasting nature, but steamboats changed all that. Their stacks spewed forth clouds of smoke and cinders, and shorelines of timber were ravaged for the fuel. When coal, and later diesel oil, replaced wood as fuel, the residue from the combustion was deposited in their wake. This became particularly bad in harbors and channels where the slicks of coal dust and diesel oil were concentrated. Although not intentional, oil spills also occurred. Much of this eventually mixed with sediment on the harbor floor and along ship channels. Some of this toxic material eventually made its way into the food chain through fish, such as catfish, known to be bottom feeders. When the Corps of Engineers deepened harbors or channels, dredging operations disturbed pollutants, mixing them with the water. In addition, the polluted sediment was removed and dumped either on the shoreline or off-shore, which spread the toxic material to previously uncontaminated areas. As ships grew larger, their passage through the Lakes created bigger wakes, disrupting life patterns along shorelines.[16]

Fortunately, strong efforts have been made in recent years to address these and other environmental problems on the Lakes. The costs have been enormous so far, and the problems are far from being resolved. Dealing with the issue of discharging ballast water from foreign vessels, for example, still has not been fully addressed. Moreover, new challenges to the environment continue to appear. We might ask how we should we react to the damages done over the past decades by the system created to deliver iron ore. Could that have been accomplished without the environmental damage that accompanied it? Probably much of it could have been avoided, but to have done so would have required people at the time to possess the knowledge and insight of more modern generations. That would be asking a lot of any people, let alone a nation in the midst of a remarkable industrial revolution. Moreover, 19th century Americans believed that God had chosen the country, the first true democracy, to serve as a model for decadent Europe and backward countries elsewhere. John Winthrope's 17th century vision of the nation as the "city on the hill," and its 19th century incarnation as "Manifest Destiny," imbued Americans with a sense of righteousness and entitlement that directed the course of the nation well into the 20th century. Moreover, He had shown His favor towards them by providing the country with lands of boundless wealth. To ignore such riches would be an affront to God. Such attitudes became revealed in the conquest of people, land, and resources. By our standards today, much of what occurred was heavy-handed, short-sighted, selfish, and, in the light of the costs to correct some of the problems created, counter–productive. Yet, judging the people of history by our standards and with our knowledge demonstrates an equally unforgivable arrogance. While we can learn from their errors of judgment, it is unfair to condemn our ancestors' choices unless we use their own knowledge and standards to do so. The damage done to the Lakes by our ancestors, then, was unfortunate, maybe callous, but rarely malicious. Continuing to undermine or destroy the environment today, however, given what we know, is unforgivable.

In *The Progress of America, Discovery by Columbus to the Year 1846*, John MacGregor, quoting from "a Buffalo periodical," wrote, "the present month completes a quarter of a century since the first steamer was launched upon the western lakes. During that period changes of vast magnitude have been affected by the application of the mighty agent, steam. Dense forests, which frowned from the margin of the great lakes, have been felled, to give place to thriving villages." In addition, "the moody aboriginal occupant" has been banished from the area to "wander beyond the limits of the Mississippi." These and other changes "have characterized the introduction of steam upon the lakes." Although these observations were published in 1847, three years after William Burt's discovery of iron near Lake Teal, MacGregor's paean to steam concentrated on its contribution to the development of "the fertility and abounding resources of the prairies," which "have become the granary of the world." Little could he have imagined the "vast magnitude" of change that was about to transform the Lakes in the coming decades. Yet, he was prescient when he remarked on "the independent, inquiring spirit, which so distinctly marks the habits of the people of this country." The transformation poised to unfold in the coming decades was sparked by just such a people. What they accomplished helped to redirect the course of the nation.[17]

Chapter Notes

Introduction

1. *Chicago Tribune* (n.d.), quoted in "The 'Boom' in Iron," *Cleveland Plain Dealer*, January 13, 1880.

2. Richard J. Wright, *Freshwater Whales: A History of the American Shipbuilding Company and Its Predecessors* (Kent, OH: Kent State University Press, 1969); Walter Havighurst, *Vein of Iron: The Pickands Mather Story* (Cleveland: World, 1958); Peter White, "Development of the Lake Superior Region," *Sault Ste. Marie Evening Star*, August 3, 1905 (reprinted in *Inland Seas* 11 [1955]: 99); Alexander McDougall, "Autobiography of Alexander McDougall," *Inland Seas* XXIII (1967): pp. 91–103, 199–216, 282–301 and XIV (1968): pp. 16–33, 138–147.

3. Allan Nevins, *John D. Rockefeller: The Heroic Age of American Enterprise* (New York: Charles Scriber's Sons, 1940) and *Study of Power: John D. Rockefeller, Industrialist and Philanthropist*, 2 vols. (New York: Scribners, 1953). Railroads were the first entities large enough to generate public concern, prompting state and federal governments to consider regulation. Lewis Haney concluded that the nation generally supported railroad expansion until 1850; afterward people sought to limit what they perceived as the unrestricted growth of a powerful monopoly. Their interest changed, asserted Haney, from demands for more railroads to appeals for better ones. In 1870 "the spirit of positive regulation" began to dominate over aid to railroads. (Lewis Henry Haney, *A Congressional History of Railways in the United States, 1850–1887* [Madison: University of Wisconsin Press, 1910]. Reprinted in *Bulletin of the University of Wisconsin*, no. 342, part of *Economics and Political Science Series*, Vol. 6, no. 1, pp. 7–8.) Government regulation in the late 19th century was slow to expand to other industries. While many seemed eager to legislate moral standards (i.e., the Women's Christian Temper-

ance Movement), most people viewed the rise of American business as a positive movement that served to enrich the nation as a whole.

4. W. W. Rostow, *The Stages of Economic Growth: A Non-Communist Manifesto* (Cambridge, MA: Cambridge University Press, 1971); John A. Garraty, *The New Commonwealth, 1877–1890* (New York: Harper Torchbooks, 1968), p. 85; Robert William Fogel, *Railroads and American Economic Growth: Essays in Econometric History* (Baltimore, MD: The John Hopkins University Press, 1964), pp. 4, 6–7.

5. Kenneth Warren, *The American Steel Industry, 1850–1970: A Geographic Interpretation* (Oxford: Clarendon Press, 1973), pp. 88–108, 115–117.

6. Thomas J. Misa, *A Nation of Steel: The Making of Modern America, 1865–1925* (Baltimore, MD: The Johns Hopkins University Press, 1995); Carl Rakeman, "Historic Roads."

7. F. G. Fassett, ed., The *Shipbuilding Business in the United States of America* (New York: The Society of Naval Architects and Marine Engineers, 1948).

Chapter 1

1. "William Austin Burt," http://www.geo.msu.edu/geo333/burt.htmL, pp. 2–3.

2. A number of variables, such as the deviation between compass north and magnetic north or the influence of nearby metallic objects, meant that anyone using a magnetic compass constantly had to make adjustments to take such things into account. Burt's solar compass avoided this by comparing the location of the sun in relation to the surveyor's position on earth. After adjusting the compass for the sun's declination on that particular day, calculated from tables and the surveyor's degree of latitude, he moved an indicator to the approximate time of day and rotated the instrument until it

pointed directly at the sun. As the rays of sunlight passed through the lens, the surveyor could
use sighting vanes on the compass to align with
the true meridian. One obvious drawback, however, was that it needed the sun to function
properly, reducing its value on cloudy days or at
night. "William Austin Burt," http://www.
geo.msu.edu/geo333/burt.htmL, pp. 1–2; *The
National Cyclopedia of American Biography*,
XVIII (New York: James T. White & Company,
1922), p. 367; R. A. Brotherton, "Discovery of
Iron Ore: Negaunee Centennial (1844–1944),"
Michigan History, XXVIII (1944): p. 199.

3. William A. Burt and Jacob Houghton,
"The Needle Compass," Walter Havighurst,
ed., *The Great Lakes Reader* (The Macmillan
Company, 1966), pp. 92–93. Jacob Houghton
was the brother of early Michigan geologist and
explorer Douglass Houghton. He served as the
barometer man on Burt's survey team. "The
Compass Needle," p. 93. If Houghton's recollections are correct, the weather must have improved from the time the party awoke, as the
solar compass required at least some sunlight to
operate effectively.

Before he died in 1858, Burt added to his list
of inventions the equatorial sextant and the "ty-
pographer," the first practical typewriting machine produced in the United States. *National
Cyclopedia of American Biography*, pp. 367–368.

4. "William Austin Burt," http://www.ge
o.msu.edu/geo333/burt.htmL, p. 3; R. A.
Brotherton, "Discovery of Iron Ore: Negaunee
Centennial (1844–1944)," *Michigan History*,
XXVIII (1944): p. 199.

5. Edmund Jefferson Danziger, Jr., *The
Chippewas of Lake Superior* (Norman, OK: Uni-
versity of Oklahoma Press, 1979), pp. 87–89.
The United States government began acquiring
the lands along the southern and western shores
of Lake Superior in 1820 with the Treaty of
Sault Ste. Marie, in which the Chippewas ceded
a 16-square-mile area along the Falls of St.
Mary's. In the 1836 Treaty of Washington, the
Ottawa and Chippewa relinquished territory in
the eastern portion of the Upper Peninsula from
Sault Ste. Marie to the Chocolate River. The
Treaty of La Pointe in 1842 found the Chippewas giving the remainder of the Upper Peninsula to the United States. Finally, two treaties,
La Pointe (1854) and Washington (1855), gave
the United States control of northern Minnesota. In the coming decades these lands
yielded millions of tons of iron ore from mines
located there. Charles J. Kappler, *Laws and
Treaties, Vol. II (Treaties)* (Washington: Government Printing Office, 1904), pp. 187–188, 450–
456, 542–545, 648–652, and 685–690.

6. William D. Patterson, *Beginnings of the
American Rectangular Land Survey System,
1784–1800* (Columbus, OH: The Ohio Historical Society, 1970), pp. 35–36. The meridians
ran north from Vincennes on the Wabash River
to Lake Michigan and north from the mouth of
the Great Miami River. These are the current
western and eastern borders of Indiana. Patterson provides a thorough, well-documented
background of surveying and mapping in the
early years of the nation's history.

7. "The Toledo War," (http://www.geo.ms
u.edu/geo333/toledo_war.html), pp. 1–3.

8. J.W. Scott, "Troubles in Toledo," Walter Havighurst, ed., *Land of the Long Horizons*
(New York: Coward-McCann, Inc., 1960), pp.
291–295. Scott, an early editor for the city's
first newspaper, *The Blade*, also remembered
how Toledo's reputation for malarial outbreaks
and other scourges was used by other lake ports
to dissuade people from traveling there because
they viewed the city as a potential competitor;
"The Toledo War," pp. 3, 5–6.

9. Ibid., pp. 6–7.

10. *Coureurs de bois* (literally "runners of
the woods") were French trappers who
lived amongst the Native Americans in the
upper lakes, often inter-marrying with them.
Voyageurs annually traveled from settlements
like Montreal on the St. Lawrence in over-
sized canoes to collect furs from the *coureurs
de bois* and Indians for shipment back to France.
This trade influenced fashion throughout
Europe and proved so lucrative for France
that furs came to be known as "gold of the
woods."

Reuben G. Thwaites, ed., *The Jesuit Relations
and Allied Documents: Travels and Explorations of
the Jesuit Missionaries in New France, 1610–1791*
(Cleveland, OH: Burrows Brothers Co., 1896–
1901), p. 219; Mentor L. Williams, ed., *Schoolcraft's Narrative Journal of Travels Through the
Northwestern Regions of the United States extending from Detroit through the Great Chain of American Lakes to the Sources of the Mississippi River
in the Year 1820* (East Lansing, MI: Michigan
State University, 1992), pp. 128, 131. Schoolcraft
provides the interested reader with a thorough
analysis of the geology, customs of the native
peoples, and the plants and animals of the Lake
Superior region in the early 1800s; John T. Blois,
Gazetteer of the State of Michigan (Sydney L.
Rood & Co., 1840), p. 41.

11. Alexander Henry, *Travels and Adventures
in Canada and the Indian Territories between the
Years 1760 and 1776* (New York: I. Riley, 1809),
pp. 226–235.

12. Philo Everett, "Finding the Iron Moun-

tains," Havighurst, *The Great Lakes Reader*, p. 95.

13. R. A. Brotherton, "Story of Philo Everett's Trip from Jackson, Michigan, to Marquette in 1845," *Inland Seas* #1 (October 1945): pp. 23–28, #2 (January 1946): pp. 45–49. A contemporary of Everett, John R. St. John, offers a colorful account of his trip along the southern Lake Superior shoreline in 1845. It is quite detailed, even describing the type of clothing and equipment one needed to survive such a trip. *A True Description of the Lake Superior Country; Copper Mines and Working Companies* (Grand Rapids, MI: Black Letter Press, 1846; reprinted in 1976), pp. 12–26.

14. Schoolcraft observed, "The forest trees are white and yellow pine, hemlock, spruce, birch, poplar, and oak, with a mixture of elm, maple, and ash, upon the banks of the rivers. The coast is very elevated, — in some places mountainous, — generally sterile, — and dangerous to navigate." Williams, *Narrative Journal of Travels*, p. 137.

15. Douglas Houghton led a geological survey of southern shore of Lake Superior in 1840. His report of large deposits of copper led many to the region to seek their fortune, this despite his fear that "it may prove the ruin of hundreds of adventurers, who will visit it with expectations never to be realized." Douglas Houghton, "The Mineral Veins," in Havighurst, *The Great Lakes Reader*, pp. 60–61. Copper then was particularly valuable because builders of ocean-going vessels used it on the hulls to protect them from damage and deterioration. Copper was also used to sheath roofs and was a necessary component for making bronze. The challenges initially faced by copper miners on the Keweenaw can be understood by tracing the development of the Norwich Mine, which was located in a particularly remote and isolated part of the peninsula. See Larry Lankton, *Cradle to Grave: Life, Work, and Death at the Lake Superior Copper Mines* (New York: Oxford University Press, 1991), pp. 15–16; Larry Lankton, *Beyond the Boundaries: Life and Landscape at the Lake Superior Copper Mines, 1840–1875* (New York: Oxford University Press, 1997), pp. 38–39.

16. Williams, ed., *Schoolcrafts's Narrative Journal of Travels*, p. 137; Alexander McDougall, "The Autobiography of Alexander McDougall," reprinted in *Inland Seas* XXIII (1967): p. 100 and XXIV (1968): p. 20; U.S. Congress, House of Representatives, *Congressional Globe: Appendix*, 51st Congress, 1st Session, 1886, p. 34.

17. For a thoughtful analysis of the emerging philosophical movement in 19th century America, including the influence of Ralph Waldo Emerson, see Louis Menand, *The Metaphysical Club* (New York: Farrar, Straus, and Giroux, 2001).

18. See, for example, Polk's veto message of the 1846 river and harbors bill, U.S. Congress, Joint Committee on Printing, *A Compilation of the Messages and Letters of the Presidents* (New York: Bureau of National Literature, Inc., 1897), pp. 2310–2316.

19. John Hope Franklin, "The Southern Expansionists of 1846," *Journal of Southern History* 25 (1959): pp. 325, 326–328; Charles Grier Sellers, Jr., "Who Were the Southern Whigs?" *American Historical Review* LIX (January 1954): pp. 335–346. Franklin noted that about 20 southern congressmen, mostly young and new in 1846, could be regarded as strongly supporting expansion as nationalists rather than sectionalists (pp. 330, 333).

20. Of course tariffs indirectly influenced the prices of domestic products as well. U.S. manufacturers, freed from the pressures of foreign competition, did little to cut their own costs. Rather, they usually set their prices at or just below those of foreign producers, which frequently generated windfall profits for them but artificially high prices for consumers.

21. Henry Nash Smith, *The American West as Symbol and Myth* (Cambridge, MA: Harvard University Press, 1978), pp. 147–151; Emory Q. Hawk, *Economic History of the South* (New York: Prentice-Hall, Inc., 1934), pp. 312–313; Herbert Wender, *Southern Commercial Conventions, 1837–1859* (Baltimore, MD: Johns Hopkins Press, 1930), pp. 12, 19–21, 23, 32, 50, 57.

22. Tocqueville to his brother Edouard, May 28, 1831; quoted in George Wilson Pierson, *Tocqueville in America* (Baltimore, MD: The Johns Hopkins University Press, 1996), p. 81.

23. Zachariah Allen, *The Science of Mechanics* (Providence, RI: n.p., 1829), quoted in Nathan Rosenberg, *Technology and American Economic Growth* (New York: Harper & Rowe, 1972), footnote, p. 66.

24. Paul Paskoff, *Industrial Evolution: Organization, Structure, and Growth of the Pennsylvania Iron Industry, 1750–1860* (Baltimore, MD: the Johns Hopkins University Press, 1983), p. 8; Cecil Bining, *Pennsylvania Iron Manufacturing* (Harrisburg, PA: Pennsylvania History and Museum Commission, 1973), p. 49. Fritz Redlich, in his introduction to Johan Lundstrom's *Soderfors Anchor-Works History* (Boston, MA: Baker Library, Harvard Graduate School of Business Administration, 1970), believes that the location of iron deposits was not as important to locating early iron works as Paskoff and Bining do (p. 11).

Fred Albert Shannon, *The Economic History of the People of the United States* (New York: the Macmillan Company, 1934), p. 262. See also Irene Neu, *Erastus Corning: Merchant and Financier, 1794–1872* (Ithaca, NY: Cornell University Press, 1960), p. 49 and Struthers Burt, *Philadelphia: Holy Experiment* (New York: Rich and Cowan, 1947), pp. 188–190.

25. Paul F. Paskoff, "Introduction" in Paul F. Paskoff, ed., *Iron and Steel in the Nineteenth Century* (New York: Facts on File, 1989), p. xvi; Kenneth Warren, *The American Steel Industry, 1850–197-: A Geographic Interpretation* (Oxford: Clarendon Press, 1973), p. 14; Shannon, *Economic History*, pp. 224–225; Warren, *American Steel Industry*, p. 13; F. W. Taussig, *The Tariff History of the United States* (New York: G. P. Putnam's Sons, 1888), pp. 50–59. The April 24, 1846, *Cleveland Herald* reported that the "present tariff" on iron had revived and increased the iron business. The article pointed to six furnaces in north-central Kentucky and 17 in south-central Ohio, noting that "all are profitably engaged." Collectively they manufactured about 37,500 tons of pig iron (sold at $30 per ton) and employed about 12,000 people. *Annals of Cleveland* (Cleveland, OH: WPA Project #16823, 1938), p. 126.

26. Paskoff, "Introduction," pp. xvi–xvii; Shannon, *Economic History*, p. 263. This was the result of the efforts of David Thomas who borrowed an English process known as the "hot-blast" method. While he initially used the idea in a small charcoal furnace, he became frustrated with the limited amount of output because of its size. Charcoal is fragile and too much of it in one furnace will cause it to pulverize itself. In 1839, he built the first of his furnaces designed to use anthracite; he followed this with three more the next year. By 1845 he had built ten, all in the East near anthracite coal fields. Paskoff, "Introduction," p. xviii. Also see, Glyndon G. Van-Deusen, *The Jacksonian Era* (New York: Harper and Rowe, 1963), pp. 116–118.

27. Paskoff, "Introduction," p. xviii.

28. Peter Temin, *Iron and Steel in Nineteenth Century America* (Cambridge, MA: The M.I.T. Press, 1964), p. 2; Census Office, "The Manufacture of Coke," in *Special Report*, p. 22. British iron makers had begun using coke in the 1730s, and had become common throughout Britain within the next 20 years.

29. George Rogers Taylor, *The Transportation Revolution, 1815–1860* (New York: Rinehart & Co., Inc., 1951), p. 226; Joseph D. Weeks, "Manufacture of Coke," published by The Department of the Interior, Census Office, in *Special Report* (Washington: Government

Printing Office, 1884), p. 23, reprinted an advertisement from the May 27, 1813, *Pittsburgh Mercury* in which a newly arrived immigrant offered his services:

To Proprietors of blast-furnaces:

John Beal, lately from England, being informed that all blast-furnaces are in the habit of melting iron with charcoal, and knowing the great advantage it is to proprietors is induced to offer his services to instruct them in the method of converting stone coal into *coke*. The advantage if using coke will be so great that it cannot fail becoming general if put to practice. He flatters himself that he has had all the experience that is necessary in the above branch to give satisfaction to those who feel inclined to alter their mode of melting iron.

John Beal, *Iron Founder Iron Trade Review* January 12, 1884, p. 23.

Taylor, *Transportation Revolution*, p. 226. Weeks ("Manufacture of Coke," in *Special Report*) reprinted the following excerpt of a report delivered to the Pennsylvania senate by S. J. Packer, chairman of a special committee on coal, on March 4, 1834. "The coking process is now understood and our bituminous coal is quite as susceptible of this preparation and produces as good coke as that of Great Britain. It is now used to a considerable extent by our iron manufacturers in Centre county and elsewhere." Weeks considered Packer's conclusion somewhat optimistic since the first documented account of the successful use of coke in the production of pig iron was William Firmstone in 1835. And even into the late 1830s, Weeks notes that "other attempts were made to use coke at Pennsylvania furnaces; but they were unsuccessful or unfortunate" (pp. 24–25).

30. Weeks, "Manufacture of Coke," in *Special Reports*, pp. 26, 31.

31. Weeks reported that an analysis by a chemist of the H. C. Frick Coke Company found that the sulfur content of their coal was 0.784 percent, while the fixed (inherent) carbon content was 59.616 percent. Following coking, the sulfur content dropped to 0.746 percent, but the amount of carbon in the coke rose to 87.25 percent (pp. 26, 31).

32. Frank C. Harper, *Pittsburgh of Today: Its Resources and People*, Vol. II (New York: The American Historical Society, Inc., 1931), pp. 559–560, 574; Temin, *Iron and Steel in Nineteenth Century America*, p. 93.

33. Andrea Sutcliffe, *Steam: The Untold Story of America's First Great Invention* (New York: Palgrave Macmillan, 2004), p. 10; U.S.

Department of the Interior. Census Office. T. C. Purdy, "Report on Steam Navigation on the United States," in *Report on the Agencies of Transportation in the United States, including the Statistics of Railroads, Steam Navigation, Canals, Telegraphs, and Telephones*, Vol. IV. (Washington: Government Printing Office, 1883), p. 1.

34. Before the Erie Canal, residents of Ohio had three choices for transporting goods to the East Coast. They could go overland to Lake Ontario and then ship it by boat down the St. Lawrence River to the Atlantic. But the St. Lawrence had rapids and froze early. Or, they could haul it through the Appalachian Mountains by mule or cart. With little more than rough trails, this option took months and was the least economical method. Finally, there were the internal river systems, ending with the trip down the Mississippi to New Orleans.

35. Quoted in Sutcliffe, *Steam*, p. xii. Alexis de Tocqueville recorded a conversation with South Carolinian and ex-ambassador to Mexico Joel Roberts Poinsett in 1832 that bears on this issue. Poinsett stated, "There is a general feeling among us [Americans] that prevents our aiming at the durable in anything; there reigns in America a popular and universal faith in the progress of the human mind. They are always expecting that improvements will be discovered in everything, and in fact they are often right. For instance, a few years ago I asked the builders of steamboats for the North River why they made their vessels so fragile. They answered that, as it was, the boats would perhaps last too long because the art of steam navigation was making daily progress. As a matter of fact, the vessels, which steamed at 8 or 9 miles an hour, could no longer a short time afterwards sustain competition with others whose construction allowed them to make 12 to 15," in George Wilson Pierson, *Tocqueville in America* (Baltimore, MD: The Johns Hopkins University Press, 1996), p. 645. Purdy, "Report on Steam Navigation," pp. 1–2; Sutcliffe, *Steam*, p. xiii. Andrea Sutcliffe offers a finely researched and compelling narrative about the Fitch-Rumsey competition in *Steam*. She also notes that the confusion and duplicity surrounding this issue was instrumental in creating the first U.S. patent act.

36. Curt Wohlerber, "Robert Fulton," *American Heritage*, 42 (May-June 1991): pp. 74, 78–79; Seymour Dunbar, *A History of Travel in America* (New York: Tudor Publishing Company, 1937), p. 341; See Sutcliffe, *Steam*, for a closer look at the struggles Fulton faced trying to fend off competitors and maintain his state-granted monopolies (pp. 206, 207, 211–219).

37. J.L. Ringwalt, *Development of Trans-*

portation Systems in the United States (New York: Johnson Reprint Corp., 1966), p. 18 (Ringwalt was originally printed in 1888); to understand the impact of the Livingston-Fulton monopoly on the lakes see the *Sandusky* (Ohio) *Clarion*, June 5, 1822, p. 2, and September 4, 1822, p. 1.

Joan Biskupic and Elder Witt, *Guide to the U.S. Supreme Court*, 3rd ed., Vol. I (Washington, D.C.: Congressional Quarterly, Inc., 1977), pp. 90–91. Although it ruled that navigation fell under the meaning of commerce, it did not address whether states could regulate areas Congress did not regulate, or whether Congress and the states could co-regulate. This decision allowed states to continue to control internal commerce. Congress did not immediately begin exercising the regulatory power the court had given it. This only occurred in the 1880s when the interstate operations of railroads and corporations became so powerful that the federal government was forced to intervene.

R. E. Seavoy, *The Origins of the American Business Community, 1784–1855* (Westport, CT.: Greenwood Press, 1982), p. 247; U.S. Congress, *Congressional Globe*, 28th Cong., 2nd Sess., February 22, 1845, p. 328.

38. J.B. Mansfield, ed., *History of the Great Lakes* (Chicago, IL: J.H. Beers & Co., 1899), p. 393; *The Buffalo Journal*, May 26, 1818, quoted in Grace Hunter, "Life on Lake Erie a Century Ago," *Inland Seas* (Summer 1966): p. 197; William Hodge, "The Pioneer Lake Erie Steamboats," in *Papers Concerning Early Navigation on the Great Lakes* (Buffalo: Bigelow Brothers, 1883), pp. 28–30; "Steamships on Lake Erie, January 1936," *Bethel Magazine* (January 1836), reprinted in *The Buffalo Spectator* (1836), reprinted in *Freshwater* (Vol. 5, #1 [1990]): pp. 16–17.

Despite the state awarded monopoly, Livingston and Fulton were quickly learning that enforcing their rights was difficult. There were simply too many inventors and entrepreneurs scattered around to keep up with them all. These battles with violators of the monopoly plagued Fulton and his heirs for years. Mary A. W. Palmer, a passenger on the ship's first trip in 1817 and on its last in 1821; quoted in Havighurst, *Great Lakes Reader*, p. 295; Purdy, "Report on Steam Navigation," p. 669; Dunbar, *Travel in America*, pp. 403–404.

39. U.S. Army, War Department. Corps of Engineers and the U.S. Shipping Board. *Transportation on the Great Lakes* (Washington: U.S. Government Printing Office, 1926), p. 28; "Steamships on Lake Erie," *Bethel Magazine*, pp. 18–19. An article in the *Detroit Advertizer*, reprinted in the October 13, 1847, *Cleveland*

Weekly Herald, reported that the steamer *Detroit,* running between Detroit and Sault Ste. Marie, broke her walking beam, which caused considerable damage to her cylinder. She made safe harbor by "running under canvas" (Rutherford B. Hayes Presidential Center, Great Lakes Collection, Box 2, "Orth's History of Cleveland," File 3, pp. 1847–59). Dunbar suggests that there might have been even more steamships, at least along the East Coast, if shipbuilders could have avoided the legal entanglements involving the efforts of Fulton and his heirs to control exclusive rights over certain geographic areas. *History of Travel in America,* pp. 383–387, 395–396.

Considerable confusion exists regarding details and specifications of vessels on the Lakes and elsewhere during the early decades of the 19th century. While the *Bethel Magazine* reported that lake vessels were pretty much evenly divided between high pressure and low pressure boilers, the *American Railroad Journal* (May 15 and June 1, 1841, reprinted in *Inland Seas,* Spring 1992, p. 51) stated, "The larger lake boats have generally low pressure engines, while those of the western rivers are almost exclusively provided with high pressure engines." Harlan I. Hanley, however, writing in the December 1981 *Journal of Economic History* concluded, "The high pressure steam engine came to dominate the American scene [because it] was particularly well adapted to American conditions. It was powerful, flexible, lightweight, cheap, and simple in comparison with the Boulton-and-Watt-type [low pressure] engine preferred in England." And even though fuel was more expensive in England, this did not pose a problem in America (pp. 262–263).

In *The Abandoned Ocean: A History of United States Maritime Policy* (Columbia, SC: University of South Carolina Press, 1999), Andrew Gibson and Arthur Donovan point out that early steamships initially flourished on fresh water rivers and lakes because early steam engines lacked condensers. Since these engines relied on fresh water to operate, boats needed to have a water supply constantly available to them. Those on inland waterways could simply take the water from the lakes and rivers they cruised. Ocean-going vessels could use sea water, but its brine quickly created a residue that required that the engine be shut down for cleaning. While sea-going ships could carry their own fresh water supplies, the holding tanks required took up room and limited the range of these vessels. Englishman Samuel Hall invented a surface condenser in 1830, which allowed steam exhaust from the engine to be recy-

cled back into water and returned to the boiler. This made steam power more appealing for open water steamers (p. 48).

40. Between 1830 and 1860 the population of Chicago rose from 0 to 109,000, Cleveland's from 1,000 to 43,000 and Detroit's from 2,000 to 45,000. Fred Albert Shannon, *The Economic History of the People of the United States* (New York: The Macmillan Company, 1934), p. 183; See Capt. D. P. Dobbins, "List of Vessels on the Lakes Prior to 1806," (compiled from the account book of Buffalo merchant Dan'l Dobbins), *Inland Seas,* 13 (Spring 1957): p. 70.

41. Garth Wilson, "The Evolution of the Great Lakes Ship," *Freshwater,* 5, #2 (1990): p. 5. The last fully rigged brigantine on the lakes, the *Robert Burns,* proved the vulnerability of this type of vessel when it sank in the Straits of Mackinac on November 16, 1869. The Straits have shoals and reefs at either end, and require diligence to avoid stranding during passage. These obstacles could prove fatal during strong gales, especially for square-riggers like the *Robert Burns* that were unable to respond quickly enough in the narrow channel. In Charles E. Felter, "The Wreck of the Brig *Sandusky*: A Story Dating Back 142 Years," *Ye Olde Fishwrapper* (September 1990): pp. 22–23.

42. Wilson concluded that this arrangement was, and remained, an integral feature of the English schooner rig. It fell out of favor along the Atlantic Coast during the 19th century. To Wilson, then, this combination of sails was more a traditional design than a true innovation. ("Evolution," p. 10). While there are numerous technical books about sailing and sailing vessels, much of this information came from a contemporary source: Captain Howard Patterson, *Illustrated Nautical* Dictionary (New York: Howard Patterson, 1893).

43. Anyone who doubts that the Great Lakes are capable of storms every bit as violent as the ocean would do well to read Herman Melville's *Moby Dick.* In "The Town-Ho's Story," Melville—a sailor with years of experience to his credit—related the story of Steelkilt, a "Lakeman." Part of this narrative follows:

> they [the Great Lakes] are swept by Borean and dismasting blasts as direful as any that lash the salted wave; they know what shipwrecks are, for out of sight of land, however inland, they have drowned full many a midnight ship with all its shrieking crew. Thus, gentlemen, though an inlander, Steelkilt was wild-ocean born, and wild-ocean nurtured; as much of an audacious mariner as any.

Annals of Cleveland (Cleveland, OH: WPA Project #14066, 1936), p. 290.

Bernard E. Ericson, "The Evolution of Great Lakes Ships: Part II," *Inland Seas*, 25 (1969): p. 201. John P. Beck noted that during the antebellum period on the lakes, ships were smaller and their crews could handle most cargoes with little difficulty. After the Civil War, ships became bigger and crews grew more reluctant to assist with cargo loading and unloading. This was particularly true when it came to loading bulk cargo like iron ore. As the ore entered these newer ships by chutes, a group of "trimmers" were hired to distribute and level the cargo in the holds. This was a critical task since ships could capsize if the weight of the cargo was not correctly balanced. ("They Fought for their Work: Upper Peninsula Iron Ore Trimmer Wars," *Michigan History*, 73 [1989]: pp. 26–27).

44. Blois, *Gazeteer of the State of Michigan*, p. 104; Marvin A. Rapp, "New York's Trade on the Great Lakes, 1800–1840," *New York History* (January 1958): pp. 22–24; Shannon, *Economic History*, p. 191. Besides grain moving eastward, these vessels also brought meat, lumber, hides, and copper. They returned with commodities and manufactured goods. In 1990 a wreck believed to be the *Forester*, a small schooner that went aground on a deserted beach along northern Lake Michigan in 1846, was discovered by local residents. Careful analysis by archaeologists revealed that it was carrying 6,500 bushels of grain and sundry other items. It may be typical of the type of schooner operating in the lakes during the 1830s and 1840s, and provides a valuable time capsule of the period's maritime history. See John R. Halsey, "The Reeck of a Small Ship," *Michigan History Magazine* vol. 75 (March/April 1991): pp. 31–36.

Cleveland Herald, July 7, 1847 [*Annals of Cleveland*, Cleveland, OH: WPA Project #16823, 1938), p. 234]. Some grains were converted into whiskey during this period, in part, because it was easier to transport.

45. Ivan H. Walton stated that ideally these shipbuilders preferred oak for the hull and planking and pine for the masts. Nevertheless, they used what they had available, some boats coming off the ways constructed completely of pine or cedar. ("Developments on the Great Lakes, 1815–1943," *Michigan History* 27 [1943]: p. 89). H. C. Inches, "Wooden Shipbuilding," *Inland Seas*, 7 (Spring 1951): pp. 3–12. This essay by a Great Lakes sailor relates first-hand accounts of shipbuilding on the lakes. The article provided much of what follows concerning the construction of wooden ships, unless otherwise noted. Richard J. Wright, "A History of

Shipbuilding in Cleveland, Ohio," *Inland Seas* 12 (Winter 1956): p. 236.

46. While these losses were unusually high, they represent the potential for disaster that lake sailors faced each time they left port. Mansfield, ed., *History of the Great Lakes*, pp. 710–711.

47. These figures were quoted in John MacGregor, *The Progress of America from the Discovery of Columbus to the Year 1846* (London: Whittaker & Co., 1847), p. 778. Again, these figures are estimates and should be understood as such. Beaumont quoted in Pierson, *Tocqueville in America*, p. 294.

Several terms commonly used by Great Lakes sailors might cause some confusion. "Lower Lakes" generally refers to those lakes further along the flow of fresh water to the Atlantic Ocean. The reader should understand that the waters of the Great Lakes flow from Lake Superior through the St. Mary's River into Lake Huron, where they meet water from Lake Michigan to the west and from Georgia Bay to the east. Together this water flows south to the St. Clair River. Here it courses its way through the river to Lake St. Clair, then south through the Detroit River to Lake Erie. Erie's outlet, the Niagara River, enters Lake Ontario. Finally, lake waters enter the St. Lawrence River at the eastern end of Lake Ontario and flow northeastward to the Gulf of St. Lawrence and into the north Atlantic.

"Upbound" and "downbound" also can cause some confusion. If one views the Great Lakes system as a giant river, "upbound" compares with "upstream" and "downbound" with "downstream." Therefore, a ship departing Two Harbors, Minnesota, with a load of iron ore "downbound" for Conneaut, Ohio, would travel with the flow of lake water toward the lower lakes. In this case, the ship would cross Lake Superior, through the St. Mary's River, down Lake Huron, through the St. Clair River, Lake St. Clair, and the Detroit River into Lake Erie, and eastward across the lake to Conneaut. Should this vessel, however, have Gary, Indiana, as its destination; it would travel "downbound" into Lake Huron. But once it turned west into the Straits of Mackinac and then Lake Michigan, the vessel would be "upbound" until it reached Gary. This follows the purest geographic usage in which there is no "up" or "down" per se regarding movement on the planet. But one can indicate water direction as "up" or "down" based on whether one travels with or against the flow of the water.

48. L. Klein contributed an article entitled "Notes on the Steam Navigation upon the Great Northern Lakes" in *American Railroad Journal* (published in two installments on May 15 and

June 1, 1841) detailing his observations of early steamboat commerce and costs on the lakes. He provides considerable information on the *Erie*, which he describes as "one of the finest and fastest." Later he notes that "she carries principally passengers 600 in all." But, he wrote, "She is not intended for carrying freight, but takes it sometimes on deck." (Reprinted in *Inland Seas*, vol. 48 [Spring 1992]: pp. 51–54); Grace Hunter, "Life on Lake Erie a Century Ago," *Inland Seas*, 22 (Spring 1966): p. 26.

49. Quoted in Pierson, *Tocqueville in America*, p. 290n; Hunter, "Life on Lake Erie," pp. 26–27.

50. Klein, "Notes on Steam Navigation," p. 51.

51. Hunter, "Life on Lake Erie,"(Spring 1966), pp. 25, 27–28 and (Summer 1966), pp. 111, 112–114.; Purdy, "History of Steam Navigation," p. 11; MacGregor, *The Progress of America*, p. 774; John Mullett to Sylvester Sibley, April 1834, Burton Historical Collection, Detroit Public Library, quoted in Milo M. Quaife, *Lake Michigan* (New York: Bobbs-Merrill Company, 1944), chapter 15, endnote #3. For a detailed presentation of all American and Canadian steamships operating on Lake Erie in 1836 see article in the *Black Rock Advocate*, March 31, 1836, reprinted "Steamboats on Lake Erie, January 1836" in *Freshwater*, Vol. 5, #1 (1990): pp. 16–19.

52. Fremont, Ohio. Rutherford B. Hayes Presidential Center. The Frank E. Hamilton Collection, in the Charles E. Frohman Collection. A contemporary account of the elegance found on the passenger steamer *Hendrick Hudson* can be found in the May 12, 1847, *Cleveland Weekly Herald* (Rutherford B. Hayes Presidential Center, Great Lakes Collection, Box 2, Orth's History of Cleveland," File 3, pp. 1847–20 & 21).

53. Richard J. Wright, "A History of Shipbuilding in Cleveland, Ohio," *Inland Seas*, 12 (Winter 1956): pp. 237–238.

54. John G. B. Hutchins, *The American Maritime Industries and Public Policy, 1789–1914* (Cambridge, MA: Harvard University Press, 1941), p. 337. British ship-building subsidies were accomplished through a contractual operation system. This found the government contracting steamships for routes established by the Crown, such as carrying mail (pp. 337–338).

55. Ibid., pp. 330–331, 448; Association for Great Lakes Maritime History, *The Newsletter*. Vol. X, #1, March 1993: p. 6: John Codman, *A Letter Addressed to the Honorable John Lynch, Chairman of the Special Congressional Committee of the U.S. Senate on the Navigation Interest: Advocating the Expediency of Purchasing Iron Ships and Steamers in Scotland, Being the Result of a Recent Visit and Extended Observation.* (Boston: A. Williams & Co., 1869), pp. 3–4.

56. Richard F. Palmer and Anthony Slosek, "The *Vandalia*: First Screw Propeller on the Lakes," *Inland Seas*, 44 (Winter 1988): pp. 237, 251; David Plowden, *End of an era: The Last of the Great Lakes Steamboats* (New York: W.W. Norton & Co., 1992), p. 17.

57. Inches, "Wooden Ship Building," p. 7; Walton, "Developments on the Great Lakes," pp. 81–82; Purdy, "Report on Steam Navigation," p. 4; "Steamboats on Lake Erie, January 1836," *Freshwater*, Vol. 5, #1 (1990): p. 18; *Cleveland Daily Herald* beginning November 26, 1847 (Rutherford B. Hayes Presidential Center, Great Lakes Collection, Box 2, "Orth's History of Cleveland," File 3, pp. 1847–69 through 72, 1847–77 through 79).

58. Henry Hall, "Report on the Ship-building Industry of the United States," (a special report in the *Tenth Census of the United States, 1880*, Vol. VIII Washington: Government Printing Office, 1884), p. 148. For a contemporary biography of Ericsson, see *Harper's Weekly*, XXXI, #1567 (Saturday, January 1, 1887): p. 10. Like many of his contemporaries, Ericsson produced a prodigious number of inventions. These included important advancements on the steam engine, the first revolving gun turrets for warships, and an apparatus for making salt from brine. He may be best remembered for designing the *Monitor*, the Federal vessel with an iron-sheathed gun turret that fought the Confederate iron-clad *Merrimac* off Hampton Roads, Virginia, on March 9, 1862.

59. "Steamboats on Lake Erie, January 1836," *Freshwater*, vol. 5, #1 (1990): p. 18; Palmer and Slosek, "*Vandalia*," pp. 241–243, 245; Blois, *Gazetteer of the State of Michigan*, p. 108. The *Vandalia* was able to sail from Lake Ontario into the upper lakes because the Canadians had completed the Welland Canal around Niagara Falls in 1829.

60. Richard F. Palmer and Anthony Slosek, "The *Vandalia*: First Screw propeller on the Lakes," *Inland Seas* 44 (1988): pp. 237, 251.

61. Hall, *Report on the Ship-building Industry*, pp. 168–169; Ted McCutcheon, Millecoquins, "Wreck *Forester* Project Update," comments made at the Annual Meeting of the Association of Great Lakes Maritime History, Tobermory, Ontario, September 14, 1991. (As of the date of this publication, the identity of the ship indicated as the *Forester* remains uncertain. The cargo this vessel carried, however, is not in

question.) Also, see, Henry N. Barkenhausen, *Focusing on the Centerboard.* Manitowoc, WI: Manitowoc Maritime Museum, 1990.

62. *NorthWestern Journal* and the *Detroit Journal and Michigan Advertiser,* quoted in Halsey, "The Reeck of a Small Vessel," pp. 34–35.

63. Arthur M. Woodford, *Charting the Inland Seas* (Detroit, MI: U.S. Army Corps of Engineers, 1991), p. 12.

64. *Professional Papers of the Corps of Engineers,* United States Army, #24, 1882, reprinted in Frank A. Blust, "The U.S. Lake Survey, 1841–1974," *Inland Seas,* 32 (Summer 1976): p. 92; *Cleveland Daily Herald,* December 6, 1847 (Rutherford B. Hayes Presidential Center, Great Lakes Collection, Box 2, "Orth's History of Cleveland," File 3, pp. 1847–75 &76; U.S. Congress, House. Congressman Conger speaking for Harbor and River Appropriations. H. Res. 2092, 41st Cong., 2nd Sess., June 13, 1870, *Congressional Globe,* Appendix, pp. 476–477.

65. William Hodge, *Papers Concerning Early Navigation on the Lakes* (Buffalo, NY: Bigelow Brothers, 1883), pp. 42–43.

66. Inches, "Wooden Ship Building," p. 7.

67. *New York Daily Tribune,* June 6, 1847, p. 2; June 24, 1847, p. 2; *Cleveland Weekly Herald,* September 8, 1847 (Rutherford B. Hayes Presidential Center, Great Lakes Collection, Box 2, "Orth's History of Cleveland," File 3, pp. 1847–53).

68. Jerome K. Laurent, "Sources of Capital and Expenditures for Internal Improvements in a Developing Region: The Case of Wisconsin Lake Ports, 1836–1910," *Exploration in Economic History* 13 (1976): p. 184. The author provides a detailed analysis of funding for the six principal Wisconsin ports on Lake Michigan; Forest S. Hill, *Roads, Rails, and Waterways: The Army Engineers and Early Transportation* (Norman, OK: University of Oklahoma Press, 1957), pp. 159, 177, 192; Thomas D. Odle, "The Commercial Interests of the Great Lakes and the Campaign Issues of 1860," *Michigan History* (March 1956): p. 5.

Although the need for lighthouses in British North America became obvious as early as 1716 in Boston, there were still only 13 in existence along the entire Atlantic coast by 1788. All of them had been built by the individual colonies and were later managed by their respective state. In 1789 the Federal government requested that the states cede control of all these lighthouses, the process being completed by 1795. Initially, the government did not know where the responsibility for lighthouse oversight should be located. Between 1789 and 1852 regulation

bounced back and forth from the Secretary of the Treasury and the Commissioner of Revenue. From 1852 until 1910 the Lighthouse Board assumed responsibility. Since that time, the United States Coast Guard has overseen the country's lighthouses. David W. Francis, "Early Lighthouse Construction on the Great Lakes: A Case Study," *Inland Seas* 44, #4 (1988): pp. 290–291.

69. Goodrich, *Government Promotion,* pp. 9–10, 12–14, 295–296. The author distinguishes between exploitative enterprises, where reasonable returns on investments could be expected immediately, and developmental enterprises, which were undertaken to encourage settlement and to generate new economic activity. The speculative nature of the latter often made private investment capital difficult to find and the return on that investment delayed. If one adds to this the size and geographic challenges of the young country, it becomes clear how important it was for the federal government to assist in internal improvements.

Laurent noted that in the period before 1865 that the rivers and harbors acts "were concerned with engineering feasibility and cost considerations; none of the authorizing provisions required that commercial considerations be taken into account in preparing survey reports" ("Sources of Capital and Expenditures," pp. 186, 188).

Hill, *Roads, Rails, and Waterways,* p. 177; Larson, *History of Great Lakes Navigation,* p. 5. Larson concluded that the Corps of Engineers was permitted to undertake harbor improvements in the lakes because there were too few civilian engineers available, the Corps gained valuable firsthand knowledge that could benefit the nation in time of war, and harbors were important for our national defense.

70. John W. Larson, *History of Great Lakes Navigation* (Washington: U.S. Government Printing Office, 1983), p. 3; Laurent, "Sources of Capital and Expenditures, p. 183; Carter Goodrich, *Government Promotion of American Canals and Railroads, 1800–1890* (New York: Columbia University Press, 1960), pp. 15–16. Gallatin's enthusiastic support of federal funds for internal improvements may have had to do with his background. An immigrant from Switzerland, he was no doubt accustomed to the European tradition of government aid for roads and canals. This sense of government responsibility for such enterprises most certainly influenced his thinking on internal improvements. (See Goodrich for a brief discussion of European funding for improvements, p. 6); Congress, *Messages and Papers of the Presidents,*

p. 2185; Hill, *Roads, Rails, and Waterways*, pp. 184–185.

71. U.S. War Department, Corps of Engineers, United States Army, and the United States Shipping Board, *Transportation on the Great Lakes*. (Washington: Government Printing Office, 1926), p. 244; Lake Carriers Association, *Annual Report* (Cleveland, OH: Lake Carriers Association, 1909), chart, "Yearly Shipments of Iron Ore from Various Ranges of Lake Superior District," p. 122; Peter Temin, *Iron and Steel in Nineteenth Century America* (Cambridge, MA: The M.I.T. Press, 1964), pp. 93, 189, 195; Stephen Blossom, "The Frontier: Handmaiden to Giants," *Inland Seas*, Vol. 39 (Fall 1983): p. 4; Paul Henry Landis, *Three Iron Mining Towns* (New York: Arno Press, 1970), p. 14.

Chapter 2

1. Mansfield, ed., *History of the Great Lakes*, pp. 202, 204–205; Mentor L. Williams, "The Chicago River and Harbor Convention, 1847," *Mississippi Valley Historical Review* 35 (March 1949): p. 608.

2. Congress, *Messages and Papers of the Presidents*, p. 2314; Mansfield, *History of the Great Lakes*, p. 204.

3. Thomas D. Odle, "The Commercial Interests of the Great Lakes and the Campaign of 1860," *Michigan History* (March 1956): pp. 17, 20–22; Williams, "The Chicago River and Harbor Convention," pp. 622–625. The 1845 Memphis Convention sought, as did those southern commercial conventions before and after it, to gain more control over exportation of the region's agriculture production, especially cotton. Part of this plan envisioned an improved and expanded transportation system throughout the South using railroads and canals. Under the leadership of South Carolina's John C. Calhoun, the convention asked Congress to appropriate funds for, along with 17 other projects, navigational improvements to the Mississippi River. Even a strict-constructionist like Calhoun was convinced that such improvements were a key component in the South's plans to open up the nation's interior wealth, including the Great Lakes, to southern ports for shipment overseas. But even his role as chairman of a select Senate committee to review the recommendations was not enough to convince Calhoun's fellow senators to support any of the convention's resolutions. The House refused to even hear them. (Wender, *Southern Commercial Conventions*, pp. 50, 55, 57, 64–66.)

4. U.S. Congress, House. Graham H. Chapman speaking for a motion to amend an appropriations bill to fund certain harbors on the western lakes, 24th Congress, 2nd Session, February 27, 1837, *Congressional Globe*, Appendix, p. 221.

5. Ralph D. Williams, *The Honorable Peter White: A Biographical Sketch of the Lake Superior Iron Country* (Cleveland, OH: Freshwater Press, Inc., 1905, reprinted 1986), pp. 19–21.

6. Ibid., pp. 21–22.

7. Ibid., pp. 22, 34, 49–50; Henry Oliver Evans, *Iron Pioneer: Henry W. Oliver, 1840–1904* (New York: E.P. Dutton & Co., 1942), p. 181. Horace Greeley took a detour to the Lake Superior copper region while on his way to the Chicago River and Harbor Convention in 1847. Although he was enthusiastic about the volume and quality of the copper, he was quick to note problems associated with mining of any kind along Lake Superior's southern shores. Such ventures, he concluded, must be very expensive because of the high cost of labor and supplies, and the lack of local markets. All of these shortcomings were the result of the region's isolation. *New York Tribune*, July 10, 1847, p. 2.

8. Kenneth Warren, *The American Steel Industry, 1850–1970: A Geographic Interpretation* (Oxford, OH: Clarenton Press, 1973), p. 44; Lewis Beeson, ed., Edward Brewster, "From Illinois to Lake Superior and the Upper Peninsula by Steamer in 1852," *Michigan History* 33 (1949): p. 333.

9. Williams, *The Honorable Peter White*, p. 49

10. Williams, *The Honorable Peter White*, p. 49, 56; U.S. Department of Interior, Census Office, 10th Census, Joseph D. Weeks, "The Manufacture of Coke," in Vol. X, *Special Reports*, 1884, p. 31. A correspondent writing to the *Fremont* (Ohio) *Journal* from the region in 1863 said that vessels bound for Marquette used coal from eastern Ohio as ballast. In an article submitted nearly a month later, he described the mining operations of the three companies then operating south of Marquette this way. "The mines might better be called 'quarries' than mines. Indeed the hills from which the ore is taken are nothing but vast masses of (ore) piled up like rocks and covered over with a few inches of earth. Remove this earth, and thousands of tons of ore lie beneath your feet. Any stone-quarry will give you a good idea of these iron mines, provided you imagine the stone to be of a color very near that of new iron." And, he added, "The ore is said to contain from sixty to seventy-five percent of iron." (*Fremont Journal*, September 18 and October 16, 1863.)

11. Ibid., pp. 56, 59.

12. Lake Carriers' Association, *The 1910 An-*

nual *Report of the Lake Carriers' Association* (Cleveland, OH: Lake Carriers' Association, 1911), p. 2; Williams, *The Honorable Peter White*, pp. 61–62. For an account of the controversy, see pp. 62–68; John A. Burke, "Barrels to Barrows, Buckets to Belts: 120 Years of Iron Ore Handling on the Great Lakes," *Inland Seas* 31 (1975): pp. 268–269.

13. Ibid., pp. 75–76.

14. U.S. Army, Corps of Engineers, "Formation of the Lakes" (Form #GPO 643–886) (Duluth: U.S. Army Corps of Engineers, Detroit District, n.d.).

15. U.S. Army, *Report of the Chief of Engineers: U.S. Army, 1920, Part III, Miscellaneous Reports* (Washington: Government Printing Office, 1920), p. 107; Williams, ed., *Schoolcraft's Narrative Journal of Travels*, pp. 94–96. The Treaty of Paris (1783) ending the American Revolution placed the boundary line between the new United States and the British colony of Canada through the Great Lakes. This line used the St. Mary's River as a convenient part of the boundary.

For a contemporary discussion of how Native Americans of the Great Lakes constructed canoes, see Thomas L. McKenny, *Sketches of a Tour to the Lakes* (Baltimore, MD: Fielding Lucas, Jr., 1827), pp. 319–320.

16. McKenny, *Sketches of a Tour to the Lakes*, pp. 191–192; John H. Forster, "Lake Superior Country," *Collections of the Pioneer Society of the State of Michigan*, VIII, 1885 (Lansing, MI: Michigan Pioneer Society, 1907) p. 136; Ivan H. Walton, "Developments on the Great Lakes, 1815–1943," *Michigan History* 27 (November 6, 1988): p. 116.

17. Thomas H. Smith, *The Mapping of Ohio* (Kent, OH: Kent State University Press, 1977), p. 220; Williams, *The Honorable Peter White*, p. 105; Janet Lewis, *The Invasion* [a narrative of the Johnston family of St. Marys], quoted in Walter Havighurst, ed., *The Great Lakes Reader* (New York: The Macmillan Company, 1966), pp. 256–258.

18. Clark F. Norton. "Early Movement for the St. Mary's Falls Ship Canal," *Michigan History* 39 (1955): p. 259, ff; John N. Dickinson, *To Build a Canal: Sault Ste. Marie, 1853–1854 and After* (Columbus, OH: Ohio State University Press, 1981), pp. 8, 21–22; Charles T. Harvey, "Pioneer Sault Canal," *Marine Review*, August 4, 1904, reprinted in *Semi-Centennial Reminiscences of the Sault Canal (Lake Superior), 1852–1855*, compiled by S.V.E. Harvey and A. E. H. Voorhis (Cleveland: Press of J.B. Savage, 1905).

19. Memoir of Lewis Marvill, quoted in Williams, *The Honorable Peter White*, pp.

101–102; William H. G. Kingston, *Western Wanderings*, selected portions reproduced in *Michigan History* 39 (1955): pp. 287, 292; *New York Tribune* (Volume VII, #72), July 2, 1847.

20. *Lake Superior News & Mining Journal* (Sault Ste. Marie, Michigan), 1948; Dickinson, *To Build a Canal*, pp. 24–26;

21. U.S., Congress, Senate, *Congressional Globe*, 31st Congress, 1st Session (August 6, 1850), p. 1532 and (August 30, 1850), p. 1718.

22. U.S. Congress, Senate, *Congressional Globe*, 31st Congress, 1st Session (August 30, 1850), pp. 1719–1720; U.S. Congress, Senate, *Congressional Globe*, 32nd Congress, 1st Session (April 14, 1852), Chart, "Statement of Public Lands Sold, and Otherwise Disposed of, to the 30th of September 1851; Showing, also, the Lands Remaining Unsold and Undisposed of at that Date," p. 1066.

23. Dickinson, *To Build a Canal*, pp. 26–28; Congress, *Messages and Papers of the President*, pp. 2626–2627; U.S. Congress, *Congressional Globe*, 32nd Congress, 1st Session (August 26, 1852), "The Laws of the United States, Public Acts of the 32nd Congress," p. xi; U.S. Army, War Department, Letter from the Secretary of War on the Saint Mary's River and Saint Mary's Canal, January 26, 1882, in House Exec. Doc. #54, 47th Congress, 1st Session, p. 4. For a brief summary of how the lands were eventually dispersed, see Irene D. Neu, *Erastus Corning: Merchant and Financier, 1794–1872* (Ithaca, NY: Cornell University Press, 1960), pp. 151–152.

24. Peter White, in "The Iron Region of Lake Superior," listed the six other investors: John F. Seymour, James F. Joy, J. W. Brooks, J. V. L. Pruyn, John M. Forbes, and Eratus Corning. [*Collections of the Pioneer Society of the State of Michigan*, Vol. VIII. (Lansing, MI: Michigan Pioneer Society, 1907), p. 154]. Dickinson concluded that most had experience with transportation systems. Forbes, Brooks, and Corning were major stockholders in the Michigan Central railroad, with Joy and Pruyn probably also holding shares in that railroad. As costs quickly began to outpace the sale of the land, Michigan Central profits, Dickinson believes, made up part of the shortfall. [Dickinson, *To Build a Canal*, pp. 38, 100.]; Marcus Cunliffe, *The Nation Takes Shape* (Chicago, IL: the University of Chicago Press, 1959), p. 106; Williams, *The Honorable Peter White*, p. 107.

25. Williams, *The Honorable Peter White*, pp. 109–111. (Williams reproduced Ward's letter in its entirety.); Dickinson, *To Build A Canal*, pp. 36, 38.

26. Williams, *The Honorable Peter White*, pp. 111, 113.

27. Ibid., p. 66. Dickinson recounts in detail these and other problems that plagued the workers constructing the locks. (p. 59, passim); Kingston, *Western Wanderings*, p. 292; Merlin D. Wolcott, "Marblehead Limestone for the Soo Locks," *Inland Seas*, 32 (Summer 1976): pp. 105–111; Elijah Calkins, "Report of St. Mary's Falls Ship Canal," in "Statement of Receipts and Expenditures of St Mary's Falls Ship Canal, 1857," pp. 72–73, quoted in Philip P. Mason, ed., "The Operation of the Sault Canal, 1857," *Michigan History* 39 (#1, 1955): pp. 69–70. Calkins also reported that "sabotage" by disgruntled locals was continuing with damage done to property used by lock personnel and to a temporary beacon light at the west end of the canal (pp. 72–73).

28. Dickinson, *To Build A Canal*, pp. 96, 100–107.

29. U.S. Army, War Department, Corps of Engineers. *Report of the Chief of Engineers, 1920*, Part III, *Miscellaneous Reports*. (Washington: Government Printing Office, 1920), p. 3932; Poe's quote in Joseph E. and Estelle E. Bayliss, *River of Destiny: The Saint Marys* (Detroit, MI: Wayne State University Press, 1955), pp. 106–107, quoted in Wolcott, "Marblehead Limestone for the Soo Lock:" p. 111; Williams, *The Honorable Peter White*, pp. 77–78. Harvey's success with the canal opened up other opportunities. In the late 1850s, he organized a group of Eastern investors to start and run several iron furnaces near Marquette. He was also instrumental in helping to bring the first railroad to Lake Superior. In 1868, his future seemed assured when he built an experimental section of the world's first elevated railroad in New York City. Although the project was successful, his rights were suppressed by a rival group and he spent the next 25 years unsuccessfully attempting to recover those rights. He also served as the chief engineer on several railroad projects later in the century. He died in New York in 1912 at the age of 83. Charles Thompson Harvey Papers, GLMS-17, The Center for Archival Collections, Bowling Green State University.

30. John H. Forster, "Lake Superior Country," in *Collections of the Pioneer Society of the State of Michigan*, Vol. VIII, 1885 (Lansing, MI: Michigan Pioneer Society, 1907), p. 136; Williams, *The Honorable Peter White*, p. 78.

31. *Report of the Chief of Engineers, 1920*, p. 3933; Dickenson, *To Build a Canal*, p. 136. See Chapter 3, note 27, for an explanation of registered tonnage.

32. War Department, *Letter from the Secretary of War on the Saint Mary's River and Saint Mary's Falls Canal*, pp. 4–5.

33. U.S. Army, War Department. Corps of Engineers and U.S. Shipping Board. *Transportation on the Great Lakes*, Table No. 21, "Statement of commerce through both the American and Canadian canals at Sault Ste. Marie, Michigan and Ontario, for each year from first opening in 1855" (Washington: U.S. Government Printing Office, 1928), pp. 60–61; Elisha Calkins, "Report of St Mary's Falls Ship Canal, 1857," *Michigan History* 39 (1959): pp. 76–80; S. P. Ely, "Historical Address," in *Pioneer Collections. Report of the Pioneer Society of the State of Michigan*, Vol. VII, 1886 (Lansing, MI: Thorp & Godfrey, State Printers & Binders, 1904), p. 168; *Lake Superior Journal*, August 15, 1857, in Williams, *The Honorable Peter White*, n.pp. 124–125; Crowell and Murray, *The Iron Ores of Lake Superior: Containing Some Facts of Interest Relating to Mining and Shipping of the Ore and Location of Principal Mines* (Cleveland, OH: Penton Publishing Co., 1914), p. 31; *Fremont (Ohio) Journal*, September 18 and October 16, 1863.

34. S. P. Ely, "Historical Address," p. 169; Williams, *The Honorable Peter White*, p. 36.

35. Norman Beasley, *Freighters of Fortune: the Story of the Great Lakes* (New York: Harper & Brothers Publishers, 1930), p. 107; John P. Beck, "They Fought for their Work: Upper Peninsula Iron Ore Trimmers Wars," *Michigan History* 73 (1989): p. 26; Burke, "Barrels to Barrows," pp. 268–269; *Cleveland Leader*, June 6, 9, 17, 21, 24, & 28, 1862 [In *Annals of Cleveland, 1818–1935* (Cleveland, OH: Cleveland WPA Project #14066, 1937), pp. 612–613]. For a first-hand account of the early construction and evolution of the Marquette ore docks, see D. H. Merritt, "History of the Marquette Ore Docks," a paper delivered at the joint meeting of the Michigan Pioneer and History Society and the Marquette County Historical Society, August 23, 1918. ("Harbors — N," The Frank E. Hamilton Collection, in the Charles E. Frohman Collection, Rutherford B. Hayes Presidential Center, Freemont, Ohio.)

36. D. H. Merritt, "History of the Marquette Ore Docks," a paper read by Dr. T. A. Feich at the joint meeting of the Michigan Pioneers and Historical Society and the Marquette County Historical Society, August 23, 1918. (A photocopy of a published version found in the Frank Hamilton Collection, Rutherford B. Hayes Presidential Center, Volume "Harbors — E" Burke, "Barrels to Barrows," p. 268; *Lake Superior Journal*, August 15, 1857, quoted in Williams, *The Honorable Peter White*, n.p. 125, 126–127.

37. Burke, "Barrels to Barrows," p. 269; H.

E. Hoagland, *Wage Bargaining on Vessels of the Great Lakes* (Urbana, IL: University of Illinois Press, 1917), pp. 105–106, quoted in Charles P. Larrowe, *Maritime Labor Relations on the Great Lakes* (East Lansing, MI: Labor and Industrial Relations Center, Michigan State University, 1959), p. 16; John R. Commons, "Types of American Labor Unions: The Longshoremen of the Great Lakes," *The Quarterly Journal of Economics*, XX (November 1905): p. 61; "Longshore work — Treasurer of the International Longshoremen's Association, in *Report of the Industrial Commission on Transportation* (Washington: Government Printing Office, 1901), p. cclxx.

38. Jacob Dolson Cox, Sr., *Building and American Industry: The Story of the Cleveland Twist Drill Company and Its Founder* (Cleveland, OH: The Cleveland Twist Drill Company, 1951), pp. 49–50.

39. F. W. Taussig, *The Tariff History of the United States* (New York: G. P. Putnam's Sons, 1888), pp. 58–59; Shannon, *Economic History of the People of the United States*, pp. 224–225; n.a., "The Tariff on Iron and Steel Justified by Its Results," in *Tariff/Iron & Steel*, John Sherman Collection, The Rutherford B. Hayes Presidential Center, Fremont, Ohio; Robert William Fogel, *Railroads and American Economic Growth: Essays in Economic History* (Baltimore, MD: The Johns Hopkins Press, 1964), pp. 135, 232–233. Fogel contends that the domestic iron industry in the 1840s did not depend on the railroad market. This certainly supports the conclusion that U.S. mills were indifferent to the needs of the railroads because of their local focus, as well as their lack of expertise in pioneering production methods then being used by the British mills (pp. 131–135). John P. King, president of the Georgia Railroad Company, directed a memorial to the U.S. Senate in 1844 requesting that the 1842 tariff be repealed. He too argued that the tariff did little to encourage development in the domestic iron industry. But, King concluded, being forced to use taxed British iron "cripple(s) and embarrass(es) railroad enterprise." "Memorial of the Georgia Railroad Company, January 16, 1844," Serial Set, sen doc 58 (28–1), p. 432.

40. Lewis Henry Haney, *A Congressional History of Railways in the United States, 1850–1887* (Madison, WI: University of Wisconsin Press, 1910), p. 39; Shannon, *The Economic History of the People of the United States*, p. 263; Nathan Rosenberg, *Technology and American Economic Growth* (New York: Harper and Rowe, 1972), p. 73; Henry V. Poor, *Sketch of the Rise and Progress of the Internal Improvements, and of the Internal Commerce of the United States*

(New York: H. V. & H. W. Poor, 1881), pp. xxiv–xxvi; Irene D. Neu, *Erastus Corning: Merchant and Financier, 1794–1872* (Ithaca, NY: Cornell University Press, 1960), pp. 72–73, 79. The July 17, 1839, Toledo *Blade* reported that one could travel the 775 miles from Toledo to New York in three days and 15 hours as follows: Toledo to Buffalo by steamboat (39 hours), Buffalo to Rochester by stage and railroad (nine hours), Rochester to Auburn by stage (eight hours), Auburn to Albany by railroad (12 hours), Albany to New York by steamboat (nine hours). In addition, there was a total of nine hours of delays between Buffalo and New York. [Clark Waggoner, ed., *History of the City of Toledo and Lucas County* (Toledo, OH: Munsell & Company, Publishers, 1888)].

41. Haney, *Congressional History of Railways*, pp. 40–41, 44; Poor, *Sketch of the Rise and Progress of the Internal Improvements*, p. xxv.

42. Fogel, *Railroads and American Economic Growth*, pp. 2–3; Kathleen Bruce, *Virginia Iron Manufacture in the Slave Era* (New York: The Century Co., 1931), pp. 280–290; Emory Q. Hawk, *Economic History of the South* (New York: Prentice-Hall, Inc., 1934), pp. 328–329, 332–333, 336–337, 343–344; Henry V. Poor, *Manual of the Railroads of the United States for 1890* (New York: H. V. & H. W. Poor, 1890), Chart, "Statement showing mileage of railroads in each State and groups of States at various periods since 1835," p. vi, xxii–xxiv.

43. Hawk, *Economic History of the South*, p. 341; Dunbar, *History of Travel in America*, appendix C; Fogel, *Railroads and American Economic Growth*, p. 206; Neu, *Erastus Corning*, pp. 70–71; *Vide Iron Age*, August 16, 1883, in James H. Bridge, *Inside History of the Carnegie Steel Company* (New York: The Aldine Book Company, 1903), pp. 72–73n.

44. Rosenberg, *Technology and American Economic Growth*, pp. 76–77; Warren, *American Steel Industry*, pp. 11–13, 15; Temin, *Iron and Steel in Nineteenth Century America*, p. 2, 55; Fogel, *Railroads and American Economic Growth*, p. 125; Secretary of the Treasury, *Report on Commerce and Navigation* (Washington: U.S. Government Printing Office, 1853), pp. 70–71, 178–179. The report added that German production through the Zollverein to the American markets was minimal, the total for both iron and steel for the fiscal year ending June 30, 1852, amounting to only $322,813 (p. 316).

45. Lake Carriers' Association, *Annual Report, 1909* (Detroit, MI: P.N. Bland PTG. Co., 1910), pp. 122, 125; *Cleveland Leader*, February 20 and June 1, 1865 [*Annals of Cleveland* (Cleveland, OH: WPA Project #14066, 1937), p. 185.].

46. *Cleveland Herald,* June 9, 1847 [*Annals of Cleveland* (Cleveland, OH: WPA Project #16823, 1938), p. 232]; Poor, *Sketch of the Rise and Progress of the Internal Improvements,* p. xix; War Department, Corps of Engineers, U.S. Army and the United States Shipping Board Transportation Series No. 2, *Transportation in the Mississippi and Ohio Valleys* (Washington: U.S. Government Printing Office, 1929), p. 172; Henrietta M. Larson, *The Wheat Market and the Farmer in Minnesota, 1858–1900* (New York: Henrietta M. Larson, 1926), pp. 17–19, 25–26.

47. Louis C. Hunter, *Steamboats on the Western Rivers: An Economic and Technological History* (Cambridge, MA: Harvard University Press, 1949), p. 547; Ronald D. Tweet, *History of Transportation on the Upper Mississippi and Illinois Rivers,* Navigation History NWS-83–6 (n.p.: National Waterways Study, U.S. Army Engineer Water Resources Support Center, Institute for Water Resources, 1983), p. 40; Brig. Gen. B. F. Kelly to Maj. Gen. George B. Mc-Clellan, November 6, 1861. Serial Set, House misc. doc. 15 (37–3), p. 1171; "Payments to Railroads for Transportation of Troops," Letter from Sect. of War Stanton to House, May 16, 1862, Serial Set, House, ex. Doc. 114 (37–2), p. 1137; *Cincinnati Gazette* quotations in George Edgar Turner, *Victory Rode the Rails* (New York: Bobbs-Merrill Company, Inc., 1953), pp. 90–91.

48. *Cleveland Leader,* January 15 and January 26, 1863, and December 5, 1864 [*Annals of Cleveland* (Cleveland, OH: WPA Project # 14066, 1937), pp. 471, 252]; J.M. Callahan, "The Northern Lake Frontier during the Civil War," in the *Annual Report of the American Historical Association, 1896* (Washington: U.S. Government Printing Office, 1897), pp. 342–343; Poor, *Sketch of the Rise and Progress of the Internal Improvements,* p. xvii; J. B. Mansfield, ed., *History of the Great Lakes* (Chicago, IL: J. H. Beers & Co., 1899), pp. 698, 705.

49. *Buffalo Commercial Advertiser,* February 26, 27, March 7, 1863, and March 3, 1865; the *Detroit Tribune* was quoted in the October 26, 1861, *Cleveland Leader,* February 15, 1864 [*Annals of Cleveland* (Cleveland, OH: WPA Project #14066, 1937), pp. 252–253].

50. Mansfield, *History of the Great Lakes,* p. 690, 692; *Cleveland Leader,* August 4, 1862 [*Annals of Cleveland* (Cleveland, OH: WPA Project #14066, 1937), p. 613]; Henry Hall, "Report on the Ship-building Industry of the United States," 1884, p. 218; John G. B. Hutchins, *The American Maritime Industries and Public Policy, 1789–1914* (Cambridge, MA: Harvard University Press, 1941), p. 443.

51. Hutchins, *American Maritime Industries*

and Public Policy, pp. 330–331, 448; John Codman, *A Letter Addressed to the Honorable John Lynch* (Boston, MA: A. Williams & Co., 1869), p. 4.

52. Alexander Smith, "Shipbuilding," in *Reports,* Twelfth Census, Vol. X, *Manufactures,* Part IV (Washington: Government Printing Office, 1902), p. 209; Hutchins, pp. 398–399, 441–442; John Harrison Morrison, *Iron and Steel Hull Steam Vessels of the United States, 1825–1905* (Salem, MA: The Steamship Historical Society of America, 1945), p. 16; R. A. Fletcher, *Steamships and their Story* (London: n.p., 1910), p. 339; Dingle Report, 1882 (House Report 1827, 47–2, vol. 1, Serial Set 2159) pp. 3–4. The report also attributes British shipbuilding and trade success to the active support of Parliament. The government encouraged ship interests by providing "liberal" pay for shippers who undertook mail routes around the empire. The Crown even guaranteed 78 percent dividends to shipping interests. "The merchant shipping laws of the United Kingdom were revised, so as to remove every burden from her merchant marine, and afford every possible facility for gaining possession of the ocean." Unquestionably, such support came at an opportune moment, as new technology encouraged the move from wood and sail to iron and steam.

53. Hutchins, *American Maritime Industries and Public Policy,* pp. 443–444, 447–448; Lamar T. Beman, Compiler, *Ship Subsidies* (New York: H. W. Wilson, 1923), p. 24. It is interesting to note that the British government seemed less enthusiastic about iron hulls than commercial shippers. Early in 1863, a debate in the House of Commons found the members in "vigorous" debate over the Admiralty's policy of maintaining obsolete [wooden] vessels following the experience of the Americans in favor of iron plated ships during the Civil War. In the end, the House agreed to continue the existing policy. *Buffalo Commercial Advertiser,* March 23, 1863.

54. Charles Warren, *The Supreme Court in United States History* (Boston, MA: Little, Brown, and Company, 1932), pp. 239–240; Hampton L. Carson, *The Supreme Court of the United States: Its History* (Philadelphia, PA: John Y. Huber Company, 1891), p. 365; Congress, *Messages and Papers of the Presidents,* pp. 2801–2802.

55. U.S. Congress, House, Graham H. Chapman speaking for a motion to amend an appropriations bill to fund certain harbors on the western lakes, 24th Congress, 2nd Session, February 27, 1837, *Congressional Globe,* Appendix, p. 221.

56. U.S. Congress, *Messages and Letters of the Presidents*, p. 2804; Andrew T. Brown, "The Great Lakes, 1850–1861," *Inland Seas* 6 (Winter 1950): pp. 185–186; Odle, "The Commercial Interests of the Great Lakes and the Campaign of 1860": pp. 11–12.

Chapter 3

1. Williams, *The Honorable Peter White*, p. 147; "Yearly Shipments of Iron Ore from Various Ranges of the Lake Superior District," in Lake Carrier's Association, *Annual Report, 1909*, p. 122.
2. Williams, *The Honorable Peter White*, pp. 147–149.
3. John A. Burke, "Barrels to Barrows, Buckets to Belts: 120 Years of Iron Ore Handling on the Great Lakes," *Inland Seas*, vol. 31, #4 (Winter 1975): pp. 270–271.
4. American Iron and Steel Association, *Annual Statistical Report* (Philadelphia, PA: American Iron and Steel Association, 1879), pp. 17, 32, quoted in Thomas J. Misa, *A Nation of Steel: The Making of Modern America, 1865–1925* (Baltimore, MD: The Johns Hopkins University Press, 1999), p. 4, n. 7. Peter Dobkin Hall, *The Organization of American Culture, 1700–1900: Private Institutions, Elites, and the Origins of American Nationality* (New York: New York University Press, 1982), pp. 227–236, 242, 246. Hall bases his conclusions concerning a postwar return to sectionalism, in part, on the experiences of the nation's railroads. While the Transcontinental Railroad required an organization that was national in scope, railroads that followed tended to overexpand and duplicate routes. Consequently, they "were engaged in frantic efforts to gain returns on their investments, often an impossible task." This lack of profitability, he concluded, sparked the depression of 1873. Only efforts in the late 1870s by investment bankers like J.P. Morgan and Henry Lee Higginson spurred cooperative efforts that helped the nation's railroads to recover (p. 246).
5. "American Industries, No. 33: Manufacture of Rolled Iron," *Scientific American* (March 6, 1880): p. 149.
6. "Veto of an act making an appropriation for deepening the channel over the St. Clair Flats," James Buchanan, February 1, 1860, in U.S. Congress, *Messages and Letters of the Presidents*, p. 3131; F.J. Walsh, "The St. Clair Delta, White Star Magazine (1924): pp. 23–25.
Besides the North and South Passes, there was the Middle Pass and the Pass of the "Cheval a'bout around." George C. Meade, Capt., Topographic Engineers, to Lt. Col. James Kear-

ney, Superintendent Lake Survey, December 19, 1856, in "Report on St. Clair Flats," *Senate Executive Reports*, #46, 34th Cong., 3rd Sess., Vol. VIII, p. 4.
E.C. Martin remembered a trip through the Flats aboard the *Sam Ward* in May 1847. "We steamed up the St. Clair Flats and laid over until daylight as it was not considered safe to undertake to cross after dark as the channel was very crooked and the water very shallow, making it necessary to have the skill and judgment of an experienced navigator and requiring daylight and fair weather." "Leaves from an Old-Time Journal," in *Michigan Pioneer and Historical Collections*, Vol. XXX (Lansing, MI: Michigan Pioneer and Historical Society, 1906), p. 405.
LaSalle captained the first European vessel, the *Griffin*, through the Great Lakes in 1679. He was accompanied by the Recollet friar, Louis Hennepin, who kept a journal of the ship's voyage to Green Bay. Although the *Griffin* mysteriously disappeared on its return trip, Hennepin survived with LaSalle. Following his return to France, he published *A New Discovery of a Vast Country in America*, which recalled (and sometimes exaggerated) many of his adventures in New France, including his trip aboard the *Griffin*. He wrote that Lake St. Clair "is very shallow, especially at its mouth. The Lake Huron falls into this St. Claire by several [channels], which are commonly interrupted by Sands and Rocks. We sounded [measured the depth of the water with a weighted line] all of them, and found one [no doubt the North Channel] at last about one League [approximately three nautical miles] broad without any Sands, its depth being every where from three to eight fathoms [18 to 48 feet] water." Louis Hennepin, *A New Discovery of a Vast Country in America, Extending above Four Thousand Miles, Between New France and New Mexico; with a Description of the Great Lakes, Cataracts, Rivers, Plants, and Animals. Also, the Manners, Customs, and Languages of the several Native Indians; and the Advantages of Commerce with those different Nations.* (London: M. Bentley, F. Tonson, H. Bonwick, T. Goodwin, and S. Manship, 1698), p. 65.
7. Andrew T. Brown, "The Great Lakes, 1850–1861," *Inland Seas* (Fall 1951): p. 185; "Leaves from an Old Time Journal," p. 405; Kenneth Stampp, *America in 1857: a Nation on the Brink* (New York: Oxford University Press, 1990), p. 23. Apparently, the money promised to the Buffalo Board of Trade by the various cities at the 1855 Buffalo Convention for clearing the North Channel proved inadequate. *The Buffalo Commercial Advertiser*, September 3, 1855, reported that, although Buffalo had

pledged $10,000, Milwaukee $3,000, and Chicago $5,000, the project was behind by $7,000.

8. Odle, "The Commercial Interests of the Great Lakes and the Campaign Issues of 1860," p. 5; "A.W. Whipple to J.J. Abert, Annual Report, October 1, 1859," in *Letters and Reports Sent Relating to Projects, 1859–1895*, Vol. 2, St. Clair Flats; Corps of Engineers, Detroit District, Record Group 77, National Archives and Records Administration (hereafter NARA), Chicago, Illinois. Whipple stated that Congress appropriated $100,000 for the St. Clair project in 1856. Yet, President James Buchanan said in his veto several months later that only $45,000 had been earmarked for the work. "Veto of an act making an appropriation for deepening the channel over the St. Clair Flats," *Messages and Papers of the Presidents*, pp. 3131, 3135, 3137. Buchanan argued that, when the 1856 appropriation bill for dredging the Flats reached him, the "object had already been accomplished by previous appropriations, but without my knowledge." This is a curious statement since only a year before the Buffalo convention had met out of desperation over the Pierce veto of funds for improvements to the Flats (p. 3131).

9. "Annual Report of Improvement of Saint Clair Ship Canal, Michigan, for the fiscal year ending June 30, 1879," in *Letters and Reports Sent Relating to Projects, 1859–1895*. The majority of the ships passing between the river and lake chose the new channel, although many continued to rely on the old one. O.M. Poe, in charge of the canal in 1873, recorded that while 5,858 schooners and 3,153 steamers made passage through the new canal, 1,695 schooners and 1,064 steamers used the old North channel. The Engineers continued to focus their maintenance efforts on newer canals. While the locks at Sault Ste. Marie were designed to be 13 feet deep, the lower water levels on the lakes at the time made the effective depth 11½ feet. U.S. Army, Corps of Engineers, *Report of the Chief of Engineers: U.S. Army, 1920*, Part III, *Miscellaneous Reports* (Washington: Government Printing Office, 1920), p. 3932.

10. Speech of O.D. Conger, June 13, 1870, in *Appendix to the Congressional Globe*, 41 Cong., 2nd Sess. (City of Washington: Office of the Congressional Globe, 1870), pp. 475–477. Despite its recent generosity, Congress demanded a change in the way the Army Corps of Engineers reported their survey findings and recommendations for improvements. Before 1865, the Corps was "concerned [solely] with engineering feasibility and cost considerations." After the war, Congress began mandating that

reports begin including the impact of proposed improvements on commercial development, as well as harbors that could be redesigned as harbors of refuge. Clearly, the constitutional issue regarding the federal government's role in facilitating economic development had been resolved. Jerome K. Laurent, "Sources of Capital and Expenditures for Internal Improvements in a Developing Region: The Case of Wisconsin Lake Ports, 1836–1910," *Explorations in Economic History*, 13 (1976): pp. 179–201.

The figure given for the St. Mary's River and the locks at Sault Ste. Marie considers only the amount spent by the federal government. Since the locks were still owned by the state of Michigan, it does not take into account the money spent by the state for maintenance of the locks. Had the federal government been responsible for the upkeep, the appropriations no doubt would have been greater.

It is also interesting to note that a statement showing the total appropriations for river and harbor projects between 1824 and 1875 states that only $625,560 had been spent on the St. Clair Flats. Even this reduced amount would place it far above most other expenditures around the country. "Statement of total appropriations for each work of river and harbor improvement appropriated for from 1824 to and including the river and harbor act of March 3, 1875," in *Appropriations for River and Harbor Improvements*, 44th Cong., 1st Sess., p. 5. The starting date of 1824 in this analysis corresponds with the tariff bill sponsored that year by Henry Clay. This tariff was a key component of what Clay called his American System. This program sought to create an integrated national economy, in which internal improvements played a key role.

11. "Annual Report of Operations for the fiscal year ending June 30, 1877, Improvement of Saint Clair Flats Ship Canal, Michigan," and "Annual Report of Improvements of Saint Clair Ship Canal, Michigan, for the fiscal year ending June 30, 1879," in *Letters and Reports Sent Relating to Projects, 1859–1895*. There was a palpable anger emerging from the reports of the Corps of Engineers regarding the damage done to pilings by propellers, especially tugs. From the perspective of the Engineers, "they [the propellers] deliberately elected to work damage to the United States rather than run a risk of the safety of their own property." Complaints by the Engineers and the increased maintenance costs caused by such action finally prompted Congress to enact a law in August of 1876 that fined vessel owners who "willfully and unlawfully [injure] piers, breakwaters, or other works of the United States

in the improvement of rivers and harbors" ("Annual Report, 1877"). The Annual Report of June 30, 1879, recounted the total costs associated with the canal between 1867 and 1879 as $586,111.56. Most of that amount—$472,837.84—was for construction, but approximately $100,000 was expended to deepen the canal to 16 feet beginning in 1873.

12. U.S. Congress. *Congressional Record*, House, 51st Cong., 1st Sess. August 22, 1890 (Washington: Government Printing Office, 1890), pp. 9031–9032; "Portage and Lake Superior Canals Collection," GLMS 18, Historical Collections of the Great Lakes, in the Center for Archival Collections, Bowling Green State University.

13. *Congressional Record* (August 22, 1890), p. 9032; "Portage Lake Ship-Canal," *The New York Times*, October 17, 1873.

14. F. G. Fassett, Jr., ed., *The Shipbuilding Business in the United States of America* (New York: The Society of Naval Architects and Marine Engineers, 1948), Table 4, "Shipyard Statistics," p. 69 and Table 7, "Number and Gross Tonnage of Sailing, Steam Vessels, Canal boats and Barges Documented on the Great Lakes in Specified Years, 1868–1942," pp. 76–77.

15. *American Artisan*, quoted in "Manufactures of Pittsburgh," *Cleveland Daily Plain Dealer*, January 8, 1867.

16. Weeks, "Manufacture of Coke," in *Special Reports*, pp. 26, 31; Temin, pp. 197, 200. Weeks provides a detailed look at the coking process in the Connellsville region at the time (p. 32).

Weeks reported that an analysis by a chemist of the H. C. Frick Coke Company found that the sulfur content of their coal was 0.784 percent, while the fixed (inherent) carbon content was 59.616 percent. After coking, the sulfur content had dropped to 0.746 percent, but the level of carbon had actually risen to 87.25 percent.

17. Frank C. Harper, *Pittsburgh of Today: Its Resources and People* (New York: The American Historical Society, Inc., 1931), Vol. 2, pp. 559–560, 574; Temin, *Iron and Steel*, p. 93.

18. Misa, *Nation of Steel*, pp. 4–5, Figure 1.6, p. 16; Henry V. Poor, *Manual of the Railroads of the United States for 1890* (New York: H. V. & H. W. Poor, 1890), "Statement showing mileage of railroads in each State and groups of States at various periods since 1835," p. vi.

19. Temin, *Iron and Steel*, Table C.6, "Production of Rolled Iron and Steel," p. 272; U.S. Bureau of the Census. William G. Gray, "Iron and Steel," in *Twelfth Census*, Reports, Vol. X, *Manufactures*, Part IV (Washington: Government Printing Office, 1902), p. 72.

20. Herbert J. Brinks, "The Era of Pig Iron in the Upper Peninsula of Michigan" *Inland Seas* 25 (1969): pp. 228–229.

21. Ernest H. Rankin, "Fayette" *Inland Seas* 19 (1963): pp. 204–208.

22. Rankin, "Fayette"; Brinks, "The era of Pig Iron," pp. 228–231.

23. I am indebted to Thomas J. Misa's *A Nation of Steel* for much of the information on Henry Bessemer and early commercial steel production. See pp. 5–14.

24. Misa, pp. 15–23. The Bessemer Association was the outgrowth of disagreements arising out of a dispute over patent rights. Besides Bessemer's process, several others had American patents on similar methods. By the mid-1860s the struggle threatened the development of commercial steel production in the country. In a closed-door settlement, the parties agreed to divide licensing fees. While the group did not operate mills, they were in a position to not only collect and distribute license fees but also able to control the number of licenses awarded. After several name changes, it became known as the Bessemer Association (pp. 19–21). Temin concludes that in 1880 86 percent of all steel produced in the United States was Bessemer, and that 83 percent of this steel went to the railroads. (*Iron and Steel in the Nineteenth Century*, p. 285).

25. U.S., Department of the Interior. Census Office, Tenth Census. *Report on the Mining Operations of the United States, with Special Investigations into the Iron Resources of the Republic* (Washington: Government Printing Office, 1886): p. 19.

26. War Department, Corps of Engineers, U.S. Army and United States Shipping Board, *Transportation on the Great Lakes*, "Yearly shipments of iron ore from Lake Superior ranges compared with total production of United States," p. 265; Richard J. Wright, "A History of Shipbuilding in Cleveland, Ohio." *Inland Seas*, Vol. 12 (Winter 1956): pp. 36–37.

27. Bernard E. Ericson, "The Evolution of Great Lakes Ships: Part II, Steam and Steel," a paper delivered at the Cleveland, Ohio, meeting of the Society of Naval Architects and Engineers, January 24, 1968, and published in *Inland Seas*, 25 (1969): p. 202; Williams, *Peter White*, p. 181; Wright, *Freshwater Whales*, p. 5; Patrick Labadie, "Peas in a Pod: Some Recent Exercises in Comparative Anatomy of Wooden Lakes Craft," a paper presented at the Annual Meeting of the Association for Great Lakes Maritime History, Perrysburg, Ohio, September 21, 1989; Lawrence A. Pomeroy, Jr., "The Bulk Freight Carrier," *Inland Seas* Vol. 2, #3 (July 1946): p. 192; Richard J. Wright, "A His-

tory of Shipbuilding in Cleveland, Ohio," *Inland Seas* Vol. 12, #4 (Winter 1956): p. 37; The Lake Carriers' Association, "History of the Iron Ore Trade," in *1910 Annual Report* (Cleveland: The Lake Carriers' Association, 1910), p. [pp. 101–117].

Iron ships can carry about 20 percent more than a wooden ship of the same dimensions. This estimate came from the Scottish shipbuilding company of William Denny and Brothers in 1868. John Codman, *A Letter Addressed to the Honorable John Lynch, Chairman of the Special Congressional Committee of the United States Senate on the Navigation Interest: Advocating the Expediency of Purchasing Iron ships and Steamers in Scotland, Being the Result of a Recent Visit and Extended Observation* (Boston, MA: Williams & Co., 1869), pp. 24–26.

"Tonnage" is a confusing term, since it can refer to weight sometimes but can also mean capacity. "Displacement tonnage" represented the weight of a vessel determined by its displacement of water. Displacement referred to the Archimedean Principle that a floating body displaced an amount of liquid equaling the weight of the floating body. "Deadweight tonnage" meant the total carrying capacity of a ship in tons. Builders used an "old measuring rule"—adopted by Congress in 1790—to determine the tonnage of their vessels. It was calculated by using the formula:

$$\frac{\text{Length} - 3/5 \text{ Breadth} \times \text{Breadth} \times \text{Depth}}{95}$$

Not surprisingly, the weight of cargoes varied and caused considerable difference in tonnage records.

In 1864 Congress enacted a new system of measurement to alleviate this confusion. It was simply a standard of measurement, not of carrying power, in which 100 cubic feet equaled one ton capacity. This method followed an age-old method originally based on the number of barrels, called "tuns," of wine that a ship could carry. This "tunnage" became gross registered "tonnage." Net tonnage is the gross tonnage with areas that do not produce revenue—crews' quarters, machinery, and fuel—deducted.

As a result, there were a wide variety of "tonnages" that became possible aboard a single ship. A typical 10,000 ton deadweight cargo vessel also has the following tonnages:

Displacement tonnage	14,000
Deadweight tonnage	10,000
Gross tonnage	7,000
Net tonnage	4,800

"Gross tonnage" was the basis for many marine rules and regulations, and for assessment of drydock fees. This was the measurement referred to as "registered tonnage." This figure generally amounted to approximately ⅔ of the deadweight tonnage. Canadian Shipbuilding and Ship Repairing Association, Ottawa, Canada, *Newsletter*, #4 (April 1961); reprinted in *Inland Seas*, 22 (Summer 1966): p. 154. Also, William Pidgeon, Letter to the Editor, *Inland Seas*, 22 (Spring 1966): p. 77.

28. Osborne Howes, "Commerce on the Great Lakes," *Harper's Weekly, Supplement* (April 13, 1889): pp. 293–296.

29. Alexander McDougall, "The Autobiography of Alexander McDougall," *Inland Seas* XXIII (Winter 1967): p. 200; *Cleveland Herald* (July 28, 1880); John G. B. Hutchins, *The American Maritime Industries and Public Policy, 1789–1914* (Cambridge, MA: Harvard University Press, 1941), pp. 452–453, 455. Although most shipbuilders seemed to ignore iron hulls during the 1870s, the Buffalo yards did launch a few: the *Alaska* (1871), the *Cuba* (1872), the *Arabia* (1873), and the *Arundell* (1878). Only in 1880 did another lake city (Wyandotte, Michigan) begin building iron hulled ships. It should be noted, however, that most of the iron hulled boats that had been produced around the lakes were under 100 feet, mostly tugs and harbor vessels. [*Thirty-second Annual List of Merchant Vessels of the United States* (Washington: Government Printing Office, 1900), Part III, "Iron and Steel Vessels of the United States," pp. 315–334].

30. "Iron Shipbuilding in the United States," *New York Tribune*, Saturday, April 7, 1877.

31. "The St. Mary's Falls Canal," *Scientific American*, Vol. LIII, #25 (December 19, 1885): p. 386; "Deeper Water," *Chicago Inter Ocean* (January 22, 1880), n.p.; "Statement of commerce through both American and Canadian canals at Sault Ste. Marie, Mich., and Ontario, for each year form first opening in 1855," *Report of the Chief of Engineers: U.S. Army, 1920*, pp. 3926 and 3927.

32. Cove [W. H. Gorrill], "Lake and River" *Toledo Commercial*, July 25, 1868. It would be years before outdoor lighting was installed along the St. Mary's and at the locks. In an 1882 report from the Secretary of War to Congress, W. P. Craighill, Lt. Col. of Engineers, concluded that the inability of ships to pass through the St. Mary's River at night generated a loss to navigation in one year of $254,800. U.S. Congress. House. *Letter from The Secretary of War Transmitting Reports on the Saint Mary's River and St. Mary's Falls Canal.* Ex. Doc. 54, 47th Cong., 1st sess., pp. 8–9.

33. Congress. House. *Letter from The Secretary of War*, 47th Cong., p. 5, 7.

34. Ibid., pp. 5–6; "The St. Mary's Falls Canal," *Scientific American*, p. 386.

35. Congress. House,, *Letter from The Secretary of War*, 47th Cong., pp. 7–9; "Report of Major G. Weitzel, Corps of Engineers, Bvt. Maj. Gen., U.S.A., Office in charge for the fiscal year ending June 30, 1881, with other documents relating to the works," in *Report of the Chief of Engineers, U.S. Army*, appendix JJ. (Washington, U.S. Government Printing Office, 1881), pp. 2264–2265.

By the 1870s, Canadian and Americans had begun cooperating in operations on the lakes, which formed part of their common border. In 1872, for example, they signed a treaty that allowed the United States access to the St. Lawrence River, which gave Great Lakes shippers an outlet to the Atlantic Ocean, and permitted Canadians free operations on Lake Michigan, the only Great Lake not shared by the two nations.

36. U.S. Army. War Department. Corps of Engineers. *Report of the Chief of Engineers*, Vol. I, "Improvements of the Detroit River" (Washington: Government Printing Office, 1875), pp. 281–286; U.S. Army. War Department. Corps of Engineers. *Report of the Chief of Engineers*, Vol. I, "River and Harbor Improvements: Detroit River, Michigan" (Washington: Government Printing Office, 1909), p. 777; Odle, "The Commercial Interests of the Great Lakes and the Campaign Issues of 1860," p. 4.

37. The Comstock letter can be located in the Corps of Engineers, *Report of the Chief of Engineers*, "Improvements on the Detroit River" (1875), pp. 283–284.

38. Ibid.

39. Joan Biskupic and Elder Witt, *Guide to the U.S. Supreme Court*, Vol. I, 3rd ed. (Washington, D.C.: Congressional Quarterly Inc., 1997), pp. 92–94.

Chapter 4

1. "Two New Propellers," *Cleveland Herald*, January 24, 1884; *Inland Lloyd's* (London: Lloyd's of London, 1885) and *Lloyd's* (London: Lloyd's of London, 1916); John Harrison Morrison, *Iron and Steel Hull Vessels of the United States, 1825–1905* (Salem, MA: The Steamboat Historical Society of America, 1945), p. 25; Richard J. Wright, *Freshwater Whales: A History of the American Shipbuilding Company and Its Predecessors* (Kent, OH: The Kent State University Press, 1969), p. 103.

The *Syracuse* was 267 feet in length, 38.5 feet at the beam, with a depth of 15.8 feet. Her net tonnage was registered at 1,677. The *Boston* was nearly four feet shorter with a beam of 36 feet; her net tonnage was 1,669. [U.S., *Thirty-Second Annual List of Merchant Vessels of the United States* (Washington: Government Printing Office, 1900), pp. 317, 332.]

Mild steel, while stronger than iron, was capable of being bent or pounded into various shapes. It contained only a small amount of carbon.

2. The *Chicago Times* reflected on the Panic of 1873 in a review of commerce on the lakes in a July 1880 article:

The Panic of 1873 rolled its enormous weight upon the flourishing interest, and it crushed out nearly every vestige of life in it. The crash was general and none escaped save the few lucky ones who, when the "boom" was at its zenith, exchanged their perishable property for filthy lucre, and bore it away to rest amid the tumult of the dreadful disaster. In less than four months vessel property of nearly every description became next to worthless. And until last season no substantial evidence of returning prosperity was noticeable. (Reprinted in the *Cleveland Herald*, July 28, 1880)

3. *New York Daily Tribune*, April 7, 1877; *Engineering Magazine*, August, 1891, quoted in *Marine Review*, August 6, 1891: p. 4; *American Economist* (n.d.), quoted in *Maine Review*, August 20, 1891: p. 4.

4. John G. B. Hutchins, *The American Maritime Industries and Public Policy, 1787–1914* (Cambridge, MA: Harvard University Press, 1941), p. 456; *American Economist* (n.d.), quoted in *Marine Review*, August 20, 1891: p. 4. "Launch of the *Atlanta*," *Harper's Weekly* (October 25, 1884): p. 701. An article in the August 30, 1884, *Harper's Weekly* discussing the plans to launch the first of four steel cruisers for the Navy noted that the United States languished behind other countries that now have steel ships in active duty. The editors noted that even Brazil had recently commissioned the steel-hulled *Riachuelo*. (p. 568.)

In a paper delivered to the 1884 International Engineering Congress, Joseph R. Oldham noted that East Coast shipbuilders had been "governed by ... regulation societies" that followed strict guidelines, which effectively restricted creativity. Lake builders, on the other hand, were freer, leading to greater "variety" in lake craft. This helps explain, in part, the lack of innovation on the part of East Coast builders. [Joseph R. Oldham, "Comparison of the Types of Steamers on the Great Lakes with Regard to Strength, Efficiency, and Location of Machinery," in *Proceedings of the International Engineering Congress*, Vol. II, paper XXXVII, pp. 1–19. Edited by George W. Melville (New York: John Wiley & Sons, 1894), p. 13.]

5. Peter Temin, *Iron and Steel in Nineteenth Century America* (Cambridge, MA: The M.I.T Press, 1964), p. 196; George H. Ely, *Iron Ores: Arguments and Statistics Presented to the U.S. Tariff Commission* (Philadelphia, PA: National Executive Committee Iron Ore Producers, 1882), p. 14.

6. 1880 Log of the Schooner *Thomas Gawn*. The *Gawn* had a successful career for a wooden schooner. It was launched at Lorain, Ohio, in 1872 and operated until 1926, when it was removed from the Rouge River as a total wreck. Captain W. Henry Wallace was with the *Gawn* for only the 1880 season. (Historical Collections of the Great Lakes: Great Lakes Vessels Index. Bowling Green State University Library, Bowling Green, Ohio.)

There were 1,459 sailing ships and 931 steamers registered on the "Northern Lakes" in 1880. [U.S. Department of Commerce, Bureau of Navigation, *Report of the Commissioner of Navigation* (Washington: Government Printing Office, 1897), p. 292.]

Captain Thomas provided no details of the unloading process. We can assume, however, that a donkey engine was employed because it usually took longer than two days to unload a schooner without one.

7. Although only shipped from one port— Marquette, the volume of iron ore in 1873 reached 1,162,458 tons. U.S. Army. War Department. Corps of Engineers, and U.S. Shipping Board. *Transportation on the Great Lakes*, chart of "Yearly shipments of iron ore from Lake Superior compared with total production of the United States" (Washington: U.S. Government Printing Office, 1926), p. 265.

While the *Hackett* was powered by steam, she continued to carry sail rigging. This practice allowed smaller wooden propellers to save fuel by running under sail with a favorable wind. In addition, sails provided an alternative if the steam engine failed. Finally, some continued to employ their spars and rigging in unloading operations. As a result, many lake steamers carried rigging into the 1890s. Still, the growth of vessel size, along with a continuing reduction of rigging during the 1870s and 1880s, allowed for more creativity in unloading.

Schooners, too, continued to haul bulk cargo into the 20th century. And, although it must

have proved tedious for the operators of the rigs, "Tom Collins" could be used to unload sailing vessels. A supplement to the April 13, 1889, *Harper's Weekly* provides an illustration of a Brown rig unloading three schooners at Cleveland's New York, Pennsylvania, and Ohio (NY-PANO) dock (pp. 294–295).

8. The *Cleveland World*, *"The Cleveland World's History of Cleveland* (Cleveland, OH: The *Cleveland World*, 1896), pp. 382–384; *The National Cyclopedia of American Biography*, vol. 33 (New York: James T. White & Company, 1947), pp. 242–243; Williams, *Honorable Peter White*, pp. 189–190; John A. Burke, "Barrels to Barrows, Buckets to Belts: 120 Years of Iron Ore Handling on the Great Lakes," *Inland Seas* 31 (1975): p. 271.

9. "The Iron Ore Trade," *Cleveland Herald*, November 3, 1884; "Hoisting Iron Ore," *Cleveland Herald*, December 10, 1884. While labor problems forced Brown to wait a year before he could assemble his first "Tom Collins," he was able to erect one much faster under normal conditions. The October 20, 1891, *Marine Review* (Vol. IV, #8) reported that Brown unloaders destroyed by a tornado at the Tonawanda Iron and Steel docks were expected to be rebuilt in three weeks.

10. Burke, "Barrels to Barrows," p. 271; Frank E. Kirby and A. P. Rankin, "The Bulk Carrier of the Great Lakes," *Inland Seas* 34 (1978): p. 220. To follow the alterations made to the original "Tom Collins," see U.S. Patent Office, *Specifications and Drawings of Patents Issued from the United States Patent Office, May 30, 1871—June, 1912* (Washington: Government Printing Office, 1872–1913), #231,767 (August 31, 1880), #s 281,011 and 281,446 (July 10, 1883), #295,727 (March 25, 1884), #s 300,689 and 300,690 (June 17, 1884), #s 302,705 and 302,706 (July 29, 1884), #311,285 (January 27, 1885), #314,424 (March 24, 1885), #315,235 (April 7, 1885), and #315900 (April 14, 1885). Also see "The Brown Hoisting Apparatus" in *The Cleveland Herald*, January 20, 1884.

Brown's invention was equally adept at unloading coal, limestone, sand, and a variety of other bulk materials. He established the Brown Hoist and Conveying Company in 1883 to further refine ore unloading. His work attracted the interest of a number of manufacturing and shipbuilding firms from around the world. Representatives from England's Vickers Sons & Maxim in England and Germany's Krupp Iron Works visited Brown's Cleveland firm for ideas and inspiration. In 1887 the Cleveland Shipbuilding Company contracted with Brown's firm to build a traveling crane to move unwieldy material during vessel construction. Three years later he built similar machines for the Chicago Shipbuilding Company. When he died in 1911, Brown held nearly 100 patents in a variety of fields. For example, he built the first cantilevered shipbuilding crane and trestle at Newport News, Virginia, in 1898. Seven years later he designed and built wireless radio antennae in Massachusetts and Scotland, which, at the time, were the highest such masts ever erected. [*National Cyclopedia*, p. 343; *Marine Review*, III (01/08/1891), pp. 3–4, quoted in Wright, *Freshwater Whales*, pp. 12–13; Brown Hoisting Machinery Company, *"Brownhoist" General Catalogue* (Cleveland, OH: Brown Hoisting Machinery Company, 1919), p. 9.]

11. The Elstner Publishing Company, *The Industries of Cleveland* (Cleveland, OH: The Elstner Publishing Company, 1888), p. 119; Eric Hirsimaki, "The Huron Hustler," *Nickel Plate Road Magazine*, XXII (Winter/Spring 1988): pp. 12–13; Burke, "Barrels to Barrows," p. 273; "Hoisting Iron Ore," *Cleveland Herald*, December 10, 1884.

12. Williams, *Honorable Peter White*, p. 190; Burke, "Barrels to Barrows:" p. 272; "The Iron Ore Trade," *The Cleveland Herald*, November 3, 1884. Aspin's patent (#275,849) was recorded on April 17, 1883, and included the names B.F. Porter and J.P. Bloom. Patent Office, *Specifi-cations of Patents*, Vol. 576 (Washington: Government Printing Office, 1883), pp. 1286–1287. The Fleming-Stovering unloader used "buckets, when loaded [that were] carried back on a simple wooden truss and emptied where desired."

13. Burke, "Barrels to Barrows:" p. 272. Burke tells of a variation of the Champion hoist built on a forgotten Cleveland dock by an unknown inventor, probably in the mid-1880s. Instead of stopping at vertical like Aspin's creation, this system allowed the boom to arc 180 degrees, from dockside to off-dock storage. "It is suspected," concluded Burke, "that the rigs never worked well, if at all" (pp. 272–273).

14. *The Cleveland World's History of Cleveland* (Cleveland, OH: The Cleveland World, 1891), 273; Burke, "Barrels to Buckets," p. 273.

Brown's initial success with the "Tom Collins" encouraged him to establish the Brown Hoist and Conveying Company in Cleveland in 1883. With his father Fayette Brown serving as president, the company designed and built variations of the "Tom Collins," as well as other specialized machinery involved in conveying and manufacturing. The initial capital investment of $100,000, noted the *World's History of*

Cleveland, built "one of the most notable manufacturing organizations of Cleveland, and indeed, the country" (p. 384).

15. Burke, "Barrels to Barrows," p. 274.

16. "Commerce on the Great Lakes," *Harper's Weekly* (April 13, 1889): pp. 293–296; Henry Penton, "Low Cost of Lake Transportation," *Marine Review* 58 (December 1928): p. 37; W. Livingston to Harvey Brown, August 5, 1889, Harvey H. Brown Papers (MSS 3342), Western Reserve Historical Society, Cleveland, Ohio.

Shipping on the Great Lakes is subject to seasonal changes. Since the lakes contain fresh water and are located above the 40th parallel, they usually freeze over during winter. This was particularly true in the colder average temperatures of the late 19th century. Most shippers on the lakes planned on seven to eight months of clear sailing each year.

17. John R. Commons, "Types of American Labor Unions: The Longshoremen of the Great Lakes," *The Quarterly Journal of Economics*, XX (November 1905): p. 66. Commons explains that under the old system workers received around $600 per year. Those doing clean up earned around $500 per year. The younger, stronger workers preferred shoveling into the old-style buckets; the older men seemed pleased to work for less money on clean up.

18. John Garraty, *The New Commonwealth: 1877–1890*. (New York: Harper Torchbooks, 1968), p. 128; Charles P. Larrowe, *Maritime Labor Relations on the Great Lakes*. (East Lansing, MI: Labor and Industrial Relations Center, Michigan State University, 1959), p. 15. Garraty provides examples of the decline in the cost of living and increased wages that generally accompanied the industrialization of the country beginning in the late 1870s. By the 1880s, he observed, real wages were up about 25 percent.

Ore trimmers were employed on ore and coal docks to make sure that a sailing ship's bulk cargo was properly leveled in the hold. Failure to do so meant that the vessel would ride unevenly and could prove difficult to handle, especially in bad weather. See John Beck, "They Fought for their Work," *Michigan History* (January/February 1989): p. 27.

19. John P. Beck, "They Fought for their Work: Upper Peninsula Iron Ore Trimmer Wars," *Michigan History* 73 (1989): pp. 26–27); Edward S. Warner and Colleen (Oihus) Warner, "Lives and Times in the Great Lakes Commercial Trade Under Sail," *Hayes Historical Journal* (Fall 1991): p. 6, 7, 11. The excerpted portions were quoted from R. L. Polk, *Directory of the*

Marine Interests of the Great Lakes (Detroit, MI: R.L. Polk & Company, 1884), p. 422, and from the Warners' article. The latter used the financial accounts of the schooner *W. S. Lyons*, 1871, found in the archives of the Great Lakes Historical Society, Vermilion, Ohio. The authors also noted that, even though Congress had mandated the establishment of marine hospitals, seamen were assessed a fee, known as "hospital dues," to cover their medical costs if they were admitted in an emergency. This, of course, reduced their already meager rate of pay even further (p. 10).

20. Eric Arnesen, "American Workers and the Labor Movement in the Late Nineteenth Century," in Charles W. Calhoun, Ed., *The Gilded Age: Essays on the Origins of Modern America*. (Wilmington, Delaware: Scholarly Resources, Inc., 1996), p. 42.

21. Jay C. Martin, "The Principle of Beneficence: The Early History of the International Ship Masters' Association, 1886–1917," *Hayes Historical Journal* (Fall 1991): pp. 29–31; R. L. Polk, *Directory of the Marine Interests of the Great Lakes* (Detroit: R. L. Polk & Co., 1884), p. 420: *Preamble, Constitution and By-laws of the Ship Carpenters and Caulkers Protective Association of the City of Cleveland* (Cleveland, OH: Fairbanks, Benedict & Co., 1861), The Western Reserve Historical Society, Cleveland, Ohio.

It is clear from their preamble that the ship carpenters and caulkers had other issues in mind when they formed their association. "Certain vagaries have been adapted in the modern constitution and formation of society, upon which have been based false and repulsive distinctions, calculated to elevate wealth above labor in the social and political scale, and to reduce the producers to a grade where preferments and honors will never reach them. Such causes and such affects," they continued, "are, in our opinion, anti-republican and inconsistent with the true spirit of American institutions; and require at least an effort on our part to overthrow them, before the consequences shall be more fully established and more disastrously entailed upon the ship carpenters and caulkers of the city of Cleveland." They concluded, "We recognize no rule of action or principle that would elevate wealth above industry, or the professional man above the mechanic. We pledge ourselves, individually and collectively, to every laudable means to carry out the principle of equal rights and equal privileges in society."

Great Lakes sailors also sought to influence the federal government on safety issues. A Jan-

uary 1888 convention in Toledo, Ohio, which brought together delegates that represented "more than 5,000 seamen of the great chain of lakes," delivered a resolution to Congress asking that the Treasury Department be more diligent in preventing the overloading of ships on the lakes. Such a practice, they insisted, contributed to the loss of 73 ships, $2.5 million of cargo, and 204 lives in 1887. (U.S. Congress, *Misc. Doc. # 190*, "Overloading of Vessels on Great Lakes, etc.," 50th Congress, 1st Session, February 9, 1888).

22. Lake Carriers Association (GLMS 44, Box 117), Center for Archival Collections, Bowling Green State University. The minutes of the Cleveland Vessel Owners contain a handwritten record of all their meetings. It is also periodically augmented with newspaper clippings that provide details of resolutions passed in their meetings.

23. Ibid. George H. Ely, *American Iron Ores: Arguments and Statistics Presented to the United States Tariff Commission* (Philadelphia, PA: National Executive Committee, Iron Ore Producers, 1882), pp. 11, 13, 16. Ely had also written about rail freight charges from Lake Erie to the Pennsylvania furnaces were about the same as the charges from the Atlantic coast, where the imported ore arrived. In addition, he noted that ocean freight costs from Spain were low because American shippers backhauled Spanish ore to avoid returning empty. Finally, imported ore was less expensive because Spanish miners were paid less than their American counterparts.

The 1884 treaty with Spain sought to ease trade restrictions between the United States and the Spanish colonies of Cuba and Puerto Rico. Some Americans had invested in iron mines in Cuba and the Association realized that this ore could have a negative impact on the Lake Superior mining industry, which was an important customer of the vessel owners. The threat made by the importation of foreign ores was real. In the late 1880s, the Pennsylvania Steel Company, for example, obtained an interest in the Juragua mines in Cuba, which sent ore to the firm's subsidiary, the Maryland Steel Company, located on Chesapeake Bay. It began producing Bessemer steel in 1891. ("Progress of the Maryland Steel Company," *Scientific American*, July 23, 1891: p. 56.)

The Association also fought to establish a uniform method of steering vessels in 1887. This was a safety issue caused by two different designs employed in steering lake vessels. Simply put, one method turned the vessel in the direction the pilot turned the wheel; the other turned the ship in the opposite direction he turned the wheel. For pilots changing ships, this could be a serious problem, especially in emergency situations where one had to react without thinking.

24. Jerome K Laurent, "Trade Associations and Competition in Great Lakes Shipping: The Pre–World War I Years," *International Journal of Maritime History*, Vol. IV, no. II (December 1992): pp. 118–120; "Agency History," Lake Carriers' Association, GLMS-44, Historical Collections of the Great Lakes, Jerome Library, Bowling Green State University, Bowling Green, Ohio.

25. Ibid., pp. 121–122.

26. Walter Havighurst, *Vein of Iron: The Pickands Mather Story* (Cleveland, OH: The World Publishing Co., 1958), p. 43; *Toledo Blade*, December 23, 1867, from an article reprinted by the *Marquette Star*(n.d.). But, as George Ely wrote, none of these mines would have survived without protective tariff that ensured their profitability. (*American Iron Ore*, pp. 7, 10).

27. Ibid., pp. 9–11, 15–16, 18–24; Polk, *Directory of the Marine Interests of the Great Lakes*, p. 259. The iron merchants in Cleveland in the 1870s and 1880s clustered in the area around St. Clair and Water (now W. 9th) streets.

28. Havighurst, *Vein of Iron*, pp. 34–36, 38–39, 41, 45, 47.

29. Pickands, Mather, and Company, Annual Statements, Container 1, Folders 1 (1889) and 2 (1891), The Western Reserve Historical Society, Cleveland, Ohio. The term "back-haul" refers to cargo carried by ships on their return voyages. This helps offset expenses that would accrue if the vessel returned "in ballast," that is, without cargo. In other words, it helps ensure the ship's profitability.

30. Corps of Engineers and United States Shipping Board, *Transportation on the Great Lakes*, p. 265; Lake Carriers' Association, *1910 Annual Report of the Lake Carriers' Association* (Cleveland: Lake Carriers' Association, 1910), pp. 4–5. The four Lake Superior mining ranges in 1884 were the Marquette, Menominee, Gogebic, and Vermilion. The latter two had only begun operation that year.

31. Misa, *A Nation of Steel*, pp. 39–40; Henry V. Poor, *Manual of the Railroads of the United States for 1890* (New York: H. V. & H. W. Poor, 1890), pp. vi, viii; Temin, *Iron and Steel in Nineteenth Century America*, pp. 222–223.

32. "Making Bessemer Rails," *Harper's Weekly* (April 10, 1886): p. 238.

33. Temin, *Iron and Steel in Nineteenth Century America*, p. 223; U.S. *Congressional Record*,

51st Congress, 1st Session, Senate, September 1, 1890 (Washington: Government Printing Office, 1890), p. 9459; "The Increasing Use of Steel Castings," *Scientific American* (July 17, 1880): p. 42; Paul F. Paskoff, ed., *Iron and Steel in the Nineteenth Century* (New York: Facts on File, 1989), p. xxxvii; Dennis Cashman, *America in the Age of Titans: The Progressive Era and World War I* (New York: New York University Press, 1988), p. 347; "Steel Tow Lines," *Scientific America* (September 14, 1878): p. 168.

34. Misa, *A Nation of Steel*, pp. 95–97.

35. "The Clapp-Griffiths Steel Process," *Scientific American* (March 27, 1886): p. 195.

36. "The Use of Steel for Structural Purposes," *Scientific American* (May 15, 1880): p. 304; "The Clapp-Griffiths Steel Process," *Scientific American* (March 27, 1886): pp. 195–197; "The Basic Steel Process," *Scientific American* (July 24, 1886): pp. 48–49. Thomas Misa's *A Nation of Steel* provides a detailed account of the struggle to develop structural steel in the late 19th century. His discussion of Bessemer steel's weaknesses and the development of Open Hearth steel are particularly recommended. See Chapter 2, "The Structure of Cities, 1880–1900," pp. 45–89.

37. Walter Miller, "Marine Engineering on the Great Lakes — Past and Present," *Beeson's Marine Directory* (Chicago: Harvey C. Beeson, 1897), p. 245; Commissioner of Navigation, *Report of the Commissioner of Navigation to the Secretary of the Treasury* (Washington: Government Printing Office, 1897), chart of registered gross tonnage by year (1868–1897) for the Lakes, p. 292.

38. U.S. Congress, House, Representative Theodore E. Burton, "The Great Lakes," a speech delivered before the 52nd Congress, 2nd Session, February 5, 1891, *Congressional Record: Appendix*, pp. 142–143. An article in the *Duluth (Minnesota) Daily News* of May 8, 1892, supports much of what Keep presented in his memorial to Congress, citing a cost of 1.3 mills per ton-mile for ships and the same 9.22 ton-miles for railroads. The savings enjoyed by using ore carriers, however, was $135,800,000, an amount almost three times as great as Keep's calculations. The figures presented in both cases should be understood not as exact amounts, but rather as indications of a more general nature. Still, the advantages of water transport over rail were considerable. Of course, as the size of ships increased and they were capable of hauling even larger cargoes, the savings became even greater.

The option of using rail transportation necessarily had to consider Chicago only. At that time, there was no bridge across the Straits of Mackinac and the technology to construct one did not exist. Therefore, hauling ore from the Upper Peninsula by rail to the Straits, off-loading it on barges to cross the Straits, and reloading it again on rail cars for the trip south defeated the purpose. Using Canadian rails presented another set of even more formidable geographic obstacles, as well as potential political problems. Any ore traveling by rail, then, had to first arrive in Chicago before moving east.

39. Hutchins, *American Maritime Industries and Public Policy*, pp. 318–319; telephone conversation with C. Patrick Labadie, then director, Canal Park Marine Museum, Duluth, Minnesota, May 23, 1991; W. A. McDonald, "Composite Steamers Built by the Detroit Drydock Company," *Inland Seas*, 15 (Summer 1959): pp. 114–116; Codman, *Letter to John Lynch*, p. 24. Traditionally members of the Great Lakes maritime community have disagreed on just what constitutes a composite ship. Mr. Labadie provided an example in a subsequent telephone conversation on January 6, 1992. The *Monarch*, which sank off Isle Royale (Lake Superior) in 1906, used a number of iron straps to reinforce its wooden hull. The *Monarch's* frame, however, was wooden. At that time, park rangers, relying on insurance records, categorize the ship as composite. Most maritime historians, however, reserve the term for ships with metal frames and wooden planking. Such conflicting classifications have helped to cloud our understanding of the evolution of ship construction.

40. *Chicago Inter Ocean* (January 14, 1880); The *Detroit Free Press*, April 1880, reprinted in *The Cleveland Herald*, July 1, 1880; Hall, "Report on the Ship-building Industry of the United States," p. 140; U.S., Department of the Interior, *Report of the Commissioner of Navigation, 1897*, Chart 10 B, "Number and Gross Tonnage of Sailing Vessels, Steam Vessels, Canal Boats, and Barges, on the Northern Lakes, From 1868 to 1897." This report included canal boats, used in the extensive canal system feeding Lake Erie, in this total because their operations often took them into lake ports. By the 1880s, they numbered between 500 and 700, but their combined gross tonnage never exceeded 72,000.

41. Wright, "History of Shipbuilding in Cleveland," p. 113; Mansfield, *History of the Great Lakes*, p. 413; Hall, "Report on the Ship-building Industry of the United States," pp. 169, 218; John Harrison Morrison, *Iron and Steel Hull Steam Vessels of the United States, 1825–1905* (Salem, MA: The Steamship Historical Society of America, 1945), p. 17.

Wright also noted that Cleveland shipbuilder George Washington Jones played a major role in the *Onoko*. Earlier he had devised the "Deacon's arch" that had allowed wooden sidewheelers to gain extra length without breaking in two. He was also the first builder to launch ships sideways instead of bow first. And he also built the *Empire* in 1844. It was the first steamboat over 1,000 tons launched in the United States (pp. 237–239).

42. Morrison, *Iron and Steel Hull Steam Vessels*, pp. 24–25; "Steel Ships," *Scientific American* (March 20, 1886): p. 185.

43. Hutchins, *American Maritime Industries and Public Policy*, p. 457; "Representative Houses: Cleveland's Leading Mercantile, Manufacturing and Financial Concerns," in *The Industries of Cleveland* (Cleveland, OH: The Elstner Publishing Co., 1888), pp. 56–57; Hall, "Report of the Ship-building Industry of the U.S.," p. 167. The issue of operating efficiency had been growing in importance the mid-1870s, according to the January 22, 1880, *Chicago Inter Ocean*. "Each season," the article continued, "since then has witnessed the commissioning of vessels and steamers of dimensions larger than any craft that was afloat the previous season, until now we have what we allude to as monster propellers. Steamers and vessels that half a dozen years ago were considered very large are now only medium." These larger boats, of course, were limited in size by the dimensions of important locks and channels they were forced to use. The impetus behind the push for ever-larger vessels centers, in part, on railroads seeking to attract business in bulk items and commodities away from the lake carriers with cheaper rates. Economies of scale and cheaper cost-per-mile rates enjoyed by larger boats generally prevented the railroads from succeeding.

The May 20, 1891, *Marine Review* further noted that the coastal builders had been protected since 1792 by a federal law that prohibited the registration of foreign-built ships under the United States flag. This led to complacency on the part of coastal builders that discouraged experimentation and allowed the more aggressive lake shipyards to help meet coastal demands for steel vessels (p. 4). Horace See, writing in the August 1891 *Engineering Magazine*, freely admitted that the Eastern shipbuilder could learn "many a lesson" from the lake builder of iron ships.

44. Oldham, "Comparison of the Types of Steamers on the Great Lakes," pp. 1–19; "Steel Ships," *Scientific American* (March 20, 1885): p. 185.

45. J. F. Froggett, "Shipping on the Great Lakes is an Indispensable Asset to Business," *Marine Review* (July 1928): p. 79; U.S. Congress, House, Congressman Burton speaking on "The Great Lakes," 52nd Cong., 2nd Sess., February 5, 1891, *Congressional Record*, Appendix, Vol. 22; U.S. War Department, Corps of Engineers, United States Army, and the United States Shipping Board, *Transportation on the Great Lakes* (Washington: Government Printing Office, 1926), p. 29; "New Steel Steamship," *Chicago Inter Ocean*, January 2, 1886; *Marine Review* (October 22, 1891) and (March 19, 1891); Robert P. Porter, "Cleveland: Its Industrial Status in Relation to Traffic of the Great Lakes," address to Cleveland Board of Industry and Improvement, April 26, 1892 (Cleveland, OH: Cleveland Board of Industry and Improvement, 1892), p. 9; Morrison, *Iron and Steel Hull Steam Vessels*, pp. 25–26. The *Chicago Inter Ocean* observed that, even though constructed of steel, the *Spokane* had three masts and was schooner rigged. Opportunities to run under sail with a favorable wind to save fuel or as an alternative power source in the case of engine failure remained important considerations in the minds of lake shippers.

46. Miller, "Marine Engineering on the Great Lakes — Past and Present," pp. 245–246; Morrison, *Iron and Steel Hull Steam Vessels*, p. 26.

47. Froggett, "Shipping on the Great Lakes," p. 79; Arthur M. Woodford, *Charting the Inland Seas: A History of the U.S. Lake Survey* (Detroit, MI: U.S. Army Corps of Engineers, Detroit District, 1994), pp. 69, 72; U.S. Army. War Department. Corps of Engineers. "Report of the Chief of Engineers," (Washington: Government Printing Office, 1909), p. 756; "The St. Mary's Falls Canal," *Scientific American* (December 19, 1885): p. 386. The article noted that German and Russian engineers had visited the canal recently; one, General Barminsky of the Imperial Russian Engineers, concluded after a two-day inspection "that [the Weitzel Lock] is the most effective work of its kind in the world." The article also contains details regarding the dimensions, design, and construction of the 1881 lock.

48. U.S. Congress. House. A memorial concerning funding of improvements at new lock at Sault Ste. Marie, August 2, 1890, *Congressional Record*, 52nd Cong., 1st sess., 21: 8293; U.S. Army, Corps of Engineers, Report of the Chief of Engineers, 1909, Vol. I, p. 756.

49. Woodford, *Charting the Inland Seas*, pp. 64, 68–71; Frank A. Blust, "The U.S. Lake Survey, 1841–1974," *Inland Seas* (Summer 1976): p. 95.

50. Waldon Fawcett, "The Most Remarkable Year in the History of the Great Lakes," *Harper's Weekly* (September 29, 1900): p. 915.

Chapter 5

1. Lake Carriers' Association, "Yearly Shipments of Iron Ore from Various Ranges of Lake Superior District," in *Annual Report of the Lake Carriers' Association, 1909* (Cleveland, OH: Lake Carriers Association, 1909), p. 122; J. Bernard Walter, *The Story of Steel* (New York: Harper & Brothers Publishers, 1926), p. 18.

2. U.S. Department of the Interior. Census Office. William G. Gray, "Iron and Steel," in *Twelfth Census*, Reports, Vol. X, *Manufactures, Part IV.* (Washington: Government Printing Office, 1902), pp. 4, 5 60, 61, 244). Pennsylvania's production, of course, was divided between the western Pittsburgh mills and the eastern mills outside of Philadelphia. But the growth was centered in the West, particularly with the Carnegie Steel Corporation. Already in the early 1880s, western Pennsylvania out produced mills in the eastern part of the state by nearly 25 percent. The disparity only grew during the coming decades. James M. Swank, "Statistics of Iron and Steel Production," *Tenth Census of the United States, 1880* (Washington: Government Printing Office, 1883), Chart "Statistics of Iron and Steel Production," p. 6.

3. The information on Alexander McDougall, unless otherwise noted, came from his autobiography. It was published in installments in *Inland Seas* XXIII (Summer 1967): pp. 91–103 (Fall 1967): pp. 199–216 (Winter 1967): pp. 282–301; XIV (Spring 1968): pp. 16–33 (Summer 1968): pp. 138–147.

4. The quotations were from the Winter 1967 *Inland Seas*, p. 282.

McDougall's design truly was radical, which begs the question, what might have influenced him? The *Toledo Blade* article, like his autobiography, provides little insight, stating only that "the builder claims that [it was] a result of his long study of plans and theories." The August 21, 1880, *Harper's Weekly* offers one tantalizing possibility in an article entitled, "The Russian Imperial Steam-Yacht" (pp. 539–540). The two illustrations accompanying the article show what the editors term "an extraordinary novelty in ship-building." They describe her hull as "something between oval and rhomboid, or rather in the shape of a turbot; at its widest part the breadth is 153 feet — more than three-fifths of the length. The depth of the fish-like raft in the centre is 18 feet, and *the waterline is only 6 feet above the lowest point"* (emphasis added). The turbot-like lower portion has a flat bottom of 14,500 square feet. "At the edges the surface trends out and upward, all around the ship, toward the waterline." Here, "a change is made in the direction of the curves. The outward slope is *succeeded by a slope inward"* (emphasis added). The ship was built of steel with a double bottom at the Clyde shipyard of John Elder & Co., Govan, for Alexander II of Russia. Might this article, published a few years before McDougall began considering his new design, offer a clue about the inspiration for his boats? A flat bottom for operating in shallow water while carrying a heavy load, the lack of any freeboard, and the rounded hull above the waterline were all features found in his design. McDougall himself says nothing about the inspiration for his remarkable, if flawed, boat.

5. Rick Lydecker, *Pigboat, the Story of the Whalebacks* (Superior, Wisconsin: Head of the Lakes Maritime Society, Ltd., 1981), p. 4; "The Big Cigar Ship" Toledo *Blade* (July 17, 1888): p. 2.

6. Winter 1967 *Inland Seas*, p. 283; *Chicago Tribune*, May 19, 1893. Wetmore's letter was reproduced in Allan Nevins, *John D. Rockefeller*, Vol. II (New York: C. Scribner's Sons, 1940), pp. 374–375.

7. Winter 1967 *Inland Seas*, pp. 294–295; Edward Huntington Dwight, "The New Whaleback Boats" (*Harper's Weekly*, September 5, 1891): p. 675.

McDougall's desire to demonstrate that his boats could haul more than iron ore was important because it would allow his whalebacks to participate in the high volume of grain shipments on the lakes in the 1890s. J. B. Mansfield reported that nearly 33.5 million bushels of wheat left Chicago in the holds of lake boats in 1892, dwarfing 6.7 million bushels leaving that city by rail that same year. Lake ships that same year also enjoyed a more than two-to-one advantage over railroads in hauling corn out of Chicago. (*History of the Great Lakes*, pp. 532–533).

8. Dwight, "The New Whaleback Boats," pp. 672, 675; Walter van Brunt, ed., *Duluth and St. Louis County: Their Story and People*, Vol. I (Chicago and New York: The American Historical Society, 1921), p. 289; Wright, *Freshwater Whales*, p. 7; *Inland Seas* (Winter 1967), p. 285.

9. Lydecker, *Pigboat*, pp. 10–11. Lydecker

also noted other shortcomings of the whaleback design. The rounded decks meant that spillage during loading and unloading was often lost. Furthermore, the clamshell buckets of unloading machines, like Brown's "Tom Collins," often dented the deck plates to the point that hatch covers were not watertight, a dangerous situation for a boat expected to have her decks awash while underway. McDougall introduced stanchions in the *John Ericsson* and *Alexander Holley,* both with 48-foot beams, but these supports caused problems as expected. The Barge Company then launched the *Alexander McDougall,* but the ship's 50-foot beam was made possible by compromising the whaleback design by employing a conventional bow to overcome the design problems. Whalebacks, while not always popular with crews because of their rough ride, remained in use around the world for some time. The last whaleback, the *Meteor* (originally the *Frank Rockefeller*) remained in active service until 1967. It was then placed on permanent display in Superior, Wisconsin.

10. Wright, *Freshwater Whales*, pp. 146–147; "Built on the Lakes for Ocean Service," *Marine Review*, XXV (January 30, 1902): pp. 21–23; Smith, "Shipbuilding," in *Twelfth Census*, p. 210. The consolidation of Great Lakes shipbuilders was part of what historians call the Great Merger Wave, which began with the Depression of 1893 and lasted until 1904. See Glenn Porter, "Industrialization and the Rise of Big Business," in Charles W. Calhoun, ed., *The Gilded Age: Essays on the Origins of Modern America* (Wilmington, DE: Scholarly Resources, Inc., 1996), pp. 1–18.

11. Walter Havighurst, *Vein of Iron: The Pickands Mather Story* (Cleveland: The World Publishing Company, 1958), pp. 75, 93; Walter van Brunt, ed., *Duluth and St. Louis County*, pp. 57, 59–61.

12. Paul de Kruif, *Seven Iron Men* (Minneapolis: University of Minnesota Press, 2009), pp. 77–83, 92–95, 101–107. [See excerpt in Havighurst, *Great Lakes Reader*, pp. 122–131.]

13. War Department, *Transportation on the Great Lakes*, p. 246; Paul Henry Landis, *Three Iron Mining Towns* (New York: Arno Press, 1970), pp. 12–13; *Harper's Weekly*, January 12, 1895: pp. 30–31. The article also contains a detailed map of the Mesabi Range mining district that locates the 40-acre mining claims occupied at the time. The Mesabi Range eventually doubled to 100 miles in length.

The destination of the iron ore sent from the Lake Superior mines, including the Mesabi, in 1897 was broken down for the year 1897 by A. I. Findley, editor of the *Iron Trade Review.*

Total volume of Lake Superior iron ore shipped: 12,469,637 tons (70 percent of national total)

Destination
- 10,120,906 tons to Lake Erie ports*
- 2,094,739 tons to Chicago
- (balance to foreign trade)

*Lake Erie Ports	Tons
Toledo	416,438
Sandusky	79,792
Huron	198,231
Lorain	355,188
Cleveland	2,456,704
Fairport	912,879
Ashtabula	3,001,914
Conneaut	495,327
Erie	1,311,526
Buffalo/Tonawanda	797,446

Quoted in Mansfield, *History of the Great Lakes*, pp. 566–567)

14. U.S. Bureau of the Census. *Fourteenth Census of the United States*. Table 9, "Production of Iron Ore: 1879 to 1920," in *Mines and Quarries, 1919* (Washington: Government Printing Office, 1922), p. 337; U.S., War Department, *Transportation on the Great Lakes* (Washington: U.S. Government Printing Office, 1926), p. 246; Allen Nevins, *John D. Rockefeller: The Heroic Age of American Enterprise*, Vol. II (New York: Charles Scribner's Sons, 1940), pp. 371–372, 393–394; van Brunt, ed., *Duluth and St. Louis County*, Vol. I, pp. 292, 399–404; *Autobiography*, Winter 1967, *Inland Seas*, p. 289. According to McDougall, he "was in the field looking after mining and other developments, tie contracts and what not, and I had a good deal to do with the [Duluth, Missabe and Northern] railroad construction." In addition, he recounted, "I remember writing [Wetmore], 'Rockefeller is king in oil; his son can be king of iron.' I repeated that hint in several quarters where it would get to Rockefeller" (p. 290).

15. Nevins, *John D. Rockefeller*, p. 396. Nevins argues that Rockefeller perpetrated no fraud against the Merritts, pp. 383–384; van Brunt, ed., *Duluth and St. Louis County*, Vol. I, pp. 404–405, 407–408. Although John D. Rockefeller is generally associated with the formation and expansion of Standard Oil, this venture into the iron ore business was not his first. He had previously invested $250,000 in the Vermilion Range, had money invested in McDougall's Barge Company, and had taken interest in other iron ore property in the early 1890s. (p. 405).

16. van Brunt, ed., *Duluth and St. Louis County*, pp. 408–409; George Harvey, *Henry Clay Frick: The Man* (Privately printed, 1936; copyright, 1928, by Charles Scribner's Sons), pp. 188–191; Andrew Carnegie to Board of Managers, Carnegie Steel, April 18, 1894, quoted in James H. Bridge, *Inside History of Carnegie Steel* (New York: The Aldine Book Company, 1903), p. 259. Harvey suggests that Carnegie's apprehension concerning investments in mining trace back to his company's experiments with iron ore mining in the Tyrone region of Pennsylvania years before.

17. Harvey, *Henry Clay Frick*, pp. 191–195; Nevins, *John D. Rockefeller*, p. 398.

18. Ibid., pp. 197–199; van Brunt, *Duluth and St. Louis County*, p. 411. Weeks, "The Manufacture of Coke," pp. 27, 31–32.

19. Jean Strouse, *Morgan: American Financier* (New York: Random House, 1999), pp. 396–397, 399.

20. Strousse, *Morgan*, pp. 397–398. The Allen description of Gary was from *The Great Pierpont Morgan* (New York: Harper and Brothers, 1949), p. 164, quoted by Strousse on p. 397.

21. Strousse, *Morgan*, pp. 399–400; Ida Tarbell, *Life of Elbert H. Gary: the Story of Steel* (New York: D. Appleton and Company, 1925), p. 111.

22. Strousse, *Morgan*, p. 400; Joseph Frazier Wall, *Andrew Carnegie* (Pittsburgh, PA: University of Pittsburgh Press, 1970), pp. 776 *passim*, 783–785.

23. Carnegie believed strongly, "It is a nobler ideal that man should labor, not for himself alone, but in and for a brotherhood of his fellows, and share with them all in common." He published an essay in the *North American Review* in 1899, elaborating on this philosophy. It was later reprinted in a British periodical under the title, "The Gospel of Wealth." Carnegie eventually gave away much of his fortune to construct hundreds of public libraries around the United States and to purchase countless church organs in Europe. ("Andrew Carnegie, 'Wealth,' June, 1889," in Richard Hofstadter, ed., *Great Issues in American History: From Reconstruction to the Present Day, 1864–1969* [New York: Vintage Books, 1969], pp. 87–92).

24. Strousse, *Morgan*, p. 401; Misa, *Nation of Steel*, p. 165; Wall concludes that Morgan's decision to stop Carnegie by buying him out "has always been clouded in mystery and legend." As far as Morgan's seat on Schwab's right at the banquet, Wall believes it was planned, but by whom remains uncertain. *Carnegie*, pp. 784–785.

25. Strousse, *Morgan*, p. 403. In his autobiography, Carnegie spends very little time discussing the sale of his companies. But, ever the

competitor, he notes that, although U.S. Steel "netted sixty millions" in their year of operation, his company expected to show a profit of $70 million that same year, if he had retained ownership. Andrew Carnegie, *The Autobiography of Andrew Carnegie* (Boston, MA: Northeastern University Press, 1986), p. 245. Wall concluded that Carnegie's decision to sell his holdings could not have been an easy one. Yes, it freed him for his philanthropic work, but he also stood on the verge of controlling the world's steel market within five to ten years. Wall, *Carnegie*, p. 788.

A sub-current underlay this seemingly smooth transaction. Carnegie profoundly disliked Morgan. A strong puritanical streak in Carnegie was deeply offended by Morgan's reputation as a womanizer. This compounded a mutual mistrust that had developed earlier arising out of business dealings between the two. According to Strousse, Schwab feared this mutual antagonism might prevent him from closing the deal. In the end, Carnegie apparently saw that the philanthropic good he could accomplish outweighed any moral qualms he had with Morgan. (Strousse, p. 402; Misa, *Nation of Steel*, pp. 165, 166).

26. Strousse, *Morgan*, pp. 404–406; Charles M. Schwab, "What May Be Expected in the Iron and Steel Industry," *North American Review* (May 1901): p. 661; Misa, *Nation of Steel*, p. 166.

27. Misa, *Nation of Steel*, 75–76, 83–85; James W. Swank, "The Manufacture of Open-Hearth Steel," in *Statistics of iron and Steel Production*, 10th Census (Washington: Government Printing Office, 1883), p. 128.

28. Swank, "The Manufacture of Open-Hearth Steel," 127–128; Misa, *Nation of Steel*, pp. 77, 83.

29. E. T. Evans to Henry T. Abbott. Reprinted in U.S. Congress, *Congressional Record: Appendix*, 51st Congress, 1st Session, 1890, p. 34; "The Steel Steamer *Choctaw*," *Scientific American* (August 20, 1892): p. 115; War Department, Corps of Engineers and United States Shipping Board, *Transportation on the Great Lakes*, p. 29; U.S. Congress, House, Speech of Representative Theodore E. Burton of Ohio, February 5, 1891, *Congressional Record, Appendix*, 52nd Congress, 2nd Session, p. 142. Burton also provided the following information. The combined value of the steel vessels in 1886 was $694,000 (an average of $116,000 per ship), but increased in 1890 to $11,964,500 (an average of $176,000 per ship).

30. F.G. Fassett, Jr., ed., *The Shipbuilding Business in the United States of America*, chart on page 76 compiled from U.S. Department of Commerce (New York: The Society of Naval Architects and Naval Engineers, 1948), p. 76; R. L. Newman, "Construction of Lake Steamers," a paper delivered to the Civil Engineers Club of Cleveland, printed in *Marine Review* (March 3, 1898): p. 8; Havighurst, *Vein of Iron*, p. 87; Smith, "Shipbuilding," *Reports*, Twelfth Census, Vol. X, *Manufactures*, part IV, p. 210. Smith noted that lake ships traveled fewer miles between ports than did blue water vessels, therefore making it possible for them to undertake more trips. On the other hand, weather prevented them from operating for more than seven or eight months out of the year, while ocean ships could sail the better part of the year.

The remarkable increase in average gross tonnage with such a small increase in the number of steam vessels can be understood if one considers the impact of steel-hulled bulk carriers. Clearly the majority of steamers by 1900 were still wooden-hulled and subject to the size limitations that had always plagued such vessels. But the steel ships had no such restraints. Although far fewer in number, their rapidly expanding dimensions were great enough to increase the average gross tonnage of all steamships by 50 percent.

Shippers employing larger bulk carriers generally preferred to haul iron ore instead of grain because it was more profitable. An article entitled "Advantages in the Ore Trade" (*Marine Review*, August 6, 1891) noted that, while the per day gross for carrying grain from Chicago to Buffalo was slightly higher than hauling iron ore from Escanaba to Cleveland, towing charges in Chicago, plus the added risks of the Chicago River, "more than counteracted the difference of $10 a day in favor of the grain" (p. 4).

31. Jewell R. Dean, "The Wilson Fleet: Freight Pioneers" *Inland Seas*, 2 (July 1946): p. 164; Havighurst, *Vein of Iron*, p. 88; Alexander C. Meakin, *Master of the Inland Seas: The Story of Captain Thomas Wilson and the Fleet That Bore His Name* (Vermillion: The Great Lakes Historical Society, 1988), p. 20; *Marine Review*, Vol. IV (July 9, 1891): p. 8. Tomlinson and Minch were shipbuilders and ships' captains responsible for important contributions to Great Lakes navigation during the later decades of the 19th century.

32. Havighurst, *Vein of Iron*, p. 85 passim. For details of the Bessemer Fleet, see Roger M. Jones, "The Rockefeller Fleet," *Inland Seas* 3 (Fall 1947): pp. 131–136. Allan Nevis's *John D. Rockefeller: The Heroic Age of American Enterprise*, discusses the creation of the Bessemer Fleet from Rockefeller's perspective, quoting liberally from his *Random Reminiscences* (pp. 404–410).

33. Smith, "Shipbuilding," *Twelfth Census, Reports*, Vol. X, *Manufactures*, pp. 223–224; Naomi R. Lamoreaux, *The Great Merger Movement in American Business, 1895–1904* (New York: Cambridge University Press, 1987), pp. 2–3. There is some inconsistency in the capitalization figures. Part of this can be attributed to the authorized capitalization of the American Shipbuilding Company, which was $30 million. The actual capitalization was closer to $14 million.

34. Wright, "A History of Shipbuilding in Cleveland, Ohio": p. 115; "Built on the Lakes for Ocean Service," *Marine Review* XXV (January 30, 1902): p. 21.

35. Harry F. Myers, "Remember the 504's," *Inland Seas* 44 (Summer 1988): p. 78; Lake Carriers' Association, "History of the Iron Ore Trade," in *1910 Annual Report of the Lake Carriers' Association* (Cleveland, OH, and Detroit, MI: Lake Carriers' Association, 1910), p. 115; Lake Carriers' Association, *1908 Annual Report*, p. 116; John Foord, "The Great Lakes and Our Commercial Supremacy" *North American Review* (August 1898): APS Online, p. 155; Smith, "Shipbuilding," in *Manufacturing*, Part IV, Twelfth Census, Tables 10, 11, 12, p. 223; Hall, "Report on the Shipbuilding Industry of the United States," Tenth Census, Vol. VIII, p. 169; Frank E. Kirby, "Shipping on the Great Lakes" *Engineering* XCII (July 1911): p. 63; James C. Mills, *Our Inland Seas: Their Shipping and Commerce for Three Centuries* (Chicago: A. C. McClug, 1910), p. 302; Inches, "Wooden Ship Building," pp. 5–6. Inches also provides a summary of the various steps involved in the construction of a wooden steamer.

As early as 1891 the Great Lakes dominated other regions of the United States in the production of large steel vessels. Walter Miller, speaking to the International Engineering Congress in 1894, quoted figures from the U.S. Treasury Department that reported that in the category of ships 1,000–2,500 feet the Great Lakes fleet numbered 310 ships (512,788 gross tons). The rest of the country combined had 213 ships (319,751 gross tons). Walter Miller, "Ship-Building and Engineering on the Great Lakes," in *Proceedings of the International Engineering Congress*, Vol. II, paper XXXVI, edited by George W. Melville (New York: John Wiley & Sons, 1894), p. 8. Miller was the superintending engineer for Cleveland's Globe Iron Works. His published essay contains detailed plans for various boilers, engines, and ships built by Globe Iron.

In 1909 Robert Curr delivered a paper entitled "Shipbuilding on the Great Lakes" to the annual meeting of the Society of Naval Architects and Marine Engineers. This highly detailed but invaluable study of the construction of lake bulk carriers was published in the Society's *Transactions*. The reader can learn how a Great Lakes bulk carrier of the period was constructed—from laying the keel to fitting her out. The uninitiated will require a nautical dictionary to keep up. [*Transactions* 16 (New York: Society of Naval Architects and Marine Engineers, 1909), pp. 195–209, plates, pp. 86–114.

36. "New Lake Steamers," *Scientific American*, reprinted from *Marine Review* (January 16, 1892): p. 34; Lawrence A. Pomeroy, "The Bulk Freight Vessel" *Inland Seas* (July 1946): p. 193; *Cleveland Plain Dealer*, January 5, 1880; U.S. Congress, House, *Congressional Record*, , 51st Congress, 1st Session (August 22, 1890), p. 9040; Havighurst, *Vein of Iron*, p. 86; Lake Carrier's Association, *Annual Report—1899*, p. [needs further research].

37. Richard Gebhart, "The Coming of the Yellow Monster," *Telescope*, Vol. XXXIX, #6 (November-December 1991): pp. 149–151; William C. Fischer and Christopher K. Lohmann, ed., *W. D. Howells: Selected Letters, Vol. 5, 1902–1911* (Boston, MA: Twayne Publishers, 1983), p. 224.

38. Myers, "Remembering the 504's," p. 78; Kirby, "Shipping on the Great Lakes," p. 222; "The Coming of the Yellow Monster," *Telescope* (November-December 1991): pp. 150–152.

39. A. F. Lindblad, "A Critical Analysis of the Factors Affecting Safety and Operation on the Bulk Freight Vessels of the Great Lakes," Ph.D. dissertation, University of Michigan, 1924. Reprinted in *Marine Review* (October, November, December 1924, February 1925), Table III—"Calculations for Curves in Figure 10"; Ivan H. Walton, "Developments on the Great Lakes, 1815–1943" *Michigan History* 27 (1943): p. 125.

40. Lawrence A. Pomeroy, Jr., "The Bulk Freight Vessel," *Inland Seas* 2 (July, 1946): p. 197. The Fay, Spofford, Thorndike quote came from *Great Lakes Commerce and the Port of Oswego* (Oswego, NY: *Palladium-Times*, 1925), 1: E-69—E-70. Their report does caution that World War I was being fought during two of the years under discussion, 1916—1918, and freight rates were "abnormally high." James C. Mills, *Our Inland Seas: Their Shipping and Commerce for Three Centuries* (Chicago: A. C. McClug, 1910), p. 294

41. Kirby and Rankin, "The Bulk Carrier of the Great Lakes," p. 223; Lindblad, "Critical Analysis," Pt. 3, p. 1. The loss of the 729-foot *Edmund Fitzgerald*, fully loaded with 26,013

tons of taconite (iron ore pellets) and caught in 30-foot seas northwest of Whitefish Point, Lake Superior, in 1975, again raised the question of extending the length of bulk carriers. Underwater cameras that surveyed the wreck in 1989 showed that the *Fitzgerald* was in two pieces on the bottom. If the ship had been caught in a trough between the waves, it is conceivable that her extended length — straining under 26,000 tons of cargo — might have caused her to buckle and break apart. On the other hand, the empty 640-foot *Carl D. Bradley* broke in two during heavy seas in 1958. William Ratigan concluded that ships running empty ride high in the water and are even more likely to snap if caught in a trough. *Great Lakes Shipwrecks and Survivals* (Grand Rapids: Wm. B. Eerdmans Publishing Company, 1977), pp. 340–341, 347–352; War Department, Corps of Engineers and U.S. Shipping Board, *Transportation on the Great Lakes*, p. 37.

42. Foord, "The Great Lakes and Our Commercial Supremacy" (n.p.); U.S. Bureau of the Census. Special Reports, "Transportation by Water" (Washington: Government Printing Office, 1906), Table 39, "Congressional appropriations for the survey, improvement, and maintenance of the harbors, channels, and tributary streams of the Great Lakes and St. Lawrence River, by localities and periods," pp. 154–155 (Note: total congressional appropriations for the St. Lawrence River through 1907 amounted to $3,462,683.); *Harper's Weekly* (Vol. XXXV, #1790) (April 11, 1891): p. 270.

43. U.S. Congress. House. Congressman Theodore E. Burton speaking on "The Great Lakes," 52nd Cong., 2nd sess., February 5, 1891. *Congressional Record*, Appendix, Vol. 22, p. 143; "Ship Channel Between the Great Lakes." Letter transmitting a report of Col. O. M. Poe, Chief of Engineers to House, 51st Cong., 2nd sess., January 24, 1891. Vol. 33, Ex. Doc. 207, pp. 1–11 (serial 2863).

44. U.S. Department of Commerce. Bureau of the Census. Alexander Smith, "Shipbuilding," in *Twelfth Census*, Reports, Vol. X, *Manufactures*, Part IV. (Washington: Government Printing Office, 1902), p. 211; Commissioner of Navigation, *Report of the Commission of Navigation to the Secretary of the Treasury* (Washington: Government Printing Office, 1897), p. 8.

45. U.S. Congress. *Congressional Record*, House, 51st Cong., 1st Sess., May 22, 1890 (Washington: Government Printing Office, 1890), pp. 9031, 9033; "Portage and Lake Superior Canals Collection," GLMS 18, Historical Collections of the Great Lakes, in the Cen-

ter for Archival Collections, Bowling Green State University.

46. *Sandusky Register* (April 18, 1898): p. 5; "Improving Ore Handling Equipment at Lorain," *Marine Review* (July 21, 1898): p. 9.

47. *Sandusky Register* (April 14, 1898): p. 4; Lake Carriers' Association, *Annual Report, 1899*, pp. 15–17; Lake Carriers' Association, *Annual Report, 1904*, p. 11; Waldon Fawcett, "The Most Remarkable Year in the History of the Great Lakes," *Harper's Weekly* (September 29, 1900): p. 915; Harvey C. Beeson, *Beeson's Sailor's Handbook and Inland Marine Guide, 1901* (Cleveland, OH: Harvey C. Beeson, 1901), p. 181; Lake Carriers' Association, *Annual Report, 1910*, pp. 94–96. For the reader interested in following the improvements to each channel and harbor separately, see John W. Larson, *History of Great Lakes Navigation*. Washington: Superintendent of Documents, U.S.G.R.O., 1983.

48. Arthur Woodford, *Charting the Inland Seas: a History of the U.S. Lake Survey* (Detroit, MI: U.S. Army Corps of Engineers, Detroit District, 1994), pp. 64, 68–71, 79–80; Frank A. Blust, "The U.S. Lake Survey, 1841–1974" *Inland Seas* (Summer 1976): p. 95; Geo. P. McKay, Sect. of Cleveland Vessel Owners Association, to L. A. Grant, Acting Sect. of War (n.d.), reprinted by Committee of Rivers and Harbors under title "Obstruction to Navigation of the Great Lakes," Serial Set, 52nd Cong. 1st Sess., H. Ex. Doc., Vol. 29, n. 9–28; Lake Carriers' Association, *Annual Report, 1907*, pp. 64–66.

49. War Department, *Transportation on the Great Lakes*, p. 265. In some cases, the smaller harbors simply could not accommodate the larger new ships. The *Annual Report, 1909*, of the Lake Carriers Association, commenting on the dock facilities at Ashtabula, Ohio, concluded that "the old machinery [probably Brown rigs] has handled, and if the ships had not outgrown the capacity of the old slips, could handle very well between four and five million tons of ore per year" (p. 55). Harbors like Ashtabula continued to receive ore, but it arrived in smaller ships and was unloaded with older, more traditional equipment.

50. Waldon Fawcett, "The Most Remarkable Year in the History of the Great Lakes," *Harper's Weekly* (September 29, 1900): p. 915; Elroy McKendree Avery, *A History of Cleveland and Its Environs: The Heart of New Connecticut, Vol. III, Biography* (Chicago, IL: The Lewis Publishing Company, 1918), p. 130.

51. Burke, "Barrels to Barrows," pp. 274–275; Wright, *Freshwater Whales*, p. 153; Williams, *Honorable Peter White*, p. 203; "Ore Unloading Machines for Use at Receiving Docks"

Engineering News , Vol. 54, # 5 (August 3, 1905): pp. 125–126.

George Hulett had designed unloading equipment for some time before introducing his revolutionary rig. An article in the April 9, 1891, *Marine Review* mentioned dock improvements at Huron, Ohio, and referred to ore hoists and conveyors "of Hulett pattern made by the McMyler Co. of Cleveland" (p. 1). He also received a patent (#516,053) for a devise to unload railroad cars in 1894 (U.S. Patent Office, *Specifications and Drawings*, March 6, 1894, pp. 520–522).

52. Dwight Boyer, "Those Magnificent Huletts," *The Cleveland Plain Dealer Sunday Magazine*, July 6, 1969: p. 22; Burke, "Barrels to Barrows," pp. 274, 275; "Ore Unloading Machines for Use at Receiving Docks," p. 126; Williams, *Honorable Peter White*, p. 203; Eric Hirsimaki, "The Huron Hustler," *Nickel Plate Road Magazine* (Winter/Spring 1988): p. 25.

53. Burke, "Barrels to Barrows," p. 276; War Department, *Transportation on the Great Lakes*, pp. 38–39. Thomas W. Gerdel, writing in the March 24, 1991, *Cleveland Plain Dealer*, stated that the *Hennepin* was the first self-unloader in 1902 (Section E, p. 4).

54. The Frank E. Hamilton Collection, the Charles E. Frohman Collection, Rutherford B. Hayes Presidential Center, Fremont, Ohio.

Chapter 6

1. Stetson Conn, Rose C. Engelman, and Byron Fairchild, *The United States Army in World War II, The Western Hemisphere: Guarding the United States and Its Outposts* (Washington: U. S, Government Printing Office, 1964), pp. 102–103; Paul T. Hurt, Jr., "Vacation Voyages on Inland Seas," *Inland Seas*, Vol. 7, # 4 (Winter 1951): p. 258.

2. Ibid., 103; George J. Joachim, *Iron Fleet: The Great Lakes in World War II* (Detroit, MI: Wayne State University Press, 1994), pp. 60–62. German innovation in strategy and military technology had surprised and awed the world when war broke out in 1939. The seeming invincibility of the Wehrmacht created early in the conflict an exaggerated fear of German capabilities. While fleets of heavy German bombers appearing over New York, or the Soo Locks, may seem far-fetched in hindsight, it seemed quite plausible to Americans still reeling from the Pearl Harbor humiliation. According to Joachim, War Department was most fearful of an attack by German paratroopers intent upon destroying the locks. (p. 64).

3. Conn, et al, *United States Army*, pp. 103–105.

4. Ibid., p. 105; Joachim, *Iron Fleet*, p. 69.

5. Conn, et al, *United States Army*, p. 102.

6. John G. B. Hutchins, *The American Maritime Industries and Public Policy, 1789–1914* (Cambridge, MA: Harvard University Press, 1941), p. 461; Bernard E, Ericson, "The Evolution of Great Lakes Ships: Part II, Steam and Steel," presented at the Cleveland, Ohio, meeting of the Society of Naval Architects and Engineers, January 24, 1968 (printed in *Inland Seas*, Vol. 25, # 3 (1969): p. 203; Plowden, *End of an Era*, p. 27.

7. Plowden, *End of an Era*, p. 28; Thomas W. Gerdel, "Great Lakes Shipping," *Cleveland Plain Dealer*, March 24, 1991, pp. 1,4.

8. Plowden, 19, 20, 29; Kenneth Miller, "Geared Turbine Ore Carriers for the Great Lakes," *The Ohio State Engineer* (May 1938): pp. 12, 14; Duncan Haws, *Ships and the Sea: A Chronological Review* (New York: Thomas Y. Crowell Company, Inc., 1975), p. 180, *Van Nostrand's Scientific Encyclopedia* (Princeton: D. Van Nostrand Company, Inc., 1968), p. 517.

9. Plowden, *End of an Era*, p. 8. As of this printing, Congress has authorized funding for a second "Poe-sized lock," which would replace the Davis and Sabin locks. Between 1972 and 2007, 1,000-footers have come to dominate the U.S. Great Lakes fleet, hauling nearly 70 percent of all freight carried on the Lakes. Since only the expanded Poe lock can handle 1,000-footers, any damage it might experience would seriously curtail commerce on the Lakes. (Lake Carriers Association, *2007 Position Papers*, www.lcaships.com/2007pspp.pfd, p. 14).

10. Jacques Lesstrang, *Cargo Carriers of the Great Lakes: the Saga of the Great Lakes Fleet—North America's Fresh Water Merchant Marine* (Boyne City, MI: Harbor House Publishers, 1977), pp. 131, 133, 143–144. A new design change with the ships like the *James R. Barker* in 1975 found the forward island, including the pilot house, incorporated into an "all-aft" design. Here the crew of 30 is housed in quarters of comfort unimaginable a century earlier. There is even an elevator to move the crew quickly among the five different decks. Most of the living spaces are air conditioned. The ship even has its own sewage treatment facility and holding tank. (pp. 135–136)

11. Warner Olivier, "The Coming Crisis in Iron," *Saturday Evening Post*, Vol. 215, # 20 (November 14, 1942): p. 22.

12. Ibid., 122; William Ashworth, *The Late, Great Lakes* (New York: Alfred A. Knopf, 1987), p. 88.

13. "Semi-Centennial of Sault Ste. Marie Canal," *Marine Review* (February 6, 1902): p. 16. Excerpts of the Poe letter cited were included in this article.

According to the 1900 *Report of the Industrial Commission on Transportation*, "railways [frequently reduced] their freight rates during the season of navigation on the Great Lakes in order to compete" with lake vessels. This occurred, however, primarily in the grain business. Moreover, railroads often owned "their own lines of lake boats." But most of them carried general merchandize, which paid a higher freight rate, rather than bulk cargoes subject to lower rates. (*Report of the Industrial Commission on Transportation*, Vol. IV [Washington: Government Printing Office, 1900], pp. 162–163).

14. Ashworth, *Late, Great Lakes*, pp. 88–89; John H. Judd, "Life in the Lakes," in *Decisions for the Great Lakes*, A. Donald Misener and Glenda Daniel, eds. (Hammond, IN: Purdue University Calumet, 1982), p. 76E. Part of the problem with the asbestos deposits in western Lake Superior has to do with the lake's "water flushing time." This is understood as "the average length of time that individual molecules or ions of water remain in the lake before being transported out by the outflowing rivers." In the case of Lake Superior, water flushing time is 165 years. By way of comparison, flushing time for Lake Erie is two-and-a-half years. Since much of the asbestos is lying on the bottom, it is impossible to know if much of that will be picked up and carried out. And even if it is, the asbestos will simply be transferred to another series of lakes and rivers. Once created, a problem like this persists until natural deterioration occurs, hence the estimate of millennia before it goes away. (W. M. Schertzer, "How Great Lakes Water Moves," in *Decisions for the Great Lakes*, p. 53)

15. Fred L. Synder, *Zebra Mussels in Lake Erie: The Invasion & Its Implications*, Fact Sheet 045. (Columbus, OH: Ohio Sea Grant College Program, 1989), pp. 1–4. The method by which zebra mussels ingest plankton has led to improved water clarity in Lake Erie. Research in 1995 found "an array of once-absent plants which apparently were energized by sunlight penetrating clear waters." This is particularly ironic because this lack of clarity was the result of other detrimental activity—farm run-off, dredging, industrial dumping—over the years. But, as Jeffrey Reutter, director of the Ohio Sea Grant program, concluded at the time: "The ultimate impact on the ecosystem from zebra mussels has not been reached. We're not even close to a steady state. It's changing very quickly" ("Underwater Plants Return as Zebra Mussels Improve Lake Erie Clarity," *Tiffin* [Ohio] *Advertiser-Tribune* [November 27, 1995]).

16. Ashworth, *Late, Great Lakes*, p. 101.

17. John MacGregor, *The Progress of America, Discovery by Columbus to the Year 1846*, Vol. II (London: Whittaker &Co., 1847), p. 776.

Bibliography

Primary

Unpublished

Cass, Lewis Papers. William L. Clemens Library, University of Michigan, Ann Arbor, Michigan.

Conneaut Harbor (Ohio) Chapter, International Longshoreman's Association, Finnish Ore Handlers, Local No, 220, Minutes of general meetings, 1901–1908. (Translated by Eli N. Hirsimaki). Original in the possession of Eric Hirsimaki.

Hamilton, Frank E. Hamilton Collection, in the Charles E. Frohman Collection. Rutherford B. Hayes Presidential Center, Fremont, Ohio.

Hyzer, Peter C., and Clifford A. Auve, "Great Lakes Connecting Channels and Soo Locks," a paper presented to the Society of Naval Architects and Marine Engineers, Chicago, Illinois, October 18, 1957. Center for Archival Collections, Bowling Green State University, Institute for Great Lakes Research, Bowling Green Ohio.

Locke Family Collection. Rutherford B. Hayes Presidential Center, Fremont, Ohio.

Portage Lake and Lake Superior Canals Collection. Institute for Great Lakes Research, Center for Archival Collections, Bowling Green State University, Bowling Green, Ohio.

Propeller *W. R. Stafford*: Logbook (1890–1896). Institute for Great Lakes Research, Center for Archival Collections, Bowling Green State University, Bowling Green, Ohio.

Shelbourne (William Petty, 1st Marquis of Lansdowne, 2nd Earl of) Papers. William L. Clemens Library, University of Michigan, Ann Arbor, Michigan.

Williams, Samuel Papers. William L. Clemens Library, University of Michigan, Ann Arbor, Michigan.

Published

"Advantages in the Ore Trade." *Marine Review.* (August 6, 1891): p. 4.

American Iron and Steel Association. *Annual Statistical Report.* Philadelphia: American Iron and Steel Association, 1879.

Addams, Jane. *Twenty Years at Hull House.* New York: James W. Linn, 1938.

Babcock and Wilcox Company. *Forged Steel Water-Tube Marine Boiler.* New York: Babcock and Wilcox Co., 1901.

_____. *Marine Steam.* New York: Babcock and Wilcox Co., 1928.

Bancroft, William L. "Memories of Captain Samuel Ward." *Michigan Pioneer and Historical Collections*, Vol. 21 (18921): pp. 336–337.

"The Basic Steel Process." *Scientific American*, Vol. LV, no. 4 (July 24, 1886): pp. 48–49.

Beeson, Harvey C. *Beeson's Sailors Handbook and Inland Marine Guide.* Published Annually between 1888 and 1921. Chicago, IL: Charles C. Beeson.

"Big Cigar Ship." *Toledo Blade*, July 17, 1888.

Blois, John T. *Gazetteer of the State of Michigan.* Detroit, MI: Sydney L. Rood & Co., 1840.

Board of Lake Underwriters. *Marine Register, 1863.* A copy in the Frank E. Hamilton Collection, in the Charles E. Frohman Collection. Rutherford B. Hayes Presidential Center, Fremont, Ohio.

Brewster, Edward. "From Illinois to Lake Superior and the Upper Peninsula by Steamer in 1852," ed., Lewis Beeson. *Michigan History* 33 (1949): pp. 328–336.

Brown Hoisting Machinery Company. "*Brownhoist*": *General Catalogue.* Cleveland, OH: Brown Hoisting Machinery Company, 1919.

Brough, Bennett H., ed. *The Journal of the Iron and Steel Industry, General Index.* London: E. & F. N. Spon, 1902.

Buffalo Commercial Advertiser

"Built on the Lakes for Ocean Service." *Marine Review*, XXV. (January 30, 1902): pp. 21–23.

Burt, William A., and Jacob Houghton. "The Needle Compass." In *The Great Lakes Reader*. Ed., Walter Havighurst, pp. 92–93. New York: The Macmillan Company, 1966.

Calkins, Elijah. "Report of the St. Mary's Falls Ship Canal, 1857." In "The Operation of the Sault Canal, 1857." Edited by Philp P. Mason. *Michigan History* 39 (1955): pp. 69–70.

Canadian Shipbuilding and Ship Repair Association, Ottawa. *Newsletter*, 4 (April 1961). Quoted in *Inland Seas*, No. 22 (Summer 1966): p. 154.

Carnegie, Andrew. *The Autobiography of Andrew Carnegie*. Boston, MA: Northeastern University Press, 1986.

Chicago Inter Ocean

"Clapp-Griffiths Steel Process." *Scientific American,* Vol. LIV, No. 13 (March 27, 1886): pp. 191, 196–197.

Clarke, Thomas C. "Avenues of Western Trade." Hunt's *Merchant Magazine*, XXXV (August 1856): 146–160. Quoted in Andrew T. Brown. "The Great Lakes, 1850–1861." *Inland Seas*, 7 (Fall 1951): p. 188.

Cleveland (Ohio) *Herald*

Codman, John. *A Letter Addressed to the Honorable John Lynch, Chairman of the Special Congressional Committee of the United States Senate on the Navigation interest: Advocating the Expediency of Purchasing Iron Ships and Steamers in Scotland, Being the Result of a Recent Visit and Extended Observation.* Boston: A. Williams & Co., 1869.

"Commerce on the Great Lakes." *Harper's Weekly* (April 13, 1889): pp. 293–296.

"Complimenting Lake Builders." *Marine Review*, August 6, 1891, p. 4.

Cove [W. H. Gorrill]. "Lake and River." *Toledo Commercial*. (July 25, 1868).

Cox, Jacob Dolson, Sr. *Building and American Industry: The Story of the Cleveland Twist Drill Company and Its Founder.* Cleveland, OH: The Cleveland Twist Drill Company, 1951.

Crowell and Murray. *The Iron Ores of Lake Superior: Containing Some Facts of Interest Relating to Mining and Shipping of the Ore and Location of Principal Mines.* Cleveland, OH: Penton Publishing Co., 1914.

Curr, Robert. "Lake Ship Yard Methods of Steel Ship Construction." *Marine Review* 35 (May 30, 1907): pp. 40–42.

_____. "Shipbuilding on the Great Lakes." In *Transactions*, pp. 16, 195–209, plates 86–114. New York: Society of Naval Architects and Marine Engineers, 1909.

Daily Gazette, Vol. 1, no. 4, Detroit, Michigan Territory, Friday, August 15, 1817. Reprinted in *The American Magazine and Historical Chronicle* 4 (Autumn-Winter, 1988–1989): pp. 55–56.

Daily Graphic, The (New York)

"Deeper Water." *Chicago Inter Ocean* (January 22, 1880): n.p.

De Warville, J. P. Brissot. *New Travels in the United States of America.* Bowling Green, OH: Historical Publications Company, 1919.

Dwight, Edward Huntington. "The New Whaleback Boats." *Harper's Weekly.* (September 5, 1891): pp. 672, 675.

Elstner Publishing Company. *The Industries of Cleveland.* Cleveland, OH: The Elstner Publishing Company, 1888.

Ely, George H. *Arguments and Statistics Presented to the U.S. Tariff Commission.* Philadelphia, PA: National Executive Committee Iron Ore Producers, 1882.

Ely, S. P. "Historical Address," delivered on July 4, 1876. Reprinted in *Report of the Pioneer Society of the State of Michigan, 1886*, VII (pp. 165–173). Lansing, MI: Thorp & Godfrey, 1904.

Everett, Philo. "Finding the Iron Mountains." In *The Great Lakes Reader*, ed., Walter Havighurst, pp. 95–99.

Fischer, William C., and Christop R. Lohmann, eds. *W. D. Howells: Selected Letters*, Vol. 5, 1902–1911. Boston, MA: Twayne Publishers, 1933.

Fondue du Lac (Wisconsin) *Reporter*

Foord, John. "The Great Lakes and Our Commercial Supremacy." *The North American Review* (August 1898): pp. 155–164.

Forster, John H. "Lake Superior Country." In *Collections of the Pioneer Society of the State of Michigan*, Vol. VIII, 1885. Lansing, MI: Michigan Pioneer Society, 1907.

Frank Leslie's Illustrated Newspaper

Fremont (Ohio) *Journal*

Griswold, Stanley. "Ancient Naval Fight on Lake Erie." *Nile's National Register* 9 (October 14, 1815). Reprinted in *Inland Seas* 7 (Spring 1951): pp. 113–114.

Harper's Weekly

Harvey, Charles Thompson. Papers, GLMS-17. The Center for Archival Collections. Bowling Green State University, Bowling Green, Ohio.

Hayes, J. D. "The Niagara Ship Canal," a published paper. Buffalo, NY: Printing House of Matthews and Warren, 1865.

Hennepin, Louis. *A Description of Louisiana.* New York: John G. Shea, 1880.

_____. *A New Discovery of a Vast Country in America, Extending above Four Thousand Miles,*

Between New France and New Mexico; with a Description of the Great Lakes, Catar-acts, Rivers, Plants, and Animals. Also, the Manners, Customs, and Languages of the Several Native Indians: and the Advantages of Commerce with Those Different Nations. London: M. Bentley, F. Tonson, H. Bonwick, T. Goodwin, and S. Manship, 1689.

Henry, Alexander. *Travels and Adventures in Canada and the Indian Territories between the Years 1760 and 1776.* New York: I. Riley, 1809.

Hodge, William. *Papers Concerning Early Navigation on the Lakes.* Buffalo, NY: Bigelow Brothers, 1883.

"Hoisting Iron Ore." *Cleveland Herald*, December 10, 1884.

Houghton, Douglas. "The Mineral Veins," an excerpt from his 1840 survey of Michigan's Upper Peninsula. In *The Great Lakes Reader*, ed., Walter Havighurst, 60–61. New York: Macmillan Company, 1966.

"Hudson Suspension Bridge, The." *Harper's Weekly*, May 10, 1890, p. 361.

Hughes, Sarah Forbes, ed. *Letters and Recollections of John Murray Forbes*, 2 volumes. Boston, MA: Houghton, Mifflin and Company, 1899.

Hurt, Paul T., Jr. "Vacation Voyages on Inland Seas. *Inland Seas* 7 (1951): pp. 257–263.

"Improving Ore Handling Equipment at Lorain." *Marine Review* (July 21, 1898): p. 9.

"Increasing Use of Steel Castings." *Scientific American*, Vol. XLIII, No. 3 (July 17, 1880): p. 42

Iron and Steel Institute. *The Iron and Steel Institute in America in 1890: Special Volume of "Proceedings."* London: E. and F. N. Spon, n.d.

Iron and Steel Institute in America in 1890, The. London: E. & F. N. Spon, n.d.

"Iron Ore Trade." *Cleveland Herald*, November 3, 1884.

Iron Trade Review.

Ise, John, ed. *Sod-house Days: Letters from a Kansas Homesteader, 1877–1878.* Lawrence, KS: University of Kansas Press, 1986.

Kappler, Charles J. *Indian Affairs: Laws and Treaties, vol. II, Treaties.* Washington: Government Printing Office, 1904.

Kingston, William H. G. *Western Wanderings*, selected portions reproduced in *Michigan History* 39 (1955): pp. 282–297.

Lake Carriers' Association. "Agency History." GLMS-44. Center for Archival Collections, Institute for Great lakes Research. Bowling Green State University, Bowling Green, Ohio.

Lake Carriers' Association. *Annual Report of the Lake Carriers' Association.* Cleveland, OH, and Detroit, MI: Lake Carriers' Association, 1885–present.

Lake Superior Journal, Saturday, November 13, 1852. Reprinted in *Inland Seas* 8 (Winter 1952): p. 291.

Lake Superior News & Mining Journal "Launch of the *Atlanta*." *Harper's Weekly.* (October 25, 1884) p. 701.

Lewis, Janet. "The Battle of the Millrace." In *Great Lakes Reader*, pp. 256–258. Edited by Walter Havighurst. New York: Macmillan Co., 1966.

Lindblad, A. F. "A Critical Analysis of the Factors Affecting Safety and Operation of the Bulk Freight Vessels of the Great Lakes." Ph.D. Dissertation, University of Michigan, 1924. Reprinted in *Marine Review* (October, November, December 1924, February 1925).

Livingston, W. Letter to Harvey Brown. August 5, 1889. MSS 3342, Harvey H. Brown Papers. Western Reserve Historical Society. Cleveland, Ohio.

Lloyd, William Stokely. "Our Lake Commerce." *Harper's Weekly*, September 21, 1895, p. 897.

Lloyd's of London. *Inland Lloyd's.* London: Lloyd's of London, 1885.

Lloyd's of London. *Lloyd's.* London: Lloyd's of London, 1916.

"Making Bessemer Rails." *Harper's Weekly*, Vol. XXX, no. 1529 (April 10, 1886): p. 238.

"Manufactures of Pittsburgh." *Cleveland Daily Plain Dealer*, January 8, 1867.

Marine Review

Martin, E. C. "Leaves from an Old Time Journal." In *Michigan Pioneer and Historical Collections*, vol. XXX. Lansing, MI: Pioneer and Historical Society, 1906.

Massey, H. "Traveling on the Great Lakes when Detroit Was Young," *The Detroit Free Press.* Reprinted in *Report of the Pioneer Society of the State of Michigan, 1836*, VII. Lansing, MI: Thorp & Godfrey, 1904, pp. 131–133.

McDougall, Alexander. *The Autobiography of Alexander McDougall.* Reprinted in *Inland Seas*, XXIII (1967): pp. 91–103, 199–216, 282–301 and XIV (1968): pp. 16–33, 138–147.

McKenney, Thomas L. *Sketches of a Tour to the Lakes.* Baltimore, MD: Fielding Lucas, Jr., 1827.

Melville, George W., ed., *Proceedings of the International Engineering Congress, Division of Marine and Naval Engineering and Naval Architecture*, 2 volumes. New York: John Wiley and Sons, 1894.

Merritt, D. H. "History of the Marquette Ore Docks," a paper read by Dr. T. A. Feich at the

joint meeting of the Michigan Pioneer and
Historical Society, August 23, 1918, at Mar-
quette, Michigan. A published version, from
the Frank E. Hamilton Collection, is in the
Charles E. Frohman Collection, Rutherford
B. Hayes Presidential Center, Fremont, Ohio.
Michigan Pioneer and Historical Collection
Miller, Walter. "Marine Engineering on the
Great Lakes — Past and Present." In *Beeson's
Marine Directory.* Chicago, IL: Harvey C.
Beeson, 1897, pp. 245–246.
_____. "Ship-Building and Engineering on the
Great Lakes." In *Proceedings of the Interna-
tional Engineering Congress,* Vol. II, Paper
XXXVI, ed., George W. Melville. New York:
John Wiley & Sons, 1894.
Morrison, Lauchlin P. "Recollections of the
Great Lakes, 1874–1944." *Inland Seas* IV: pp.
173–183, 219–227; V: pp. 48–51, 106–110;
VI: 43–46, 105–110, 185–188, 258–262; VI:
pp. 46–53, 118–127.
Mullet, John to Sylvester Sibley, April 1834.
Burton Historical Collection, Detroit Public
Library. Reprinted in Milo Quaife, *Lake
Michigan.* New York: Bobbs-Merrill Co.,
1945, Chapter 15, endnote 3.
Mushkat, Jerome. "Mineral and Timber
Prospects in Upper Michigan: The 1858
Diary of John V. L. Pruyn." *Inland Seas* 30
(1974): pp. 84–89.
"New Lake Steamers." *Scientific American*
(reprinted from *Marine Review*) (January 16,
1892): p. 34.
"New Steel Steamship." *Chicago Inter Ocean*
(January 2, 1886): n.p.
New York Daily Tribune
New York Times
Newman, R. L. "Construction of Lake Steam-
ers." A paper delivered to the Civil Engineers
Club of Cleveland and printed in *Marine Re-
view.* (March 3, 1898): p. 8.
Nile's National Register
"Not by a Dam Site." *Beeson's Handbook, 1901.*
Chicago, IL: Harvey C. Beeson, p. 181.
Oldham, Joseph R. "Comparison of the Types
of Steamers on the Great Lakes with Regard
to Strength, Efficiency, and Location of Ma-
chinery." In *Proceedings of the International
Engineering Congress,* Vol. II, paper XXXVII,
pp. 1–19. Edited by George W. Melville. New
York: John Wiley & Sons, 1894.
"Ore Unloading Machines for Use at Receiving
Docks." *Engineering News,* Vol. 54, No. 5
(August 3, 1905): pp. 125–126.
Palmer, Mary A. W. "The Short Life of the
Walk-in-the-Water. In *Great Lakes Reader,* pp.
295–299. Edited by Walter Havighurst. New
York: Macmillan Co., 1966.

Patterson, Captain Howard. *Patterson's Illustrated Nautical Dictionary.* New York:
Howard Patterson, 1891.
Penton, Henry. "Low Cost of Lake Transportation." *Marine Review,* 58 (December 1928):
pp. 37–39.
Phillips, Barnet. "The Construction of Great
Buildings." *Harper's Weekly,* April 12, 1890,
pp. 282–283.
Pickands, Mather, and Company. Annual State-
ments. Container 1, Folders 1 (1889) and 2
(1891). The Western Reserve Historical Soci-
ety, Cleveland, Ohio.
Pickering, Timothy Manuscript, Burton His-
torical Collection, Detroit Public Library.
Reprinted in *Inland Seas,* Vol. 1 (October
1945): p. 15.
Poe, Orlando M. Interview in *Marine Review,*
IV August 6, 1891, p. 6.
Polk, R. L. *Directory of the Marine Interests of the
Great Lakes.* Detroit: R. L. Polk & Company,
1884.
Poor, Henry V. *Sketch of the Rise and Progress of
the Internal Improvements, and the Internal
Commerce of the United States.* New York: H.
V. & H. W. Poor, 1881.
Porter, Robert P. "Cleveland: Its Industrial Sta-
tus in Relation to Traffic of the Great Lakes."
Published address to Cleveland Board of In-
dustry and Improvement, April 26, 1892.
Cleveland, OH: Cleveland Board of Indus-
try and Improvement, 1892.
"Progress of the Maryland Steel Company." *Sci-
entific American* (July 23, 1891): p. 56.
"Protect the Lime Kiln's Crossing." *Marine Re-
view,* IV (October 15, 1891): p. 4.
"Representative Houses: Cleveland's Leading
Mercantile, Manufacturing and Financial
Concerns." In *The Industries of Cleveland.*
Cleveland, OH: The Elstner Publishing Co.,
1888.
Richardson, James D., ed. *A Compilation of the
Messages and Papers of the Presidents,* 20 vol-
umes. New York: Bureau of National Liter-
ature, Inc., 1897.
"Russian Imperial Steam-Yacht." *Harper's
Weekly.* (August 21, 1880): pp. 539–540.
St. John, John. *A True Description of the Lake
Superior Country.* New York: Wm. H. Gra-
ham, 1846; reprint edition, Grand Rapids,
MI: Black Letter Press, 1976.
"St. Mary's Falls Canal." *Scientific American*
LIII, no. 25 (December 19, 1885): p. 386.
Sandusky (Ohio) *Register*
Schoolcraft, Henry Rowe. *Narrative Journal of
Travels through the Northwestern Regions of the
United States extending from Detroit through
the Great Chain of American Lakes to the*

Sources of the Mississippi River in the Year 1820. Ed., Mentor L. Williams. East Lansing, MI: Michigan State University Press, 1992.

Scientific American

Scott, George. *Scott's New Coast Pilot for the Lakes.* Detroit, MI: Detroit Free Press Printing Company, 1895.

Ship Carpenters and Caulkers Protective Association of the City of Cleveland. *Preamble, Constitution and By-laws of the Ship Carpenters and Caulkers Protective Association of the City of Cleveland.* Cleveland, OH: Fairbanks, Benedict & Co., 1861. (Copy located at Western Reserve Historical Society, Cleveland, Ohio.)

"Steamboats on Lake Erie." *Bethel Magazine.* January 1836. Reprinted in *Black Rock Advocate*, March 31, 1836, 3. Reprinted in *Freshwater* 5 (1990): pp. 16–19.

"Steel Steamer *Choctaw*." *Scientific American.* (August 20, 1892): p. 115.

"Steel Tow Lines." *Scientific American* (September 14, 1878): p. 168.

"Tariff on Iron and Steel Justified by Its Results." In (n.a.) *Tariff/Iron and Steel*, John Sherman Collection. Rutherford B. Hayes Presidential Center. Fremont, Ohio.

Thayer, Gordon W., ed. "The Great Lakes in the *Nile's National Register*." (*Inland Sea* carried this as a regular section in many of its early editions.)

Thomas Gawn, Schooner. Log. 1880. Center for Archival Collections, Institute for Great Lakes Research: Great Lakes Vessels Index. Bowling Gren State University, Bowling Green, Ohio.

Thompson, Merwin Stone. *An Ancient Mariner Recollects.* Oxford, OH: Typoprint, Inc., 1967.

Thompson, Thom. S. *Thompson's Coast Pilot and Sailing Directions for the North-Western Lakes.* Detroit, MI: Wm. A. Scripps, 1878.

Thwaites, Reuben G. ed. *The Jesuit Relations and Allied Documents: Travels and Explorations of the Jesuit Missionaries in New France, 1610–179,* 73 volumes. Cleveland, OH: Burrows Brothers Co., 1896–1901.

Toledo (Ohio) Blade

"Two New Propellers." *Cleveland Herald*, January 24, 1884.

"Use of Steel for Structural Purposes." *Scientific American*, Vol. XLII, No. 20 (May 15, 1880): p. 304.

"A Very Old Petition to Congress." *Marine Review*, October 8, 1891, p. 10.

Ward, Eber. "The Remarkable Family of Ward." An oral interview reprinted in *Inland Seas* 17 (1961): pp. 58–60.

Ward, Eber. "The Soo Locks." In *Great Lakes Reader*, 279–280. Edited by Walter Havighurst. New York: Macmillan Co., 1966.

Wetherell, James. Letter, September 15, 1815. Reprinted in Frank H. Severance, ed. *Publications of the Buffalo Historical Society*, XXIV. Buffalo, NY: Buffalo Historical Society, 1920.

White, Peter. "Development of the Lake Superior Region." *Sault Ste. Marie Evening Star*, August 3, 1905. Reprinted in *Inland Seas* 11 (Summer 1955): pp. 92–102.

_____. "The Iron Region of Lake Superior." In *Collections of the Pioneer Society of the State of Michigan*, Vol. VIII. Lansing, MI: Michigan Pioneer Society, 1907, pp. 145–161.

Government Documents

Andrews, Israel D. *Report on the Trade and Commerce of the British North American Colonies, and Upon the Trade of the Great Lakes and Rivers.* Washington: Beverly Tucker, Senate Printer, 1854.

Barter, Mr. "Longshore work — Great Lakes," a report of the secretary-treasurer of the International Longshoremen's Association. Published in *Report of the Industrial Commission of Transportation*, X. Washington: Government Printing Office, 1901.

Birkinbine, John. "Iron Ore," a special report in *Mines and Quarries, 1902.* U.S. Bureau of the Census. Washington: Government Printing Office, 1905.

Commissioner of Navigation. *Report of the Commissioner of Navigation to the Secretary of the Treasury.* Washington: Government Printing Office, 1897. "Chart of registered gross tonnage by year (1868–1897) for the lakes," p. 292.

Gray, William G. "Iron and Steel," a special report included in *Industries*, Vol. X, *Manufactures*, Part IV. U.S. Bureau of the Census. Washington: Government Printing Office, 1902.

Hall, Henry. "Report on the Ship-building Industry of the United States," a special report in the *Tenth Census of the United States, 1880*, Vol. VIII. Department of the Interior. Bureau of the Census. Washington: Government Printing Office, 1884.

Industrial Commission on Transportation. *Report of the Industrial Commission on Transportation*, Vol. IV. Washington: Government Printing Office, 1900.

Lewis, Joseph D. "Great Lakes and St. Lawrence," in *Transportation by Water.* Department of Commerce and Labor. Bureau of the Census. Washington: Government Printing Office, 1906.

Newcomb, H. T. *Changes in the Rates of Charge for Railway and Other Transportation Services,* Bulletin No. 15. Department of Agriculture, Division of Statistics. n.p. 1901.

Purdy, T. C. "Report on Steam Navigation in the United States," in *Report on Agencies of Transportation in the United States, including the Statistics of Railroads, Steam Navigation, Canals, Telegraphs, and Telephones,* Vol. IV. Department of the Interior. Census Office. Washington: Government Printing Office, 1883.

Smith, Alexander. "Shipbuilding," in *Twelfth Census, Reports,* Vol. X, *Manufactures,* Part IV. Bureau of the Census. Washington: Government Printing Office, 1902.

Stacey, Francis N. "Great Lakes and St. Lawrence River," in *Transportation by Water, 1916.* Department of Commerce. Bureau of the Census. Washington: Government Printing Office, 1920.

Swank, James M. ""Statistics of Iron and Steel Production." In *Tenth Census of the United States, 1880.* Washington: Government Printing Office, 1883.

Tunell, George Gerard. *Statistics of Lake Commerce.* Secretary of the Treasury. Bureau of Statistics. Washington: Government Printing Office, 1898.

_____. *Transportation on the Great Lakes of North America.* House Document No. 277, 55th Cong., 2nd Sess., 1998.

United States. Army Corps of Engineers. A. N. Lee to G. Weitzel, November 24, 1875, in *Report on Detroit River, December 31, 1875.* House Exec. Doc. 39, 44th Cong., 1st Sess., X: p. 3.

_____. _____. A. W. Whipple to J. J. Albert, Annual Report, October 1, 1859. In *Letters and Reports Sent Relating to Projects, 1859–1895,* Vol. 2, St. Clair Flats. Corps of Engineers, Detroit District, Record Group 77, National Archives and Records Administration (hereafter NARA), Chicago, Illinois.

_____. _____. A. W. Whipple to J. J. Abert, January 8, 1857, in *Report on St. Clair Flats.* Senate Exec. Report 46, 34th Cong. 3rd Sess., VIII: pp. 12–16.

_____. _____. "Formation of the Lakes, a Fact Sheet." Detroit District: U.S. Army Corps of Engineers, n.d.

_____. _____. G. Weitzel to A. A. Humphreys, November 26, 1875, in *Report on Detroit River, December 31, 1875.* House Exec. Doc. 39, 44th Cong., 1st Sess., X: p. 2.

_____. _____. George C. Meade to James Kear-

ney, December 19, 1856, in *Report on St. Clair Flats.* Senate Exec. Report 46, 34th Cong., 3rd Sess., VIII: p. 6–11.

_____. _____. J. J. Abert to C. M. Conrad, May 28, 1852, *Report on Improvement of the St. Clair Flats, May 31, 1852.* Senate Exec. Doc. 76, 32nd Cong., 1st Sess., XI: p. 2.

_____. _____. James Kearney to J. J. Abert, December 24, 1856, in *Report on St. Clair Flats.* Senate Exec. Doc. 46, 34th Cong., 3rd Sess., VIII: p. 4.

_____. _____. "Report of Major G. Weitzel, Corps of Engineers, Bvt Maj. Gen., U.S., Office in charge for the fiscal year ending June 30, 1881, with other documents relating to the works." In *Report of the Chief of Engineers, U.S. Army,* appendix J.J. Washington: U.S. Government Printing Office, 1881.

_____. _____. *Report of the Chief of Engineers, 1920,* Part III, *Miscellaneous Reports.* Washington: Government Printing Office, 1920.

_____. _____ and United States Shipping Board. *Transportation of the Great Lakes.* Washington: U.S. Government Printing Office, 1926.

_____. _____ and United States Shipping Board Transportation Series n. 2, *Transportation in the Mississippi and Ohio Valleys.* Washington: U.S. Government Printing Office, 1929.

_____. _____. *Special Reports.* "Transportation by Water." Washington: Government Printing Office, 1906.

_____. Bureau of the Census. *Statistical Atlas of the Twelfth Census of the United States, 1900.* Washington: Government Printing Office, 1903.

_____. Commissioner of Navigation. *Thirty-Second Annual List of Merchant Vessels of the United States.* Washington: Government Printing Office, 1900.

_____. Congress. *Congressional Globe.*

_____. _____. *Congressional Record.*

_____. _____. Misc. Doc no. 190, "Overloading of Vessels on Great Lakes, etc." 50th Cong., 1st Sess., February 9, 1888.

_____. _____. House. Brig. Gen. B. F. Kelly to Maj. Gen. George B. McClellan, November 6, 1861. Serial Set, H., misc. doc. 15 (37–3), p. 1171.

_____. _____. _____. Congressman Edward Wade in report from Committee of Commerce, *Improvements of the Navigation of the Northern and Northwestern Lakes, etc.* House Report 316, 34th Cong., 1st Sess., August 2, 1856, Vol. III.

_____. _____. _____. Congressman Omar D. Conger speaking for the river and harbor appropriations. House report 2092, 41st Cong., 2nd Sess., June 13, 1870, Vol. 92.

_____. _____. _____. Congressman Samuel P. Snider speaking for River and Harbor Bill. House Report 9486, 51st Cong., 1st Sess., August 22, 1890. Vol. 21, part 9.

_____. _____. _____. Congressman Theodore E. Burton speaking on "The Great Lakes," 52nd Cong., 2nd Sess., February 5, 1891. Appendix, Vol. 22, 143.

_____. _____. _____. Dingle Report, 1882. Serial Set, H. Rep. 1827 (47–2).

_____. _____. _____. E. T. Evans to Henry L. Abbott, November 23, 1886, in *Portage Lake Canals*, House Report 1025, Appendix A, "Casualties on the South Shore of Lake Superior." 51st Cong., 1st Sess., Appendix, pp. 34–39.

_____. _____. _____. George P. McKay, Sect. of Cleveland Vessels Owners Association, to L. A. Grant, Acting Sect. of War (n.d.). Reprinted by Committee of Rivers and Harbors under the title "Obstruction to Navigation of the Great Lakes," Serial Set, 52nd Cong., 1st Sess., H. Ex. Doc., Vol. 29, pp. 9–28.

_____. _____. _____. "Letter from the Secretary of War Transmitting Reports on the Saint Mary's River and St. Mary's Falls Canal." Ex. Doc. 54. 47th Cong., 1st Sess., pp. 8–9.

_____. _____. _____. A Letter from the Western Iron Ore Association, August 2, 1890, favoring improvements to Sault Ste. Marie Ship-Canal. 52nd Cong., 1st Sess., Vol. 29: p. 8293.

_____. _____. _____. "Payment to Railroads for Transportation of Troops." Letter from Sect. of War Stanton to House, May 16, 1862. Serial Set, H. ex. Doc. 114 (37–2), p. 1137.

_____. _____. _____. Report of the Board of Engineers on Deep Waterways between the Great Lakes and the Atlantic Tide Waters. House Document 149. 56th Cong., 2nd Sess., 1901.

_____. _____. _____. Report on the Geology and Topography of a Portion of the Lake Superior Land District in the State of Michigan. Exec. Doc. 69, 31st Cong., 1st Sess., 1850.

_____. _____. _____. Resolution by Cleveland Vessel Owners' Association supporting takeover of Lake Superior Ship Canal, October 12, 1886, Exec. Doc. 1025, 51st Cong., 1st Sess., Appendix B, p. 44.

_____. _____. _____. "Ship Channel Between the Great Lakes." A letter transmitting a report of Col. O. M. Poe, Chief of Engineers, January 24, 1891. Serial Set, Exec. Doc. 207, 51st Cong., 2nd Sess.

_____. _____. Joint Committee on Printing. *A Compilation of the Messages and Letters of the Presidents*. New York: Bureau of National Literature, Inc., 1897.

_____. _____. _____. Senate. Chart: "Statement of Public Lands Sold and Otherwise Disposed of, to the 30th of September 1851." 32nd Cong., 1st Sess., April 14, 1852.

_____. _____. _____. "Memorial of the Georgia Railroad Company, January 16, 1844." Serial Set, sen. doc. 58 (28–1), p. 432.

_____. _____. _____. National Waterways Commission. *Final Report of the National Waterways Commission*, Senate Doc. 469. 62nd Cong., 2nd Sess., 1912.

_____. _____. _____. Senator Lewis Cass in response to President Pierce's veto of the bill entitled, "An act to remove obstructions to navigation in the mouth of the Mississippi River at the Southwestern Pass and Pass a' l'Outre." 34th Cong., 1st Sess., July 7, 1856. Appendix.

_____. Department of Commerce. Bureau of Foreign and Domestic Commerce. *Statistical Abstract of the United States*. Washington: Government Printing Office, 1930.

_____. _____. Bureau of the Census. *Fourteenth Census of the United States: 1920*, Vol. XI, *Mines and Quarries, 1919*. Washington: Government Printing Office, 1922.

_____. _____. Bureau of Navigation. *List of Merchant Vessels of the United States*. Washington: Government Printing Office, 1868 forward.

_____. _____. _____. *Report of the Commissioner of Navigation, 1897*. Washington: Government Printing Office, 1897.

_____. Department of the Interior. Census Office. *Compendium of the Tenth Census of the United States, 1880*. Washington: Government Printing Office, 1883.

_____. _____. _____. *Compendium of the Eleventh Census of the United States, 1890*. Washington: Government Printing Office, 1892.

_____. _____. _____. "Report on the Statistics of Steam and Water Power Used in the Manufacture of Iron and Steel During the Census Year Ending May 31, 1880," in *Report on Power and Machinery Employed in Manufactures*. Washington: Government Printing Office, 1888.

_____. _____. _____. *Tenth Census of the United States, 1880: Report on the Mining Operations of the United States*, Vol. X. Washington: Government Printing Office, 1882.

_____. _____. _____. Bureau of Statistics. *Statistical Abstract of the United States*. Washington: U.S. Government Printing Office, 1890–1896.

_____. Department of the Treasury. *Report of*

the Commissioner of Navigation to the Secretary of the Treasury, 1897. Washington: Government Printing Office, 1897.
_____. Industrial Commission on Transportation, Vol. IX. "Longshore work — Great Lakes," a report from Mr. Barter, sect.-treas. of the International Longshoremen's Association, CCLXIX-CCLXXII, Washington: Government Printing Office, 1901.
_____. Patent Office. *Specifications and Drawings of Patents Issued from the U.S. Patent Office, May 30, 1871–June 1912.* Washington: Government Printing Office, 1872–1913.
_____. War Department. "Letter from the Secretary of War on the Saint Mary's River and Saint Mary's Canal, January 26, 1882." In H. Ex. Doc. 54, 47th Cong., 1st Sess., p. 4.
Weeks, Joseph D. "The Manufacture of Coke," in *Census Bureau: Special Report.* Department of the Interior. Census Office. Washington: Government Printing Office, 1884.

Miscellaneous

Herdendorf, Charles E. "Environments of the Great Lakes." Seminar, Bowling Green State University, September 21, 1988.
Hirsimaki, Eric to Bruce Bowlus, December 14, 1991.
Labadie, C. Patrick, Director, Canal Park Marine Museum, Duluth, Minnesota. Telephone conversations, May 23, 1991, and January 6, 1992.
_____. "Peas in a Pod." A paper delivered at the annual meeting of the Association for Great Lakes Maritime History, Toledo, Ohio, September 23, 1989.
Martin, Jay. "Construction and Use of Scows on the Great Lakes, 1825–1865." Unpublished paper delivered at the Annual Meeting of the Association of Great Lakes Maritime History, Tobermory, Ontario, Canada, September 14, 1991.
McCutheon, Ted. "Miieconquins Wreck *Forester* Project Update," Comments made at the Annual Meeting of the Association of Great Lakes Maritime History, Tobermory, Ontario, Canada, September 14, 1991.
Pidgeon, William. Letter to the Editor, *Inland Seas* 22 (Spring 1966): p. 77.

Secondary

Books

Andreas, Alfred Theodore. *History of Chicago* (3 volumes). Chicago, IL: By the author, 1884–1886.

"Andrew Carnegie, 'Wealth,' June 1889." In *Great Issues in American History: From Reconstruction to the Present Day, 1864–1969,* ed. Richard Hofstadter, 87–92. New York: Vintage Books, 1969.
Armes, Ethel. *The Story of Coal and Iron in Alabama.* Cambridge, MA: The University Press, 1910.
Arnesen, Eric. "American Workers and the Labor Movement in the Late Nineteenth Century." In *The Gilded Age: Essays on the Origins of Modern America,* ed. Charles W. Calhoun, pp. 39–61. Wilmington, DE: Scholarly Resources, 1996.
Ashworth, William. *The Late, Great Lakes: An Environmental History.* New York: Alfred A. Knopf, 1987.
Avery, Elroy Mckendree. *A History of Cleveland and Its Environs: The Heart of New Connecticut,* Vol. III. *Biography.* Chicago, IL: The Lewis Publishing Company, 1918.
Backert, A. O., ed. *The ABC of Iron and Steel.* Cleveland, OH: The Penton Publishing Company, 1921.
Bald, F. Clever. *Michigan in Four Centuries.* New York: Harper & Rowe, 1961.
Barcus, Frank. *Freshwater Fury.* Detroit, MI: Wayne State University Press, 1960.
Barkenhausen, Henry N. *Focusing on the Centerboard.* Manitowoc, WI: Manitowoc Maritime Museum, 1990.
Barry, James P. *Ships of the Great Lakes: 300 Years of Navigation.* Berkeley, CA: Howell-North Books, 1973.
Bauer, K. Jack. *A Maritime History of the United States.* Columbia, SC: University of South Carolina Press, 1988.
Bayliss, Joseph E., and Estelle L., and Milo Quaife. *River of Destiny: The St. Mary's.* Detroit, MI: Wayne State University Press, 1955.
Beasley, Norman. *Freighters of Fortune: The Story of the Great Lakes.* New York: Harper & Brothers Publishers, 1930.
Beman, Lamar T., Compiler. *Ship Subsidies.* New York: H. W. Wilson, 1923.
Beston, Henry. "The Golden Age of the Canoe." In *Great Lakes Reader,* ed. Walter Havighurst, pp. 31–37. New York: Macmillan Co., 1966.
Bining, Cecil. *Pennsylvania Iron Manufacture.* Harrisburg, PA: Pennsylvania Historical and Museum Commission, 1973.
Biskupie, Joan and Elder Witt. *Guide to the U.S. Supreme Court.* 3rd ed. Washington: Congressional Quarterly, Inc., 1977.
Boyer, Dwight. *Ghost Ships of the Great Lakes.* New York: Dodd, Mead & Company, 1968.
Bridge, James H. *Inside the History of the*

Carnegie Steel Company. New York: The Aldine Book Company, 1903.

Briggs, Asa, ed. The Nineteenth Century: The Contradictions of Progress. London: Thames and Hudson, 1970.

Bruce, Kathleen. Virginia Iron Manufacture in the Slave Era. New York: The Century Co., 1931.

Burt, Struthers. Philadelphia: Holy Experiment. New York: Rich and Cowan, 1947.

Callahan, J. M. "The Northern Lake Frontier during the Civil War." In The Annual Report of the American Historical Association, 1896. Washington: U.S. Government Printing Office, 1897.

Carson, Hampton L. The Supreme Court of the United States. Philadelphia, PA: John Y. Huber Company, 1891.

Cashman, Dennis. America in the Age of Titans: The Progressive Era and World War I. New York: New York University Press, 1988.

Chandler, Alfred D. "The Beginnings of 'Big Business' in American Industry." In The Rise of Big Business, ed. Glenn Porter, 335–367. Syracuse, NY: Syracuse University Press, 1970. First published in Business History Review XXXIII (Spring 1959): pp. 1–31.

_____. The Invisible Hand: The Managerial Revolution in American Business. Cambridge, MA: Harvard University Press, 1977.

Chapman, H. H. The Iron and Steel Industries of the South. Tuscaloosa, AL: University of Alabama Press, 1953.

Cleveland World's History of Cleveland. Cleveland, OH: The Cleveland World, 1891.

Conn, Stetson, Rose C. Engelman, and Byron Fairchild. The United States Army in World War II, The Western Hemisphere: Guarding the United States and Its Outposts. Washington: U.S. Government Printing Office, 1964.

Croil, James. Steam Navigation and Its Relation to the Commerce of Canada and the United States. Toronto: Wm. Briggs, 1898.

Cunliffe, Marcus. The Nation Takes Shape. Chicago, IL: The University of Chicago Press, 1959.

Curwood, James Oliver. The Great Lakes: The Vessels that Plough Them, Their Owners, Their Sailors, and Their Cargoes. New York: G. P. Putnam's Sons, 1909.

Daddow, Samuel H., and Benjamin Bannon. Coal, Iron, and Oil. Philadelphia, PA: J. B. Lippincott & Co., 1866.

Danziger, Edmund J. The Chippewas of Lake Superior. Norman, OK: University of Oklahoma Press, 1979.

Decker, Leslie E. Railroads, Lands, and Politics. Providence, RI: Brown University Press, 1964.

De Kruif, Paul. Seven Iron Men. New York: Harcourt, Brace, & Co., 1929.

Dickenson, John N. To Build A Canal: Sault Ste. Marie, 1853–1854 and After. Columbus, OH: Ohio State University Press, 1981.

Dunbar, Seymour. A History of Travel in America. New York: Tudor Publishing Company, 1937.

Ellis, William Donohue. Land of the Inland Seas: The Historic and Beautiful Great Lakes Country. New York: Weathervane Books, 1974.

Evans, Henry Oliver. Iron Pioneer: Henry W. Oliver, 1840–1904. New York: E. P. Dutton & Co., 1942.

Fassett, F. G., Jr., ed. The Shipbuilding Business in the United States of America. New York: The Society of Naval Architects and Marine Engineers, 1948.

Finlay, J. L., and D. N. Sprague. The Structure of Canadian History. Scarborough, Ontario: Prentice-Hall Canada, Inc., 1984.

Fisher, Douglas A. Steel Making in America. n.p.: U.S. Steel Corporation, 1949.

Fisher, William C., and Christopher K. Lohmann, eds. W. D. Howells: Selected Letters, 1902–1911, Vol. 5. Boston, MA: Twayne Publishers, 1983.

Fletcher, R. A. Steamships and their Story. London: n.p., 1910.

Fogel, Robert William. Railroads and American Economic Growth: Essays in Econometric History. Baltimore, MD: The Johns Hopkins Press, 1964.

Friedman, Leon and Fred L. Israel. The Justices of the United States Supreme Court 1789–1969: Their Lives and Major Decisions, 4 volumes. New York: R. R. Bowker, 1969.

Garraty, John A. The New Commonwealth, 1877–1890. New York: Harper Torchbooks, 1968.

Gephart, William F. Transportation and Industrial Development in the Middle West, Vol. XXXIV, #1 of Studies in History, Economics and Public Law, edited by the faculty of Political Science of Columbia University. New York: Columbia University, 1909.

Gibson, Andrew and Arthur Donovan. The Abandoned Ocean: A History of United States Maritime Policy. Columbia, SC: University of South Carolina Press, 1999.

Gibson, Arrell Morgan. The American Indian: Prehistory to the Present. Lexington, KY: D. D. Heath and Company, 1980.

Ginger, Ray. Age of Excess: The United States from 1877–1914, 2nd ed. New York: Macmillan Publishing Co., Inc., 1975.

Goodrich, Carter. *Government Promotion of American Canals and Railroads, 1800–1890*. New York: Columbia University Press, 1960.

Great Lakes Commerce and the Port of Oswego. Oswego, NY: *Palladium-Times*, 1925.

Greenwood, John O. *The Fleet Histories Series*, Vol. I. Cleveland, OH: Freshwater Press, Inc., 1990.

Hall, Peter Dobkin. *The Organization of American Culture, 1700–1900: Private Institutions, Elites, and the Origins of American Nationality*. New York: New York University Press, 1982.

Haney, Lewis Haney. *A Congressional History of Railways in the United States, 1850–1887*. Madison: University of Wisconsin Press, 1910. Reprinted in *Bulletin of the University of Wisconsin*, #342, part of the *Economics and Political Science Series*, 6: pp. 1–336.

Harper, Frank C. *Pittsburgh of Today, Its Resources and People*, 4 volumes. New York: The American Historical Society, Inc., 1931.

Harvey, George. *Henry Clay Frick: The Man*. Privately printed, 1936. Copyright by Charles Scribner's Sons, New York, 1928.

Hatcher, Harlan. *A Century of Iron and Men*. New York: The Bobbs-Merrill Co., Inc., 1950.

_____. *Lake Erie*. New York: Bobbs-Merrill Company, 1945.

Havighurst, Walter, ed. *The Great Lakes Reader*. New York: Macmillan Co., 1966.

_____. *Long Ships Passing*. New York: Macmillan Co., 1944.

_____. *Vein of Iron: The Pickands Mather Story*. Cleveland, OH: World Publishing Company, 1958.

Hawk, Emory Q. *Economic History of the South*. New York: Prentice-Hall, Inc., 1934.

Haws, Duncan. *Ships and the Sea: A Chronological Review*. New York: Thomas Y. Crowell Company, Inc., 1975.

Hill, Forest S. *Roads, Rails, and Waterways: The Army Engineers and Early Transportation*. Norman, OK: University of Oklahoma Press, 1957.

Hirsimaki, Eric. *The Lakers*. North Olmstead, OH: Mileposts Publishing Company, 1987.

Hoagland, H. E. *Wage Bargaining on Vessels of the Great Lakes*. Urbana, IL: University of Illinois Press, 1917.

Hunter, Louis C. *Steamboats on the Western Rivers: An Economic and Technological History*. Cambridge, MA: Harvard University Press, 1949.

Hutchins, John G. B. *The American Maritime Industries and Public Policy, 1789–1914*. Cambridge, MA: Harvard University Press, 1941.

Joachim, George J. *Iron Fleet: The Great Lakes in World War II*. Detroit, MI: Wayne State University Press, 1994.

Judd, John H. "Life in the Lakes." In *Decisions for the Great Lakes*, eds. A. Donald Misener and Glenda Daniel, pp. 65–70. Hammond, IN: Purdue University Calumet, 1982.

LaFayette, Kenneth D. *Flaming Brands: Fifty Years of iron Making in the Upper Peninsula of Michigan, 1848–1898*. Marquette, MI: Northern Michigan University Press, 1977.

Lake Carrier's Association. "History of the Iron Ore Trade." In *1910 Annual Report of the Lake Carrier's Association*, Cleveland, OH, and Detroit, MI: Lake Carrier's Association, 1910.

Lamoreaux, Naomi R. *The Great Merger Movement in American Business, 1895–1904*. New York: Cambridge University Press, 1987.

Landis, Paul Henry. *Three Iron Mining Towns*. New York: Arno Press, 1970.

Landon, Fred. *Lake Huron*. New York: Bobbs-Merrill Company, 1944.

Lankton, Larry. *Beyond the Boundaries: Life and Landscape at the Lake Superior Copper Mines, 1840–1875*. New York: Oxford University Press, 1997.

_____. *Cradle to Grave: Life, Work, and Death at the Lake Superior Copper Mines*. New York: Oxford University Press, 1991.

Larrowe, Charles P. *Maritime Labor Relations on the Great Lakes*. East Lansing, MI: Labor and Industrial Relations Center, Michigan State University, 1959.

Larson, Henriette M. *The Wheat Market and the Farmer in Minnesota, 1858–1900*. New York: Henrietta M. Larson, 1926.

Larson, John W. *History of Great Lakes Navigation*. Washington: U.S. Government Printing Office, 1983.

Laurent, Jerome King. *The Development of Harbors, Waterborne Shipping and Commerce at Six Wisconsin Ports on Lake Michigan Through 1910*. Ann Arbor, MI: University Microfilms International, 1976.

LesStrang, Jacques. *Cargo Carriers of the Great Lakes*. Boyne City, MI: Harbor House Publishers, 1985.

Livesay, Harold C. *Andrew Carnegie and the Rise of Big Business*. Boston, MA: Little, Brown and Company, 1975.

Lydecker, Ryck. *Pigboat: The Story of the Whalebacks*. Superior, MI: Head of the Lakes Maritime Society, Ltd., 1981.

Lytle, William M. (Compiler). *Merchant Steam Vessels of the United States, 1807–1868*. Mystic, CT: The Steamship Historical Society of America, 1952.

M'Cabe, Jas. D. *Illustrated History of the Great*

Republic. Toledo, OH: O. A. Browning & Co., 1871.

MacGregor, John. *The Progress of America, from the Discovery of Columbus to the Year 1846*. London: Whittaker & Co., 1847.

Mansfield, J. B., ed. *History of the Great Lakes*, 2 volumes. Chicago, IL: J. H. Beers & Co., 1899.

Mason, Philip. *The History of Great Lakes Transportation*. Ann Arbor, MI: Brown-Branfield, 1957.

McCormac, Eugene I. *James K. Polk*. Berkeley, CA: University of California, 1922.

McPherson, James M. *Battle Cry of Freedom*. New York: Oxford University Press, 1987.

Meakin, Alexander C. *Master of the Inland Seas: The Story of Captain Thomas Wilson and the Fleet That Bore His Name*. Vermilion, OH: The Great Lakes Historical Society, 1988.

Melville, Herman. *Moby Dick*. New York: The Library of America, 1983.

Mills, James C. *Our Inland Seas: Their Shipping and Commerce for Three Centuries*. Chicago: A. C. McClug, 1910.

Mills, John M. *Canadian Coastal and Inland Steam Vessels, 1809–1930*. Providence, RI: The Steamship Historical Society of America, Inc., 1981.

Misa, Thomas J. *A Nation of Iron and Steel: The Making of Modern America, 1865–1925*. Baltimore, MD: The Johns Hopkins University Press, 1999.

Morrison, John H. *History of American Steam Navigation*. New York: Stephen Daye Press, 1958.

_____. *Iron and Steel Hull Vessels of the United States, 1825–1905*. Salem, MA: The Steamboat Society of America, 1945.

National Cyclopedia of American Biography. New York: James T. White & Company, 1922.

Neu, Irene D. *Erastus Corning: Merchant and Financer, 1794–1872*. Ithaca, NY: Cornell University Press, 1960.

Nevins, Allan. *John D. Rockefeller: The Heroic Age of American Enterprise*. New York: Charles Scribner's Sons, 1940.

_____. *Study of Power: John D. Rockefeller, Industrialist and Philanthropist* (2 volumes). New York: Scribners, 1953.

Nute, Grace Lee. *Lake Superior*. New York: Bobbs-Merrill Co., 1944.

Orth, Samuel P. *A History of Cleveland*, 3 volumes. Cleveland, OH: The S. J. Clarke Publishing Co., 1910.

Paskoff, Paul. *Industrial Evolution: Organization, Structure, and Growth of the Pennsylvania Iron Industry, 1750–1860*. Baltimore, MD: The Johns Hopkins University Press, 1983.

_____, ed. *Iron and Steel in the Nineteenth Century*. New York: Facts on File, 1989.

Pearson, Henry Greenleafe. *An American Railroad Builder, John Murray Forbes*. New York: Houghton Mifflin Company, 1911.

Pierson, George Wilson. *Tocqueville in America*. Baltimore, MD: The John Hopkins University Press, 1996.

Plowden, David. *End of an Era: The Last of the Great Lakes Steamboats*. New York: W. W. Norton & Co., 1992.

Pounds, Norman J. G. *The Geography of Iron and Steel*. London: Hutchinson and Company, Ltd., 1959.

Quaife, Milo M. *Lake Michigan*. New York: Bobbs-Merrill Company, 1944.

Ransom, Roger L. "Public Canal Investment and the Opening of the Old Northwest." In *Essays on Nineteenth Century Economic History*, eds. David C. Klingman and Richard R. Vedder, Athens, OH: Ohio University Press, 1976.

Ratigan, William. *Great Lakes Shipwrecks & Survivals*. Grand Rapids: Wm. B. Eerdmans Publishing Company, 1977.

Redlich, Fritz. "Introduction." In *Soderfors Anchor-Works History*. Ed. Johan Lundstrom, Boston, MA: Baker Library, Harvard Graduate School of Business Adminsitration, 1970.

Reimann, Lewis C. *Between the Iron and the Pine: A Biography of a Pioneer Family and a Pioneer Town*. Ann Arbor, MI: Northwood Publishers, 1951.

Ringwalt, J. L. *Development of Transportation Systems in the United States*. New York: Johnson Reprint Corp., 1966.

Rosenberg, Nathan. *Technology and American Economic Growth*. New York: Harper and Rowe, 1972.

Rostow, W. W. *Stages of Economic Growth: A Non-Communist Manifesto*. Cambridge, MA: Cambridge University Press, 1971.

Sargent, John H. *Development of Cleveland's Harbor*. Cleveland, OH: Western Reserve Historical Society, 1892.

Schertzer, W. M. "How Great Lakes Waters Move." In *Decisions for the Great Lakes*, eds A. Donald Misener and Glenda Daniel, 51–63. Hammond, IN: Purdue University Calumet, 1982.

Seavoy, R. E. *The Origins of the American Business Community, 1784–1855*. Westport, CT: Greenwood Press, 1982

Shannon, Fred Albert. *The Economic History of the People of the United States*. New York: The Macmillan Company, 1934.

Smith, Henry Nash. *The American West as Symbol and Myth*. Cambridge, MA: Harvard University Press, 1978.

Smith, J. Russell. *The Story of Iron and Steel*. New York: D. Appleton and Company, 1926.

Smith, Thomas H. *The Mapping of Ohio*. Kent, OH: Kent State University Press, 1977.

Synder, Fred L. *Zebra Mussels in Lake Erie: The Invasion & Its Implications*. Columbus, OH: Ohio Sea Grant Program, 1989.

Stampp, Kenneth M. *America in 1857: A Nation on the Brink*. New York: Oxford University Press, 1990.

Stanton, Samuel Ward. *Great Lakes Steam Vessels, #1: American Steam Vessels Series*. Meriden, CT: Meriden Gravure Co., 1962.

Strouse, Jean. *Morgan: American Financier*. New York: Random House, 1999.

Sutcliffe, Andrea. *Steam: The Untold Story of America's First Great Invention*. New York: Palgrave Macmillan, 2004.

Tanner, Helen Hornbeck, ed. *Atlas of Great Lakes Indian History*. Norman, OK: University of Oklahoma Press, 1987.

Tarbell, Ida. *Life of Elbert H. Gary: The Story of Steel*. New York: D. Appleton and Company, 1925.

Taussig, F. W. *The Tariff History of the United States*. New York: G. P. Putnam's Sons, 1888.

Taylor, George Rogers. *The Transportation Revolution, 1815–1860*. New York: Rinehart & Co., Inc., 1951.

Temin, Peter. *Iron and Steel in Nineteenth Century America*. Cambridge, MA: The M. I. T. Press, 1964.

Tripple, John. "Big Businessmen and a New Economy." In *The Gilded Age*, ed. H. Wayne Morgan, Syracuse, NY: Syracuse University Press, 1970.

Turner, George Edgar. *Victory Rode the Rails*. New York: Bobbs-Merrill Company, Inc., 1953.

Tweet, Ronald D. *History of Transportation on the Upper Mississippi and Illinois Rivers*, Navigation History NWS-83–6. N.p.: National Waterways Study, U.S. Army Engineer Water Resources Support Center, Institute for Water Resources, 1983.

Van Brunt, Walter, ed. *Duluth and St. Louis County: Their Story and People*, Vol. 1. Chicago, IL, and New York: The American Historical Society, 1921.

Van Deusen, Glyndon G. *The Jacksonian Era, 1828–1848*. New York: Harper & Row, 1963.

Van Nostrand's Scientific Encyclopedia. Princeton, NJ: D. Van Nostrand Company, Inc., 1968.

Waggoner, Clark, ed. *History of the City of Toledo and Lucas County*. Toledo, OH: Munsell & Company, 1888.

Wall, Joseph Frazier. *Andrew Carnegie*. Pittsburgh, PA: University of Pittsburgh Press, 1970.

Walter, J. Bernard. *The Story of Steel*. New York: Harper & Brothers Publishers, 1926.

Ward, David. *Cities and Immigrants: A Geography of Change in Nineteenth Century America*. New York: Oxford University Press, 1971.

Warren, Charles. *The Supreme Court in United States History* (2 volumes). Boston, MA: Little, Brown, and Company, 1932.

Wender, Herbert. *Southern Commercial Conventions, 1837–1859*. Baltimore, MD: Johns Hopkins Press, 1930.

Whiffen, Marcus. *American Architecture Since 1870*. Cambridge, MA: M. I. T. Press, 1981.

Williams, Ralph. *The Honorable Peter White*. Cleveland, OH: Penton Publishing Company, 1907.

Williamson, Jeffrey G. "The Railroads and Midwestern Development, 1870–1890: A General Equilibrium History." In *Essays in Nineteenth Century Economic History: The Old Northwest*, eds. David C. Klingman and Richard K. Vedder, Athens, OH: Ohio University Press, 1975.

Witt, Elder, ed. *Guide to the U.S. Supreme Court*. Washington: Congressional Quarterly, Inc., 1979.

Woodford, Arthur M. *Charting the Inland Seas*. Detroit: U.S. Army Corps of Engineers, 1991.

Workman, James C. "Shipping on the Great Lakes." In *Historical Transactions 1893–1943*. New York: The Society of Naval Architects and Marine Engineers, 1945.

Wright, Richard J. *Freshwater Whales: A History of the American Shipbuilding Company and Its Predecessors*. Kent, OH: The Kent State University Press, 1969.

Newspaper and Periodical Articles

"American Industries, n. 33: Manufacture of Rolled Iron." *Scientific American* (March 6, 1880).

Annals of Cleveland. Cleveland, OH: WPA Project no. 16823, 1938.

Atkins, Kenneth S. "*Le Griffon*: A New View." *Inland Seas* 46 (Fall 1990): pp. 162–169.

Baker, Wallace J., Jr. "On Manitoulin Island." *Inland Seas* 3 (October 1947): pp. 211–217.

Beck, John P. "They Fought for their Work: Upper Peninsula Iron Ore Trimmer Wars." *Michigan History* 73 (1989): pp. 24–31.

Blossom, Stephan A. "The Frontier: Handmaiden to Giants." *Inland Seas* 39 (1983): pp. 4–20.

Blust, Frank A. "The U.S. Lake Survey, 1841–

1974." *Inland Seas* 32 (Summer 1976): pp. 91–104.

Boyer, Dwight. "Those Magnificent Huletts." *The Cleveland Plain Dealer Sunday Magazine* (July 6, 1969): pp. 22–23.

Brinks, Herbert J. "The Era of Pig Iron in the Upper Peninsula of Michigan." *Inland Seas* 25 (1969): pp. 225–234.

Brotherton, R. A. "Discovery of Iron Ore: Negaunee Centennial." *Michigan History* 28 (April-June 1944): pp. 199–213.

_____. "Iron Money." *Inland Seas* 3 (1947): pp. 193–195.

_____. "Story of Philo Everett's Trip form Jackson, Michigan, to Marquette in 1845." *Inland Seas* 1 (October 1945): pp. 23–28, and 2 (January 1946): pp. 45–49.

Brown, Andrew T. "The Great Lakes, 1850–1861." *Inland Seas* 6 (1950): 99–103, 161–165, 185–189.

Burke, H. N. "Weather and the Great Lakes." *Inland Seas* 13 (Summer 1957): pp. 138–141.

Burke, John A. "Barrels to Barrows, buckets to Belts: 120 Years of iron Ore Handling on the Great Lakes." *Inland Seas* 31 (1975): pp. 266–277, 298–299.

Calkins, Elijah. "Report of St. Mary's Falls Ship Canal, 1857." *Michigan History* 39 (1957): pp. 71–80.

Canadaian Shipbuilding and Ship Repairing Association, Ottawa, Canada. *Newsletter*, 4 (April 1961). Reprinted in *Inalnd Seas* 22 (1966): 154.

Chicago Sunday Tribune

Cleveland Plain Dealer

Commons, John R. "Types of American Labor Unions: The Longshoremen of the Great Lakes." *The Quarterly Journal of Economics* XX (November 1905): pp. 59–85.

Dean, Jewell R. "The Wilson Fleet, Freight Pioneers." *Inland Seas* 2 (July 1946): pp. 159–164.

Dickson, Kenneth R. "The Schooner *David Dows*" *Metropolitan* (March 1988): pp. 63–67.

Dobbins, D. P. "List of Vessels on the Lakes Prior to 1806" *Inland Seas* 13 (1957): p. 70.

Dutton, Fred W. "Life on the Great Lakes: A Wheelman's Story." *Inland Seas* 39 (1983): pp. 256–275.

Edwards, Thomas S. "Strangers in a Strange Land: The Frontier Letters of John and Anna Graves." *Hayes Historical Journal* 4 (Summer 1987): pp. 16–28.

England, R. W. "The Engineer." *Inland Seas* 1 (1945): pp. 11–13.

Ericson, Bernard E. "The Evolution of Great Lakes Ships: Part I — Sail." *Inland Seas* 25 (1969): pp. 91–104, 129.

_____. "The Evolution of Great Lakes Ships: Part II — Steam and Steel." *Inland Seas* 25 (1969): pp. 199–212, 220–221. (Originally presented at the meeting of the Society of Naval Architects and Marine Engineers, Cleveland, Ohio, January 24, 1968.)

Felter, Charles E. "The Wreck of the Brig *Sandusky*: A Story Dating Back 142 Years." *Ye Olde Fishwrapper* (September 1990): pp. 22–23.

Fitzpatrick, R. W. "On the Great Lakes." *Cosmopolitan* XXV (May 1898).

Fleming, Roy F. "The Search for La Salle's Brigantine *Le Griffon*." *Inland Seas* 8 (1952): pp. 223–228.

Francis, David W. "Early Lighthouse Construction on the Great Lakes: A Case Study." *Inland Seas* 44 (1988): pp. 290–299.

Franklin, John Hope. "The Southern Expansionists of 1846." *Journal of Southern History* 25 (1959): pp. 323–338.

Froggett, J. F. "Shipping on the Great Lakes Is an Indispensable Asset to Business." *Marine Review* 58 (1928): pp. 78–82.

Gebhart, Richard. "The Coming of the Yellow Monster." *Telescope*, XXXIX, No. 6 (November-December 1991): pp. 149–151.

Gilmore, James. "The St. Lawrence River Canal Vessels," Part II. *Inland Seas* 12 (1957): pp. 17–23.

Halsey, Harlon I. "The Choice between High-Pressure and Low-Pressure Steam Power in America in the Early Nineteenth Century." *The Journal of Economic History* XLI (1981): pp. 723–744.

Halsey, John R. "The Reeck of a Small Vessel." *Michigan History Magazine* 75 (March-April 1991): pp. 30–36.

Hardy, George R. "The David Dows." *Inland Seas* 1 (1945): p. 54.

Harp, Gillis J. "A Republic of Social Industrialism: The Reform Thought of T. B. Wakeman." *Hayes Historical Journal* IX (spring 1990): pp. 5–19.

Harvey, Hank. "A Century of Shipbuilding." *Toledo Magazine* (October 15–21, 1989): pp. 4–6.

Henrickson, Merle. "Michigan Lumberman's Shipping: Impact of Western Problems on the Development of a Constituency for the Republican Party, 1840–1860." *Chronicle* 26 (Fall 1990): pp. 2–7, 19–20.

Hirsimaki, Eric. "The Hulett Story." *Inland Seas* 47 (1991): pp. 82–95.

_____. "The Huron Hustler." *Nickel Plate Road Magazine* XXII (Winter-Spring 1988): pp. 4–36.

_____. "The Ore Docks." *Inland Seas* 47 (1991): pp. 165–178.

Hodge, William. "The Pioneer Lake Erie Steamboat." In *Papers Concerning Early Navigation on the Great Lakes*. Buffalo, NY: Bigelow Brothers, 1883, pp. 23–44.

Hoogenboom, Ari and Olive. "Alfred T. White: Settlement Worker and Housing Reformer." *Hayes Historical Journal* IX (Fall 1989): pp. 5–31.

Hoopes, Roy. "It Was Bad Last Time Too: The Credit Mobilier Scandal of 1872." *American Heritage* (February-March 1991): pp. 58–59.

Hunter, Grace. "Life on Lake Erie a Century Ago." *Inland Seas* 22 (1966): pp. 17–28, 111–120, 196–207.

Inches, H. C. "The Copper Country and the Keweenaw Waterway." *Inland Seas* 8 (1952): pp. 155–159

_____. "Wooden Ship Building." *Inland Seas* VII (1951): pp. 3–12.

_____, and Chester J. Partlow. "Great Lakes Driftwood: Schooner Scows." *Inland Seas* 20 (1964): pp. 289–294.

Inkster, Tom H. "McDougall's Whalebacks." *American Neptune* 25 (1965): pp. 168–175.

Jacobs, Fred B. "Shipbuilding Science Makes Rapid Strides During the Past Fifty Years." *Marine Review* 58 (July 1928): pp. 40–45, 110.

"John Ericsson." *Harper's Weekly*. January 1, 1887, p. 10.

Jones, Roger M. "The Rockefeller Fleet." *Inland Seas* 3 (1947): pp. 131–136.

Kirby, Frank E. "Shipping on the Great Lakes." *Engineering* XCII (July 1911): pp. 62–63.

Kirby, Frank E., and A. P. Rankin. "The Bulk Carrier of the Great Lakes." *Inland Seas* 34 (1978): pp. 218–223.

Klein, L. "Notes on the Steam Navigation Upon the Great Northern Lakes." *American Railroad Journal* (May 15 and June 1, 1841): n.p. Reprinted in *Inland Seas* 48 (1992): pp. 49–58.

Laurent, Jerome K. "Sources of Capital and Expenditures for Internal Improvements in a Developing Region: The Case of Wisconsin Lake Ports, 1836–1910." *Exploration in Economic History* 13 (1976).

_____. "Trade Associations and Competition in Great Lakes Shipping: The Pre-World War I Years." *International Journal of Maritime History* IV (December 1992): pp. 118–120.

Lee, Don. "Bones in the Bay." *Sandusky* (Ohio) *Register* 166 (October 11, 1988): pp. 1–2.

Martin, Jay. "The Principle of Beneficence: The Early History of the International Ship Masters' Association." *Hayes Historical Journal* XI (1991): pp. 5–12.

Mason, Phillip. "The Operation of the Sault Canal, 1857." *Michigan History* 39 (1955): pp. 69–80.

McDonald, W. A. "Composite Steamers Built by the Detroit Drydock Company." *Inland Seas* 15 (1959): pp. 114–116.

Miller, Kenneth. "Geared Turbine Ore Carriers for the Great Lakes." *The Ohio State Engineer* (May 1938): pp. 12–14.

Murphy, Rowley. "Discovery of the Wreckage of the *Griffon*" *Inland Seas* 11 (1955): pp. 232–42, and 12 (1956): pp. 43–53.

_____. "The *Griffon* Wreckage at Tobermory." *Inland Seas* 12 (1956): pp. 275–285.

Murray, Thomas E. "Some Recollections." *Inland Seas* 2 (1946): pp. 28–32.

Myers, Frank A. "The Tobermory *Griffon* vs. the Manitoulin *Griffon*." *Inland Seas* 12 (1956): pp. 68–69.

Myers, Harry F. "Remembering the 504's." *Inland Seas* 44 (1988): pp. 76–93.

Norton, Clark F. "Early Movement for St. Mary's Falls Ship Canal." *Michigan History* 39 (1955): pp. 257–280.

Norton, Harold F."Developments in Shipbuilding." In *Historical Transactions 1893–1943*. New York: Society of Naval Architects and Marine Engineers, 1945.

Odle, Thomas D. "The Commercial Interests of the Great Lakes and the Campaign Issues of 1860." *Michigan History* (March 1956): pp. 1–23.

Olivier, Warner. "The Coming Crisis in Iron." *Saturday Evening Post*, Vol. 215 (November 14, 1942): pp. 22, 122–123.

"Orth's History of Cleveland." Frank E. Hamilton Collection, in the Charles E. Frohman Collection. The Rutherford B. Hayes Presidential Center. Fremont, Ohio.

Palmer, Richard F. "First Steamboat on the Great Lakes." *Inland Seas* 44 (1988): p. 7–20.

_____, and Anthony Slosek. "The *Vandalia*: First Screw Propeller on the Lakes." *Inland Seas* 44 (1988): p. 236–252.

Pankhurst, J. F. "The Development of Shipbuilding on the Great Lakes." *Transactions of the Society of Naval Architects and Marine Engineers* 1 (1893): pp. 252–262.

Plowden, David. "The Last of the Old 'Lakers' Are Steaming Off into History." *Smithsonian* 22 (October 1991): pp. 34–47.

Pomeroy, Lawrence A., Jr. "The Bulk Freight Vessel." *Inland Seas* 2 (1946): pp. 191–200.

Rapp, Marvin A. "New York's Trade on the Great Lakes, 1800–1840." *New York History* (January 1958): pp. 22–24.

Sandusky (Ohio) *Clarion*

Schwab, Charles M. "What May Be Expected in

Iron and Steel." *North American Review* (May 1901): pp. 655–664.

Scott, J. W. "Troubles in Toledo." In *Land of the Long Horizons*, ed., Walter Havighurst, pp. 291–295. New York: Coward-McCann, Inc., 1960.

Sellers, Charles Grier, Jr. "Who Were the Southern Whigs?" *American Historical Review* LIX (1954): pp. 335–346.

Shonette, Donald G. "Heyday of the Horse Ferry." *National Geographic* (October 1989): pp. 548–556.

"Steamboats on Lake Erie, June 1836." *Bethel Magazine* (January 1836): n.p.; reprinted in *Buffalo Spectator* (1836): n.p.; reprinted in *Freshwater* 5 (1990): p. 16.

Tappenden, Richard P. "A Possible Solution to the Mystery of the *Griffin*." *Inland Seas* 2 (1946): pp. 1–6.

Thayer, Gordon W. "Fifty Years Ago on the Lakes: Gene Herman's Early Days." *Inland Seas* 1 (1945): pp. 41–44.

Telescope

Tyler, Polly. "Hosea Rogers, Builder of Boats." *Inland Seas* 3 (1947): pp. 33–39, 66–70, 155–160.

Walsh, F. J. "The St. Clair Delta." *White Star Magazine* (1924): p. 23–25.

Walton, Ivan H. "Developments on the Great Lakes, 1815–1943." *Michigan History* 27 (1943): pp. 72–142.

Walton, Thomas. "The Dreaded Gales of November." *The* (Toledo) *Blade*, Section D (November 6, 1988): pp. 1, 3.

Warner, Edward S., and Colleen (Oihus). "Lives and Times in the Great Lakes Commercial Trade Under Sail." *Hayes Historical Journal* (Fall 1991): pp. 5–16

Waterbury, George A. "The Woodburners." *Inland Seas* 3 (1947): pp. 208–210.

Wax, Anthony C. "Calumet and Helca Copper Mines: An Episode in the Economic Development of Michigan." *Michigan History* 16 (Winter 1932): pp. 5–41.

Williams, Mentor L. "Chicago River and Harbors Convention of 1847." *Mississippi Valley*

Historical Review 35 (March 1949): pp. 607–626.

Wilson, Garth. "The Evolution of the Great Lakes Ship.: *Freshwater* 5 (1990): pp. 4–15.

Wohlcott, Merlin. D. "Marblehead Limestone for the Soo Locks." *Inland Seas* 32 (1976): pp. 105–111.

Wohleber, Curt. "Robert Fulton." *American Heritage* 42 (May-June 1991): pp. 74, 78–79.

Wright, Richard J. "A History of Shipbuilding in Cleveland, Ohio: *Inland Seas* 12 (1956): pp. 232–242, 13 (1957): pp. 29–37, 110–117.

Miscellaneous

Annals of Cleveland. Cleveland, OH: Works Progress Administration

Puotinen, Arthur E. "Finnish Radicals and Religion in Midwestern Mining Towns, 1865–1914." Ph.D. diss., University of Chicago, 1973.

Rakeman, Carl. "Historic Roads." This is a series of 93 paintings owned by the United States Department of Transportation currently on loan to the Texas Transportation Institute and on display in their building on the campus of Texas A & M University, College Station, Texas.

Stevens, Wystan. "Islands of Invention." (Leaflet) Lansing, MI: Historical Society of Michigan, n.d.

Wright, Richard J. "'Pig Pen Port:' Conneaut, Ohio," an unpublished paper in the Frank E. Hamilton Collection, in the Charles E. Frohman Collection. Rutherford B. Hayes Presidential Center, Fremont, Ohio.

Electronic Sources

Lake Carrier's Association, *2007 Position Papers*, 14. www.lcaships.com/2007pspp.pdf.

"The Toledo War," http/www.geo.msu.edu/g eo333/Toledo_war.html, 1–3.

"William Austin Burt," http/www.geo.msu/ geo333/burt.html, 2–3.

Index

Numbers in **bold italics** indicate pages with photographs or illustrations.